SELF-GUIDED

European
Cities

SELF-GUIDED

European Cities

*With 100 illustrations and photographs
in color and black and white; 62 maps*

LANGENSCHEIDT PUBLISHERS, NEW YORK

Publisher:	Langenscheidt Publishers, Inc.
Managing Editor:	Lisa Checchi Ross
General Editor:	Donald S. Olson
U.S. Editorial Adaptation:	Patricia Bayer, Stephen Brewer, Gertrude Buchman, Donald S. Olson
U.S. Editorial Staff:	Linda Eger, Dana M. Schwartz
Original German Text, Illustrations, and Cartography:	Adapted by Polyglott-Redaktion from various editions of Polyglott-Reiseführern for publication as *Polyglott Städteführer Europa*. U.S. cartographic adaptations by Dan McAleese
Cover Design:	Diane Wagner
Cover Photographs:	Image Bank Bavaria
Text Design:	Irving Perkins Associates
Production:	Ripinsky & Company
Photographs:	No. 1, Image Bank/Slaughter; No. 2, Bavaria/Heine Stillmark; No. 3, No. 4, Heidi Weidner; No. 5, Image Bank/Vergani; No. 6, Christa Proells; No. 7, Luxembourg Tourism Office; No. 8, Spanish Tourism Office; No. 9, Witt; No. 10, Bavaria/Leidmann; No. 11, French Tourism Office; No. 12, Mauritius/Salek; No. 13, Image Bank/Gordon; No. 14, Image Bank/Feulner; No. 15, Austrian Tourism Office; No. 16, Eugen-Egon Hüsler
Translation:	German Language Service
Letters:	We welcome your comments and suggestions. Our address: Langenscheidt Publishers, Inc. 46-35 54th Rd. Maspeth, N.Y. 11378

Manufactured in the United States of America
10 9 8 7 6 5 4 3 2 1

ISBN: 0-88729-208-9

Contents

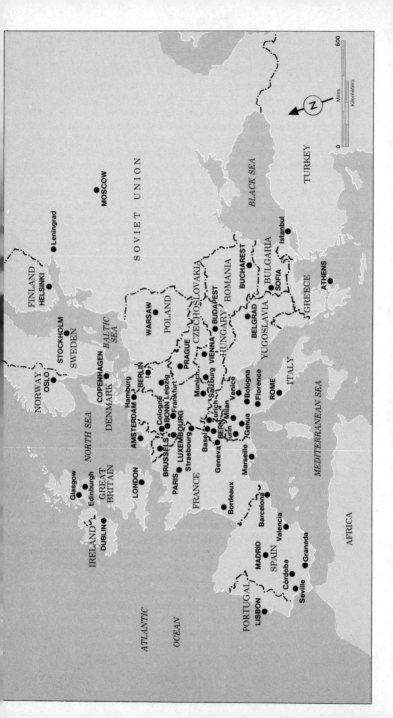

Foreword

At one time, the education of a well-bred young American man or woman included a Grand Tour of Europe's great cities. The whirlwind trip was taken on an elegant ocean liner and entailed up to several months of shuttling from city to city to absorb hundreds of years of art, architecture, culture, and history before returning home.

In E. M. Forster's *A Room with a View*—quite possibly the best novel ever written about traveling—a British clergyman living in Florence takes a dim view of Americans abroad: "We residents sometimes pity you poor tourists not a little," he tells a visitor, "handed about like a parcel of goods from Venice to Florence, from Florence to Rome. . . they mix up towns, rivers, palaces in one inextricable whirl. You know the American girl in *Punch* who says: 'Say Poppa, what did we see at Rome?' And the father replies: 'Why, guess Rome was the place where we saw the yaller dog.' "

Obviously, the sardonic ractoneur of Forster's novel does not understand Americans at all. If we are a bit fervent in our European travels, it is only because our romance with the great cities of Europe is of such long standing. The foggy streets of Dickensian London, Paris in the heady years just after the war (the Paris, that is, of F. Scott Fitzgerald and Ernest Hemingway), the cafés along the Danube as it flows through Budapest, the intellectually rife Vienna of Freud and Wittgenstein—these places loom as large to an American as do the Rocky Mountains and that deep gash we call the Grand Canyon to a European.

European cities have hypnotically lured Americans for decades with their old world charm and history. It is difficult to name a man or woman of American letters who has not crossed the Atlantic and sent reports to an eager audience back home. When the humorist Robert Benchley first saw Venice, he cabled his editor in New York, "Streets full of water. Please advise." While living in Paris, Edith Wharton wrote her masterful novels about the American way of life. Mark Twain, that most American of writers, made the Grand Tour in 1869. Writing home from Florence, he observed of the Arno, "It would be a very plausible river if they pumped some water into it." Henry James was in Florence the same year and remarked more fervently, "She sat beside her little river like the treasure house she has always been."

In today's hard-driving world, few of us have time for the leisurely Grand Tour of yesteryear, but our love affair with Europe has not cooled. We still flock to Europe by the millions to marvel at the history and culture that predates our own by thousands of years. Only now we do it on the run—we sandwich in a couple hours of sightseeing in Munich between business meetings; we have a 12-hour layover between connecting flights in Madrid; or we have only two weeks of vacation time in which to see all of Italy. Planning an efficient itinerary for such trips can be a nightmare.

Langenscheidt's Self-Guided European Cities is an inventory of the treasures to be seen in 50 of Europe's great cities. It is an extremely useful armchair companion that you will want to consult over and over again as you prepare for your trip to Europe, be it the time-honored Grand Tour pilgrimage or a brief glimpse between business appointments. For each city, we present a concise, essential description and an easy-to-use, alphabetically arranged directory to *all* its important sights. A fact-filled "Practical Information" chapter lists addresses of information offices and other useful data. Long before departure, an Italy-bound traveler will be able to determine which ruins to visit in Rome, which Florentine museums merit a full morning's visit, and which churches in Venice should not be missed. Also, in these pages you will discover little-known treasures—where to buy licorice in Amsterdam, the most interesting Byzantine church in Istanbul, the almshouse where the notorious Don Juan died in Seville—that you will want to add to your itinerary.

Using this Guide

This guide is a quick reference to help you plan, organize, and enjoy your trip to Europe. Fifty European cities have been arranged alphabetically from Amsterdam to Zurich. Within each chapter, there is a brief history of the city to provide background for the sights you will be seeing, followed by an alphabetical listing that describes the major attractions and nearby excursions. A map of each city is keyed to the text and is accompanied by a legend that includes additional points of interest.

Langenscheidt's writers also offer a subjective guide to the most appealing sights within each city. Our unique three-star system appears throughout the guide:

> ***Worth a special trip—don't miss it!
> **The most important sights on the tour
> *Highlights

Major sights appear in boldface for easy reference, while other notable attractions appear in italics. Numbers in parentheses correspond to locations on the maps. The "U" symbol on some maps indicates a subway stop.

The guide concludes with a Practical Information chapter that will help you plan your trip, prepare you for customs procedures, and provide you with other helpful information. Also included are the addresses of tourism offices, embassies, and consulates in the various European cities.

Notes and Observations

We can think of no better companion to this book than one of the European country guides from Langenscheidt's Self-Guided series. Each guide includes extensive, step-by-step, stone-by-stone walking tours of major cities. And, in the happy event that your travels take you beyond the city gates, each provides detailed driving tours across the country.

Travel information, like fruit, is perishable. We've made every effort to double-check information in this guide. But museums and other attractions do shut down for renovation, so be sure to check ahead whenever possible.

We welcome your comments and updates of our information. Please write us at:

Langenscheidt Publishers, Inc.
46–35 54th Road
Maspeth, N. Y. 11378

Amsterdam

Amsterdam, population 679,000, is a city of unique charm and easygoing temperament. Compact and yet cosmopolitan, by turns raucous and serene, it's like no other city in Europe. Whether you're gliding down one of the famous floodlit canals in a glass-roofed boat, snacking on a fresh herring at a busy outdoor market, or strolling through a quiet 17th-century neighborhood of gabled row houses, the special spirit of Amsterdam—a spirit that comes from the sea and a long history of social freedom—rises up to greet you. Amiable, helpful, conversant in English, and stubbornly practical, the Dutch have been making visitors to Amsterdam feel welcome for hundreds of years.

History

Located close to the North Sea at the confluence of the Amstel and Ij rivers, the city took its name seven centuries ago from a protective wall or "dam" that was built across the Amstel to help keep out the sea. This "dam in the Amstel"—constructed when the city was nothing more than a fishing village—was only the first in a series of remarkable planning and engineering feats that have shaped the size and topography of Amsterdam over the centuries. Reclaimed from the ever-advancing sea, the city literally stands on underwater pilings.

An intermediary port for international trade, Amsterdam grew quickly and established its own fleet of ships to compete in the foreign marketplace. The city, needing more room for the ever-growing business of cargo storage, began construction of its first canals at the end of the 14th century. In the century that followed, as Amsterdam's importance grew, stone towers were erected at strategic points to serve as fortifications.

Ironically, Protestantism was taking hold just at the time when the Dutch provinces came under the rule of the Catholic king of Spain in the early 16th century. When Philip II became king of Spain in 1555, Holland's Protestant heretics were vigorously persecuted; religiously inspired violence became rife throughout the country. Amsterdam, loyal to Spain, did not officially join in the cause for freedom from Spanish rule until 1578. A year later the Treaty of Utrecht was signed, providing the foundation for what would eventually become the Kingdom of the Netherlands.

The enterprising and commercially minded Dutch sailed the route to what is now Indonesia before 1600; as soon as they had established trade there, a seemingly inexhaustible source of wealth from the East Indies began to fill the coffers of the recently established (1602) Dutch East Indies Company. The Dutch West Indies Company was founded in 1621 and traded with New Amsterdam (now New York City) and Brazil.

Amsterdam now became the world's leading port and boasted an enormous fleet of its own. As the city extended its influence, establishing colonies worldwide, it also began to attract foreigners escaping religious persecution in their own countries. With its reputation for tolerance and its commercial prosperity, the city continued to grow. Its canals (called *grachten*, or, literally, graves) were extended in three semi-circular belts that surrounded the old town: The Herengracht (Gentlemen's Canal); the Keizersgracht (Emperor's Canal); and the Prinsengracht (Prince's Canal); remain primary arteries—and prime real estate—today. You'll see goods still being transported along these and the approximately 100 other canals on flat barges called *schuten*.

Amsterdam's "Golden Age" lasted throughout the 17th century and was based on the shipping trade, in all its guises. Prosperous merchants began to build the gabled canal houses that so beguile visitors today. Some of the canal houses are princely mansions, but most of them are charmingly modest—and some are downright tiny.

The wealthy bourgeois citizens of Amsterdam invested in more than real estate, however: They strongly supported the arts that flourished in this period. It was said, in fact, that Amsterdam had as many painters as bakers. The most famous artist to work in the city was, of course, Rembrandt van Rijn, who spent 46 years here. (His house is open to the public and many of his paintings, etchings, and drawings may be seen in Amsterdam's museums.)

The burgeoning civic pride of the Protestant Amsterdammers was also expressed in architecture; work began on what is now the Royal Palace in 1648. It was completed seven years later.

Amsterdam's glorious Golden Age ended in the 18th century as, inevitably, foreign powers broke the city's powerful trading monopolies. A period of decline followed, with French revolutionary troops briefly occupying the city, and Louis Bonaparte—Napoleon's younger brother—installed as King of Holland. The Dutch House of Orange was called back from exile in 1813, and Prince William of Orange was proclaimed the country's first king.

The 19th century was a period of social progress for Amsterdam. The social welfare system that currently characterizes Amsterdam and all of Holland, was established at that time.

During the First World War, the Netherlands maintained its neutrality; it attempted to do so again in the Second World War. This position was thwarted, however, when it was invaded by German forces who occupied the area from 1940 to 1945. In 1941, the working population of Amsterdam mounted a strike to protest the deportation of the city's Jews—the only time a city in occupied Europe dared to show open solidarity with its

Jewish fellow citizens. The famous house where the family of Anne Frank hid in a secret attic from 1942 until 1944 evokes this tragic period. Allied forces liberated the country in 1945.

Postwar recovery was aided by the growing prominence of Amsterdam as a diamond center, an industry that was started here in the 1570s. In recent years, Amsterdam's popularity has made it Europe's fourth largest tourist center. Home to some of the world's outstanding cultural institutions—among them, the Concertgebouw Orchestra, the Rijksmuseum, and the van Gogh Museum—Amsterdam is a city proudly linked to its past, but firmly and confidently dedicated to the present and future.

Attractions

Amsterdam boasts an excellent and economical public transportation system. Buy a *strip ticket* at any tobacconist, post office, railway station, or the VVV ticket office across from the Central Station; it can be used on the bus, tram, and metro, and is far cheaper than buying an individual ticket on the buses and trams themselves. For any stop within the Centrum, or town center, punch three strips on your ticket.

If you want to reach your destination in fast but romantic style, you can rent a water taxi to speed you through the maze of canals. Check for landing points throughout the city. A fascinating way to explore this city of waterways is by canal bike. Easy to peddle and maneuver, they are available to rent from four different locations in the city. You can take a canal cruise from one of several different locations. They run throughout the day. Some offer candlelight tours with wine and dinner.

Amsterdam is a city where the bicycle is still the king of transportation, and the sight remains undeniably picturesque. Please remember that bicyclists often have their own lanes and don't like pedestrians in them.

Tickets for most major cultural events can be purchased in the ticket office of the Stadsschouwburg, on the main Leidseplein.

Lunch or tea in the top-floor restaurant of Metz & Co. department store on Leidestraat and Keizersgracht provides a unique bird's-eye view out and over the rooftops and canals. Another atmospheric place for drinks, tea or a snack is the famous American Hotel, just off the Leidseplein.

The biggest and best outdoor market in Amsterdam is held Monday through Saturday on Albert Cuypstraat. Sample a fresh herring at one of the fish stands, or buy a bag of freshly made waffles with honey, baked and filled on the spot—no sweeter treat to be found.

Licorice is a somewhat surprising speciality of Amsterdam, and licorice-lovers should visit Jacob Hooy's shop at 12, Kloveniersburgwal to sample an amazing array of sweet or salty, lavender or honey-filled licorices. (A good gift idea.)

Allard-Pierson Museum, Oude Turfmarkt 127: Well-displayed articles of everyday life from ancient Greece, Egypt, Rome, Crete, and West Asia are featured in this museum.

Amstelkring Museum (Our Lord in the Attic) [10], Oudezijds Voorburgwal 40: The only remaining "secret" church in the city, this unusual structure was set up in the attics of three adjoining 17th-century canal houses at the time of the Reformation, when Catholic worship was forbidden.

Amsterdam Historical Museum, Kalverstraat 92: Now beautifully restored, the museum is situated in what served for 400 years as the municipal orphanage. Particularly interesting is the permanent exhibition relating to the history of Amsterdam from the 13th century to the present.

Anne Frank House [15], Prinsengracht 263: The famous teenage diarist Anne Frank hid in this house with her Jewish family from 1942 until August 1944, when they were discovered and taken to a concentration camp in Bergen-Belsen.

Begijnhof [3], Kalverstraat: Often missed by visitors because it's hidden from the street by closed doors, this charming and typically Dutch *hofjes* (a small housing development built for the poor by wealthier citizens) is a quiet, enclosed courtyard surrounded by 16th- and 17th-

Begijnhof

century homes in which the elderly poor still live.

Centraal Station (main train station): The busy transportation hub of the city, this brick building was built by architect H.P. Berlage in 1903 and set the standard for modern Dutch architecture. You can take a canal and harbor cruise from here, or catch one of the trams that will take you into the Centrum.

City Hall and Opera House, Waterlooplein: Even if you're not scheduled to see an opera or a ballet, Amsterdam's newest architectural addition is worth visiting for its modern architecture and site-planning.

The **Concertgebouw,** Museumplein: One of the greatest concert halls in Europe, the Concertgebouw is blessed with superb acoustics and is the home of the renowned Concertgebouw Orchestra.

Dam Square: This site where the city began some 800 years ago is considered the "heart of Holland," and is an appropriate setting for the *national monument,* dedicated in 1956 by Queen Juliana. Several important buildings are located on or near the busy square, including the **Royal Palace** [1], known in its time as the "eighth wonder of the world" because of its size and construction on 13,659 wooden pilings. This splendid Dutch Classical building began life in the mid-17th century as Amsterdam's town hall and law courts, and is open to the public in the summer. ***New Church** [2], next to the Royal Palace, was actually new in 1408, and since 1814, has been the scene of many Dutch coronations, most recently Queen Beatrix's in 1980. Many of Holland's most distinguished citizens are buried in this Late Gothic edifice.

Fleamarket [6], Valkenburgerstraat: Although lacking in

Royal Palace and New Church

charm, this locale remains a good place to poke around for that one treasure you've been waiting a lifetime to find.

Fodor Museum, Keizersgracht 609: The place to go for modern art exhibitions by contemporary Amsterdam artists.

Jewish Historical Museum, Nieuwmarkt 4: Part of the renovated Hoogduitse Synagogue complex since 1987, this museum is dedicated to Jewish culture, both past and present.

*Jordaan: Settled by French Huguenots in the 17th century, this lively working-class neighborhood has attracted a fair number from Amsterdam's artistic community. Their presence is signaled by the area's intriguing craft studios and workshops, specialty stores, cafes, pubs, and restaurants. One of the oldest "brown cafes" (*bruine kroeg,* the Dutch equivalent of an English pub) in Amsterdam, *De Reiger,* is located at Nieuwe Leliestraat 34, and is a good place to sample the famous Dutch gin called *jenever.*

Leidseplein: For decades, this busy square and its surrounding streets have been a meeting place for natives and tourists alike. Full of outdoor bars, ethnic restaurants, clubs, and cafes, you can indulge in a meal or some leisurely people-watching over afternoon coffee. The area is landmarked by the 19th-century **Stadsschouwburg,** the city's municipal theater and a convenient information center for every cultural event in the city. Streetcars are the only vehicles allowed on *Leidsestraat,* which leads out of the square, so window-shopping along this busy street is a pleasure. *Bali,* Leidsestraat 95, is one of many specialty restaurants serving *rijstafel* (rice table)—an absolute must in Amsterdam.

Munttoren (the mint) [4]: Built in 1490 as a city gate and rebuilt in 1620, this old tower adjoins the *floating flower market* on the Singel canal; a traditional Dutch tune plays on the tower's carillion every half-hour. **Rembrandtsplein,** one block from the mint, takes its name from the statue of the great artist in its cen-

ter; there's nothing very "artistic" around here, however, and the area is basically known for its nightlife.

Amsterdam Attractions:
1. Royal Palace
2. New Church
3. Begijnenhof
4. Munttoren
5. Willet Holthuysen Musem
6. Fleamarket
7. Rembrandt's House
8. Zuiderkerk
9. Oude Kerk
10. Amstelkring Museum
11. Schreierstoren
12. Rijksmuseum
13. Vincent Van Gogh Museum
14. Westerkerk
15. Anne Frank House

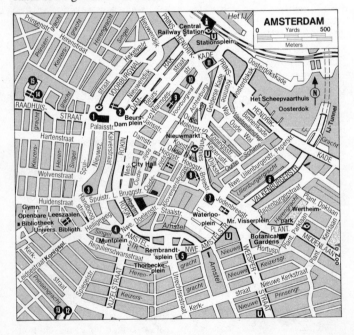

Oude Kerk (Old Church) [9]: The city's oldest church stands somewhat incongruously in the center of Amsterdam's busy red-light district. The ladies you see sitting in the windows around here close their curtains only when they're not "in business."

Rembrandt's House, [7] Jodenbreestraat 4–6: The painter Rembrandt van Rijn lived in this luxurious house in the old Jewish quarter from 1639 until 1658. Furnished with 17th-century furniture, the house contains an almost complete collection of the master's etchings, as well as illustrative paintings and memorabilia from his life.

***Rijksmuseum [12], Stadhouderskade 42: The largest and richest museum in the country: In addition to a breathtaking collection of works by the Old Masters (including Rembrandt's famous "Night Watch" and works by Vermeer and Frans Hals), the museum provides an exhaustive overview of the art and cultural development of the Netherlands.

Schreierstoren (Weepers' Tower) [11]: Once situated directly on the harbor and a part of the city walls, the tower takes its name from the tears of the sailors' wives who would wave goodbye to their sea-going husbands from here. It is said that Henry Hudson set sail to Nieuwe Amsterdam (now New York City) from this site in 1609.

Stedelijk Museum, Paulus Potterstraat 13: Housing the latest in international contemporary art, as well as earlier modern masterpieces by artists such as Cézanne, Picasso, and Matisse, the Stedelijk remains an exciting and provocative museum.

Museum Van Loon, Keizersgracht 672: A perfectly preserved residence in two adjoining 17th-century canal houses; its collections of medals and family portraits are particularly noteworthy.

***Vincent van Gogh Museum [13], Paulus Potterstraat 7: The museum is dedicated to the genius of this Dutch artist. Besides displaying some of van Gogh's well-known paintings, the museum provides insights into various aspects of his personality through letters and other documentation.

Waag (Weighing House) [17]: With its seven eye-catching turrets and circular interior, this intrigu-

Westerkerk

ing edifice stands in the center of Nieuwmarkt Square; it was originally a city gate. The Surgeons' Guild dissected and experimented with the bodies of criminals here in the 17th century—scenes that Rembrandt immortalized on canvas.

Westerkerk (West Church) [14]: Former Crown Princess Beatrix and Prince Claus of the Netherlands were married in this massive structure (built between 1620 and 1630), and Rembrandt was buried here. Its steeple, generally open for a few hours every day in the summer, provides the highest observation deck in the city.

Willet Holthuysen Museum [5], Herengracht 605: Another splendid 17th-century canal house with a lovely 18th-century garden.

Zuiderkerk [8]: Built in the early 17th century, this was the first church constructed here after the Reformation. Its tower, the Zuidertoren, is considered to be the most beautiful in Amsterdam.

Athens

The birthplace of democracy has its share of crippling traffic, pollution, and government scandals, but despite these 20th-century woes, cosmopolitan—and still profoundly classical—Athens (AΘHNAI, or Athinai) is one of the most evocative and exciting cities in Europe. Although Greece's roots in its Golden Age are visible everywhere, its Byzantine and Middle Eastern legacies are evident as well, making Athens a city of many cultures. With its picture-perfect weather, it is also a city for all seasons. The white-marble majesty of the Parthenon alone is worth the trip—viewed up close or from afar, ideally over an al fresco dinner at a restaurant with a breathtaking Acropolis view. The bustling Agora, or marketplace, is another highlight of this now-sprawling metropolis of over three million, as are the ubiquitous monuments and ruins, the museums, the food, and the nightlife. Part of Greater Athens is its port, Piraeus, one of the Mediterranean's busiest harbors and best known to tourists as the starting-off point for Greek island-hopping.

History

Athens stands on a plain between the mountains of Parnes, Pentelikon, and Hymettos, at the foot of the Acropolis, or "high city." According to Greek mythology, Athens was named after the goddess Athena, who made an olive tree (the symbol of peace and bounty) grow on the Acropolis. The legendary Phoenician king Kekrops built a city at the foot of the hill some four millennia ago, and around 1300 B.C. Theseus was said to have united the 12 villages of Attica, making Athens the capital of the new state.

Athens grew quickly, first developing as an artistic center of Greece in the eighth century B.C. around the time of the unification of Attica under Athens. By the start of the sixth century, the center of the Archaic style of sculpture moved from the Cyclades to Athens, concurrent with Solon's giving the city a democratic constitution (594 B.C.), as well as reorganizing its agriculture, expanding its trade, and reforming its currency. The next leader, Pisistratos, and his sons, laid down the roots of the Athenian Empire, also securing the city's foremost position in literature (by publishing Homer) and drama (by founding a theatrical festival).

During the Persian Wars, Athens was badly plundered; Xerxes and his men pushed through Thermopylae and eventually sacked the Acropolis. But the city regained leadership in Greece by defeating the Persians at sea (Salamis, 480 B.C.) and on land (Plataea, 479 B.C.). Later in the century, under Pericles, Athens flourished both financially and culturally: The Parthenon was completed under Phidias's direction in 438 B.C., the rest of the buildings on the "holy hill" were erected in the decades that followed, and the talents of Sophocles, Thucydides, and other great thinkers emerged.

Athens began suffering a decline during the Peloponnesian Wars (431–404 B.C.), when rival Sparta assumed supremacy until the early fourth century. In 338 B.C., Philip II of Macedonia defeated the Greeks at Chaeronea, and Macedonia ruled Athens until 168 B.C., when the Romans took over after the fall of Perseus. Rome allowed the city to retain many privileges and hence continue to thrive until Sulla sacked and conquered it in 86 B.C. Athens experienced its final period of flourishing under Emperor Hadrian in the second century A.D.

When the Roman Empire was divided in 395 A.D., Athens, along with the rest of Greece, came under Byzantine rule. From 1204 to 1456, Frankish Crusaders and their descendants resided there as dukes. The city then fell to the Ottoman Empire of the Turks, who held Athens until the Greek War of Independence (1821–1829). For a short time, Nafplion was the capital of liberated Greece, but Athens replaced it in 1834, when the newly elected King Otto of Bavaria chose to reside there. At the time, Athens was a poor, desolate enclave of some 6,000 refugees who lived amid the remnants of the once-glorious and often-plundered Acropolis. In less than a century, however, it grew once more into a prosperous city, whose progress was temporarily halted by the two world wars (British and French troops occupied it during World War I; the Germans held it from 1941 to 1944).

From the 1960s onward, Athens has expanded considerably in both area and population, with rapid industrialization contributing to the growth. Although the latter has no doubt benefited the growing masses, it has also created a major pollution problem. But somehow the "chemical cloud" that so often envelops Athens has not managed to dissipate this eminent survivor's proud and noble aura.

Attractions

Academy [8], Sina Avenue: Built in 1859 from Theophilus von Hansen's design and financed by the Greco-Austrian Baron Sina, the Hellenic Academy is a replica of Vienna's Parliament. Its massive statues of Apollo and Athena occupy two of the Ionic columns and the façade is covered with Pentelic marble which has been painted and gilded, à la classical architecture.

***The Acropolis [17], entrance off Dionysiou Areopagitou Street: The country's premier attraction—and one of the world's best-known sights—the Acropolis is usually the first stop on every visitor's itinerary. A superficial tour takes about two hours, but to really get to know the place, you should spend several hours absorbing the majesty and history (and ignoring whatever scaffolding, swarming tourists, and other distractions surround you). There is a *son-et-lumière* spectacle on summer nights, but try to come on your own at sundown, preferably when a full moon is rising—the Acropolis is at its most magical and impressive on such an evening.

The hill of the Acropolis was probably settled around 3500 B.C., and the king of Attica resided here by 1400 B.C. Parts of the palace and the immense 10-meter- (33-foot-) high wall encircling the plateau on the hill remain intact. The bastion on which the Nike Temple is built also existed at that time. Beginning around 800 B.C., the Acropolis became an almost exclusively sacred area with no residential precincts.

The first Parthenon was built around 590 B.C., and some 70 years later the old Athena Temple was constructed. Reconstruction of the Acropolis began soon after the final victory over the Persians, with Pericles presenting his massive building plan to the Athenians in 456 B.C. Since that Golden Age (the Parthenon was completed under Phidias's direction in 438 B.C., the other major buildings were constructed in the ensuing decades) the Acropolis has variously been looted, burned, occupied, destroyed, and rebuilt. What you see today, though a pale ghost of its original glory, nonetheless casts a giant shadow on its visitors.

Atop the Acropolis, the major attractions are:

Acropolis Museum: Displayed here is a wealth of finds unearthed on the Acropolis since 1834, as well as front sections of the Erectheion, Parthenon, and Nike Temple. In Room IV is a bevy of sixth-century B.C. Korae, statues of draped maidens presented as votive offerings to Athena, while the Nike Temple's pediment figures—including handsome genuflecting giants—are displayed in Room V. Room VIII features those parts of the Parthenon frieze not removed by Lord Elgin to London in the early 19th century, and Room IX is home to the surviving caryatids of the Erectheion (those supporting the actual nearby building are sturdy casts with metal cores).

Beulé Gate: Named after the French archaeologist who discovered it in 1852, this gate is situated at the entranceway of the Acropolis. Its two square turrets were built in the mid-third century A.D., under the Roman Emperor Valerian.

*Erectheion: One of the most perfect examples of Greek architecture—and under continuous restoration since 1909—the Erectheion succeeded the Old Temple of Athena as the shared shrine of that goddess and Poseidon-Erectheus. As part of Pericles' extensive building program, it was designed by Mnesikles and finished around 408 B.C. A wooden idol of Athena was once housed here, as well as an eternally burning golden lamp and a bronze palm tree. The "supporting cast" of the south portico, a sextet of caryatids, are perhaps the Acropolis's best-known denizens—even though the six you see today are all modern casts.

Monument of Agrippa: This

second-century B.C. marble plinth, 9 meters (29 feet) high, once bore a quadriga and probably honored a Pergamene chariot victory during Eumenes II's reign. Statues of Cleopatra and Antony occupied the plinth, but were blown down in 31 B.C.; they were replaced by the group dedicated to the consul Marcus Agrippa in 27 B.C.

Nike Temple: In the square cella of this small temple stood the cult idol of Athena Nike, with a pomegranate in her right hand, and a helmet in her left. A marble reproduction replaced an Archaic statue, which was probably of wood. Kallikrates designed the original temple, which was completed around 425 B.C.; it was pulled down by the Turks in 1686, but reconstructed in the 19th century.

*Parthenon: Built from 447–438 B.C., the Parthenon (its name means "Hall of the Virgin," referring to one of its rooms) stands as the most perfect edifice of classi-

cal antiquity; even as a ruin, it is incomparably beautiful. You must use your imagination, however, to conjure up the original, which functioned as both a house of worship and the state treasury: Almost all the decorative exterior sculptures are gone, as well as the brilliant colors with which the entire structure was once painted, the bronze festoons, the golden escutcheons, the marble floors, the coffered ceilings, and the chryselephantine statue of Athena, replete with detachable robe of pure gold. Still, the unique harmony of this Doric building—a masterpiece of work by Iktinos (architect), Kallikrates (builder), and Phidias (sculptor)—remains for all to appreciate.

*Propylaea: Master planner Pericles envisioned this massive entrance portico—built in 437–32 B.C. according to Mnesikles' design—as "a radiant diadem" topping "the citadel of the gods." Constructed of Pentelic marble, with the exception of some decorative details in black Eleusinian stone, the structure remained almost fully intact up to the 13th century A.D., when it functioned as the palace of the Byzantine bishop. The Turkish Aga was a later occupant. In subsequent centuries it suffered some damage, but most of the colonnaded gateway still stands.

Sanctuary of Artemis Brauronia: This shrine, a stoa with two extended wings, was dedicated to the bear goddess (among the votive offerings that have been found

Nike Temple

here was a carved bear). Within the shrine is a pedestal of a monumental bronze representation of the Trojan Horse.

Agii Theodori [11], Klafthmonos Square: Built in the 12th century on a cruciform foundation dating from a century earlier, Agii Theodori is most likely the oldest of Athens' Byzantine churches. Early Arabic calligraphy features on its brick and stone walls, and there is also a later belfry.

Agora [21], Theseion Square: Once the hub of Athens' community life, the ancient marketplace is a treasure trove of ruins, from the Theseion (see separate entry)—Greece's finest extant temple—to the two-story, colonnaded Stoa of Attalos II. The latter, built in the second century B.C. by the Pergamene king and reconstructed by the Americans in the 1950s, is today the site of the *Agora Museum*, with its large collection of vases, sculptural fragments, and other pieces unearthed in the area.

Areopagos [18], western slope of the Acropolis: The "Hill of Ares," supposed site of the trial of the god of war for the murder of Poseidon's son, gave its name to the council of nobles who meted out criminal justice, especially for killings. It is also the rock at whose base the Apostle Paul preached to the Athenians (a bronze tablet commemorates his speech).

Asklepieion [27], southern slope of the Acropolis: The sanctuary of Asklepios, god of healing, was dedicated in 418 B.C.; a

new Asklepieion was built in the next century, devoted to the god's sister, Hygieia. More visible on the site, however, are the remains of a fifth- or sixth-century Byzantine church.

Athenian Cemetery [16], Anapafseos Street: Athens' main

Athens Attractions:
1. Omonia Square
2. Syntagma Square
3. National Garden
4. Zappeion
5. Parliament (Vouli)
6. Schliemann's House
7. Roman Catholic Cathedral
8. Academy
9. University
10. National Library
11. Agii Thodori
12. National Historical Museum
13. Stadium
14. Royal Palace
15. Evzones' Barracks
16. Athenian Cemetery
17. Acropolis
18. Areopagos
19. Philopappos Hill
20. Pnyx Hill
21. Agora
22. Keramikos Cemetery and Museum
23. Olympieion
24. Hadrian's Arch
25. Lysikrates Monument
26. Theater of Dionysos
27. Asklepieion
28. Stoa of Eumenes II
29. Odeon of Herodes Atticus
30. Cathedral of Athens
31. Small Mitropoleos
32. Roman Agora
33. Library of Hadrian
34. Folk Museum
35. Kapnikarea
36. Metamorphosis Church
37. National Archaeological Museum
38. Benaki Museum
39. Byzantine Museum
40. Lykavittos
41. Gennadeion Library
42. Moni Petraki

cemetery contains a multitude of ornate tombs, including the mausoleum of archaeologist Heinrich Schliemann (1822–1890), decorated with Trojan scenes, and the tomb of fellow archaeologist Adolf Furtwängler (1853–1907), featuring a marble replica of a sphinx he discovered on Aegina.

Benaki Museum [38], Vassilissis Sofias Avenue: Antoine Benaki spent some 35 years amassing his diverse collection; he presented it to the nation in 1931. Among the museum's myriad treasures are Copper and Bronze Age artifacts; Archaic, Hellenistic, and modern jewels; Byzantine handiwork and icons; the earliest known El Greco; Coptic textiles; Chinese ceramics, and Greek costumes and folk art.

**Byzantine Museum [39], Vassilissis Sofias Avenue: The 19th-century Villa Ilissia, once the home of the American-born Duchess of Piacenza, is now the treasure house of a collection of Byzantine sculpture, furniture, icons, frescoes, textiles, and other artworks and objects. Also displayed are reproductions of a basilica of the fifth–sixth centuries, an 11th-century cruciform church, and a post-Byzantine mosque-type church.

Cathedral of Athens [30], Mitropoleos Square: Otherwise known as the Mitropoleos, Athens' principal Greek Orthodox church is an unsightly behemoth, incorporating parts of 72 destroyed churches that were pieced together from 1840 to 1855.

Evzones' Barracks [15], Irodou Attikou Street: The famous white-skirted guards reside here.

Gennadeion Library [41], Gennadiou Street: A handsome 1926 structure of Naxian marble, the library has a central portico of eight columns and two wings. It is part of the nearby American School of Classical Studies.

Hadrian's Arch [24], corner of Amalias and Olgas avenues: This second-century A.D. Roman arch of Pentelic marble bears the frieze inscription: "This is Athens, the ancient city of Theseus" on the northwest side facing the Acropolis; "This is the city of Hadrian and not of Theseus" on the southeast side.

Kapnikarea [35], Ermou Street: This 11th-century cruciform church's name—meaning "Our Lady of the Robe"—may have something to do with the fact that it is located in an area teeming with drapers' shops, as it probably did in the Middle Ages. Its dome is supported by four recycled Roman columns, and its frescoes are neo-Byzantine. It was lovingly restored by Athens University in 1834, to which it belongs.

*Keramikos Cemetery and Museum [22], 148 Ermou Street: Cemeteries have existed in this spot, just outside old Athens' walls, since the 12th century B.C. An ancient Potters' Field was on the site, as well as a more well-to-do Street of Tombs, which displayed the handsome funerary stelae of affluent Athenians.

Kolonaki Square: Set away from the hustle and bustle of the city center, this square is the center of Athens' most elegant neighborhood. The area features excellent restaurants and shopping.

Library of Hadrian [33], Aiolou Street: Located in the old Roman Agora, the library was once a huge rectangle enclosing a courtyard of, according to the historian Pausanias, "a hundred splendid columns." A much-altered sixth-century basilica occupied the site until the late 19th century.

Lykavittos [40], reached by funicular from Aristipou Street or via a steep path from Loukianou Street: Rising some 277 meters (910 feet) from the Kolonaki district, Lykavittos is the highest Athenian hill. The view from the summit, which is crowned by the Chapel of Agios Georgios, is well worth the trip up, and on a clear day you can see the Peloponnese mountains to the north and the Argo-Saronic isle of Aegina to the south. In the summer, an open-air theater hosts musical and dramatic performances, and the Dionyssos restaurant is open for dinner year-round (a café and patisserie serve all day).

Lysikrates Monument [25], corner of Tripodon and Lysikratous streets: This nicely preserved building (circa 330 B.C.) has a square base of Piraeus stone, an Eleusinian marble cornice, three round steps of Hymettos marble, and six huge Corinthian columns. Such choragic monuments originally held a bronze tripod, awarded to the winners of the drama contests held in the Theater of Dionysos. The frieze of the Lysikrates Monument features the story of Dionysos and his captors, the Tyrrhenian pirates, whom he changed into dolphins.

Moni Petraki [42], Gennadiou Street: This one-time monastic cloister, now part of a theological seminary, features early 18th-century frescoes.

***National Archaeological Museum [37], 1 Tossitsa Street: Greece's largest and most important museum offers a comprehensive overview of Greek art, architecture, and culture from ancient to Roman times. A vast array of black- and red-figured ceramics, temple and funerary reliefs, bronze objects, jewelry, and countless more treasures are on view in the neoclassical structure, which also houses the Numismatic Museum and Epigraphic Museum.

National Garden [3], entrance at Amalias and Vassilissis Sofias avenues, Irodou Attikou Street: This verdant oasis in Athens' hub originated in the mid-19th century as the palace garden of Queen Amalia, wife of King Otto. Subtropical trees, peacocks, and remnants of Roman baths can be seen; it connects with the Zappeion Gardens.

National Historical Museum [12], Stadiou Street: Located in the 1858 old Parliament (Palea Vouli) building, the museum's collection features mementos of the War of Independence (1821–1828)—Byron's sword and helmet among them.

National Library [10], Panepistimiou Street: Designed in neoclassical style by Theophilus von Hansen and completed in 1891, the Pentelic marble library contains a half-million printed books and over 3,000 manuscripts, including two 10th- or 11th-century gospels from Thessalian convents.

Odeon of Herodes Atticus [29], southwest foot of the Acropolis: The second-century A.D. banker built this 32-tier, 5,000-seat Roman theater in memory of his wife, Regilla.

Olympieion [23], corner of Amalias and Olgas avenues: The archeological park behind Hadrian's Arch was once the site of the Olympieion, or Temple of Olympian Zeus. Greece's largest temple was 700 years in the making: Pisistratos laid its foundation in the sixth century B.C., Hellenistic-period construction took place, and, finally, the Emperor Hadrian revived Pisistratos's original plans. Hadrian also had an ivory and gold statue of Zeus placed in the temple and, next to it, an equally valuable one of himself. Sixteen of the original Corinthian columns survive.

Omonia Square [1]: Athens' most important and popular *platia,* or square, Omonia is a "folksy" gathering place, presided over by a rather lackluster fountain. Underneath the square is the main station of the Piraeus-Athens-Kifissia Railways, and assorted shop and cafés.

Parliament (Vouli) [5], Syntagma Square: Ludwig I of Bavaria had this somber palace built for his son, Otto, Greece's first king. Completed in 1843, it has been used since 1933 by the Greek Parliament. In a hollow square at its front is the Tomb of the Unknown Soldier, guarded over by the stylishly clad Evzones.

Philopappos Hill [19], west of the Acropolis: Antiquity's "Hill of the Muses," 147 meters (482 feet) high, is the site of the tomb of Philopappos (circa A.D. 115), a Syrian prince who lived in Athens and served as a Roman consul and praetor. The view is particularly lovely at sunset.

The Plaka, between the Acropolis and Syntagma Square: Athens' old town, a pedestrian-friendly zone—though sometimes the hordes of tourists can be more overbearing than automobile traffic—is *the* prime area for visitors, with countless souvenir shops interspersed among Roman, Byzantine, and Turkish buildings. The pace picks up in the evening, when numerous tavernas, nightclubs, discos, bars, and *bouzoukia* lure tourists and residents alike.

Pnyx Hill [20], west of the Acropolis: The 109-meter- (358-foot-) high location of Athens' Assembly, or Ecclesia, from the late sixth century to the late fourth century B.C., the Pnyx is a massive semicircular artificial terrace. Some of the retaining wall and speaker's platform still remain. An observatory can be found nearby.

*Roman Agora [32], Polignotou Street: Sometimes called the Agora of Augustus, this market was built between 10 B.C. and A.D. 2 with moneys provided by the Emperor; in its time, it was the hub of Roman civic life. A 15th-century mosque functions on the site today as an archaeological workshop.

Roman Catholic Cathedral [7], Omirou Street: This ornate Italian-style basilica (1870) is dedicated to Agios Dionysios Areopagitos (St. Dennis), the patron of Athens. Based on a design by the German architect Leo von Klenze, it was completed by the native Kaftandzoglou.

Royal Palace [14], Irodou Attikou Street: More modest than the Parliament, its predecessor as royal residence, this palace was used by the king after the 1935 restoration; more recently, it has served as the home of the President.

Schliemann's House [6], Panepistimiou Street: The Renaissance-style "Palace of Ilion" was occupied by the archaeologist of Mycenae and Troy and since 1928 has been the seat of the Areopagos, or Supreme Court of Appeal.

*Small Mitropoleos [31], Mitropoleos Square: The harmonious proportions of this small 12th-century church make it one of Athens' most beautiful Byzantine structures. Its Pentelic marble walls are set with classical blocks and reliefs, as well as fragments from sixth- or seventh-century churches. Note especially the antique frieze over the entrance (first

Small Mitropoleos

century B.C.), which depicts the celebrations of the Attic festivals.

Stadium [13], Vassileos Konstantinou Avenue: Constructed in 1895, the 70,000-seat marble stadium occupies the site of the original stone, U-shaped structure built by Lykurgos (330 B.C.), and covered with marble circa A.D. 140 by Herodes Atticus. The present stadium, a replica of its marble predecessor, was paid for by a wealthy Alexandrian Greek, George Averoff; it was the site of the first modern Olympic Games in 1896.

Stoa of Eumenes II [28], south slope of the Acropolis: This second-century B.C. foyer, whose outer colonnade once had 64 Doric columns, links the Theater of Dionysos with the Odeon of Herodes Atticus. It was built by Eumenes II, the King of Pergamon in Asia Minor, to serve as both a shelter and promenade.

Syntagma Square [2]: This elegant square, around which are situated the Parliament building and an array of elegant hotels and smart cafés, has a chic international flavor.

**Theater of Dionysos [26], southeastern foot of the Acropolis: Built in stone by Lykurgos in the fourth century B.C. (to replace an earlier theater), numerous additions and extensions were made in the Hellenistic and Roman eras; it resulted in a hodgepodge of ruins spanning three-quarters of a millennium. Considered the birthplace of Drama, the 17,000-seat theater features proscenium reliefs that depict the deeds of its patron, Dionysos (first century A.D.).

**Theseion, in the Agora at Adrianou Street: Although named after Theseus (whose exploits appear in stone, along with those of Herakles, on its frieze), this well-preserved Doric temple was dedicated in the mid-fifth century B.C. to Hephaistos, the god of blacksmiths and potters. It is thought to be the work of the same architect who designed the temples at Sounion and Rhamnous. In subsequent years, the Theseion served as a Byzantine church, a Turkish mosque, and a 19th-century cemetery for British Protestants.

Tower of the Winds, in the Roman Agora at Avrilou Street: Originally a first-century B.C. hydraulic clock (with sundial and weathervane), this handsome octagonal structure, some 12 meters (39 feet) high, is decorated with allegorical reliefs of the eight winds. Designed by the Syrian astronomer Andronikos, the tower was occupied by dervishes during Turkish rule.

University [9], Panepistimiou Street: Built from 1839 to 1942 to a design by Christian Hansen, a Danish architect, this neo-Classical structure boasts polychrome decoration and an elegant Ionic portico of creamy Pentelic marble. It is used for ceremonial purposes today, with classes held in outlying Panepistimioupoli, or University City.

Zappeion [4], in the National Garden: This 1874–1888 national exhibition building, renovated in 1959–1960, was set up by the Zappas cousins. Set amid lovely gardens also bearing the name Zappeion, is a popular café with open-air stage adjacent, as well as an outdoor movie theater.

Excursions

All four of these sights are accessible by bus, with Piraeus also connected to Athens by railway.

*Daphni, 11 km. (7 miles) northwest of Athens: Located on the Sacred Way leading from Athens to Eleusis, Daphni was the original site of the Temple of Apollo Daphneios. The Monastery of Daphni, built in the fifth or sixth century on the grounds of the earlier temple and then rebuilt in the late 11th century, was dedicated to the Virgin. Subsequently it was sacked by Crusaders, occupied by Cistercian and then Orthodox monks, and used as a barracks and asylum. The monastery was restored after World War II; today you can visit the church (circa 1080), with its handsome mosaic fragments, and the Cistercian-period cloister.

Kaisariani, 6.5 km. (4 miles) east of central Athens: The woody lower slopes of Mount Hymettos once were home to a shrine of Aphrodite and a sacred spring (which fed water to Athens before the Marathon Dam was built). In the early 11th century the Kaisariani Monastery was set up here, its Church of the Panagia (Holy Virgin) rebuilt on the site of a fifth-century basilica. Besides the church, which is in the shape of a Greek cross and includes well-preserved 17th- and 18th-century frescoes, a bakery, bathhouse, mill, and refectory can be viewed.

Piraeus, southwest of Athens: In the time of Pericles, ancient Piraeus—the port of Athens—was laid out in a grid pattern cen-

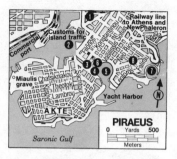

Kaisariani

tering on an agora. The harbor was connected to Athens by the walls of Themistocles, remains of which are extant. Today you arrive by rail from Athens at the *Train Station* [1], and it's a short walk to *Kantharos* [2], the Great Harbor, where ships leave for the islands as well as other Mediterranean ports, and farther abroad. If you're not heading straight for a ferry, visit the *Archaeological Museum* [3], on Harilaou Trikoupi Street, with the ruins of the Hellenic *Zea Theater* [4] directly behind. Nearby is the yacht-choked Zea Harbor, or *Pashalimani* [5]. Heading west along the harbor, you'll come upon the *Naval Museum* [6], which affords a good overview of the Greek fleet from ancient times to the present. To the east is the *Mikrolimano basin* [7], with its bobbing sailboats and fine seafood restaurants. Just north of the harbor, climb the *Kastella* or *Munichia hill* [8] for a superb view of the Saronic Gulf.

*Sounion, 70 km. (44 miles) southeast of Athens: The most southerly point of Attica, Cape

Sounion was a most appropriate location for a Temple of Poseidon. Built in the fifth century B.C. on the site of an earlier (unfinished) building destroyed by the Persians, the temple is an imposing structure, commanding a hilltop position. Byron carved his name on one of its Doric columns, 12 of which are extant. On a lower hill stand the remains of the small Temple of Athena Sounias.

Barcelona

Surrounded by mountains and the sea, Barcelona is not so much typically Spanish as fiercely Catalonian, and Catalan is the distinctive language you'll hear spoken by the natives. From an ancient Gothic Quarter with narrow, winding streets and a cathedral to sweeping mountaintop panoramic views, from age-darkened relics to the Picasso and Miró museums, Barcelona offers an eclectic feast for the eyes. A magnificent avenue—the Ramblas—runs through the heart of the old city and offers non-stop people watching. This vibrant, exciting port city was also the home of the architect Antonio Gaudí, whose brilliant *art nouveau* structures are certain to make you rethink architecture.

History

Because of its desirable location on the Mediterranean Sea, Barcelona has been fought over and occupied by various groups since prehistoric times; Phoenicians, Carthaginians, Romans, Visigoths, Moors, and Franks have at one time or another claimed the area as their own. (Traces of the Roman occupation can be seen in modern Barcelona, and the Catalan language spoken there is descended from Latin.) The Franks under Charlemagne, who had come to dispel the Moors and return Iberia to Christianity, captured Barcelona in 801 and made the city a Frankish dependency called the Spanish March. Independence was granted in 878, and by the 12th century, the count of Barcelona had become king of Aragon. As a result, Barcelona entered a prosperous, expansionist Golden Age, the fruits of which are evident in the city's marvelous medieval quarter.

The great era of world-wide exploration had begun and Catalonia, with Barcelona as its capital, was in the forefront. Christopher Columbus, whose voyage of discovery to America was financed by Ferdinand and Isabella, is traditionally said to have been greeted by the monarchs on his return from the New World in Barcelona's Placa del Rei.

But the Mediterranean eventually lost its importance as a trading zone, and by the 17th century, Barcelona, unwilling to be ruled by the king of Spain, fell under the "protection" of the king of France. Besieged, the city surrendered and begrudgingly renewed allegiance to the Spanish crown. When Barcelona later sided with the Bourbons against Spain, the city was overrun and harsh reprisals carried out, including the suppression of the Catalan language.

Industrialization came in the late 19th century and with it a resurgence of artistic and cultural vitality. Barcelona became the capital of an autonomous Catalan Republic in 1931, was repeatedly bombed by Italian planes, and fell in 1939, when Nationalist forces won the Spanish Civil War. Once again, under Franco, the Catalonian city's independent identity was firmly suppressed. Today, however, with Catalonia experiencing a renewed sense of its unique identity and history, Barcelona has become the exciting center of a regional renaissance.

Attractions

*Archeological Museum (Museu Arqueològic) [21]: On display is an outstanding collection of art and artifacts from all the peoples and cultures that have occupied Barcelona over the centuries, from the Phoenicians to the Romans.

Barri Gòtic: Barcelona's medieval quarter, crammed with ancient buildings and twisting, mysterious streets, is full of enough architectural treasures to keep you gawking and gaping for days.

*Cathedral (Catedral de Santa Eulalia) [15]: Begun in the 13th century on the highest point in old Barcelona, this magnificent structure was built in the Mediterranean Gothic style and features beautifully carved choir stalls, the 14th-century tomb of Santa Eulalia in the crypt, and a particularly lovely cloister presided over by a noisy gaggle of geese.

Church of the Holy Family (Temple de la Sagrada Familia) [11]: Left unfinished at the time of the architect Gaudí's death in 1926, this is one of the most remarkable structures in Spain— the minute you see its façade, you'll know why. For a bird's-eye view of the city, take the elevator to the top of one of the towers.

Columbus Monument (Monumento a Colom) [8]: A breathtaking panorama of the city unfolds from the top of this monument dedicated to the discoverer of the New World. A replica of his ship, the *Santa María,* is docked at the nearby wharf.

Gaudí Buildings: On the Passeig de Gracia are *Casa Batlló* (#43) and *Casa Milá* (#92), two early 20th-century luxury apartment buildings with distinctive, undulating *art nouveau* façades designed by Gaudí. *Palau Güell,* just off the Ramblas, was built for Gaudí's friend and patron Eusebio Güell, who also sponsored the audacious and wonderful *Parc Güell,* which was originally meant to be a garden city. As you stroll along its serpentine walks paved with mosaics, you'll come across gingerbread houses, one of which is the home of the *La Gaudí Museum.*

Gran Teatro del Liceu [5]: A somewhat undistinguished façade hides one of the oldest and most beautiful gilt and red plush opera houses in the world, dating from the mid-1800s.

La Ljotja [9]: A *bolsa* (or exchange) has been in existence in this spot since the 14th century, and today La Ljota houses the Barcelona Stock Exchange.

Mare de Déu de Betlem [2]: The church is less interesting than the area that surrounds it, where birds, monkeys and tropical flowers and plants are for sale.

Montjuïc: This steep hill overlooking the sea was the site of the 1929 World's Fair, and contains several interesting buildings from that time, including the recently rebuilt Mies van der Rohe Pavilion, the **Poblo Espanyol** (Spanish Hamlet) [19], a collection of houses typical of Catalonia and other Spanish provinces, and two important museums. *The* **Museum of Catalan Art** (Museu d'Art de Catalunya) [20] in the Palau Nacional is a must-see for its fabulous collection of regional medieval treasures. Not far away is the **Miró Foundation** (Fundació Miró) [23], which the artist bequeathed to his native city; several rooms are devoted to Miró's distinctive, delicate work,

Poblo Espanyol

while other areas serve as exhibition space for changing shows. To reach Montjuïc and its various attractions, you can take the funicular railway from the harbor.

Museu de la Ciutat (Museum of the History of the City) [18]: Don't bother with the maps and other documents in this palace—go underground. There you'll find a series of remarkable subterranean passages, all of which chart the Roman presence in Barcelona.

Museu Mar i Cel del Mar: Located in Sitges, a resort town south of the city, the museum is housed in a 14th-century palace and displays an excellent collection of medieval sculpture.

Museu Federico Marès [16]: An eclectic collection put together by a local sculptor, the museum has an assortment of everything from walking sticks to crucifixes.

Museu Marítim [7]: Located in a medieval shipyard known as Drassanes, the only structure of its kind in the world, the Maritime Museum presents a tribute to Barcelona's nautical history and includes a 15th-century atlas that belonged to the explorer Amerigo Vespucci. While you're in the vicinity, you might want to consider a boat tour of Barcelona's harbor.

*Museu Picasso [13]: Works spanning Picasso's entire career—and donated by him to the city—fill this extremely popular museum which is housed in two 15th-century palaces.

Palace of the Vicereine (Palau de la Virreina) [3]: Erected

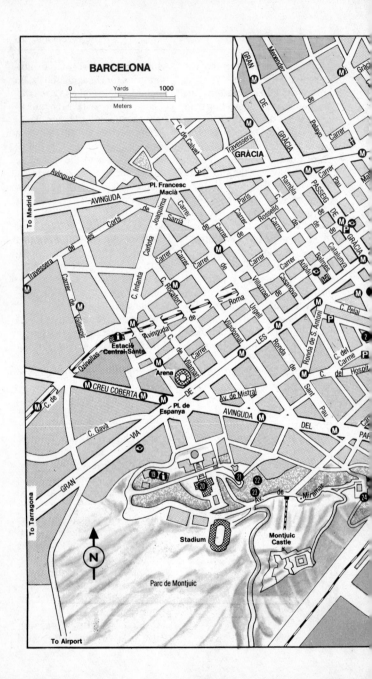

Barcelona Attractions:
1. Plaça de Catalunya
2. Mare de Déu de Betlem
3. Palace of the Vicereine
4. Santa Maria del Pi
5. Gran Teatro del Liceu
6. Sant Pau del Camp
7. Museu Marítim
8. Columbus Monument
9. La Ljotja
10. Parc de la Ciutadella
11. Church of the Holy Family
12. Santa Maria del Mar
13. Museu Picasso
14. Plaça Sant Jaume
15. Cathedral
16. Museu Federico Marès
17. Archives of the Arogòn Crown
18. Plaça del Rei/Museu de la Ciutat
19. Poblo Espanyol
20. Museum of Catalan Art
21. Archaeological Museum
22. Greek Theater
23. Miro Foundation
24. Jardins de Miramar

in 1778 by a Peruvian viceroy, this building is now the city's major exhibition center and also houses the *Museu d'Arts Decoratives* with its sumptuous collection of carpets, porcelain, glassware, furniture, and clocks.

Parc de la Ciutadella [10]: Barcelona's *Zoological Gardens*, the *Martorell Geological Museum* (Museu de Geologia "Martorell"), and the *Museum of Modern Art* (Museu d'Art Modern) are all located in this large, pleasant oasis which was once the site of the citadel.

Plaça de Catalunya: [1] One of Europe's largest and most beautiful squares, the Plaça is also one of the busiest, for it's the business center of modern Barcelona and the spot where bus, railway, and metro lines converge. There are plenty of stores in the vicinity and you can quench your thirst opposite the *Hostal Continental* at a beer hall known as the *Cervecería*, or sit at the old *Café Zurich* on Pelai and sip a coffee. At night, the fountains are brilliantly illuminated.

Plaça del Rei (King's Square) [18]: The city's most historic square, site of the *Royal Palace* (Palau Reial) and the place where, tradition has it, Columbus was greeted on his return from the New World. Forming a regal welcoming committee, the Catholic monarchs Ferdinand and Isabella may have stood on the steps of *Saló del Tinell* (Tinell Hall), one immense room, dating from the 14th century, which served as a reception and banqueting hall. Looming above the hall is the curious five-storied *Torre del Rei Marti* (King Martin's Watchtower), added in the mid-16th century. Lovers of ancient history can go to the nearby Carrer Paradis to see the remains of the Roman *Temple of Augustus.*

Plaça Sant Jaume [14]: Situated in the heart of the medieval quarter, this lovely square was built in the 1840s and contains two important older buildings. The 14th-century *Ajuntament* (City Hall) is entered through two courtyards and contains, in the Saló de las Cronicas, a striking black-and-gold mural painted in 1928 by Josep Maria Sert, and the sumptuous, recently restored Saló del Consell de Cent, where the city's ruling Council of One Hundred sat from 1372 to 1714. Facing it across the square is the *Palau de la Generalitat,* home of Catalonia's parliament, with a heavily ornamented St. George's Chapel and a roof garden patio (Patio de los Naranjos) with orange trees.

Las Ramblas: Described by some as the funkiest street in Europe, the Ramblas seems to combine attributes from New York's Times Square and East Village and London's Soho. The lively street, filled with flower stalls, frequently changes names and can be dangerous at night. It's a great place to sample a characteristic snack of the city, *pa amb tomaquet* (bread with tomato), or the ever-present *pollo al ast* (chicken on a spit). If you take the Ramblas past

Plaça de Catalunya all the way to Diagonal, you'll come to Barcelona's chic new section, filled with boutiques, beautiful restaurants, and hotels.

*Santa Maria del Mar [12]: With its stark, uncluttered grandeur and rose window, this handsome Gothic church—its cornerstone laid in 1329—impresses the spirit in a special way. If you're lucky you might be able to hear a concert or recital here.

Santa Maria del Pi [4]: Damaged during the bitter fighting of the Spanish Civil War, the church retains a 13th-century portal and an octagonal belltower from the 15th century.

Basel

With its magnificent setting on the Rhine at the junction of Switzerland,
West Germany, and France, surrounded by the Jura and Vosges mountains and the Black Forest, it's not surprising that Basel has always been a
strategic trading and cultural conduit. Switzerland's second-largest city
may have fewer than 350,000 inhabitants, but its size has in no way
diminished its importance as a long-standing intellectual and industrial
center. Its banking, chemical, and pharmaceutical firms are internationally influential, and the city annually hosts many trade fairs.

The city's physical aspects are so pleasing that any visit is bound to be
exhilarating. The great river positively rushes through it—its current so
strong that ferries use it for crossing guided only by anchoring cables.
The esplanades and the bridges afford other gratifying views of this city
that is noticeably prosperous, clean, and architecturally interesting with
the structures of the medieval, Renaissance, Baroque, or modern periods. Basel is efficient and hard-working, but also attractive and stimu-
lating to visit, and it has marvels of art to offer as well.

History

First a Celtic settlement that became a fortified Roman town called Ba-
silia in A.D. 372, Basel was attacked by rampaging Huns, and eventually
came under Burgundian rule. It later became part of the Germanic Empire. In the 13th century, an emperor's court was located here. The Ecu-
menical Council on church reform met in Basel briefly during the 15th
century. In 1460, a former Italian delegate to that council, Pope Pius II,
founded the country's first university which flourishes to this day. From
early times, luminous names have been associated with both city and
university, among them the painters Dürer and Holbein the Younger, the
physician Paracelsus and the scholar Erasmus. Nietzsche was on the
philosophical faculty, and contemporary figures like the art historians
Jakob Burck hardt and Heinrich Wölfflin, philosophers Karl Jaspers and
Karl Barth, and the novelist Hermann Hesse, have all made their contributions to the city's humanist tradition.

Attractions

The Historical Museum [4] is
housed in the beautiful 14th-
century Barfusserkirche (Barefoot
Church, so called because its resident Franciscan monks worshiped in their bare feet). The
structure was used as a warehouse
in the 19th century, but by the end
of the century had been restored
for a more fitting function as a museum; it has since undergone further restoration. The collection
includes pre-historic finds, sacred
and secular medieval art, gold

items from the cathedral treasury, 15th-century tapestries, weaponry, and Renaissance and Baroque artworks.

The **Kirschgarten Museum** [3], a four-story, 18th-century mansion, is furnished entirely in the style of the period. Among the many works of art and works of craftsmanship are an especially fine china and porcelain collection, impressive silver and tapestries, toys, and items of homely practical use.

The **Museum of Fine Arts** [2] is in the front ranks of European museums. Apart from the most extensive Holbein collection in the world, it holds many works by German, Flemish, and Swiss masters, as well as a stunning collection of modern art that represents all the great contempo-rary artists—Monet, Gauguin, Cézanne, van Gogh, Matisse, Braque, Picasso, Chagall, Léger, Gris, Klee, Arp, and Giacometti, among others.

The **Museum of Ancient Art** (Antiken Museum) houses Greek and Roman works from important private collections. It is conveniently located diagonally across from the Museum of Fine Arts. At

Basel Attractions:
 1. Cathedral
 2. Museum of Fine Arts
 3. Kirschgarten Museum
 4. Historical Museum
 5. Leonharskirche
 6. Industrial Museum
 7. Spalentor
 8. Town Hall
 9. Museums of Ethnography and Natural History
10. Cultural Hall
11. Natioanalgalerie

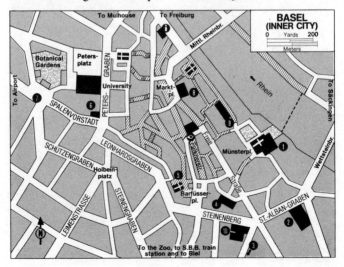

the end of the street is the *St. Alben-Tor,* a medieval city gate. Nearby, too, in a restored mill, you'll find a rather specialized *Museum of Paper, Writing, and Printing.*

The ***Cathedral** [1], or *Münster,* with its patterned roof and ruddy coloring, is Basel's landmark. It endured many disasters, both natural and man-made, before the part-Romanesque, part-Gothic cathedral was rebuilt in the 14th, 18th, and 19th centuries. The St. Gallus Portal on the north façade, parts of the so-called Wheelwindow, sections of the apse, the Chapter House, and the crypt with its Romanesque murals, remain from the original 12th-century structure.

The tympanum of the portal depicts the Last Judgment, with statues of the Evangelists and the wise and foolish virgins below the figure of Christ as the divine judge. Erasmus's tomb is here, and the 15th-century chancel, choir stalls, and crypt should be seen. The glorious panorama visible from the tower justifies the climb.

Cathedral

The **museums of Ethnography** and **Natural History** [9] are located in the cathedral square, and the **Museum of European Folklife** is on an adjacent street. The Museum of Ethnography (Museum für Volkerkunde) has collections of considerable interest from many cultures, most importantly from Central and South America, as well as one of boats from all over the world, and prehistoric objects. The Museum of Natural History (Naturhistorisches Museum) focuses largely on the fauna of Switzerland. Those more interested in human life will find the smaller works of man, such as textiles, farm paintings, and masks, in the Swiss Museum of European Folklife (Schweizerishes Museum für Volkskunde).

The **Town Hall** [8] (Rathaus) dominating the main square (Marktplatz), was built in Gothic style in the early 16th century, but has undergone a number of alterations. The colorful façade, like the walls in the inner courtyard, are decorated with frescoes. At the top of the courtyard stairs is a statue of *Munatius Planecus,* the Roman said to have established the Roman settlement in 44 B.C.

The **Spalentor** [7] is a beautifully preserved 15th-century city gate with twin towers, once part of the city's defensive wall. Nearby is one of Basel's oldest fountains, known as the "Bagpiper," possibly constructed from designs by Holbein and Dürer.

From the other side of the Rhine, on the *Oberen Rheinweg,*

you can get an embracing view of the Cathedral and the old city. Farther downriver, on the *Unteren Rheinweg*, is the **City and Cathedral Museum** (Stadt-und Munstermeum), in which the history of the city is well-documented.

Belgrade

Belgrade, the capital of Yugoslavia and Serbia, is the country's largest city, as well as its political, economic, and cultural center.

As one might expect from its turbulent history, Belgrade has lost most of its past architectural distinction and atmospheric richness. Travelers who wish to stroll among antiquities and buildings that straddle the centuries, and to discover unaltered corners of picturesque charm, may find Belgrade something of a disappointment.

Nevertheless, history looms large here, but it is one that makes manifest the appalling waste of human and cultural resources inherent in unending wars and struggles, domination and outrage, suffering and resilience, destruction and rehabilitation. The very emphasis on the modern aspects of the city sparks an understanding of how much has been destroyed over the centuries, and how the natural and accumulating heritage of the people has been likewise wrenched and distorted. There is plenty of evidence of this saddening process, both in the commemorative tablets about the city, and in the Museum of the Illegal Party Printing Works, a house in which Gestapo officers lived while at the same time, below them, resistance messages were being communicated.

No one can visit Belgrade and remain unmoved or fail to be drawn to the people themselves, whose friendliness and vivacity belies their passionate concern for their own troubled history.

History

Its strategically important position, on a site which has been inhabited for 7,000 years, accounts for its blood-stained history. In the early third century B.C., Celts founded a settlement here called Singidium. The Romans captured it in the first century B.C., and established a flourishing town. It later suffered a succession of invasions, until the Slavs settled here in the ninth century and renamed it Beligrad (White Town).

In the following centuries, the city was alternately ravaged and reestablished by the Byzantines, the Bulgarians, and the Hungarians. At last, once more under Byzantine rule, it became an important frontier stronghold; in the 13th century, it came under Serbian rule, and two centuries later became the Serbian capital. It was conquered by the Turks in the 18th century, and for the next two centuries passed back and forth between them and the Austrians.

In the early 19th century, after Serbia had successfully rebelled against Turkish oppression, Belgrade became the vital cultural, political, and administrative center of an autonomous Serbia. Austria recaptured Belgrade during World War I, but Serbia's army liberated it. Then, as capital of the newly founded Yugoslav state, it enjoyed a period of expansion, until two-thirds of the city was destroyed by German bombs in 1941. It was occupied by the Germans until combined Yugoslav and Russian forces marched on the city in October 1944.

Attractions

The **Bajrakli dzamija** (Bajrak Mosque, Mosque of Flags) [12] is the last of approximately 100 mosques that flourished in the city during the 18th century.

The ***Etnografski muzej** (Museum of Ethnography) [10] on Studentski trg, contains a rich collection of traditional costumes from every region of the country, as well as laces, textiles, tapestries, jewelry, farming tools, and other works of art and craft.

The **Muzej fresaka** (Fresco Museum) [11] has a remarkable collection of extremely skillful copies of beautiful frescoes, many of them from remote medieval Serbian and Macedonian monasteries.

Kalamegdan [1]. The largest section of this park, which overlooks Belgrade's two rivers, the Danube and the Sava, was once a great citadel. It is filled with vivid reminders of the site's occupation by Celtic, Roman, Turkish, Austrian, and Serbian forces. It was laid out as a park during the Austrian occupation (1717–1739) after the Turkish retreat, and was transformed from a fortress into a pleasure site, with a multiplicity of paths, fountains, busts of distinguished Serbs, a zoo, and an engrossing military museum. Among the sculptures is Ivan Mestrović's monument dedicated to France. The Baroque clock tower and gate, set into the medieval wall of the *Upper Fortress* (Gornji grad) [2] lead you to the museum, in which you can see not only an extensive collection of weaponry, but the so-called Roman Fountain (actually of 1731), the Monument to the Victor by Mestrović, the octagonal Turbeh (tomb) of the Turkish grand vizier Sultan Ahmed III, Damad Ali Pasha. In addition, there are two churches located here. Within the *Lower Fortress* (Donji grad), there is an 18th-century *hamam* (Turkish bath), the Gate of the Emperor Karl VI, a triumphal arch, and the Nebojsa Tower. You can gather even from this short list something of the vastness of this ancient site, which you may prefer to explore with the help of a guide.

The **Narodni muzej** (National Museum) [6] is the most important museum in the Balkans and one of Europe's finest. Its choice and beautifully presented collection covers the art and culture of Yugoslavia from prehistoric times. Needless to say, given the country's history, it is a varied and fascinating survey. There are also many more familiar sorts of works—paintings by modern European masters such as Toulouse-

Belgrade Attractions:
1. Kalemegdan
2. Upper Fortress
3. Orthodox Cathedral
4. Konak (Palace) of Princess Ljubica
5. Trg Republike
6. National Museum
7. Parliament
8. Church of Saint Mark
9. City Museum
10. Museum of Ethnography
11. Fresco Museum
12. Bajrak Mosque
13. Vuk and Dositej Museum
14. Skadarlija

Lautrec, Matisse, Picasso, Renoir, van Gogh, and others.

The **Saborna crkva** (Orthodox Cathedral [3], with its arching ceiling, was erected in the first half of the 19th century. You will find many tombs and relics of rulers, paintings, wood carvings, and an impressive painted iconostasis here.

The street known as Knez Mihailova ulica (Prince Mihailo

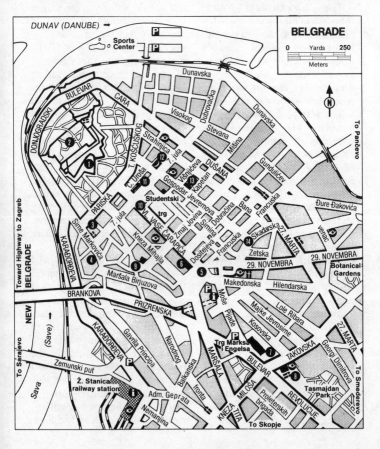

Street) leads to the lively center of Belgrade, **Terasije Square,** with its trees, fountains, cafés, hotels, restaurants, and river view.

The **Skardarlija district** [14] was the artistic center of Belgrade at the turn of the century. Today it is a popular rendezvous spot, a pedestrian zone where people gather to enjoy galleries, restaurants, and street entertainment.

The **Gradski muzej** (City Museum) [9] exhibits thousands of items pertaining to Belgrade's colorful history from ancient times to the last century.

Trg Republike (Republic Square) [5], at the heart of the city, is a good starting point for exploration. Mose Pijade Street leads from here to the **Trg Marksa i Engelsa** (Marx and Engels Square) and the Boulevar Revolucije (Boulevard of the Revolution). The domed parliament building, the **Skupstina** [7], dominates the square. In *Tasmajden Park* you will find the **Church of St. Mark** [8], containing the tombs of King Alexander and Queen Draga, who were assassinated in 1903.

Parliament

Excursions

Avala Mountain, a forested peak 15 km. (7 miles) from Belgrade, on the border of the fertile, hilly countryside of Sumadija, is a delightful venue for picnics. The country's *Tomb of the Unknown Soldier* is on the summit—another of Mestrovic's commemorative sculptures.

The four-hour hydrofoil excursion on the Danube, from Belgrade to ****Iron Gate** (Djerdap), on the Rumanian border, makes a rewarding day trip.

Berlin

For many people, Berlin conjures up an unforgettable era of pre-war decadence and post-war political intrigue—a place set apart, where the naughtiest of nightlife once flourished and where, after the Second World War, a wall was erected to separate East Berlin from West. Whatever its past sins, or perhaps because of them, West Berlin remains a special place, fast-paced and sophisticated, full of cultural vitality, great museums, and a very special ambience. Crossing what's left of the Wall and stepping into East Berlin today is as easy as showing your passport; once there, you'll find a very different-looking Berlin with its own share of attractions in a very unusual package. With the destruction of the wall and talk of reunification, Berlin—East or West—is as exciting now as it has ever been.

History

Although it recently celebrated its 750th birthday (and was mentioned in official documents as early as 1244), Berlin was not always the capital of an undivided Germany and one of Europe's great cities. The House of Hohenzollern made Berlin its home in the 15th century and continued in power as Princes-Elect for several hundred years. Under Frederick the Great (1740–1786), Berlin became established as a leading European center, but it was bombarded and occupied by both Austria and Russia during the Seven Years' War. In 1806, after the military collapse of Prussia, Napoleon entered the city and two years of French occupation ensued. Berlin became one of Europe's most important industrial cities during the reign of King Friedrich Wilhelm IV (1840–1861) and, following the defeat of Austria in 1867, finally emerged as the capital of the German Empire.

Situated at the geographical and political crossroads between Western and Eastern Europe, Berlin has often been caught in conflict between the two. Germany was declared a republic in 1918 from a window of Berlin's Reichstag, which the Nazis later burned down. Hitler wanted the city to be the showplace of the Third Reich, and the Olympic Games were held here in 1936. His grandiose plans for Berlin never got much farther, for continuous air raids began in 1943, and by 1945, the city had been seized by the Soviet Army. With the city completely besieged, Hitler committed suicide in his bunker there.

Berlin then became the headquarters of the Allied High Command and the city was divided into four sectors, each to be occupied by one of the four Allied Powers. When the Soviet Union seceded from the Allied Control Council in 1948 and blockaded the city, the famous Berlin "Air

Lift" took place. The blockade ended the following year, and the German Democratic Republic (DDR: Deutsche Demokratische Republik) was founded, with East Berlin as its capital. The Berlin Wall was erected in 1961 to stop the flow of East Berliners into West Berlin; it created yet another political crisis. In an equally dramatic turn of events on November 9, 1989, the government of the German Democratic Republic opened its borders, allowing its citizens to pass freely into the West.

West Berlin Attractions

Akademie der Künste (Academy of Arts) [15], Hanseatenweg: Founded in 1960, the academy has become one of Berlin's most important cultural centers and hosts temporary exhibitions throughout the year.

Bauhaus-Archiv [25]: A late work by Berlin-born architect Walter Gropius, this archive houses a large collection of Bauhaus School of Design objects.

Brandenburger Tor (Brandenburg Gate): An 18th-century Prussian victory arch, this famous monument now lies within

East Germany. It was reopened as a crossing point in late 1989.

Checkpoint Charlie, Friedrichstrasse 44: Once the most famous crossing-point between the two Berlins, Checkpoint Charlie also acts as a small museum of the Wall's history.

Berlin Attractions (zoo and west):
1. Zoological Gardens
2. Kaiser-Wilhelm-Gedächtniskirche
3. Europa-Centrum
4. Theater des Westens
5. Schaubühne (Playhouse)

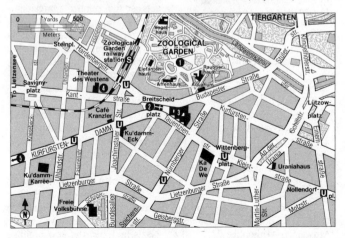

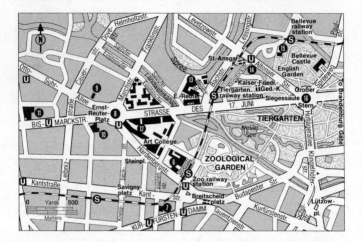

Berlin Attractions (north of zoo):
6. Art Library, Museum of Architecture
7. Jüdishe Gemeindehaus
8. Ernst Reuter Platz
9. Theater Tribüne
10. Schiller Theater
11. German Opera
12. Technical University
13. Staatliche Porzellanmanufaktur
14. Hansaviertel
15. Academy of the Arts
16. Siegessaule

Europa Centrum [3]: Berlin's largest shopping, business, and entertainment center was opened in 1965 and is home to over a hundred shops, cafes, bars, and restaurants, as well as movie theaters, a cabaret, the Palace Hotel, and the Spielbank Berlin casino. You can get an excellent view of Berlin from the 20th floor observation deck.

**Gemaldegalerie (Painting Gallery, also known as the Dahlem Museum), Arnimallee 23,27: By far the greatest art museum in Berlin, this artistic pleasure palace has enough Rembrandts and Rubens to keep you studying skin tones for a month.

Grünewald: This immense forested park in the west of the city acts as "the country" for residents of West Berlin, and provides outdoor recreational facilities of every kind, from steamer rides on Wannsee Lake to nudist beaches.

*Hansaviertel (Hansa Quarter) [14]: Severely damaged during the Second World War, this city district between the Tiergarten and Bellevue subway stations was redesigned as a model city by 48 architects from 13 different countries.

Jüdische Gemeindehaus (Jewish Community Hall) [7]: Erected in 1959 on the foundation of a synagogue destroyed by the Nazis in 1938, the new building has the portal of the old one incorporated into its structure. At nearby *Steinplatz* there is a memorial to the Victims of National Socialism (Nazism) and another memorial dedicated to the victims of Stalinism.

*Kaiser-Wilhelm Gedächtniskirche [2]: A perennial memorial to the devastation of war, this Berlin landmark is a stark amalgamation of a new church with the ruins of the earlier one which was built between 1891 and 1895.

*Kunstgewebemuseum, Tiergarten 6: This new museum displays European arts and crafts from the early Middle Ages (including the noteworthy ****Guelphs' Treasure**) up to the turn of the century.

*Kurfürstendamm: Consid- ered the most famous avenue and promenade in Berlin since 1886, and jumping with activity from morning until late at night, the "Ku-Damm," as it's called, evolved from a log road built to make it easy for the 16th-century Prince-Electors (Kurfursten) to reach their hunting lodge in the Grunewald.

Memorial to the Victims of July 20, 1944 [24], Stauffenbergstrasse 13/14: Created by

Berlin Attractions (east of zoo):

17. Schloss Bellevue
18. Congress Hall
19. Reichstag
20. Soviet Memorial
21. Philharmonie
22. National Library
23. National Gallery
24. Memorial to the Victims of July 20, 1944
25. Bauhaus-Archiv

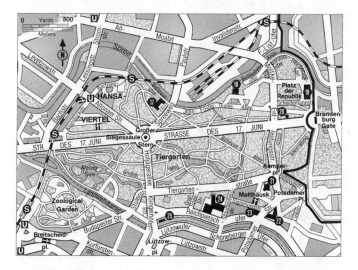

Richard Scheibe in 1953, this war memorial commemorates an abortive attempt on Hitler's life by several German officers.

*Nationalgalerie (New National Gallery) [23]: Designed by Mies van der Rohe and opened in 1968, its impressive holdings include works of the German Romantics, as well as German Impressionists, Expressionists, and Surrealists.

Philharmonie (Philharmonic Hall) [21], Matthaikirchstrasse 1: Although Herbert van Karajan, the autocratic conductor of the Berlin Philharmonic Orchestra for decades, is no longer at the podium, the orchestra is always worth hearing in this modern, acoustically sensitive hall.

Rathaus Schoneberg (City Hall): Seat of the city and state government of West Berlin, its Freedom Bell (Freiheitsglocke), presented to the city in 1950 by the Americans expressing solidarity with West Berlin, strikes the noon hour every day. A bronze plaque at the entrance commemorates John F. Kennedy's visit in 1963 and his now-famous "Ich bin ein Berliner" speech.

Reichstag [19]: An uninspiring, restored version of Germany's former parliament building, originally built in a ponderous Italian High Renaissance style in the late 19th century, the Reichstag has seen more than its share of historic moments. The German Republic was proclaimed here in 1918, and Nazis burned the building in 1933; now it's used for meetings of the two houses of the German Parliament. If the tragedies and conundrums of German history interest you, be sure to have a look at the permanent exhibit called "Fragen an die deutsche Geschichte" (Questions about German History).

Schloss Bellevue [17]: Prince Ferdinand, the youngest brother of Frederick the Great, had this palace built in 1785; the West German president calls this home when he's in Berlin.

***Schloss Charlottenburg, Louisenplatz: The largest and most beautiful palace in Berlin, it was built between 1695 and 1699 as a small pleasure seat for Sophie Charlotte, Prussia's first queen. The historical rooms have been restored and are open to the public, and behind the palace is the beautifully laid-out *Schlosspark*. Lovers of Egyptian antiquities should not miss the **Ägyptisches Museum* opposite the palace, for it's home to the exquisite ***bust of Queen Nefertiti* and one of the best preserved mummies outside of Cairo.

National Gallery

Siegessäule (Victory Column) [16]: Prussian military victories over Denmark, Austria, and France are commemorated by this column, which formerly stood in front of the Reichstag, erected in 1873 as a monument to Prussia's might and glory. Go up to the observation deck and you'll be able to view West Berlin and East Berlin.

Staatliche Porzellanmanufaktur (National Porcelain Manufacturing Plant) [13]: The imperial blue scepter of the House of Brandenburg is still used as the trademark on the porcelain made in this factory, which was acquired for the Prussian state in 1763 by Frederick the Great.

Zoologischer Garten [1]: Originally laid out in 1841, the zoo has an enormous collection of animals, and is the home of the **Berlin Aquarium*, the largest in Europe.

East Berlin Attractions

Plan to spend at least one day in East Berlin, which is the capital of the Soviet-styled DDR (Deutsche Demokratische Republik) and acts as its premiere showcase. East Berlin looks very different from West Berlin, thanks (or no thanks) to the Soviet architects who helped build it after the war. There's a conspicuous lack of capitalist glamor here (though that is rapidly changing) because the city was in very different financial straits from West Berlin, which was rebuilt with massive influxes of American and West European aid. East Berlin has major museums and over a dozen fine theaters, including the Deutsche Staatsoper (German State Opera), the Komische Oper (Comic Opera), and the famous Brecht-Bühne Berliner Ensemble. Crossing into the city for a day's visit is a routine affair at Checkpoint Charlie or any other opening in the now defunct Berlin Wall. You will need to exchange a certain amount of money (approximately 25 marks) into East German marks, and buy a one-day visa for five marks. You will not find East Berlin a city of culinary wonders and sumptuous feasting, so don't expect much on the food front unless you are prepared to pay through the nose.

Alexanderplatz [32]: Called "Alex" for short, this modern business, shopping, and communications center was named in 1805 for the Russian czar Alexander I.

Altes Museum [16]: Postwar East German art and Old Masters etchings and drawings are exhibited in this severely neoclassical building located in the museum complex known as *Museumsinsel* (Museum Island).

***Bodemuseum** [21]: Also situated on Museum Island, the Bode features an outstanding collection of Early Christian and Egyptian art.

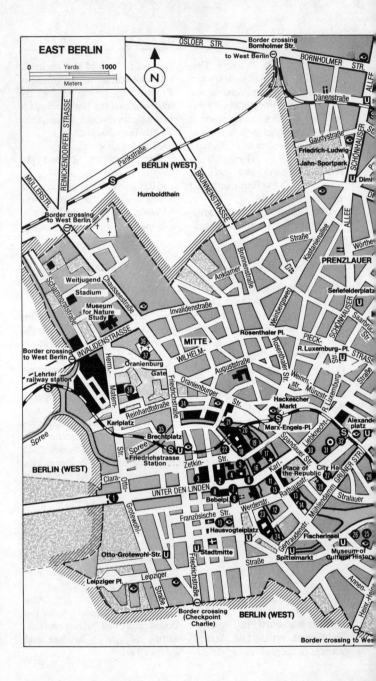

East Berlin Attractions:
1. Brandenburg Gate
2. Humboldt University
3. German State Library
4. Neue Wache
5. Maxim Gorki Theater
6. Museu für Deutsche Geschite
7. German State Opera
8. Old Library
9. Saint Hedwig's Cathedral
10. Platz der Akademie
11. Marx-Engels-Platz
12. East German Council of State Building
13. Alter Marstall (Old Stables)
14. Ribbeckhaus
15. Ministry of Foreign Affairs
16. Altes Museum
17. Cathedral
18. Neues Museum
19. National Gallery
20. Pergamonmuseum
21. Bode-Museum
22. Max-Planck-Haus
23. Jungfernbrücke
24. Gertraudenbrücke
25. Märkisches Museum
26. Märkisches Ufer
27. Rotes Rathaus (Red City Hall)
28. Nikolaikirche
29. Zur letzten Instanz (restaurant)
30. Marienkirche
31. Television Tower
32. Alexanderplatz
33. "Berolina"
34. Friedrichstadt-Palast
35. Theater am Schiffbauerdamm
36. Brecht's Residence
37. Dorotheenstädtischer Friedhof (Cemetery)
38. Deutsches Theater
39. Friedrichshain
40. Tierpark Friedrichsfelde

*Brandenburger Tor (Brandenburg Gate) [1]: This classically inspired Prussian landmark was completed in 1791 and once again acts as Berlin's Arc de Triomphe on the famous avenue *Unter den Linden.*

Deutsche Staattsoper (German State Opera) [7]: Three

times destroyed, three times rebuilt, the Opera in East Berlin is considered East Germany's best. Just beside the opera is the recently restored *Palais Unter den Linden,* formerly the palace of the crown prince.

Dorotheenstadischer Friedhof [37]: Known as the "Scholars' and Artists' Cemetery," this is the final resting place of playwright Bertold Brecht, the architect Schinkel, the philosopher Hegel, and the writer Heinrich Mann.

Humboldt University [2]: Founded by the scholarly Humboldt brothers Wilhelm and Alexander, it is now the largest university in East Germany; since its opening in 1810, and, among its distinguished faculty and alumni, had Marx and Engels (students), and Einstein (teacher).

Jungfernbrücke [23]: This small structure is the last and oldest drawbridge in Berlin, a city which once used its extensive series of canals and waterways for transportation.

Marienkirche (Church of Saint Mary) [30]: Rebuilt in the 15th century in a Late Gothic style, the church is chiefly known for its "Dance of Death" fresco.

Markisches Museum [25]: Among the several serious sections of the museum devoted to the cultural history of Berlin, you'll find one distinctly lighthearted collection of automaphones, self-playing musical instruments.

The **Markischer Ufer** (Bank of the March) [26], just across from Fischerinsel (Fischer Island), has several old Berlin houses which are being restored; you can compare the architecture of 18th-century Berlin with that of the 20th century as represented by the new apartment complexes on Fischer Island.

Marx-Engels-Platz [11]: As you might expect in a square named after two heroes of Communism, there's not a lot of glitter and glitz here—rather, it's dominated by the terrifically ugly *Palast der Republik,* the assembly hall of the lower house of the East German Parliament, which also has restaurants, a theater, and a dance hall.

Museum für Deutsche Geschichte [6]: History is written differently, according to which side of the wall you live on, and this museum, located in a lovely Baroque building on the Spree, is devoted to a Marxist view of Germany from 1789 to the present.

*Nationalgalerie [19]: First built in 1876 in the form of a Corinthian temple, the restored museum houses drawings, paintings, and sculpture from the 19th and 20th centuries.

*Neue Wache (New Guard House) [4]: Guarded by members of the People's Army, this early 19th-century building now serves as a monument to the victims of fascism and militarism.

Nikolaikirche (Church of Saint Nicholas) [28]: Beautifully restored, the church, which dates from about 1200, is Berlin's oldest building. The *Nicolai Quarter*

Market Gate of Milet

around the church, with its narrow streets, gas lanterns, and old taverns, is also worth exploring.

***Pergamonmuseum [20]: East Berlin's premiere museum, the monumental Pergamon, is named after its world-famous, block-long ****Pergamon Altar,* a Greek temple from 180 B.C. Other eye-openers are the 2,500-year-old ****Babylonian Processional Way,* the ***Market Gate of Milet,* and the ***Ishtar Gate.*

Platz der Akademie [10]: Everything here was severely damaged in the war, but the beautifully reconstructed classical *Schauspielhaus* (theater) is now a concert hall, and the 18th-century Baroque *French Cathedral* (with its *Huguenot Museum*) and the *German Cathedral* have been restored.

Ribbeckhaus [14]: Built in 1624 and once the townhouse of a local aristocratic family, it is now the sole remaining Renaissance house in Berlin.

Rotes Rathaus (Red City Hall) [27]: A landmark of Berlin, this red brick building, originally completed in 1870, has been carefully restored.

Saint Hedwig's Kathedrale, Bebelplatz: Frederick the Great, inspired by the Pantheon in Rome, designed this Roman Catholic cathedral in the 18th century.

*Unter den Linden: Old-timers still remember what was once the most popular promenade in Berlin, a boulevard lined with monumental buildings (now restored) and fragrant linden trees. Long severed from West Berlin by the Wall, it was rejoined in late 1989.

Zur Letzten Instanz (At the Last Minute) [29]: This publike restaurant near the ruins of the old city wall has been in business for 400 years.

Bern

A medieval air hangs over much of Bern, the Alp-surrounded capital of Switzerland, but there's nothing out-moded about the smart bustle and chic contemporaneity of its natives. It's a small city of about 150,000 residents, the site of an important university, as well as the administrative center for the country and the canton of Berne. The old quarter, located on a peninsula in the Aare River, is considered by many to be the best-preserved in Europe, and it's here, along the distinctive, arcaded streets with their tempting cellar shops, cafes, and restaurants, that you'll find the old heartbeat of Bern.

History

Bears once roamed in the Duke of Zähringen's private hunting grounds, where the city now stands. When the duke founded the city in the early 12th century, he named it Bärn—bear—after the first animal that was caught on a special hunt, and later incorporated the figure into the city's coat of arms. Bärn has become Bern.

In 1218, Bern became a free city of the Holy Roman Empire, and a little over a hundred years later it joined the Swiss Confederation of States. Later, the city became known for its aggressive policies of annexation. In 1848, Bern replaced Zurich as the capital of Switzerland.

Attractions

Bear Pits (Bärengraben) [8]: Living symbols of the city's name and heraldry—bears—have been housed here since the 15th century.

Bernese Historical Museum [10]: A bit of everything historical—from Celtic treasure to domestic architecture—can be found in this museum located on Helvetia Platz.

**Cathedral of St. Vinzenz (Münster St. Vinzenz) [6]: An impressive feast of Gothic architecture, the Münster was begun in 1421 and completed in 1596. The

Clock tower

tower was added in the late 19th century and you can climb it for a special view of city and mountains. Some of the saints in the portal's depiction of the Last Judgment still bear traces of their original paint. The Alps, in all their impressive glory, can be seen from the cathedral terrace.

Clock Tower (Zyttgloggeturm) [5]: If you're *pünktlich* (punctual) and arrive at four minutes before the hour, you'll see a medieval menagerie of jesters, kings, and bears appear in the tower of this old astronomical clock, one of Bern's most popular sights.

Bern Attractions:
1. Parliament Building
2. Prison Tower
3. The Museum of Fine Arts
4. French Church
5. Clock Tower
6. St. Vinzenz Cathedral
7. Rathaus (City Hall)
8. Bear Pits
9. Swiss Postal Museum
10. Bernese Historical Museum
11. Museum of Natural History
12. National Library
13. Kursaal

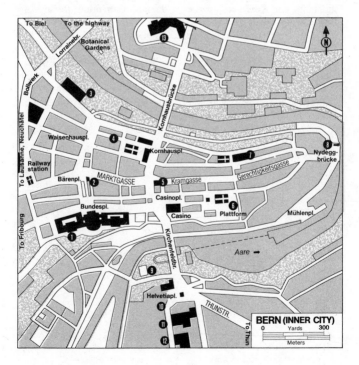

French Church (Französische Kirche) [4]: The exterior, done in an early 18th-century style, hides the surprise of a 13th-century early Gothic interior with wall paintings.

Museums on Helvetia Platz: There are museums everywhere you turn, including the *Swiss Alpine Museum,* of special interest to skiing aficionados, and the *Swiss Postal Museum* [9], a philatelic's paradise. The *National Library* [12], noted for its collection of bibles, is just south of here.

Kornhaus Platz: One of Bern's charming 16th-century fountains, the *Kindlifresserbrunnen,* graces this square named for its 18th-century granary, which now houses three small museums. The *City Theater* (Stadttheater) is one street north.

Museum of Fine Arts (Kunstmuseum) [3]: If you don't know the work of Bern-born artist Paul Klee (1878–1940), this is the place to get acquainted with it. The museum houses an enormous collection of his paintings, watercolors, and drawings, as well as a collection of French works by Delacroix, Manet, Cézanne, Matisse, and Chagall.

***Museum of Natural History** (Naturhistorisches Museum) [11]: Birds and wildlife of the Alps and Africa are dioramically displayed in their habitats.

Parliament Building (Bundeshaus) [1]: Seat of the Swiss Parliament, it was completed just after the turn of the century in a domed, Florentine Renaissance style; a colorful flower market takes place in front on Tuesdays and Saturdays.

Prison Tower (Käfigturm) [2]: A remnant of a 13th-century city wall, the tower was erected during Bern's early Expansionist period.

Bonn

The capital of the German Federal Republic is also a gateway to the Rhine Valley. Bonn is a pleasant hybrid—its center, with narrow, winding streets and old houses, feels like a small town from another era, but the presence and prestige it gains from being the seat of the government definitely instills a contemporary air and a sense of power. For the most part, however, Bonn is sober, serious, and quiet—the exception being carnival time, when the citizens let their hair down and raise many a glass of the local "Dragon's Blood" wine to their lips. As the birthplace of Beethoven, the city draws a full share of reverent music-loving pilgrims, who come to pay homage at the great composer's home or attend a concert at the annual Beethoven Festival. The surrounding area is one of the most-visited sections of the Rhine Valley.

History

Bonn's history stretches back some 2,000 years to Roman times. Under the Emperor Claudius, it was a legionnaires' camp known as *Castra Bonnensia*. The Franks took over the settlement in the fifth century, and for some 500 years, from the 13th through the 18th centuries, the powerful Prince Electors of Cologne made it their seat of power. Destroyed in the 17th century, it was rebuilt and eventually became part of the Prussian state. The *Altstadt,* or "Old Town," was destroyed in the Second World War. Bonn became the capital of the Federal Republic in 1949; ever since it has witnessed much new government-related building.

Attractions

*Beethoven's Birthplace (*Beethovens Geburtshaus*) [7]: One of the world's greatest composers was born in 1770 in this house, which now serves as the *Beethoven Museum* and displays memorabilia ranging from musical scores to ear trumpets used by Beethoven when he was going deaf.

Beethoven Hall (*Beethovenhalle*) [8]: The hall, built in 1959, resounds with the composer's music during the annual Beethoven Festival. Adjacent to it on the Rhine Promenade is the **City Opera House** (*Oper*) [9] and, just to the north, the **Kennedy Bridge** (*Kennedybrucke*) [10], spanning the Rhine and leading to *Bonn-Beuel* across the river.

Government Buildings: Lining the main highways leading into the inner city you'll find the newly built *Bundeshaus* [1], headquarters of the Federal parliament; the 19th-century *Palais Schaumburg* [2]; and the administrative

Bonn Attractions:
1. Bundeshaus
2. Palais Schaumburg
3. Villa Hammerschmidt
4. Palace of the Electors (University)
5. Poppelsdorfer Schloss
6. Marktplatz
7. Beethoven's Birthplace
8. Beethoven Hall
9. City Opera House
10. Kennedy Bridge
11. Museum of the Rhine
12. Münsterplatz
13. Old Cemetery

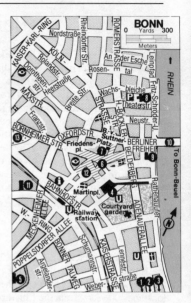

seat of the president of Germany, *Villa Hammerschmidt* [3], built between 1863 and 1865.

Marktplatz [6]: This colorful vegetable market provides a glimpse of medieval Bonn. Of the town wall, only the *Sterntor* (Star Gate) and the *Alte Zoll* (Old Customs House), which offers a splendid view of the Rhine, remain standing. The Electors had the *Town Hall* (Rathaus), with its impressive façade, built in 1738.

*Münster: The handsome spire of this heavily restored 12th-century Romanesque cathedral named for Saints Cassius and Florentius, Roman soldiers martyred for their faith in A.D. 253, rises above **Münsterplatz** (Cathedral Square) [12].

Museum of the Rhine (*Rheinisches Landesmuseum*) [11]: If you're curious to find out what your ancestors looked like, there's a prized ****Neanderthal skull** on display among other— and much later—Roman and Frankish exhibits.

Palace of the Electors (*Kurfürstliches Schloss*) [4]: One of two Baroque palaces built by the powerful Electors of Cologne, who ruled Bonn from the 13th through the 18th centuries, it has been rebuilt according to its original plan. Today it is part of the university. The ornate *Koblenzer Tor* (Gate) and the charming *Hofgarten* with its small palace (now the *Academic Art Museum*) are worth a look.

Poppelsdorfer Schloss [5]: Built between 1715 and 1740, the second palace of the Electors of Cologne is linked to the first by Poppelsdorfer Allee and contains the *Botanical Gardens* of the city.

Excursions

Königswinter: This legendary area of the Rhine Valley, located across the river from Bonn, is easily reached by local buses and trains. It is the home of the *Siebengebirge* (Seven Mountains) nature preserve, a popular hiking spot famed for its views of the Rhine and the Eiffel mountains. A good local wine called "Dragon's Blood" has been produced in the area for over 1,000 years.

Bordeaux

Bordeaux, a major harbor and industrial center on the Garonne (and linked by the Gironde to the south Atlantic coast), is best known for its red and white wines, produced by châteaux in the region and exported all over the world at the rate of some five million bottles a year. France's fifth-largest metropolis, with a population of 212,000 (over 620,000, including its suburbs), Bordeaux is also the capital of the Aquitaine region. Home to both an archbishop and a university, the city boasts elegant neoclassical buildings and grand boulevards and squares. Over a hundred years ago, Victor Hugo wrote of the charm of the old city, and his words still ring true: "Bordeaux is an original, singular, and perhaps unique city. Try to imagine a mixture of Versailles and Antwerp, and you have Bordeaux."

History

The Celtic settlement of Burdigala became a Roman merchant town, which in its heyday boasted some 60,000 residents—some of whom were the first to plant vines in this celebrated wine region. The Roman poet Decimus Magnus Ausonius, who wrote *Mosella* (a sketch of the Moselle area) and *Bissula* (the story of a young Germanic woman taken captive during a war), was born here around A.D. 310.

Bordeaux also enjoyed great importance during the period of the Visigoths, who captured it in 412, and the Franks, who occupied it from 507; its prominence continued during the three centuries of English rule which began in 1152, when Henry Plantagenet married Eleanor of Aquitaine. During this time, Bordeaux was primarily the emporium for imported goods arriving from England and for Bordeaux wines exported to England. Edward the Black Prince (1330–1376) held his court here, and his son, Richard II (1367–1400), was born in the city.

Numerous French victories endangered English rule, so the English monarchs bestowed various privileges upon the city in an effort to maintain this important foothold. In the period that followed the Hundred Years' War (1337–1453), the city paid dearly for its loyalty to England, and its special rights were reduced under French rule. Despite this, Bordeaux found such active support in its Commissariats—the highest royal administrators during the period of absolutism—that a new era of prosperity came about during the 18th century. A large number of neoclassical buildings were constructed and grand boulevards and squares were laid out, making Bordeaux one of France's most beautiful cities.

During the French Revolution, deputies of the Legislative Assembly of Bordeaux founded a moderate republican party in support of Federalism. The Girondists, as its members were known, held a majority in the

Assembly from 1791 to 1792. However, they were unable to prevail against the Montagnards, or Mountain Party—radicals led by Danton and Marat. At the instigation of the Montagnards, the Girondist leaders were hanged in 1793 as enemies of the unity of the French Republic. Accordingly, Bordeaux suffered greatly under the hostility of the Montagnards.

After the close of the Napoleonic era, Bordeaux flourished once again and continues to blossom today. It has also taken on national political significance—if only for short-lived, sporadic times—when the French government moved here from Paris in 1870–1871, 1914, and 1940.

Attractions

Basilique Saint-Michel [6], Place Canteloup: The triple-naved 14th- to 16th-century Gothic basilica of Saint-Michel has a beautiful north portal. The church boasts an impressive pulpit (1753) and a modern stained-glass window (1940) by Max Ingrand. In front is a free-standing bell tower with a 12-sided spire, *Tour Saint-Michel,* which, at 114-meters (374-feet) high, is the tallest structure in southern France. Underneath the beautifully restored 15th-century tower is the *Caveau des Momies,* a crypt of mummies *not* for the fainthearted.

Cathédrale Saint-André [8], Cours d'Alsace-Lorraine: The city's most important ecclesiastical building, the slender-spired cathedral, was erected in the Romanesque style during the 12th and 13th centuries and redesigned (and rebuilt) in the Gothic style between the 13th and 15th centuries. The 13th-century *Porte Royale* on the north side, with its sculpted tympanum of the Last Supper, is noteworthy, as is the free-standing *Tour Pey-*

Cathédrale Saint-André

Berland, a 15th-century bell tower crowned with an 1863 statue of the Virgin Mary. Inside, the choir—with its ambulatory and ring of chapels—is a masterpiece of late Gothic architecture, providing a strong contrast to the earlier 12th-century aisleless nave. The treasury is worth seeing as well.

Esplanade des Quinconces [1]: The west side of the esplanade—Europe's largest public square, measuring some 12 hectares (30 acres)—forms a semicircle, within which is an 1895–1902 memorial to the Girondists. Colossal statues of two Bordeaux natives, the essayist Montaigne (1533–1592), who was also mayor of the city for five years, and philosopher Montesquieu (1689–1755), dominate the north and south borders of the square. At the quayside, two columns are decorated with old figureheads symbolic of trade and navigation.

Grosse Cloche [7], Cours Victor Hugo: The 41-meter- (135-foot-) high gate housing the "Big Bell" of 1775—much loved by locals and rung during official festivities—was once part of the 13th-century city wall, although the present structure dates largely from the 15th century.

**Grand Théâtre [2], Place de la Comédie: The pride of the city, this neoclassical theater was built between 1773 and 1780 by Victor Louis on the site of a Gallo-Roman temple that stood until 1680. At the main entrance stand 12 Corinthian columns, and statues of the nine Muses and the goddesses Juno, Minerva, and Venus line the balustrade. The interior dazzles as well, but you can't view it without a ticket for a performance. The architect Charles Gar-

Grand Théâtre

nier borrowed details of the Grand Théâtre for the Paris Opéra.

Jardin de la Mairie [9], off Cours d'Albret: Behind the old *Palais des Rohan* (1784), now the *Hôtel de Ville* (City Hall), is this lovely garden. Two galleries, the *Musée des Beaux-Arts* and the *Musée d'Aquitaine,* are also located here.

Jardin Public [12], off Cours de Verdun: Originally planted in the 18th century, these beautiful public gardens were altered and enlarged in 1858. Besides its botanical gardens and lake, the park is the location of the *Musée d'Histoire Naturelle.*

La Bastide, on the east bank of the Garonne: This Bordeaux suburb includes the modern residential development, the *Cité de la Benauge.* The district is undergoing radical changes as a result of a current renewal program.

Maison du Vin de Bordeaux, Cours du 30-Juillet: A vast wine information center, the *Maison du Vin,* in Gabineau House, can help you decide which of the numerous wine châteaux you want to visit. Nearby is a wine megastore, *La Vinothèque,* selling a dizzying variety of wines.

Musée d'Aquitaine, 20 Cours Pasteur: Aspects of Aquitaine, from its prehistoric origins to local ethnography, are covered in this regional museum, a highlight of which is the original *Vénus de Laussel.* **Musée des Arts-Décoratifs** [10], 39 Rue Bouffard: With furniture, ceramics, metalwork, and other decorative arts on display, this museum—housed in the 1779 *Hôtel de Lalande*—covers the rich material heritage of the area, with an emphasis on the 18th century.

Bordeaux Attractions:
1. Esplanade des Quinconces
2. Grand Théâtre
3. Place de la Bourse
4. Porte de Cailhau
5. Pont de Pierre
6. Basilique Saint-Michel
7. Grosse Cloche
8. Cathédrale Saint-André
9. Musée des Beaux-Arts
10. Musée des Arts Decoratifs
11. Place Gambetta
12. Musée d'Histoire Naturelle

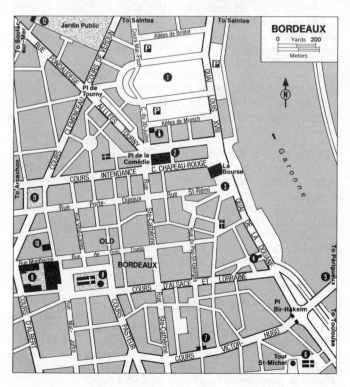

*Musée des Beaux-Arts [9], 20 Cours d'Albret: One of France's finest provincial museums, the fine arts museum is especially rich in 18th- and 19th-century French paintings, including works by Chardin, Delacroix, Renoir, and Redon. The Flemish and Dutch schools are also well represented, as are Italian artists—among them are Veronese, Titian, Perugino, and Pietro da Cortona. It also has a large collection of works by Albert Marquet (1875–1947), the landscape artist who was born in Bordeaux.

Palais-Gallien, Rue Rondaudège: Although this third-century Roman amphitheater was badly damaged during the Revolution, one handsome arched entrance remains among the ruins.

Place de Bir-Hakeim: This square is on the west bank of the Garonne and leads to the stone *Pont de Pierre.*

**Place de la Bourse [3]: Jacques Gabriel and his son, Jacques-Anges, created this square (the former *Place Royal*) and many of its surrounding buildings in the mid-18th century. Considered the loveliest square in Bordeaux, its sights include the Customs House (*Douane*), Stock Exchange (*Bourse*), and the *Musée de la Marine,* displaying model ships, figurehead, maps, and seascapes.

Place de Tourny: The magnificent tree-lined avenue, the *Allées de Tourny,* ends at this square, built between 1744 and 1748. The monument to Louis de Tourny, 18th-century disciple of urban renewal, was erected here in 1900.

Place Gambetta [11]: Although small, this is Bordeaux's liveliest square, surrounded by elegant houses dating from the reign of Louis XV (indeed, it's hard to believe that during the Revolution a busy guillotine stood here). The *Cours de l'Intendance,* the city's most elegant shopping street, begins here and runs east.

Place Jean Jaurès: This square lies at the southern end of *Quai Louis-XVIII* and the east end of *Rue Judaïque.*

*Pont de Pierre [5], off Place de Bir-Hakeim: Built between 1810 and 1822 and expanded in 1954, this 17-arched stone structure served as the city's only span until 1965. The city's two new bridges are the *Pont Saint-Jean* and *Pont d'Aquitaine.*

Porte de Cailhau [4], Place du Palais: Built in the 15th century from stones once used as ballast for sailing ships, the 34-meter- (112-foot-) high "Palace Gate" is topped with four irregular, conical turret caps.

Quai Louis-XVIII, west bank of the Garonne: Across from the *Allées d'Orleans,* at the southern end of the *Esplanade des Quinconces,* are steps leading from the *Quai* to the terrace of a parking deck, which provides a nice harbor view. Between this terrace and the one across the *Allées de Chartres* is the landing wharf for boats that cruise the harbor (June 1– September 30).

Sainte-Croix, Rue C. Sauvageau: The Romanesque façade of this church, once part of the richest abbey in France, is one of the most beautiful in the country.

Sainte-Croix

*Saint-Seurin, Place des Martyrs-de-la-Résistance: Portions of this church's choir date from the 12th century, and the elaborate south portal, with handsome, sculpted figures, dates from the 13th century. The two Romanesque bell towers were given upper stories in the 16th and 18th centuries, whereas the "fake-Romanesque" façade is from the 1800s. Worth seeing inside are 26 15th-century alabaster plaques that depict scenes from the life of the Virgin (in the *Nôtre-Dame-de-la-Rose* chapel), the stone bishop's seat, and, in the subterranean vault, sixth-century marble sarcophagi.

Brussels

Brussels breathes a prosperous, satisfied air, as well it might. The city enjoys a reputation within Europe for its grand cuisine and solid, bourgeois pleasures. Now the capital of Europe, it's a city with more ambassadors per square foot than anywhere else in the world, and a place where Eurocrats reign, serving in high-powered international organizations that have made Brussels their world headquarters (including NATO and the Common Market). This ambassadorial, Eurocratic presence has added a sophisticated veneer to Brussels over the years, but the city is also interesting as the local meeting ground for the two different languages used in Belgium: Dutch, spoken in the north, French to the south; in Brussels, both are given equal billing. Brussels offers beautiful buildings (including splendid examples of art nouveau architecture), sumptuous museums, superb dining, excellent beers, exceptional chocolates, and handmade lace.

History

The city has always been a meeting place for different cultures, located as it is on the axis of an old east-west land route between Cologne and Bruges, and a north-south river, the Senne (which now runs underground). Although the city celebrated its official millennium in 1979, recent archaeological work indicates that the area was, in fact, a busy Stone Age village as long ago as 5000 B.C.

For most of its history, Brussels has been dominated by foreign powers, starting with the Romans and the Vikings. Spain, France, Austria, England, and Holland have all claimed or used it as a pawn in European political struggles. With the patronage of Philip of Burgundy in the 15th century and Charles V of Spain in the 16th, Flemish painting, tapestry work, and lace-making reached a high peak of artistic excellence in Brussels.

In 1815, pitted against the united forces of Germany, England, and the Netherlands under the joint command of Blucher and the Duke of Wellington, Napoleon suffered his irreversible defeat at the Battle of Waterloo, which took place some 19 km. (12 miles) from the city.

The 19th century was an age of revolution throughout Europe, and the people of Brussels began their own victorious campaign to drive out the ruling Dutch in 1830. Independence brought with it a new status as capital of Belgium, and a new king, Leopold of Saksen-Koburg, the uncle of Britain's Queen Victoria. He was followed by Leopold II, who was responsible for much of the town planning that went on later in the century.

In need of its central location for army transport, Germany invaded

Brussels in both world wars. Brussels became the seat of the European Economic Community (EEC) in 1958 and, in 1967, world headquarters of NATO.

Attractions

Palais des Academies [7]:
The Prince of Orange lived in this 19th-century version of an Italian Renaissance palace before the Royal Academy moved in.

Art Nouveau Buildings:
Several important examples of this curvilinear architectural style are located in Brussels, and architectural buffs may want to track them down. The more famous examples include: *Maison Stoclet,* 281 Av. de Tervuren; the *Hôtel Solvay,* 224 Av. Louise; *Hôtel Tassel,* 6 Rue Paul-Emile Janson; the *Pullman Astoria Hotel,* 103 Rue Royale; and the *Métropole,* 31 Place de Brouckere. There are also two art nouveau restaurants, *De Ultième Hallucinatie* at 316 Rue Royale, and *Falstaff Café* at 25–27 Rue Henri Maus.

Jardin Botanique National de Belgique:
There's always something pleasurable about strolling in an old botanical garden—this one, home to exotic trees and plants, was laid out over 150 years ago and features an iron-and-glass greenhouse built in 1826.

Brussels Brewery Museum (Maison des Brasseurs),
Grand Place 10: A drinking house conveniently located next door provides samples of Brussels' rich, frothing beers at the end of the beer-making tour.

Parc de Bruxelles:
The dukes of Brabant once hunted stag and boar in this large park, which was laid out as a French garden in the late 18th century. The façade of the *Palais de la Nation* [5], meeting place of the two houses of the Belgian Parliament, overlooks the park at its northern end. At the southern end you'll find the neoclassical *Place Royale,* laid out in the 18th century and site of the *Royal Palace* (Palais du Roi) [8]. There's a superb view out over the lower town from here.

L'Eglise Notre-Dame-des-Victoires [13]:
A sumptuous Gothic style prevails in this beautiful church built during the 15th and 16th centuries.

Notre-Dame Des Victoires

Congress Column (Colonne du Congrès) [4]: Leopold I, the first king of Belgium, stands at the top of this column honoring Belgian independence; at the base, an eternal flame burns in honor of the unknown soldiers of World Wars I and II.

Palais d'Egmont [12]: The 16th-century home of a Flemish hero, Count Egmont, was classically redesigned in the 18th century. Other famous residents of this palace included Queen Cristina of Sweden and Voltaire.

Galeries St.-Hubert [2]: The first covered shopping street in Europe, the fashionable Galeries St.-Hubert has been displaying and selling goods since 1846.

Grand Sablon: Full of restaurants, antique shops, and cafes, this square is one of the best in Brussels.

*Mannekin-Pis [16]: It's said by way of scholarly explanation that this charming 17th-century statue-fountain of a little boy urinating is meant to embody the rebellious spirit of Brussels—in any case, he always makes a splash. The statue is a kind of icon of the city, and is sometimes dressed up in various military uniforms or costumes.

***Grand Place [1]: Known for centuries as the Grote Markt, this irresistible historic square is as beautiful as any in Europe, and has a special charm on Sunday mornings when it's the scene of a bird and flower market. The pride of place goes to the magnificent 15th-century **_Town Hall_ (Hôtel

Town Hall

de Ville), with Brussel's patron Saint Michael, looking down on the city from the tower. Next to the Town Hall are seven late 17th-century *_guildhalls,_ while the 16th-century _Maison du Roi,_ now home to the _City Museum_ (Musée Communal de la Ville de Bruxelles) stands opposite, with its im-

Brussels Attractions:
1. Grand Place
2. Galeries St.-Hubert
3. Cathédrale Saint-Michel
4. Congress Column
5. Palais de la Nation
6. Rue de la Loi
7. Palais des Academies
8. Royal Palace
9. Palace of Fine Arts
10. Musée Royale d'Art Ancien
11. Place du Petit Sablon
12. Palais d'Egmont
13. Notre-Dame des Victoires
14. Palais de Justice
15. Notre-Dame de la Chapelle
16. Mannekin-Pis
17. Place de Brouckère
18. Monnaie Theater
19. Stock Exchange

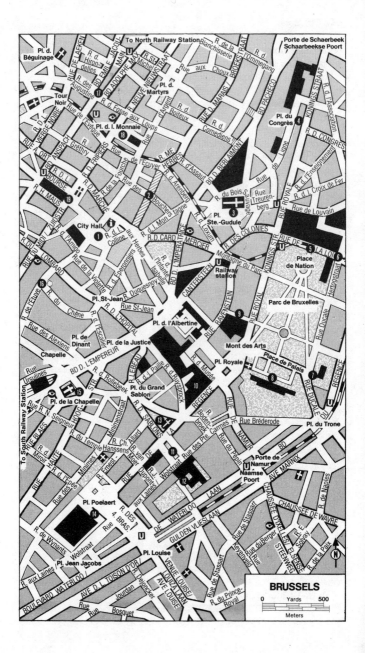

portant examples of local ceramics and silverware and the wardrobe collection of the Manneken-Pis.

Théâtre Royale de la Monnaie [18]: Located in *Brouckere Square* (Place de Brouckere) [17] and home to opera and ballet since 1816, the Monnaie was the place where Belgium's independence movement gathered force and inspiration in 1830 when a patriotic song aroused the audience to revolutionary action.

Musée d'Art Moderne: Located on the northwest corner of Place Royale, the museum showcases works by the important Belgian painters Delvaux and Magritte and other artists of the 19th and 20th centuries.

*Notre-Dame de la Chapelle [15]: Pieter Brueghel the Elder and the philosopher Spinoza are buried in this Romanesque and Gothic church located in the popular district of Les Marolles.

Palace of Fine Arts (Palais des Beaux-Arts) [9]: In this building complex with its exhibition, festival, and concert halls, movielovers will find the *Musée du Cinema,* which screens old classics daily.

Palais de Justice [14]: With its notorious reputation as the ugliest building in Europe, the symbolic intention of this building— the majesty of justice—generally gets lost; at least there's a good view.

Petit-Sablon [11]: The medieval guilds are well-represented in this old cemetery by small bronze statues, each indicative of a different trade.

**Musée Royale d'Art Ancien [10]: A rich collection of Flemish and Dutch oil paintings including works by Bruegel the Elder, Cranach, Rubens, and Van Dyke are on display in this museum located on the western corner of place Royale.

Musée Royale d'Art et Histoire: This museum in the Parc du Cinquantenaire is a must for lovers of ancient history and more recent arts and crafts.

*Saint John the Baptist (St-Jean-Baptiste-au-Beguinage): A showpiece of Flemish Baroque opulence, the church dates from the 17th century.

*Cathédrale Saint-Michel [3]: One of the oldest buildings in the city, Belgium's national cathedral sits on a hill in the center of town and is noteworthy for its splendid 16th-century stained-glass windows.

Excursions

*Waterloo: A name that still rings in history, Waterloo, 19 km. (12 miles) south of Brussels, was the scene of Napoleon's final defeat by the Duke of Wellington and General Blucher. The *Butte du Lion* monument provides a view of the battlefield, and in the town of Waterloo itself Wellington's headquarters have been made into a museum.

Bucharest

Bucharest (Bucureşti) is the capital of Rumania, as well as its economic and cultural center. Home to over two million, the metropolis takes pride in its verdant parks, handsome boulevards, and abundant rose gardens—but its crippled economy and various shortages belie the reputation it enjoyed before World War II, when it was known as the "Paris of the East." For determined visitors to this city in transition, Bucharest offers a variety of attractions, from the resident *Circul* (circus) to a triennial international music festival, from a charming museum of ceramics and glass to Manuc's Inn, an old caravanserai-turned restaurant with wooden verandas carved by the famed craftsmen of the Maramures region.

History

Legend has it that Bucharest was founded by a shepherd named Bucur, who settled in the Vlăsia forest. In reality, the area comprising today's Bucharest—which lies along the River Dîmbovita in the plains region of southeast Rumania—was settled in the third century B.C. by the Dacians, who were conquered by the Romans in the second century A.D. The name Bucharest (deriving from *bucurie,* or joy) was officially noted for the first time in a document signed by the Wallachian *voivoide* (prince), Vlad the Impaler (1431?–76)—better known as Dracula.

The history of the city is marked by rebellion, revolution, social tension, and battles of defense against Turkish occupation, the latter continuing until the 18th century. The unification of the two principalities of Wallachia and Moldavia was solidified in 1859, and Moldavian leader Alexandru Ioan Cuza was elected ruler of Rumania. In 1877, the country fought on the side of Russia in the war against the Turks, and a year later, Bucharest became the capital of independent Rumania.

Communist Party rule was established in 1949. The dictator Nicolae Ceauşescu ruled Rumania with an iron hand from 1965 until December 1989, when he and his wife were tried and executed during a popular revolution. In his campaign to make Bucharest "the first socialist capital for the new socialist man," thousands of homes and numerous historic buildings and monuments were leveled; but even the massive concrete *Centru Civic* (Civic Center) has not totally eradicated the city's past, nor uprooted its precious parklands.

Attractions

Arc de Triumf [4], Soseaua Kiseleff: Built of stone in 1935–1936—and replacing a badly con-structed structure of some 20 years earlier—the Arc resembles its Parisian namesake. It honors the Rumanian army of World War I and features the coats of arms of the country's provinces.

The Athenaeum [16], Calea Victoriei: The neoclassical home of the George Enescu National Philharmonic Orchestra was built between 1885 and 1888; its dome is decorated with lyres. The George Enescu International Festival and Competition is held here every three years, with the next scheduled to take place in 1991.

Athénée Palace Hotel, corner of Stradă Ştirbei Vodă and Calea Victoriei: This once-grand hotel used to reek of decadence and played host to espionage activities, but it is more sedate today. Still, its semi-posh interior and somewhat tacky nightclub make for quite a change from most Bucharest attractions.

Carul cu Bere (the Beer Cart), 5 Stradă Stavropoleos: The ornate neoGothic façade is an added attraction of this restaurant, whose cuisine is rich in Bucharest tradition.

Botanical Gardens [28], along Şoseaua Cotroceni: 19th-century Pioneers' Palace, as it's known today (Pioneers are the Rumanian equivalent of Boy Scouts), was originally built for Princess Marie, and is located in the park's southern section.

Calea Victorie [11]: This is Bucharest's principal thoroughfare, an avenue of architectural and cultural contrasts along which residents stroll at midday and in the early evening.

Circul, 15 Aleea Circului: Like circuses in other Eastern Bloc nations, this one has a permanent location and boasts highly skilled performers, both comic and death-defying.

Cismigiu Gardens, between Bulevard Gheorghe Gheorghiu-Dej and Ştradă Ştirbei Vodă: One of the most beautiful municipal parks in this greenery-proud city, the gardens are a popular spot for one and all, from young lovers in rented rowboats on the lake to old timers catching a quick 40 winks.

Cretulescu Church, Calea Victoriei: This 18th-century church has elaborate carvings over its entrance, patterned brickwork on its turrets, and mock arches. It is a fine example of the Brîncoveanu style of architecture, whose carved-stone motifs are borrowed from those of native woodworking.

*Curtea Veche [21], Stradă 30 Decembrie: Little remains of the "Old Court" built in the 15th century by Vlad the Impaler, but there is an underground Museum displaying the skulls of some of Vlad's victims (he decapitated his enemies and hung their heads from the city gates for all to see). More pleasing to the eye is the adjoining church, built by Mircea the Shepherd, a 16th-century Wallachian ruler. The church's foundation is in a trefoil shape, and an exquisitely proportioned tower rises over the naos.

Herăstrău Park, at the northern end of Soseaua Kiseleff: The park surrounds lovely Lake Herăstrău, the largest of the 12 lakes bordering Bucharest's northern reaches. Regattas are held here regularly, rowboats and windsurfing equipment can be rented, and a Ferris wheel is a feature of the children's playground. There are three restaurants in the park: Pescărus (specializing in fish), Miorita, and Parcul.

Manuc's Inn, Stradă 30 Decembrie: Opposite the Curtea Veche and disguised by a plain white exterior is Bucharest's premier eating establishment, originally a rich Armenian's caravanserai. The fare is traditional Rumanian, the atmosphere lively, and the surroundings handsome.

Museum of Art Collections [12], 111 Calea Victoriei: In the old Ghica Palace, collections assembled over the centuries by artists, art experts, and private individuals are on view; they all have been bequeathed to the state in order to make them accessible to the public. Films are sometimes shown here, as well.

Museum of Ceramic and Glass [13], 107 Calea Victoriei: From pre-Christian-era artifacts to a Tiffany lamp, this small museum contains over 2,000 examples of ceramics and glass, both native and foreign.

*Museum of Folk Art and **Feudal Arts Museum** [1], off Soseaua Băneasa: These two villas display the diverse collection of Dr. Minovici, engineer and connoisseur, who gave his treasures to the nation in 1945. The Folk Art Museum displays Transylvanian pottery, musical instruments, and costumes, among other things, whereas the hybrid Anglo-Italianesque Feudal Arts Museum exhibits a hodgepodge of arms and armor, furniture, stained glass, and tapestries, these mostly of Western European origin.

Museum of City History [20], 2 Bulevard Anul 1848: The past and present of the Rumanian capital are kept alive in this collection of over 100,000 objects, mostly documents, photographs, and prints. The museum is in a neoGothic pile, once a boyar's palace.

Bucharest Attractions:
1. Museum of Folk Art
2. Scînteia House
3. Exhibition Hall
4. Arc de Triumf
5. Village Museum
6. Victoria Square
7. Museum of Natural History
8. and 9. Museum of the History of the Communist Party
10. Dinamo Stadium
11. Calea Victorie
12. Museum of Art Collections
13. Museum of Ceramic and Glass
14. Piata Palatului
15. National Art Museum
16. Athenaeum
17. Theodor Aman Museum
18. University of Bucharest
19. National Theater
20. Museum of City History
21. Curtea Veche
22. Stavropoleos Church
23. Museum of the History of the Republic of Rumania
24. Civic Center
25. Central Committee
26. The People's Council of Bucharest
27. State Opera House
28. Botanical Gardens

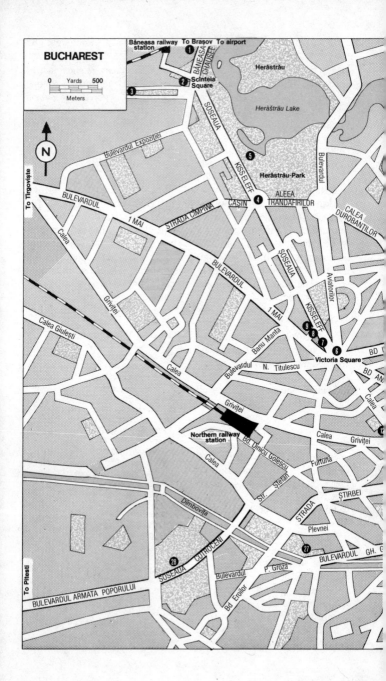

Museum of the History of the Republic of Rumania

[23], 15 Calea Victoriei: This museum of national history has a vast collection of native artifacts, including prehistoric goddess statues, Dacian jewelry, Roman arms and armor, and a treasure chamber of gold and silver objects formerly belonging to Rumanian princes. President Ceauşescu also displayed the gifts he received for his 60th birthday here.

Museum of Music, 141 Calea Victoriei: The museum is largely devoted to the life and works of native composer, conductor, and musician, George Enescu (1881–1955).

Museum of Natural History

[7], 1 Soseaua Kiseleff: This museum (whose Rumanian name includes that of Dr. Grigore Antipa, founder of ichthyology in that country) has over 300,000 objects, including the skeleton of a Moldavian dinosaur.

National Art Museum [15], 1 Stradă Stirbei Vodă, at Calea Victoriei: The edifice that houses this vast collection was originally part of the Royal Palace, built along neoclassical lines in the 1930s; construction of the museum wing began during World War II and was completed in the 1950s. On display are works of art by Rumanian masters from the 10th through 20th centuries, and objects ranging from boyars' robes to elaborate iconostases. The 19th-century paintings by Gheorghe Tattarescu and Theodor Aman are especially outstanding. Some Western European art—

Dutch porcelain, French furniture, and minor works by Old Masters—can be seen on the top floor.

National Theater [19], Stradă Tudor Arghezi: Located east of the University of Bucharest, this Colosseum-like structure is awash with quasi-Moorish motifs; it was declared a "national treasure" by Elena Ceauşescu, wife of the President, when they were in power.

Rumanian Television Building,

Aviatorilor Bulevardul: The bullet scarred Studio 4 was, in many ways, the heart of the anticommunist rebellion, where revolutionaries kept the freedom movement alive and strong before the last Ceauşescu loyalists gave up.

Russian Church, Stradă Doamnei: The onion domes of this yellow-brick, green-tiled house of worship are a joy to behold, though its interior frescoes are in need of major repair and its icons are less than lovely.

Şcînteia House [2], Şoseaua Băneasa: An arresting contemporary building in the Stalinesque style, "Spark House" is home to the Communist daily newspaper, *Scînteia*. A massive printworks is on the premises.

State Opera House [27], Bulevard Gheorghe Gheorghiu-Dej: The Rumanian Opera is the company in residence at the opera house, as well as the venue of classical music concerts.

**Stavropoleos Church [22], Stradă Stavropoleos: One of the best remaining examples of old Rumanian architecture, the church was named for the Greek monk Ioanichie, its founder, who later became the Metropolitan of Stavropolis, near Salonika, Greece. The monk first built a travelers' lodge on the site, then the little church (1724–1730). The vestibule, with its elaborate ornamentation, rests on beautiful columns, and the doors leading into the church are engraved with delicately finished wood carvings.

Theodor Aman House [17], 8 Stradă C. A. Rossetti: The Rumanian painter once occupied this house, and many of his works and possessions can be viewed. Don't miss his masterpiece, *Bulgarians Massacring the Turks,* in the National Art Museum.

University of Bucharest [18], Bulevard Republicii: Founded in 1859 after Moldavia and Wallachia were united, the university spills over with students, watched over by statues of great teachers and men of state.

**Village Museum [5], 28–30 Şoseaua Kiseleff: The *Muzeul Satului,* as it is called in Rumanian, is located in Herăstrău Park and includes an array of over 300 original structures—from peasant huts to windmills. Founded in 1936, the museum is one of Bucharest's top attractions and no wonder, since every building reconstructed here—mud-brick dwelling, shingle-roofed church, and thatched cottage alike—comprises its own miniature museum of folk history.

Village Museum

Budapest

Few cities are as beautifully and dramatically situated as Budapest. On the hilly side of the Danube sits ancient Buda, or what's left of it; on the opposite shore, where the land becomes an immense, flat plain, 19th-century Pest spreads into the distance. The two cities, along with another, called Obuda (Old Buda), became united in 1873. You'll see plenty of undistinguished new buildings along with some beautifully reconstructed old ones, but enough remains of the city and its distinctive Hungarian culture and cuisine to keep you happily occupied. Fully one-fifth of the country's population lives here, making it the political, intellectual, and artistic capital of Hungary. Budapest is also known for its spas, which offer an array of hot, natural mineral baths. Above all, it's known as a city that loves good living.

History

The Romans founded the city of Aquincum on the Danube in the first century A.D.; seven centuries later, Arpad, a Magyar chief, brought his people from the Urals and founded the Hungarian nation. The two Magyar cities of Buda and Pest steadily flourished, becoming known throughout Europe as trade and crafts centers, and reached a high point during the 40-year reign (997 to 1038) of Hungary's first king, later canonized as Saint Stephen.

Buda was fortified after the Mongols invaded and destroyed both cities in the 13th century. The two cities were steadily rebuilt, and when the Turks arrived by the 16th century, they had become quite splendid again. Buda, under the Turks, experienced 150 years of captivity and decay. After the Turkish occupation, the entire country fell to the Hapsburg Empire, where it stayed—with growing restlessness—until the end of World War I.

Hungary, under the right-wing regime of Miklos Horthy, sided with Germany in World War II and was occupied from 1944 until the Soviets arrived in 1945. In advance of their defeat, the Germans blew up whole sections of the city and all of the old bridges—some 33,000 buildings were destroyed, as was the royal palace. A Soviet regime followed. Bullet holes in some of the buildings are reminders that revolution swept through the streets of Budapest as recently as 1956, when a local freedom movement gained momentum, only to be brutally crushed by the Soviets. Yet Budapest, according to Soviet standards, remained a remarkably permissive city. In 1989, as the Soviet Union loosened its grip on Eastern Bloc countries, Hungary declared itself a republic. Its Communist Party changed its name in what appears to be a move toward a multi-party system.

The city today is changing quickly as old buildings continue to be demolished and new ones take their place. But amid the alterations, sections of old Budapest still remain, as does the Hungarian desire for the good life.

Attractions in Pest

City Park (Varosliget) [12]: There's a public spa, an artificial lake, a zoo, a botanical garden, an amusement park—and *Vajdahunyad Castle,* a building comprised of various Hungarian architectural styles and the façade of a royal Transylvanian castle. It was built for the Millennium Exhibition of 1896 and contains the *Agricultural Museum* (Mezögazdasági Múzeum).

Heroes Square (Hösök tere) [10]: The park was laid out in 1896 on the occasion of the thousand-year anniversary of the settling of the nation by Magyar tribes. It is dominated by the *Millennium Monument,* with its sculptured figures of Prince Arpad and six founding Magyars. In front of the monument is Hungary's *Tomb of the Unknown Soldier.* Standing on one side of the square, across from the *Municipal Art Gallery,* which features temporary exhibitions of modern work, is the important **Fine Arts Museum** (Szépmüvészeti Múzeum) [11]. Most modern masters are on view here, as are Greek, Roman, and Egyptian artifacts.

Inner City Parish Church (Belvárosi plébánia templom) [1]: The oldest church in Pest, originally dating from the 12th century, shows an accumulation of build-

Inner City Parish Church

ing styles, including a Muslim prayer niche. Liszt lived nearby and often played the organ.

Museum of Applied Arts (Imparmüvészeti Múzeum) [7]: The museum building is an example of Hungarian Art Nouveau; its collections include gold and silver work from the 15th to 17th centuries, Hungarian and European ceramics, Turkish carpets, and Gobelins tapestries.

Museum of Ethnography (Neprajzi Múzeum) [4]: Traditional Hungarian folk art, costumes, and furniture are on display in this museum across from the Parliament building.

*National Museum (Nemzeti

Múzeum) [8]: Historical and archaeological treasures of all kinds can be found in Budapest's oldest and most important museum, erected between 1837 and 1847 in the neoclassical style. The prehistoric skull from Vértesszölös is one of the oldest yet discovered; the Avar gold and silver work displays superb technical mastery; the famous Hungarian crown reputedly belonged to Saint Stephen, Hungary's first king; and Franz Liszt wielded the gold baton stored in one of the cases.

***Parliament (Országház)
[3]: The most famous landmark of the city sits on the Danube. Finished in 1902, after ten years of work, it is reminiscent of London's Houses of Parliament. A magnificent staircase with murals by Karoly Lotz leads from the main entrance to the domed hall, and the statues on the pillars represent Hungarian kings and princes of Transylvania.

Saint Stephen's Basilica
(Szent István templom) [5]: A landmark of Pest, this neo-Renaissance-style domed church, with its two tall spires, took 50 years to complete. During World War II, the city's most important documents were removed from the Municipal Archives to prevent their destruction; they were stored in the cellar of the basilica—one of the few bombproof locations in Budapest.

*State Opera (Állami Operaház) [9]: One of two opera houses in the city, the National was erected between 1875 and 1884

and is decorated with frescoes by Hungarian artists. The recent restoration of the architect Miklos Ybl's work, has returned the house to its former glory.

University Church (Egyetemi templom) [6]: Pest was once filled with Baroque buildings, and this is one of the most beautiful survivors. Completed in 1742, its magnificent wood carvings (oak portal, prayer benches, and pulpit) were fashioned by the Paulist monks.

Vörösmarty Tér: The center of the inner city, this spacious, lively square is filled with cafés and street musicians. Order a sumptuous sweet or coffee at the famous *Vörösmarty Café* or the elegant pastry shop *Gerbeaud*, both pleasant places to sit and people watch. Lined with shops, the *Váci utca,* the boulevard that begins on the south side of the square, is the fashion center of Budapest.

Attractions in Buda

***Castle Hill (Várhegy): The most important sites of the city are all located on Castle Hill, where reconstruction work has been going on since the end of World War II. With its narrow alleys, cobbled streets, pleasant squares, and its assortment of medieval, pastel Baroque, and neoclassical buildings, the district is a cheerful place to wander and provides good views of the Danube and neighboring Pest.

During the last days of the war, the Nazis made a last-ditch stand in the Royal Palace and blew it to smithereens when they departed. Archaeologists then discovered the foundations of a 15th-century castle underneath the rubble. Today, the Palace serves as an enormous museum complex that houses the *National Gallery,* with works by Hungarian painters and sculptors of the last two centuries; the *Museum of the Hungarian Working Class Movement;* and, in the southern block, the *Castle Museum,* which provides an excellent overview of Budapest's history.

*Amphitheater (Amfiteátrum) [21]: This theater of the Roman garrison town Aquincum was constructed in the second century and used until around 375, after which time it became a fortress. The *Museum of Ruins* at Korvin Otto utca 63 was built on the site of the ancient Roman camp, and has the remains of a villa and baths.

Matthias Church (Mátyás templom) [23]: The Hapsburg emperors were crowned kings of Hungary in this 13th-century church, which served for a time as a mosque during the Turkish occupation. If you are in Budapest on a Sunday, the High Mass celebrated here at 10:00 A.M. with orchestra and choir is a moving experience. Saint Stephen, the first king of Hungary, is commemorated by an equestrian monument southeast of the church. On your left as you leave the church is the neo-Romanesque ****Fisherman's Bastion (Halászbástya) [24], whose arcades frame memorable views of the city and the mighty Danube.

Church of Saint Anne (Szent Anna templom) [17]: The Baroque façade of this church is one of the most beautiful in Hungary.

Budapest Attractions:
1. Inner City Parish Church
2. Hungarian Academy of Sciences
3. Parliament
4. Museum of Ethnography
5. St. Stephan's Basilica
6. University Church
7. Museum of Applied Arts
8. National Museum
9. State Opera
10. Heroes Square
11. Fine Arts Museum
12. City Park
13. People's Stadium
14. Semmelweis Hospital
15. Rudas Baths
16. Citadel
17. Church of St. Anne
18. Royal Baths
19. Funeral Chapel of Gül Baba
20. Lukas Baths
21. Amphitheater
22. Kiscell Palace
23. Matthias Church
24. Fishermen's Bastion

St. Stephen's Monument and
Fisherman's Bastion

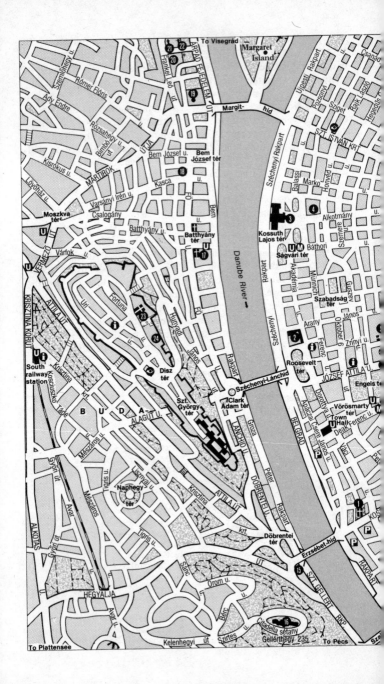

BUDAPEST

0   Yards   400

Meters

**Citadel (Citadella) [16]: Anticipating future unrest from their Hungarian subjects, the Hapsburgs had this defensive structure built in the mid-19th century. Go to enjoy the view (and the food) from the terrace restaurant and wine bar. At the foot of the hill is the impressive and recently renovated *Hotel Gellért*, dating from 1918.

*Funeral Chapel of Gül Baba (Gül Baba türbéje) [19]: Gül Baba was a dervish who died in Buda during the Turkish occupation; he was subsequently venerated as a Muslim saint.

Kiscell Palace [22]: This museum, built in the 18th century as a monastery, hosts a permanent collection called "Art and Artistry from Old Pest-Buda."

Lukas Baths (Lukács fürdö) [20]: These hot sulphurous springs have been relieving aches and pains since Roman times.

Royal Baths (Király fürdö) [18]: Built around 1556 by Pasha Mustafa Szokoli, the Baths were enlarged during the 18th century, given a neoclassical face-lift in 1826 and rebuilt in 1959.

Rudas Baths (Rudas fürdö) [15]: These radium-rich springs are located under a 16th-century Turkish dome.

**Margaret Island (Margitsziget): This large island, easily accessible from either side of the Danube, acts as Budapest's built-in summer resort and recreation zone. There are several spas, hotels, the enormous National Swimming Pool (Nemzeti Sportuszoda) and a beach. During the summer months, the center of cultural activity shifts from the city to the outdoor theaters here. The entire island, which also features a lovely rose garden, is used as a park.

Excursions from Budapest

*Aquincum: Four miles upstream from the city center are the impressive excavations of a Roman-era town known as Aquincum, one of the first settlements in the region. During the late second and early third centuries Aquincum was the capital of the Roman province of Pannonia Inferior, and at its most prosperous was inhabited by almost 100,000 people. Homes, temples, streets, and an amphitheater have been unearthed, and a **museum* on the site displays objects found during the digs.

Cologne

The massive and magnificent Gothic cathedral is reason enough to visit
Cologne, but this busy city on the Rhine offers many other riches for you
to explore. Although the city was badly damaged in the Second World
War, Cologne has completed some impressive rebuilding and today is the
fourth-largest city in Germany. There are excavated Roman ruins and
soaring churches, rich museums and small historic squares, as well as
one of the best opera houses in Germany. In February, the famous pre-
Lenten Carnival takes place and turns the city upside-down. The scented
water known as eau-de-cologne was first concocted here over a hundred
years ago, and a famous version, 4711, is still known as *Kölnisch Wasser*
(Cologne Water).

History

The longest period of early inhabitation of the area was by veteran Roman soldiers, who penetrated this part of the Rhine, ousted the Celts, and
founded a colonia (colony) from which the city's name derives. Engi-
neers first, last, and always, the Romans surrounded the town with walls,
built roads and bridges, and, with a population of 20,000, maintained
their sway for over 400 years until they were finally expelled by the
Franks and other Germanic tribes.

Flourishing trade over the centuries swelled the city's population. Cologne was part of the Hanseatic League (northern European towns band-
ed together for economic advancement and protection), and fought for
independence against its archbishop. In the 13th century, Cologne became a city-state and was ruled by a few patrician merchant families.

In 1475, Kaiser Friedrich III declared the city subject to him and
elevated it to the rank of Free Imperial City; this action gave Cologne the
right to mint its own coins. Napoleon's troops marched into the city in
1794, and seven years later, Cologne was acquired by France. At the
1815 Vienna Congress, however, the city, as part of the Rhineland, was
declared a province of Prussia.

Devastating air raids during the Second World War reduced the once-
proud city to acres of rubble: Ninety percent of the inner city was
completely destroyed. Postwar reconstruction has been constant and
considerable.

Attractions

*Altermarkt (Old Market Place):
With the once-adjacent *Heumarkt,*
the Altermarkt was the bustling
center of old Cologne. Although
the area was levelled in the war,
there are two restored 16th-

century houses at numbers 20–22 which give an indication of what the surroundings once looked like. The **Antoniterkirche** (Antonite Church) [20] was originally built around 1350, at a time when the Black Plague was devasting northern Europe.

**Dom (Cathedral of St. Peter and St. Mary) [1]: Largely spared from the ravages of the war, this splendid Gothic structure was begun in 1284 to serve as a gigantic reliquary for the remains of the Three Kings; the golden shrine may be seen within. Building continued off and on for another six hundred years. Filled with beautifully carved choir stalls, tombstones, paintings, and stained glass, the Cathedral displays its richest treasures in the *Domschatzkammer* (Cathedral Treasury) and has an observation deck for view-lovers.

*Gürzenich [19]: In the Middle Ages, this was one of the largest halls in Europe and was used for gala receptions, dancing, and banquets—events which still take place here during Carnival time. The interior, often used for concerts, and the northern section of the building were rebuilt after the war in a modern style.

Hohe Strasse: Where Roman soldiers once marched, shoppers now bustle; this pedestrians-only street was the main axis of ancient Cologne.

Museum für Östasiatische Kunst, Universitatsstrasse 100: A Japanese architect designed this modern building which exhibits the art of China, Japan, and Korea.

Neues Rathaus (New City Hall) [18]: Built in the mid-1950s on the foundations of a 17th-century building destroyed in the war, the New City Hall features an impressive stained-glass window depicting the history of the city.

Oberstolzen Haus, Rheingasse 8: Built in the early 13th century and now containing the *Industrial Art Museum,* this is the only remaining Romanesque house in Cologne.

***Römisch-Germanisches Museum [2]: Located on the site of an ancient Roman villa, this beautifully designed museum chronicles the Roman occupation of Cologne through sarcophagi, mosaics, frescoes, glass, toys, and coins. Don't miss the *Dionysus Mosaic,* the highlight of this important collection.

Roman Remains: Scattered throughout the city are small

Along the Rhine

the Tourist Information Office and the main portal of the Cathedral; and the *Romerturm,* ruins of a fortification tower, on St. Apernstrasse.

Schnütgen Museum für mittelalterliche Kunst [9]: If the treasures of the Middle Ages fascinate you, this richly endowed museum housed within the Church of St. Cecilia is certain to delight you.

Severinsbrucke (Severin Bridge): This city landmark, hanging suspended from a single pylon, was completed in 1959.

St. Andreas [3]: The philosopher-bishop Albertus Magnus is buried in a Roman sarcophagus in this triple-naved, 13th-century basilica.

*St. Gereon [5]: An important architectural monument from the Middle Ages, Saint Gereon's re-

buildings that have been erected over non-removable Roman finds. These *in situ* Roman sites include: the *Prätorium* excavations under the Neues Rathaus; the *Roman Canal* on Budengasse; the *Jewish Baths* next to the Rathaus; the architrave of the *Capitol Temple* in the foundation of Saint Maria im Kapitol; a section of the *Romertor,* the north gate of the city, between tains an early Christian vestibule-congregation hall-choir room plan.

*St. Mariä Himmelfahrt (Saint Mary of the Assumption) [21]: Pay special attention to the splendid 17th-century series of the Twelve Apostles on the columns of this Mannerist-style Jesuit church.

St. Maria im Kapitol [10]: The 11th-century foundations of this church overlooking the Rhine stand on the site of a Roman temple dedicated to Jupiter, Juno, and Minerva.

St. Maria Lyskirchen [11]: From its humble beginnings as a church where sailors from the Rhine worshiped the Virgin Mary, Saint Maria Lyskirchen has gone through several transformations, most recently in the 17th century. Its extensive collection of medieval paintings is well worth seeing.

St. Pantaleon [14]: The west wing of this royally connected church was a gift of Archbishop Bruno, Otto the Great's brother; both the archbishop and Queen Theophanu, Otto's stepdaughter, are buried here.

St. Severin [13]: One of the oldest of Cologne's churches, Saint Severin was founded in the fifth century and built on the site of a pagan and early Christian burial ground. There are beautifully carved choir stalls, old wall hangings, and a 13th-century Madonna drawn in chalk.

St. Ursula [6]: Dedicated to one of Germany's favorite saints, this 12th-century Romanesque basilica has been repeatedly altered over the centuries and has a magnificent "Golden Chamber" originally built for the veneration of holy relics.

***Wallraf-Richartz Museum and **Museum Ludwig** [17]: From serene wimpled Gothic ladies with high foreheads painted in the 14th century to pop images by Andy Warhol, these adjoined museums offer art lovers an excellent sampling of great works.

Zeughaus (Arsenal), Zeughausstrasse: Once the city arsenal, built on the remains of the Roman city walls, this early 16th-century building is now home to the interesting **Kölnisches Stadtmuseum** (City Museum of Cologne) [4] with its wide-ranging collections of old weapons, armor, and furniture.

Copenhagen

The beautiful capital of Denmark is also the largest and liveliest city in Scandinavia and a round-the-clock mecca for visitors from everywhere in the world. It occupies the northeastern shore of Zealand, the largest of the Danish islands. Copenhagen is a welcoming city ideally suited for exploration on foot, with waterfront promenades, royal palaces, pedestrian-only shopping streets, historic churches, first-class museums, open-air cafés, and Tivoli, one of the world's most famous amusement parks. It's a place of considerable local charm, graced by the statue of Hans Christian Andersen's Little Mermaid sitting on a rock in the harbor, as well as a sophisticated international playground, where "live and let live" is not only a motto but a pledge.

History

Though the city—then a small fishing village—is mentioned in official documents as early as 1043, the traditional founding date of Copenhagen is 1167 when Bishop Absalon built a fortress on the island of Slotsholmen to help protect the harbor. The town gained economic prominence a century later; in 1368, however, it was conquered and destroyed by the powerful German Hanseatic League, which wanted to monopolize all Baltic and North Sea trade.

The city became Denmark's capital early in the 15th century. When Denmark began its rule of Norway and Sweden in the same century, the royal residence was moved to Copenhagen and the city became the capital of those countries as well. The university was founded in 1479.

Copenhagen blossomed under King Christian IV (1588–1648), who was a true Renaissance figure. An indefatigable builder and planner, Christian IV was responsible for several buildings that still stand today: among them, the Stock Exchange, the Round Tower, and Rosenborg Castle. Two great fires in the following century, however, destroyed much of medieval Copenhagen.

After Denmark joined the Northern League of Armed Neutrality, its capital city suddenly found itself the victim of a surprise attack by the English under Lord Nelson. Copenhagen capitulated in 1807, when the English sent an even larger fleet and reduced what was left of the city to flames. The city that you see today mostly dates from the major rebuilding efforts that took place in the 19th century.

The 19th century was a period of constructive nationalism and social progress for Copenhagen, as citizens joined forces against the monarchy. A parliamentary constitution similar to England's was put into place in 1849. In 1894, construction of the Free Port of Copenhagen began. Hans Christian Andersen, the beloved author of countless fairy tales, and

Sören Kierkegaard, father of existentialism, both lived in Copenhagen in the 19th century.

The country remained neutral in the First World War, but when German forces occupied Copenhagen and the rest of the country from 1940 to 1945, the city became a major center of resistance. Postwar Copenhagen is a major shipyard and design center and is known for its remarkably liberal attitudes and high standard of living—the best in the world, according to a recent survey.

Attractions

*Amalienborg Palace [19]: Four separate Rococo palaces, home of the Danish royal family since 1794, frame one of the loveliest squares in Northern Europe. Alas, there's no getting inside, but when the queen is in residence you can enjoy a colorful changing of the guard at noon.

Børsen (Old Stock Exchange) [39]: This landmark Renaissance building whose spire is shaped in the form of intertwined dragon tails is a legacy from King Christian IV, Copenhagen's great builder-king.

Botansk Have [30]: Tropical and subtropical plants in the greenhouses and topless sun-worshipers on the grass in summer make this park across from Rosenborg Palace an eye-opener.

*Christiansborg Palace [34]: This impressive building stands across from the National Museum. It was erected on the site of Bishop Absalon's first fortress (medieval ruins below), once a royal residence and today the home of the Danish Parliament.

Christianshavn: Located across the Knippelsbro bridge, this lovely old district features fine 18th-century houses and the ruins of the 17th-century *bastions* [41], today a popular promenade. The Rococo *Christians Kirke* [42] has a three-story gallery, while the 17th-century Baroque *Vor Frelsers Kirke* (Church of Our Savior) [43] is distinguished by a curious external spiral staircase you can climb for an inspiriting view of the city.

**Davids Samling (David Art Collection) [29]: A remarkable collection of European and

Børsen (Stock Exchange)

Oriental art, including Danish paintings from the 19th century.

Det Kongelige Teater (Royal Theater) [16]: With low ticket prices and superb companies performing—including the Danish National Theater and the incomparable Royal Danish Ballet—a seat here is one of Copenhagen's best values.

Det Ny Teater (The New Theater) [10]: Productions here are of high artistic caliber. Just across the street is the **Bymuseum** (Municipal Museum) [11].

Gammeltorv [12]: The oldest part of Copenhagen, this ancient market square was once the site of jousting tournaments and public executions. King Christian IV had the "Caritas" ("Charity") fountain installed in 1609. The *Nytorv*, or New Market, with the early 19th-century colonnaded *Courthouse* is opposite.

Helligands Kirken (Church of the Holy Spirit) [13]: This 14th-century monastic church was given a tower in 1620 and redesigned about a hundred years later.

*Hirschsprungske Samling (Hirschsprung Collection) [32]: Paintings, watercolors, and sculptures provide a comprehensive overview of Danish art between 1800 and 1910.

Holmens Kirke (Church on the Island) [40]: Seamen in the 17th century were the first to use this Renaissance church.

Hotel Royal [6]: From June to September, the hotel hosts "Denmark Luncheons," featuring dem-

onstrations of *smorrebrod,* Denmark's fabulous open-faced sandwiches.

Kastellet (Citadel) [21]: The remains—including a windmill—of a fortress built by Christian IV in 1629.

Kunstindustrimuseet (Museum of Decorative Art) [18]: This museum, housed in what was an 18th-century hospital building, exhibits a wonderful collection of European and Oriental applied art spanning a period from the Middle Ages to the present day.

Langelinie: This favorite promenade follows the coast to the harbor, where **The Little Mermaid** (*Den Lille Havfrue*) [22] from the Hans Christian Andersen story sits on her small rock. Despite having suffered numerous indignities over the years, such as being painted and even decapitated, the Mermaid has managed to preserve her charming and tragic air of watery mystery.

Kongens Nytorv (King's New Market) [15]: Copenhagen's

The Little Mermaid

largest square features an equestrian statue of King Christian V and, on its east side, the 17th-century *Charlottenborg Palace,* now home of the Royal Academy of Art.

Marmorikirken (Marble Church or Frederik's Church) [17]: Representations of religious figures from Moses to Martin Luther adorn this church, which has an oversized dome. Two other denominations have churches nearby: The *Russiske Ortodoxe Kirke,* distinguished by its onion-shaped domes, serves the Russian Orthodox community, and *Saint Ansgar,* built in a neorenaissance style, is attended by Roman Catholics.

National Museet [33]: The largest and most important museum in Scandinavia, it counts among its many and varied treasures artifacts from the Ice Age, mysterious Viking rune stones, and the Hingdsgavl Dagger.

Nikolaj Kirke (Church of Saint Nicholas) [14]: A former medieval church, destroyed and rebuilt several times over the centuries, Saint Nicholas has now been turned into an exhibition space.

**Ny Carlsberg Glyptothek [4]: There's enough art in this monumental neoclassical building to keep you occupied for days: paintings include superb ancient Roman portraits and works by French Impressionists. The sculpture collection roams the globe from Egypt and Rome to France.

Rådhus (Town Hall) [2]: A

Copenhagen Attractions:

1. Råadhaus Pladsen
2. Town Hall
3. Tivoli
4. Ny Carlsberg Glyptothek
5. Main Train Station
6. Hotel Royal
7. Benneweis Circus
8. Sheraton Hotel
9. Church of the Sacred Heart of Jesus
10. Det Ny Teater
11. Municipal Museum
12. Gammeltorv
13. Helligånds Kirken
14. Nikolaj Kirke
15. Kongens Nytorv
16. Royal Theater
17. Marmorikirken
18. Museum of Decorative Art
19. Amalienborg Palace
20. St. Alban's Church
21. Kastellet
22. Little Mermaid
23. Church of Our Lady
24. University
25. St. Peter's Church
26. Round Tower
27. Museum of Musical History
28. Rosenborg Palace
29. David Collection
30. Botanical Garden
31. National Art Gallery
32. Hirschsprung Collection
33. National Museum
34. Christiansborg Palace
35. Theater
36. Thorvaldsen Museum
37. Royal Library
38. Arsenal
39. Børsen (Stock Exchange)
40. Holmsen Church
41. Bastions
42. Christians Kirke
43. Church of Our Savior
44. Scandinavia Skyscraper

late 19th–early 20th century red brick structure built in a compendium of styles, it has an intriguing astronomical clock that not only pinpoints the time here and on every continent in the world, but also

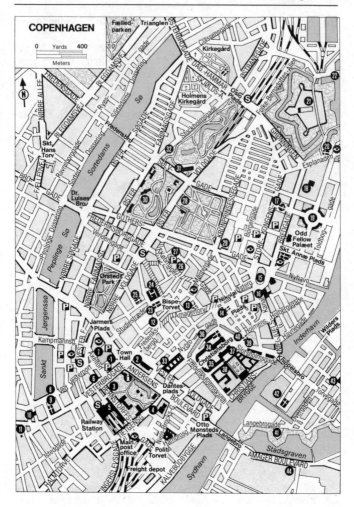

tells you what day it is according to the Julian and Gregorian calendars and whether or not you can expect an eclipse of the moon or the sun. There is a fine panoramic view from the tower.

Rådhaus Pladsen

Rådhus Pladsen (Town Hall Square) [1] is a busy place with cafés and food vendors as well as a lovely fountain, a monument to native son Hans Christian Andersen, and the tall, stone *Lur Blower's Column*—a *lur,* in case you're wondering, was an ancient trumpet.

Rosenborg Slot [28]: A Renaissance castle built by the Renaissance builder-king, Christian IV, it is now the home of the crown jewels and various other royal mementos—including Christian's pearl-studded saddle.

Runde Tårn [26]: Another part of the city's legacy from Christian IV, the round tower was built between 1636 and 1642 for use as an observatory. You can walk up the inner staircase for the view, although Peter the Great of Russia supposedly used a horse and carriage to get to the top—a privilege reserved for royalty.

Saint Peter's Church [25]: The oldest church in Copenhagen, Saint Peter's originally dates to about 1450 and has an 18th-century tower.

Sheraton Hotel [8]: The panoramic view at the top may make you feel like dancing, which is why the band is there.

Statens Museum for Kunst (National Art Gallery) [31]: A doorman wearing an old-fashioned costume admits you to this magnificent collection that ranges from Rembrandt, Rubens, and Dürer to the French Impressionists and Matisse.

Tivoli [3]: No trip to Copenhagen is complete without a visit to the world-famous Tivoli Gardens, a wonderland of lights and theaters, fireworks and amusements. Try to catch one of the many concerts that keep the park hopping from May to September.

Vor Frue Kirke (Church of Our Lady) [23]: Although it originally dates from the 13th century, this several-times-restored church with a neoclassical façade has been Copenhagen's cathedral only since 1924. The interior is graced by several marble and bronze statues by the 19th-century Danish sculptor Thorvaldsen, especially his *Christ and the Apostles.* Across the street are the main buildings of the **University** [24], which was founded in 1479.

Córdoba

The ancient city of Córdoba represented a high point in the Moorish culture that dominated Andalusia from the eighth to the 13th centuries. Moslems, Jews, and Christians lived together here, creating a center of intellectual and artistic refinement that made Córdoba one of the leading cities of Europe. The greatest monument from this period is the awe-inspiring eighth-century mosque, later dedicated as a cathedral, known as La Mezquita. Córdoba now has its share of undistinguished new buildings, but there is also an abundance of lovely squares and white-washed houses with beautiful patios (many of which are decked with flowers and opened to the public in May during the *Fiesta de los Patios*) old Arab mills, and a Roman bridge that spans the Rio Guadalquivar.

History

Before the Moors arrived from North Africa in the eighth century, Córdoba was a Roman and then a Visigoth city. The city was particularly popular with the Romans, who came in 151 B.C.: Eventually, Julius Caesar, Pompey, and Agrippa all stayed here. The surrounding fields became the deadly battlefield between the troops of Caesar and those of his rival-enemy Pompey.

Córdoba became the capital of Moorish Spain in the eighth century; it was governed as a separate emirate for about two hundred years, after which time the Caliphate of Córdoba was established. Science and philosophy flourished in the Moorish court, most notably in the persons of Averröes, an Arab scientist, and Maimónides, a Jewish doctor and philosopher. The fabulous mosque that is now Córdoba's principal tourist site was begun in the eighth century and completed in the tenth. It was said to have possessed the original copy of the Koran and a bone from the body of the Prophet Mohammed—small wonder that Moorish pilgrims flocked to its precincts by the thousands, making Córdoba one of the prime pilgrimage cities of Europe during the Dark Ages.

The city withstood several sieges by Christian armies until it was finally conquered by Saint Ferdinand in 1236. Many Castilian monarchs, including Alfons XI, Peter I, and Ferdinand and Isabella, made Córdoba their residential city. In the 16th century, Charles V angered Córdobans by setting forth plans to build a Baroque cathedral in the center of the mosque—construction proceeded, but the results were such that even the king later admitted it was a mistake.

Attractions

**Cathedral (La Mezquita) [3]: Formerly the main mosque of Western Islam, Córdoba's cathe- dral is one of Spain's greatest at- tractions and along with the Al- hambra in Granada, one of the most important Arab structures in

CÓRDOBA

0   Yards   400

Meters

Europe. Building began under Abd ar-Rahman I in the eighth century and continued for 200 years. Entering this place is a breathtaking experience and instantly reveals the high level of design and artistry achieved by the Moors: Hundreds of marble, granite, onyx, and jasper columns glint in the soft light, rising to multicolored horseshoe arches and a ceiling of tinted cedar. Before entering, pilgrims made their ceremonial ablutions in the fountains of the charming *Patio de los Naranjos* (Courtyard of the Orange Trees). The magnificent, 11th-century **Mihrab*, a prayer niche with a kind of anteroom

Former Mosque of Córdoba

known as the *makoureh,* represents the high point of the elaborate decorations found throughout the structure. Clumsily set in the midst of this beauty is the heavy Baroque *crucero* ordered by

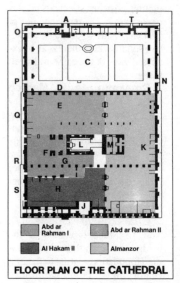

FLOOR PLAN OF THE CATHEDRAL

Charles V—it's easy to see why the townspeople lamented its presence in their fabulous building, and why even Charles regretted his decision to build it here. There is a magnificent panorama from the top of the *bell tower*, formerly the mosque's minaret.

Alcázar de los Reyes Cristianos (Royal Palace) [9]: Surrounded by magnificent gardens, this extensive complex of buildings originates in part from the Moorish period, but was completed in the 14th century. The Catholic monarchs Ferdinand and Isabella lived here for eight years, until the seizure of Granada in 1491. Antiques from Córdoba and the surrounding areas are on display, as are fine Roman mosaics depicting mythological themes.

*Calle de las Flores [2]: This picture-postcard street, its houses decorated with hanging flower baskets, leads to a small, attractive square where there is an unexpected view of the cathedral's bell tower.

Convento de la Merced [18]: A beautiful, 18th-century gate, a charming patio, and a marble staircase characterize this convent. Fire destroyed the Baroque interior of the church in 1978.

El Zoco [11]: This former Arab *souk* comes alive in summer when stalls and shops open to sell local arts and crafts souvenirs.

Guadalquivir Bridge [7]: The 16 Moorish arches of the bridge rest upon the original Roman foundations dating to the first century B.C. From the bridge

there is a lovely view of the city, which gently slopes towards the foothills of the Sierra Morena; downstream are the ruins of the old *molinos,* or Moorish mills.

Museo Arqueológico [16]: Housed within the *Palacio de los Paez* is a collection of artifacts from prehistoric to Roman times, as well as a section devoted to Iberian art.

Museo Provincial de Bellas Artes (Provincial Museum of Fine Arts) [17]: Spanish art spanning several centuries— including works by Zurbarán, Ribera, Goya, and Murillo—can be found in this museum housed in the old Hospital of Charity at the **Plaza del Potro,* with its 16th-century fountain and inn where Don Quijote was once a customer.

*Museo Taurino y de Arte Córdobés (Museum of Bull-fighting) [10]: Posters and paintings by Córdoban artists, works of leather and silver, and mementoes and memorabilia of Córdoban bullfighters fill this museum, located in two mansions surrounding a patio.

Palacio de Viana de Don Gome [20]: This former private palace with 14 inner courtyards and gardens is considered one of the most beautiful buildings in the city.

Plaza de la Tendillas [1]: The center of modern Córdoba features an equestrian statue of General Gonzalo Fernandez de Córdoba (1453–1515), known as El Gran Capitan.

Plaza de los Dolores [21]: In

the center of the square, surrounded by a Capuchin convent and the church of San Jacinto, are lanterns hanging from wrought-iron brackets that illuminate a Calvary scene.

Santa Marina de Aguas Santas [19]: This church, renowned as one of the most beautiful in Córdoba, has Romanesque portals and Gothic windows; nearby is a monument honoring the famous bullfighter Manolete.

Synagogue [12]: The only synagogue in Andalusia to survive the expulsion of the Jews by the 15th-century Catholic monarchs, it features Hebrew and Mudejar stucco work and a women's gallery.

Torre de la Calahorra (Calahorra Tower) [8]: This 14th-century tower, built to guard the entrance to the city, houses Córdoba's *Historical Museum.*

Dublin

Dublin's population may top the one-million mark, but the capital of the Republic of Ireland—picturesquely situated on the River Liffey, leading into Dublin Bay—has an easygoing, small-town charm endearing to residents and visitors alike. A rich selection of museums, colleges, theatres, churches, and historic buildings can be explored on foot around and about O'Connell Bridge; equally enticing are the entire blocks and squares of handsome 18th-century houses, their front doors painted in vivid hues and overhung with fan windows. When you tire of walking, you can find rest, refreshment, and, doubtless, a talkative Dubliner or two—the city's most valuable asset—at one of its thousands of pubs. Indeed, you'll find your senses amply sated in the welcoming city known in Gaelic as *Baile Átha Cliath* ("town at the hurdle ford")—whether your taste runs to the elegance of Georgian architecture, the gentle strains of traditional fiddles and pipes, the dark splendor of Guinness stout, or the bewitching words of Joyce and Yeats.

History

Dublin—the name derives from the Gaelic *dubhlinn,* or "dark water"—celebrated its millennium in 1988 with much fanfare and zest, which was only appropriate for a proud city with such a rich, and at times turbulent, heritage. In A.D. 140, the Greek cartographer Ptolemy referred to Dublin, which he called Eblana, as an "important settlement." St. Patrick visited Dublin in 448, and in the eighth and ninth centuries it was occupied by Vikings, who enlarged its harbor and increased its fortunes and importance. Norsemen lived here until 1014, when they fell in battle to the Irish near Clontarf. In 1169, the Normans invaded and made Dublin their citadel; three years later, Henry II of England held court here, and for hundreds of years the city was under English rule.

In the late 18th century, Dublin was at its cultural and economic peak: It had become the second most prominent city of the British Empire and one of Europe's ten major cities. Industry was on the rise, as were handsome, new buildings—Trinity College, the Four Courts, the Old Parliament House, and hundreds of private residences. But within a few decades, construction stopped, business declined, and British attention—and finances—turned to Belfast for its shipbuilding, linenmaking, and other industries.

Throughout this rise and fall—indeed, throughout centuries of English domination and subjugation—Irish nationalism, strongly fused with staunch Roman Catholicism, was quietly brewing. This nationalism became vocal and visible during the 19th century with the founding of the Gaelic League, the Irish Republic Brotherhood, and various movements and organizations in support of the cause. In 1916, the Easter Rising brought the issue to a head: Irish nationalists occupied the General Post Office and other central Dublin public buildings and were either killed on the spot or executed later by the British. The bitter Anglo-Irish War ensued, and in 1921, the Anglo-Irish Treaty established the 26 southern Irish counties as the Irish Free State (in 1949, Éire, the independent Republic of Ireland, was officially proclaimed).

Since the 1920s, Dublin has grown slowly but steadily—commercially, politically, and industrially. Sadly, in the past decade or so, many of Ireland's "best and brightest" have bypassed Dublin—and its dearth of satisfying professional work—in search of better-paying jobs abroad. This trend continues, although the last two years have witnessed an upswing in Dublin's economy that bodes well for its future.

Attractions

Abbey Theatre, Lower Abbey Street: The Abbey, Ireland's national theater, was founded in 1904 by W. B. Yeats and Lady Gregory. After the old building burned down in 1951, the present theater opened in 1966. Besides the main stage, there is the downstairs Peacock Theatre, which has lunchtime as well as evening shows.

Chester Beatty Library and Gallery of Oriental Art, 20 Shrewsbury Road: Sir Alfred Chester Beatty was an American millionaire/connoisseur who, in the 1950s, left his superb collection of Western miniatures and manuscripts, Oriental scrolls, and Persian miniatures to his adopted land. Offering a veritable history of the art of the book, from Babylonian clay tablets to *Narae-hon,* Japanese picture books of the 17th to 19th centuries, the museum is a little-known gem well worth a visit.

Christ Church Cathedral [9], Lord Edward Street: The oldest cathedral in the country, Christ Church was founded in 1038 and replaced with a new church in 1172 by Strongbow, Ireland's first English conqueror. Today only fragments remain of the Gothic building, the present church was constructed between 1871 and 1878. Of interest are a 12th-century crypt and the tombs of Strongbow and his son (during the 16th and 17th centuries, the crypt functioned as a wine cellar and tavern). The cathedral is also famous for being the site of the coronation in 1487 of Lambert Simnel "the Deceiver" as Edward VI, and for introducing the English liturgy here in 1551.

City Hall [10], Cork Hill: This domed structure in the Corinthian style was built from 1769 to 1779; its architect was Thomas Cooley. The hall's colonnaded rotunda displays monumental neoclassical sculpture, and the city's emblems, a mace and a sword, are also on view. In former times, the building functioned as the Royal Exchange (stock exchange).

The Custom House [2], Custom House Quay: This 1791 structure, considered by many the most beautiful Georgian building in Dublin, was designed by James Gandon. It was destroyed by fire in 1921 during the Anglo-Irish War, but was later restored. The main façade features a portal with Doric columns and a tympanum with allegorical figures of the Atlantic Ocean and 13 Irish rivers.

*Dublin Castle [11], Dame Street: This citadel of the city was erected by the Normans between 1208 and 1220; it was the seat of the administration during British rule. Of special interest are the *Record Tower* at the southeast corner (all that remains of the original Norman fortification); the lavish *State Apartments,* including *St. Patrick's Hall,* where the inauguration of Irish presidents takes place (the first, Douglas Hyde, was installed in 1938); the beautiful *Bedford Tower,* from which the Irish crown jewels were stolen in 1907, never to be recovered; and the former palace chapel, the *Church of the Most Holy Trinity,* built between 1807 and 1814 according to Francis Johnston's design.

Dublin Civic Museum [17], City Assembly House, South William Street: Opened in 1953, the museum contains a fascinating photographic record of turn-of-the-century Dublin.

Fitzwilliam Square: Some of Dublin's finest Georgian buildings are found along this elegant square and along adjacent Fitzwilliam Street.

The Four Courts [12], Inns Quay: Though Thomas Cooley began the design of this impressive riverside center of law in 1785, it was completed by James Gandon between 1796 and 1800. Destroyed in 1922 during the Anglo-Irish War, it was later rebuilt according to its original design. An outstanding feature of this enormous structure is its portico of Corinthian columns, crowned by statues of Moses and allegorical figures of Justice and Charity.

Gate Theatre, Parnell Square: The Gate was founded in 1928 to stage classical and international dramatic productions that were not a part of the Abbey's repertoire. The young Orson Welles, among illustrious others, appeared here.

General Post Office [1], O'Connell Street: This monumen-

Custom House

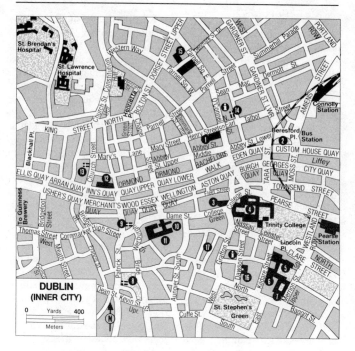

DUBLIN (INNER CITY)

0 Yards 400 · Meters

tal granite building, designed by Francis Johnston in 1818, features an Ionic arcade and statues representing Hibernia, Mercury, and Fidelity. The Post Office was the headquarters of the Irish Volunteers during the Easter Rising of 1916, which is commemorated by a statue and plaque inside. Fire destroyed part of the building during the uprising, but it was later restored.

Grafton Street: Some of Dublin's best shopping is to be found here, including *Brown Thomas* and *Switzer's,* two of the

Dublin Attractions:
1. General Post Office
2. Custom House
3. Old Parliament House (Bank of Ireland)
4. Trinity College
5. National Gallery
6. National Museum
7. Leinster House
8. St. Patrick's Cathedral
9. Christ Church Cathedral
10. City Hall
11. Dublin Castle
12. Four Courts (Supreme Court)
13. St. Michans's Church
14. St. Mary's Cathedral
15. Hugh Lane Gallery of Modern Art
16. Mansion House
17. Civic Museum

city's leading department stores, and assorted antiques shops. Stop for a coffee at *Bewley's Oriental Café*, a much-loved Dublin institution (also on Westmoreland Street).

Guinness Brewery, St. James Gate: Located in the old Liberties district of Dublin, the brewery—founded in 1759—is one of the largest in the world and one of Ireland's most important industrial enterprises. A film on the making of Guinness stout is shown Monday through Friday, followed by free samples.

Hugh Lane Gallery of Modern Art [15], Parnell Square: Located in Georgian Charlemont House since around 1930, this town house-gallery features some of connoisseur Hugh Lane's collection of contemporary art. The gallery is strongest in 19th-century French paintings and early 20th-century Irish art, including works by Jack Yeats (the poet's brother), John Lavery, and illustrator/stained-glass designer Harry Clarke.

James Joyce Tower, in Sandycove, 2 km. (1.5 miles) south of Dún Laoghaire (13 km./8 miles southeast of Dublin): Ireland's best-known author lived for a short time in the late 18th-century *Martello Tower,* originally constructed by the British as a defense in case of attack by Napoleon's forces. The opening pages of *Ulysses* feature the tower, which is now a museum housing memorabilia and documents of the author's life and work.

Kilmainham Jail Historical Museum, south of Phoenix Park: From 1796 until 1924, political prisoners were incarcerated in this formidable jailhouse. Today it serves as a memorial to the many who defied—and died over—British rule.

Leinster House [7], Kildare Street: This 1745 structure—which originally belonged to the first Duke of Leinster—has functioned since 1922 as the Irish Parliament building, where the *Seanad* (Senate) and *Dáil* (House of Commons) assemble.

Mansion House [16], Dawson Street: Since 1715, the lord mayors of Dublin have resided in this building, the site, as well, of many significant events in the history of Ireland. The 1919 Declaration of Independence and the 1921 Anglo-Irish War armistice agreement were both signed here.

Merrion Square: This elegant Georgian square once was home to W. B. Yeats (first at number 52, later number 82), and Oscar Wilde lived in number 1.

*National Gallery of Ireland [5], Merrion Square: Masterpieces of Irish as well as Continental art are a part of this national collection, which first opened its doors to the public in 1864. Italian 14th-century and Renaissance artists are well represented in the collection, as are Dutch 17th-century, Spanish, and late 18th-early 19th-century French masters. Among the outstanding works on view are a *Pietà* by Perugino, Joshua Reynolds' *Charles*

Coote, 1st Earl of Bellamont, Zurbarán's *St. Rufina,* Goya's *The Dreamer,* Rembrandt's *Rest on the Flight into Egypt,* and Poussin's *Lamentation.* The *National Portrait Gallery* area is also of interest, featuring likenesses of and by leading Irish figures, including George Bernard Shaw, W.B. Yeats (by his father, John Butler Yeats), J. M. Synge, and Brendan Behan.

National Library, Kildare Street: Both the National Library and its sister structure, the National Museum—they flank Leinster House—were designed by Sir Thomas Manly Deane; it opened to the public in 1890. Over 800,000 volumes are stored in the library, including a famous collection of maps and the Joly Collection, over 70,000 prints pertaining to the history of Ireland. The library functions primarily as an Irish research center, but its central rotunda is worth a look.

**National Museum of Ireland [6], Kildare Street: This massive institution is divided into departments of Irish antiquities, applied arts, natural science, and natural history. It is world-renowned for its superb collection of Irish artifacts, from Bronze Age gold and tools to eighth-century Celtic treasures (including the Tara Brooch and Ardagh Chalice), to early 20th-century relics of the fight for independence. There is also an Annex on nearby Merrion Row, featuring Viking objects and a display on early medieval Dublin.

O'Connell Street: This long,

Brooch of Tara

spacious thoroughfare is named after Daniel O'Connell (1775–1847), who championed Catholic Emancipation; his memorial statue stands at its south end. Balzac said he "incarnated a whole people," and, indeed, it was through his efforts that Catholics were allowed to vote, to subsequently become civil servants, and eventually be elected to Parliament. The busy, noisy length of O'Connell Street is chockablock with restaurants, cinemas, shops, travel agents, and fast-food joints; the *Irish Tourist Office* is here, as well.

Old Parliament House [3], 2 College Green: Occupied today by the Bank of Ireland, this handsome, somewhat austere building—designed in 1728–1729 by Sir Edward Lovett Pearce—originally functioned as Ireland's Parliament House. The only extant

Georgian room is the House of Lords chamber, with its splendid Dublin-glass chandelier and pair of 1733 tapestries depicting the Battle of the Boyne (1690).

Phoenix Park, western part of the city: A venue for rock concerts and cricket matches, as well as the address of the official residence of the Irish president, *Aras an Uachtarain,* this huge 712-hectare (1,700-acre) park—the largest city park in Europe—is considered one of the most beautiful public expanses in the world. Originally laid out as hunting grounds and game preserve, it opened to the public in 1747. The *Zoological Gardens,* one of Europe's oldest zoos, was founded in 1830. Near the main entrance, on Parkgate Street, are the *People's Gardens* and the 68-meter- (223-foot-) high obelisk, the *Wellington Monument.* Also on Parkgate is *Ryan's,* one of Dublin's oldest and handsomest pubs, noted for its superb Guinness and quaint "snugs," for intimate drinking and chat.

St. Audoen's Church, High Street: Dublin's oldest parish church, founded by the Normans, features three 15th-century bells. Next to the church is St. Audoen's Arch, dating to 1215 and the only surviving gate from the old city walls.

St. Mary's, The Pro-Cathedral [14], Marlborough Street: Designed by exiled patriot John Sweetman, this Roman Catholic church was built between 1815 and 1825. The main Doric portico (from the 1840s, with statues of the Virgin, St. Patrick, and Dublin's patron, St. Laurence O'Toole) was modeled after the Temple of Theseus in Athens, and the interior is based on that of St-Philippe-du-Roule in Paris. The world-famous Palestrina Choir sings the Latin Mass on Sunday mornings at 11:00.

St. Michan's Church [13], Lower Church Street: Erected during the 17th century on the site of a Viking church of 1095, St. Michan's features beautiful wood carvings and an organ on which Handel played. Don't miss the crypt vaults and their ghoulish, but fascinating, contents: The corpses contained within are almost perfectly preserved, due to the tannic acid in the dry atmosphere.

St. Patrick's Cathedral [8], Patrick Street: The early English-style cathedral was founded in 1190 and finished in 1225. The tower is a later addition, as is the pitched roof, and the building was completely restored in 1860 (it sustained heavy damages at the hands of Oliver Cromwell's troops in the 17th century). Ireland's longest church (100 meters/328 feet), St. Patrick's contains many memorials to famous personages, the most notable (to the right of the south portal) the tomb of Jonathan Swift, who served as deacon here from 1713 to 1745. Nearby is the grave of "Stella" (Esther Johnson), his lifelong love.

St. Stephen's Green: Laid out in 1880, the green is a popular recreational spot with lovely flower beds, trees, waterfalls, and a pond. Busts and statues depicting famous Irishmen are scattered throughout the park, and it is surrounded by elegant Georgian buildings. Dublin's finest hotel, the stately *Shelbourne,* stands like a citadel along the green; it has inspired the likes of Joyce, Thackeray, and Elizabeth Bowen.

*Trinity College [4], College Green: Queen Elizabeth I granted Trinity its charter in 1591, although no structures remain from that time (the Protestant university was built on the site of Augustinian All Hallows' Priory, which had been dissolved by Henry VIII). Most of the buildings seen today are from the 18th century, the earliest being the red-brick *Rubrics* (1722), where poet and alumnus Oliver Goldsmith once lived (other notable graduates include Jonathan Swift, Edmund Burke, Thomas Moore, and Oscar Wilde). The 17-hectare (40-acre) campus is an oasis of trees, grass, and stones in the middle of the city, and its architectural treasures include the college's main Palladian façade (1759), the *Examination Hall* (1787), the *museum* (1856), the *University Chapel,* and the new *Berkeley Library* (1967).

But the jewel in the university's crown is undoubtedly *Trinity College Library* (1732), which houses one of the world's finest collections of illuminated manuscripts, documents, and books—over 2.5 million specimens in all, including Egyptian papyri, ancient Greek and Latin texts, more than 140 early Irish manuscripts from the sixth century, and the magnificent *Book of Kells (eighth century), considered by many the most beautiful illuminated manuscript in the world (Joyce called it "the fountainhead of Irish inspiration"). The timber, barrel-vaulted Long Room (1860–1862), designed by Benjamin Woodward and Thomas Deane II, features two volumes of the famous Gospels, as well as the exquisite *Book of Durrow.*

Edinburgh

Edinburgh (population around 440,000), the compact yet monumental capital of Scotland, is one of the most beautiful cities in Great Britain—and many say in all of Europe. Princes Street divides Edinburgh into New Town at the north, with its carefully planned streets, elegant squares, and handsome buildings, and Old Town, dominated by the Castle and the Royal Mile (Lawnmarket, High Street, and Canongate, from the fortress to the palace of Holyroodhouse) and punctuated by labyrinthine closes and narrow, winding lanes. The city is renowned for the annual Edinburgh International Festival of art, dance, drama, film, and music and its concurrent Fringe program (featuring avant-garde performers and productions). The festival is held for three weeks in late August. Edinburgh's welcoming atmosphere and wealth of museums, theaters, concert venues, and historic buildings (not to mention its pubs!) make this city a rich and lively visitors' center all year round.

History

Rising from the volcanic Lowland hills along the Firth of Forth, the area making up present-day Edinburgh was undoubtedly inhabited in prehistoric times. The Romans settled in the western Cramond region, and, in 638, the Castle Rock site was captured by Northumbrians—the name Edinburgh may derive from that of their king, Edwin. The city's official history began in the 11th century during the reign of Malcolm Cranmore and Queen Margaret, who chose to live on Castle Rock. Their son, David I, founded the Abbey of Holy Rood on a site to the east. The medieval settlement that formed around these two areas proved vulnerable to both invaders and poverty, hence retarding its development for some three centuries. A wall was constructed around this Old Town area in 1450, and the next half-century witnessed a Golden Age in Edinburgh. The Stewarts (later Stuarts) made the Palace of Holyroodhouse their residence, and the city became the capital and seat of government. Important churches and civic structures were built, and the arts flourished and spread with the introduction of printing in 1507.

This period of prosperity ended with the Battle of Flodden Field in 1513, when James IV and hundreds of others died fighting the English (and supporting the French). The town finished constructing the Flodden Wall in 1560, the year of the Reformation. For some 250 years, this structure limited all but vertical expansion (some multi-story tenements reached as high as 12 stories). The Union of the Crowns occurred in 1603, with James VI ascending to the throne of England. A period of relative peace lasted until the 1630s, after which civil war followed (resulting in the king's execution in 1649), the occupation of Edinburgh by Cromwell and his troops in 1650, and the Restoration in 1660.

The late 17th century saw Edinburgh prosper as both a legal and medical hub. In 1707, with the Act of the Union (joining the English and Scottish Parliaments), the city began to expand its narrow boundaries, and civil strife and religious persecution virtually came to an end. The late 18th and early 19th centuries produced the so-called Scottish Enlightenment, with great men of letters, science, and the arts emerging from and enriching the city—among them the novelist Walter Scott, economist Adam Smith, architect Robert Adam, philosopher David Hume, and poet Robert Burns. When Old Town became run-down, poverty-stricken, and overpopulated, ambitious plans for the New Town were proposed and implemented. The Georgian New Town featured splendid streets and elegant squares, and helped make the Scottish capital one of the most beautiful—and progressive—in Europe.

In the 20th century, Edinburgh still flourishes as one of Europe's loveliest cities—at least within its central Old and New Town borders—and its late-summer International Festival, established in 1947, turns it into a welcome, albeit overcrowded, mecca for culture-vultures the world over.

Attractions

Calton Hill [24], off Regent Road: Besides affording lovely views, this 100-meter- (328-foot-) high hill is the site of two old observatories: Nelson's Monument (with a viewing gallery); and the 12-columned portico known as the National Monument, an unfinished (due to funds) Parthenon replica honoring Scots who died during the Napoleonic Wars.

Canongate Tolbooth [18], 163 Canongate: This picturesque 1591 building, with a turreted steeple, was originally the tolbooth (Scottish for a civic structure) for the burgh of Canongate. At first, taxes were collected here; it was eventually used for criminals' trials and as a jailhouse. Today it houses temporary exhibitions, a tartan display, and the Brass Rubbing Centre.

*The Castle [10], Castle Rock: Over the years, Scottish and

English sovereigns have occupied this 11th-century castle, located on a strategic bank of rock (the site was used as a fortress as early as the seventh century). Among the many attractions are the tiny *St. Margaret's Chapel,* one of Scotland's oldest houses of worship; *Mons Meg,* a powerful 15th-century cannon; the *Scottish National War Memorial* (dedicated to

Edinburgh Castle

the country's dead in World War II); various prisoners' quarters; the late 15th-century *Great Hall*, built for Charles IV and featuring a hammerbeam roof, and the *Palace Block*, including the Royal Treasury (with the crown jewels) and Queen Mary's Room. The *Esplanade*, a capacious paradeground set out in the 18th century, is the venue for the Military Tattoo, the Edinburgh Festival's popular presentation of taps by the Scottish Army.

Charlotte Square [32]: In 1791, Robert Adam designed this elegant Georgian square, the loveliest in Edinburgh's New Town. It centers on an equestrian statue of Prince Albert, and its buildings include *The Georgian House* (at number 7), whose lower floors have been furnished to resemble a typical residence of 1790 to 1810.

City Art Centre, 2–4 Market Street: Works of art by Scottish artists—from the 1600s to the present—comprise this municipal collection, whose best holdings are from the late 19th and 20th centuries. Temporary exhibitions are regularly on view.

Edinburgh University [30], Chambers Street to George Square: Edinburgh's Old College was established in 1581; two centuries later, Robert Adam, succeeded by William Playfair, designed the principal university buildings. Today their designs, along with Victorian and 20th-century structures, make up this eminent institution of higher learning. The university's gallery,

the *Talbot Rice Arts Centre* (Old College, South Bridge), displays Italian and Dutch paintings in its fine neoclassical interior (also an Adam/Playfair design).

The Grassmarket [25]: Once the site of witch burnings and religiously motivated hangings, this old square was also the departure point for old mail coaches. The *White Hart Inn*, frequented by Burns, Wordsworth, and other famous men, is on the north side.

Greyfriars Church and Churchyard [28], Greyfriars Place, south end of George IV Bridge: The present, much-restored church dates from 1612 (the site originally contained a 15th-century Franciscan friary). In its burial ground is a statue of Greyfriars Bobby, a Skye terrier who stood by the grave of his master, Jock Grey, for 14 years (in 1872, the dog was laid to rest beside Grey).

Heriot's School [26], Lauriston Place: George Heriot (1563–1624) was the goldsmith to James VI, and upon his death, he bequeathed his estate to the city to set up a school for orphans. The mid-17th-century building, with a symmetrical courtyard, is awash with ornate stone carving and strapwork.

**Holyroodhouse Palace [20], end of Holyrood Road and Canongate, in front of Holyrood Park: The official residence of the British sovereign while in Edinburgh, the present-day palace dates primarily from the reign of Charles II, who, in 1671, commissioned the renovation of the castle begun by James IV in the 16th century on the site of the Augustinian Abbey of Holy Rood. The Palladian-style palace, designed by Sir William Bruce, has ornate state apartments featuring lavish plasterwork ceilings, intricate carved-wood doors and frames, royal portraits, and Brussels and French tapestries. There are also historic apartments in the 16th-century round tower where you can see many objects and paintings associated with Mary Queen of Scots (who lived in the palace for six years).

Holyrood Park [21]: This huge, hilly expanse is encircled by Queen's Drive and crowned by Arthur's Seat, some 251 meters (823 feet) high and offering an impressive view westward of the city.

Huntly House [19], 142 Canongate: This 16th-century, timber-framed house is now a city museum, with displays of Edinburgh silver and glass, significant documents, and pottery, as well as a reconstructed antique kitchen and a 1920s clay-pipe workshop.

John Knox House Museum [16], 45 High Street: Built in the late 15th century by the goldsmith to Mary Queen of Scots, the town house features original oak floors and a painted ceiling from 1600. Knox, the founder of the Presbyterian Church of Scotland, is said to have lived here from 1566 until his death in 1572.

Lady Stair's House [13], Lady Stair's Close, Lawnmarket:

Manuscripts and mementoes relating to three great Scottish men of letters—Robert Burns, Walter Scott, and Robert Louis Stevenson—are displayed in this 1622 residence (Lady Stair was an occupant in the late 1700s).

The Magdalen Chapel [27], Cowgate: The original stained-glass windows survive in this 16th-century house of worship—one of Edinburgh's few remaining pre-Reformation structures; Wednesday lunch-hour concerts are regularly held here.

Museum of Childhood, High Street: Toys, games, dolls, books, costumes, and other relics and treasures of childhood are displayed in this charming museum.

National Gallery of Scotland [7], The Mound off Princes Street: William Playfair designed this neoclassical repository of European painting in the 1850s. Among its treasures are Raphael's *Bridgewater Madonna,* Titian's *Three Ages of Man,* Tintoretto's *Deposition of Christ,* and works by Velázquez, Rubens, Claude, Hals, Poussin, Gainsborough, and Turner. Modern masters include Monet, Renoir, Gauguin, van Gogh, and members of the Glasgow schools.

National Museum of Antiquities of Scotland, Queen Street: Established in the late 18th century as a museum reflecting Scottish life and culture, the collection concentrates on archaeological artifacts, from medieval Pictish Symbol Stones to the early 16th-century Montrose panels, bas-reliefs once part of a royal church pew. Arms and armor, coins, costumes, and silver from the centuries are also on display.

Outlook Tower [12], Castlehill: Various photographic exhibitions on its middle floors lead up to a rooftop *camera obscura* in this Victorian turret. Fascinating images of the city are reflected by the *camera obscura* (or periscope) onto a round, white tabletop.

Parliament Hall [15], Parliament Square: From 1639 until the union of the Parliaments in 1707, the Scottish Parliament assembled in this hall, with its handsome carved and gilt hammerbeam roof. Today the Scottish court convenes here.

Princes Street Gardens: This city park in the middle of Edinburgh's downtown district, is separated into East and West Princes Street Gardens by the Mound. It is the site of the Castle, the Walter Scott Monument, St. Cuthbert's and St. John's churches, and (in the West section) the oldest flower clock in the world, planted in 1903 and made up of some 20,000 annuals. Princes Street itself, north of the park, is a bustling thoroughfare with department stores, elegant shops, and hotels.

Royal Scottish Academy [6], The Mound off Princes Street: Temporary exhibitions are mounted throughout the year (Academy members exhibit annually from April to July) in this imposing Doric structure, designed in the 1820s by William Playfair, Edinburgh's premier Greek Revival architect.

Edinburgh Attractions:
1. Waverly Station
2. North British Hotel
3. Central Post Office
4. Register House
5. Scott Monument
6. Royal Scottish Academy
7. National Gallery
8. Saint John's Episcopal Church
9. Saint Cuthbert's
10. Edinburgh Castle
11. Scotch Whiskey Heritage Center
12. Outlook Tower
13. Lady Stair's House
14. St. Giles Cathedral
15. Parliament House
16. John Knox House
17. Moray House
18. Canongate Tolbooth
19. Huntly House
20. Holyroodhouse Palace
21. Holyrood Park
22. Old Calton Burial Ground
23. Saint Andrew's House
24. Calton Hill
25. Grassmarket
26. Heriot's School
27. Magdalen Chapel
28. Greyfriars Church
29. Royal Scottish Museum
30. University
31. Saint Andrew Square
32. Charlotte Square
33. Scottish National Gallery of Modern Art
34. Scottish National Portrait Gallery

Royal Scottish Museum [29], Chambers Street: Built in the 1850s in the wake of the Great Exhibition of 1851 in London's Crystal Palace, this museum is a spacious glass and cast-iron repository of ethnographic objects, sculpture, and decorative arts, as well as natural history, science, and technology collections. The classical, silver, and Oriental sections are especially interesting.

St. Andrew Square [31]: Though not as elegant as its west-

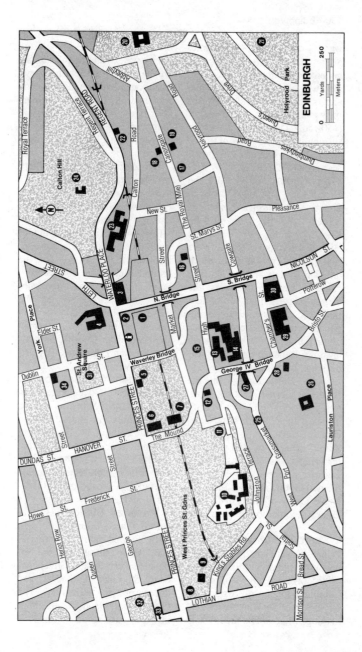

EDINBURGH

0   250
Yards
Meters

ward counterpart, Charlotte Square, St. Andrew Square is nonetheless impressive, with its many banks, insurance firms, and other commercial establishments surrounding the 45-meter- (150-foot-) high fluted column surmounted by the statue of statesman Henry Dundas, Viscount Melville (1742–1811).

St. Giles' Cathedral (The High Kirk of St. Giles) [14], High Street: Edinburgh's principal church—and the site of John Knox's famous sermons—the High Kirk has four octagonal piers supporting its crown spire, which are said to date from a Norman church. Over the centuries, the church served four denominations, and also functioned as a secondary school, prison, and office of the municipal clerk. The north aisle pre-Raphaelite window was designed by William Morris and Edward Burne-Jones. In the southeast corner is the small, richly embellished, 20th-century Thistle Chapel, with handsome, carved stalls, bronze, angel-shaped candelabra, and windows featuring coats of arms; Robert Lorimer designed the chapel in the neo-Gothic style for the Most Noble Order of the Thistle, the highest Scottish order of knighthood.

Scott Monument [5], East Princes Street Gardens: A prominent city landmark, this 60-meter (200-foot) Gothic Revival memorial spire is topped by Carrara marble statues of Sir Walter Scott and his dog, Maida. The niches hold 64 statues of characters from Scott's novels, and on the capitals are the heads of 16 Scottish poets. The monument's foundation stone was laid in 1840—eight years after the novelist's death—and four viewing platforms leading to the pinnacle afford lovely views.

**Scottish National Gallery of Modern Art [33], Belford Road: In a wooded setting west of New Town is this significant collection of contemporary art, some 3,000 works in all. Outdoor sculptures by Bourdelle, Epstein, Hepworth, and Moore dot the grounds. Inside are 20th-century Scottish, European, American, and other works. Among the movements and schools represented are the Fauves, German Expressionists, Cubists, Surrealists, Russian Primitives, Pop artists, and Minimalists.

Scottish National Portrait Gallery [34], Queen Street: Portraits of famed Scots, as well as other figures who shaped the history of Scotland, are displayed in this museum. Works date from the 16th century to the present, and artists represented include Raeburn, Gainsborough, Lawrence, and Lely.

Waverley Station [1], Waverley Place: Edinburgh's centrally located railroad station is just a stone's throw from the National Gallery, Princes Street Gardens, St. Giles' Cathedral, and dozens of other attractions. The Church of the Holy Trinity (built in 1462) once stood on this site.

Florence

Florence gave birth to the Renaissance in the 14th century. More than 600 years later, thanks to legislative limits on building and traffic in the center of the city, the medieval and Renaissance aspects still dominate it. Marble-clad churches, stately palazzi, and red-roofed buildings spread gently across the city's site on a small basin along the Arno River, all overlooked by the graceful red dome that Filippo Brunelleschi designed for the cathedral in 1420. Given the magnificent abundance of art treasures, it's no wonder that throngs of tourists flock here year-round.

History

Though the site of Florence was inhabited as early as the tenth century B.C., it was overshadowed for centuries by the larger and more important Fiesole, a nearby Etruscan city which, like Florence, later became Roman. Under Julius Caesar, Florentia ("the flourishing one") was made a veterans' colony; it began to live up to its name only when it became the Roman administrative capital of Tuscany and Umbria around the third century A.D.

Subsequently overrun by Ostrogoths, Byzantines, Lombards, and Franks, Florence became an autonomous commune in 1115. The city lost no time in destroying Fiesole (1125), establishing itself as the leading power in Tuscany, and beginning the Guelph (pro-pope) and Ghibelline (pro-emperor) conflicts that—along with plagues and famines—tore the city apart over the next few centuries.

The Medici family came to power in 1421, and the prosperity and relative political stability associated with their reign set the stage for an increased interest in the Classical age of Rome and Greece. It also spawned the secular humanism that later spread throughout Europe and became known as the Renaissance. Despite brief interruptions brought about by three banishments and the rise of the ascetic reformer Girolamo Savonarola, the Medici ruled until 1737, when Florence passed to the Austrian House of Lorraine.

Following the unification of Italy, Florence enjoyed a brief period as the national capital (1865–1871), after which its importance shifted from politics to art history and tourism. Today it serves as the regional capital of Tuscany.

Attractions

**Bargello [20]: A 13th-century palazzo built around a magnificent courtyard is home to a superlative museum of sculpture and decorative art, which includes works by Michelangelo, Cellini, Donatello, Verrocchio, and della Robbia.

***Battistero (Baptistry) [3]:

Baptistery, Duomo, and Campanile

Alternating bands of white and green marble and massive bronze doors give this beautiful 11th-century octagonal building a solid Tuscan Romanesque character. Andrea Pisano created the Gothic south door in 1330, and about 100 years later Lorenzo Ghiberti created the famous north and east doors that depict scenes from the life of Christ and the Old Testament. Magnificent 13th-century mosaics glow from the dome in the imposing interior; behind the apse you'll find the *Museo dell'Opera di Santa Maria del Fiore* (Museum of the Cathedral and its Possessions) containing works by Donatello and Michelangelo.

***Duomo (Cathedral of Santa Maria del Fiore) [1]: With the exception of Saint Peter's in Rome, this is the largest church in Italy and towers over the city from the Piazza del Duomo. Begun in 1296 by Arnolfo di Cambio, it was consecrated in 1467; the dome, huge and distinctive, is the work of Filippo Brunelleschi. The interior is surprisingly spare, which adds to its spacious elegance. Giotto designed the tall, slender, multi-marbled **Campanile** (Belltower) [2] in 1334.

**Galleria dell'Accademia (Academy of Fine Arts) [9]: Most visitors head immediately for the museum's most famous treasure, the monumental statue of *David* by Michelangelo; there are three additional pieces by him as well as paintings from the Florentine schools from the Middle Ages through the Renaissance.

***Galleria degli Uffizi (Uffizi Galleries) [17]: A former administrative building for the Medicis, built by Vasari and completed in 1580, now houses the most important collection of Florentine Renaissance art in the world. Masterpiece after masterpiece confronts the eye—works by Giotto, Cimabue, Martini, Paolo Uccello, Botticelli (including the famous *Primavera* and *The Birth of Venus*), Leonardo, Michelangelo, Raphael, and Titian. The bounty of work is so rich that it's almost impossible to take it all in. Expect lines.

Giardino di Boboli [30]: These 16th-century Italian-style gardens rise in terraces behind the Pitti Palace and are full of picturesque landscape effects such as an amphitheater, a cypress lane, and the Neptune Fountain. From the top of the hill there is a fabulous view of the city dominated by Brunelleschi's famous cathedral dome.

La Badia [19]: This tenth-century church of a former Bene-dictine abbey, with its tall Romanesque-Gothic campanile, contains masterful works by Mino da Fiesole and Filippino Lippi. The ambulatory walls are deco-rated with 15th-century frescoes depicting the life of Saint Bene-dict.

Museo Archeologico [12]: In addition to Egyptian, Roman, and Greek artifacts, the museum houses an important collection of Etruscan work.

Ognissanti [28]: Founded in 1256, the church was rebuilt sev-eral times over the centuries and contains the grave of Botticelli, whose *Saint Augustine* shares wall space with some remarkable works by Domenico Ghirlandaio.

**Orsanmichele [14]: Once an open loggia for selling cereals and grain, this building was con-verted into a lovely Gothic church in 1367.

**Ospedale degli Innocenti (Foundling Hospital) [10]: This orphanage, built by Brunelleschi in the 15th century, was the first building in Florence built in the Renaissance style. Between the arches of the colonnade, terra-cotta medallions by Andrea della Robbia depict babies in swaddling clothes.

Palazzo Medici-Riccardi [5]: This Renaissance palace with inner courtyard and chapel was built by Michelozzo in the mid-15th century for Cosimo de' Medici and eventually became the seat of the Medici rulers under Lorenzo il Magnifico; it was ac-quired in 1680 by Marquis Ric-cardi, who expanded it.

**Palazzo Pitti [29]: Impos-ing in its rusticated massiveness, the Pitti was designed by Bru-nelleschi for Luca Pitti, a rival of Cosimo de Medici; the Medicis managed to acquire it less than a hundred years later, and were re-sponsible for additional building and expanding the works of art within. When Florence was briefly the capital of Italy, it became the royal residence of King Victor Emmanuel II. The world-famous ***Galleria Palatina,* once the pri-vate collection of the Medici fam-ily, contains room after room of Italian, Flemish, and Spanish masterpieces.

*Palazzo Rucellai [27]: One of the major works of the early Re-naissance, this three-story palace with its plain façade and beautiful inner courtyard was completed in 1451 to plans by Alberti.

Palazzo Strozzi [26]: Con-sidered one of the true Renais-sance beauties of Florence, the palace, with its pleasant court-yard, was begun in 1489 and com-pleted about 50 years later.

**Palazzo Vecchio (also known as Palazzo della Signoria) [15]: Forming one end of the ***Piazza della Signoria*—the main square of Florence—and im-mediately recognizable to every-one who sees it, this massive 13th-century palace housed the original Signoria, the elected ministers of the Florentine Republic, and was then used for many years by the

Medici family. Several of the art-filled rooms are open to the public. A copy of Michelangelo's colossal *David* stands in front of the palace. To one side is the arcaded ****Loggia dei Lanzi** [16], an open-air sculpture museum that includes the violent *Rape of the Sabine Women* by Giambologna and *Perseus with the Head of Medusa* by Benvenuto Cellini.

*Piazzale Michelangelo [35]: A series of terraced steps lead up to a vast piazza surrounding a monument to Michelangelo—bronze copies of his marble statues of *David* and the allegorical figures from the Medici tombs—and one of the most celebrated views in the world: Florence and the surrounding hills. Stairs at the side of the restaurant in the piazza lead to the simple, 15th-century church of **San Salvatore al Monte** [36] and, still higher, the exquisite ***San Miniato al Monte** [37], whose distinctive green-and-white marble façade is one of the best examples of Tuscan Romanesque design in existence.

**Ponte Vecchio (Old Bridge) [18]: This famous 14th-century covered bridge has a row of shops on either side, full of lace, silver, and leather goods, and a small open square in the center with a memorial to that lusty artist-goldsmith, Benvenuto Cellini.

**San Lorenzo [4]: A Renaissance church rebuilt by Brunelleschi and Michelangelo, it's filled with paintings by Rosso Fiorentino, Filippo Lippi, Bron-

Ponte Vecchio

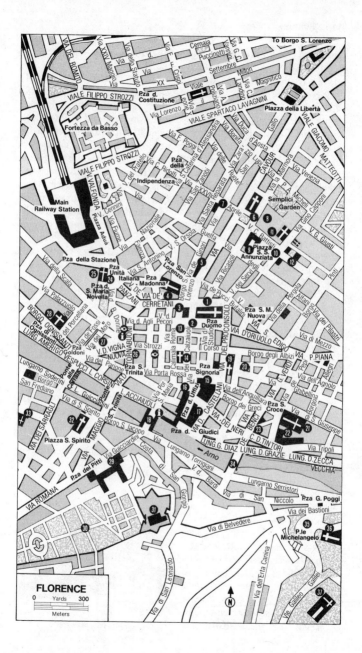

FLORENCE

0 Yards 300

Meters

zino, and two bronze pulpits that are the last works by Donatello (1460). On the Piazza di Madonna is the entrance to the *Cappella dei Principi* (Princes' Chapel), a mausoleum for the Medici grand dukes decorated with hard, brightly colored stone called *pietre dure*. A passage to the left leads to the **Sagrestia Nuova* where, on the left is the tomb of Lorenzo, Duke of Urbino, supporting Michelangelo's allegorical figures of *Dawn* and *Dusk;* to the right is another tomb with figures of *Day* and *Night*. The *Biblioteca Laurenziana,* designed by Michelangelo, is noted for its staircase and is considered one of the first examples of Mannerist architecture.

San Marco [6]: The church was started during the Romanesque period, renovated during the Renaissance, and given a Baroque façade in 1780. The adjacent *Dominican monastery* is now a museum with outstanding 15th-century works by Fra Angelico, the painter-monk whose luminous shade of blue was the envy of all who saw it.

***Santa Croce** [21]: The tombs of Galileo, Michelangelo, Machiavelli, and Rossini are found in this rebuilt 13th-century church with 19th-century façade, as are frescoes by Giotto and the *Cappella dei Pazzi* (Pazzi Chapel), a masterpiece of architecture by Brunelleschi, with terra-cotta roundels by Luca della Robbia (reached by a separate entrance). Adjacent is the **Biblioteca Nazionale** (National Library) [22].

***Santa Maria Novella** [24]: The lower part of the church façade is 14th-century Romanesque, in green and white marble, while its portal and upper portion were completed in a compatible classical style by Alberti in 1470. Generally considered to be the most important Gothic church in Tuscany, Santa Maria Novella contains numerous works of art by the likes of Pisano, Filippino Lippi, Giambologna, Ghirlandaio, Brunelleschi, Giotto, and Masaccio. In the *Chiostro Verde* (Green Cloister) next door are the frescoes considered to be Paolo Uccello's masterpieces; their green tint gives the cloister its name.

Santa Maria del Carmine [33]: This Romanesque-Gothic church was rebuilt after a fire in 1771, which fortunately did not damage Masaccio's ***frescoes* in the *Cappella Brancacci:* Painted in the early 15th century, *The Expulsion from Paradise* and *Tribute Money* profoundly influenced Re-

Santa Maria Novella

naissance painting. There are three **Cloisters** [25] next to the church with impressive frescoes.

*Santissima Annunziata (Church of the Sacred Annunciation) [11]: In the arcaded outer courtyard there are exceptionally well-preserved frescoes by Andrea del Sarto and other artists of the 15th and 16th centuries; two frescoes by Andrea Castagno enliven the walls of the inner courtyard.

Santo Spirito (Church of the Holy Spirit) [32]: Among the interior highlights of the 38 semicircular chapels in this 15th-century church designed by Brunelleschi are a *Madonna and Child With Saints* by Filippino Lippi, and the Cappella Corbinelli designed by Andrea Sansovino.

Excursions

**Fiesole, 8 km. (5 miles) from Florence: Founded in the 7th century by the Etruscans, Fiesole became an important Roman colony in 80 B.C.; it vied for predominance with Florence until 1125, when Florence captured it. Its charming views of Florence from *Piazza Mino da Fiesole,* and interesting Roman theater and baths make it a pleasant trip. The Romanesque *Duomo* (Cathedral), the 14th–15th-century *convent of San Francesco* on the site of the ancient acropolis, and the *Museo Bandini,* with Etruscan tombs and Renaissance paintings, are also noteworthy.

Frankfurt

Frankfurt-am-Main, to give it its full name, is perhaps the most "Americanized" of all European cities. Its skyline is dominated by modern high-rise office towers—most of them owned by the banks and insurance companies that have made Frankfurt one of Germany's most important financial centers. The city is one where business, often in the form of huge international trade fairs (such as the famous Frankfurt Book Fair, held each autumn), thrives and seems to grow stronger with each passing year. Several restored buildings, pleasant gardens and parks, and the old quarter of Sachsenhausen across the river Main—where you can sample the local specialty, Ebbelwei (apple cider)—lend a nostalgic air to this otherwise very contemporary metropolis.

History

Its location on the river Main in the very heart of Europe inevitably made Frankfurt an important trading post even in prehistoric times. The earliest settlers, the Celts, were defeated by German tribes, who in turn were ousted by the Romans. They fell to the marauding Franks in the fifth century. The name Frankfurt derives from the establishment of a crossing place in the river, the Franks' ford.

Charlemagne's grandson, Ludwig, made Frankfurt the capital of his German Empire; from 1152, it was the place where the German rulers of the Holy Roman Empire were elected. In time, the rulers were also crowned here.

Johann Gutenberg, inventor of moveable type, began working here in the mid-15th century and, as a result, Frankfurt became the printing center of Europe.

Frankfurt's reputation as a financial center began in the 16th century when the city was granted the right to mint money. In the 18th century, the Rothschild family opened its first bank here. Interestingly, the bankers of Frankfurt helped to finance the northern armies in America's Civil War, while the financial communities of Paris and London lent their support to the South.

Germany's greatest poet, Johann Wolfgang von Goethe, was born in Frankfurt in 1749. Disguised as a waiter, the teen-aged Goethe witnessed a banquet in the city's *Kaisersaal* celebrating the coronation of Emperor Joseph II.

St. Paul's church was the scene of the first meeting of the German National Assembly in 1848, but the city lost its independence to Prussia less than 20 years later. Nonetheless, Frankfurt remained associated with German liberalism, and registered a small voice of resistance in the early days of Hitler's Third Reich.

Athens: Parthenon

Berlin: Kaiser Wilhelm Memorial Church

Florence: Duomo and Campanile

Helsinki: Senate Square with the cathedral and Alexander II memorial

Istanbul: Mosque of Sultan Suleiman

London: Big Ben and Parliament

Luxembourg: View of the Palais Grand-Ducal

Madrid: Plaza de Oriente and Palacio Real

Allied bombs destroyed much of Frankfurt in March 1944; unlike many other German cities, Frankfurt decided not to salvage and restore what little remained of the once-medieval city. Instead, it rebuilt quickly in an undistinguished modern style, hoping that it would be chosen as the new capital of the Federal Republic—an honor that eventually went to Bonn.

Attractions

On weekends you can ride the *Ebbelwei Express,* charming, old streetcars which provide hour-long circle tours of the city and let you buy Frankfurt's famous *Ebbelwei* (apple wine) to drink along the way. There are 18 stops, including one in *Theaterplatz* and the *main railroad station,* and they leave about every 40 minutes.

Alte Oper (Old Opera House) [20]: In 1981, 100 years after it first opened, the old, bombed-out opera house on Opernplatz was reopened and now features orchestral concerts, ballet, and operetta. *Rothschild Park* [21], named after the famous Jewish banking family that came to prominence in Frankfurt, lies just north on Bockenheimeranlage.

Deutsches Architekturmuseum (German Museum of Architecture), Schaumainkai 43–43a: Anyone interested in the rebuilding of the city after the war or the development of German architecture through the centuries should pay a visit.

*Dom (Cathedral of St. Bartholomew) [1]: The building is also known as the *Kaiserdom* or Imperial Cathedral, because the German Emperors were once crowned here. It was built between the 13th and 15th centuries atop an older structure and managed to survive the Allied bombing attack that leveled the rest of Frankfurt. The interior is surprisingly undistinguished, although there are some 14th-century carved pews and 15th-century murals. Behind the cathedral is the restored 14th-century *Leinwandhaus* (Linen House), used during the medieval trade fairs as a textile showroom, and the impressive 15th-century residence known as *Steinernes Haus* (Stone House) [2], now a small museum.

*Fernsehturm (Television Tower), near Rosa Luxemburg-strasse, north of the Palm Gardens: The tallest structure in West Germany offers an observation tower providing remarkable views of the city and the Taunus Mountains; there's a cafeteria and a restaurant, too.

*Goethehaus [7]: Germany's most famous poet was born here in 1749 and spent his childhood in this house. Now reconstructed, it is furnished with period furniture and many Goethe family possessions. A museum next door offers additional documentation of Goethe's life.

Hauptwache (Guardhouse)

Frankfurt Attractions:
1. Dom (Cathedral of Saint Bartholomew)
2. Steinernes Haus
3. Römer
4. Nikolaikirche
5. Saalhof
6. Paulskirche
7. Goethehaus
8. Karmeliterkloster
9. Leonardskirche
10. House of the German Order
11. National Postal Museum
12. Bundespostmuseum
13. Liebieg House
14. Städtische Bühnen
15. Goethe Memorial
16. Monument to the Victims
17. Schiller Memorial
18. Heine Memorial
19. Beethoven Memorial
20. Alte Oper
21. Rothschild Park
22. Nebbiensches Gartenhaus
23. Eschenheimer Tower
24. Neuen Börse
25. Thurn-und-Taxis Palace
26. Hauptwache
27. Saint Catherine's Church
28. Liebfrauenkirche

[26]: A lovely Baroque building that served as a guardhouse in the 18th century, it is now a café and information center. You can reach the enormous underground shopping mall below by an escalator; the *Zeil*, Frankfurt's principal pedestrians-only shopping

St. Catherine's Church

street, also begins here. The south side of the square is bordered by the restored 17th-century *Katherinenkirche* (St. Catherine's Church) [27].

Holzhausen-Schlösschen (Holzhausen Chateau), Justinianstrasse 5: Archaeology buffs may want to visit the *Museum für Vor- und Frühgeschichte* (Museum of Early History) housed in this Regency château, once the country seat of an aristocratic family.

Karmeliterkloster (Carmelite Monastery) [8]: The state archives and the *Museum für Kunsthandwerk* (Museum of Applied Arts) are located in this reconstructed and modernized building dating originally from the 14th and 15th centuries.

Leonhardskirche (Church of Saint Leonard) [9]: This restored five-naved Gothic church dates from 1219. It is the second oldest church in the city and was almost entirely destroyed in the 1944 bombings.

Liebfrauenkirche (Church of Our Lady) [28]: A Baroque chancel was added to the original Gothic church built in the 14th and 15th centuries.

**Naturmuseum Senckenberg (Senckenberg Museum of Natural History), Senckenberganlage 25: If you've been wondering what an American diplodocus looked like, the museum's fascinating collection of prehistoric dinosaur skeletons will satisfy your curiosity.

Neuen Börse (New Stock Exchange) [24]: Across the street from the 19th-century stock exchange building and overshadowed by the Post Office Towers are the ruined portals of the *Thurn-und-Taxis Palace* [25].

Nikolaikirche (Church of Saint Nicholas) [4]: The chimes you hear three times a day come from the tower of Saint Nicholas, built in the first half of the 13th century and at one time the chapel of the Frankfurt City Council.

*Palmengarten (Palm Garden), Bockenheimer Landstrasse: Palms, orchids, cacti, and other lush subtropical plants proliferate in hothouses on the grounds of this old park laid out over 100 years ago in the English style.

Paulskirche (Church of Saint Paul) [6]: Once the meeting place in 1848 of the first German National Assembly, the church is now used for conferences and exhibitions.

Römer (Town Hall) [3]: Located next to St. Paul's on a charming square that recaptures something of old Frankfurt, you'll

Römer

see three Gothic, gabled houses that were turned into the town hall. Lining the walls of the *Kaisersaal* (Emperor's Hall) are over 50 imperial portraits; the young Goethe, disguised as a waiter, slipped into this hall to feast his eyes on the coronation celebrations for Emperor Joseph II.

Saalhof [5]: A complex of buildings—including the *Museum of History*—now surrounds the 15th-century *Renten Tower.* The original structure once served as the Hohenstaufen palace; however, only the Bergfried Palace and the beautiful *Saalhof Chapel* (dating from 1175) remain. The only half-timbered house to survive the war stands across the way.

Sachsenhausen: Across the river Main you'll find an old section of the city filled with cobbled streets and half-timbered houses, including the restored early-18th-century *Deutschordenshaus* (House of the German Order) [10] and the 14th-century *Deutschordenskirche* (Church of the German Order). The area is known for its lovely little squares and fountains and has an abundance of restaurants and *Stuben,* where you can sample Frankfurt's famous *Ebbelwei* (apple cider). Several museums lie off the Schaumainkai, including the *Bundespostmuseum* (Federal Post Office Museum) [12], the worthwhile **Städelsches Kunstinstitut und Städtische Galerie* (Stadel Institute of the Arts and Municipal Art Gallery) with its important collection of Old Masters, and the *Liebighaus,* which features a wide-ranging sculpture collection.

Untermainanlage (Lower Main River Park): The ultramodern *Städtische Bühnen* (Municipal Theaters) [14] feature a variety of theatrical venues. Just up the street, in the Gallus and Taunus Park, you'll find a host of memorials to various revered Germans, including *Goethe* [15], *Schiller* [17], *Heine* [18], *Beethoven* [19], and the *Memorial to the Victims* [16], erected in 1920.

*Zoologischer Garden (Frankfurt Zoo), Alfred-Brehm-Platz: One of the oldest zoos in Germany and one of the city's premiere attractions, it features a giant aviary, an Exotarium (aquarium with reptiles), and landscaped outdoor habitats for its large collection of animals, as well as restaurants and cafés.

Geneva

Ringed by mountains and stretching out from the shores of beautiful Lake Geneva (known as Lac Léman to natives), French-speaking Geneva is the home of several important international organizations. Precision and pride are apparent everywhere you look in this compact, lakeside city, known for its watchmaking and long Calvinist traditions. You'll find sparkling-clean streets and squares, lakeside walks with magnificent views of the Alps, well-manicured gardens, charming old quarters, and some excellent smaller museums. The city is a convenient place from which to explore the surrounding countryside.

History

For many centuries, the only bridge to span the Rhone River was located in Geneva, whose name actually means "emerging from the waters" in the ancient Ligurian language. On their seemingly endless campaigns to colonize all of Europe, the Romans, in 58 B.C., conquered the Celts who had settled the area earlier. The Franks moved in during the sixth century.

The city's reputation as an international meeting ground began with the large trade fairs that were first held in the Middle Ages. Bitter feuds between Geneva's prince bishops and the dukes of Savoy, who regarded Geneva as their territory, characterized the 15th century. The city was occupied by the invading troops of Napoleon between 1798 and 1815. In 1815, Geneva entered the Swiss Confederation as a canton in an effort to protect its newly won independence.

Geneva became known as "the Rome of the Protestants" in the 16th century, when the religious reformer John Calvin made the city his headquarters. He left an indelible imprint on the city, including building projects and the University of Geneva, which he founded in 1559. The severe austerity of Calvinism, however, forced many dissenters to leave: Geneva-born 18th-century philosopher Jean-Jacques Rousseau quit the city when his books were burned in a public square.

A century later, Geneva attracted numerous travelers making the Grand Tour of Europe, as well as literary celebrities of the day. Byron, Goethe, Dostoyevsky, and Victor Hugo are just a few of the famous writers who have strolled along Lac Léman and contemplated the surrounding mountains.

In 1864, the city became the birthplace to the International Red Cross, when the Geneva Convention was signed and made member nations responsible for the care of all sick and wounded in war. It is still headquartered here.

Attractions

Baur Collections, 8 Rue Munier-Romilly: An excellent private collection of Oriental ceramics may be seen in this home.

Cathédrale Saint-Pierre [6]: The vociferous sermons of reformer John Calvin once thundered in the austere interior of this 12th- and 13th-century cathedral, which was built in a variety of styles on the highest point of the city. Climb the north tower for a fabulous view of the city, the lake, the Jura mountains, and the Alps. Radiating out from the cathedral is Geneva's old quarter, filled with ancient streets that you'll find delightful to explore.

Calvin Auditorium: The fiery sermons of Calvinist preacher John Knox were often heard in this Gothic church. It was restored in 1959 for Calvin's 450th anniversary. The early 14th-century *Maison Tavel* (Tavel House), next to the auditorium, is the oldest house in the city and has recently opened the *Museum of Old Geneva,* providing a historical perspective of the city. You'll see the *Old Arsenal,* dating from the Napoleonic era, just across the street.

Carouge: This small, charming, quiet town within the city limits of Geneva is a perfect place to wander by day; while at night, the pubs, cafés, and small theaters offer diversion and entertainment.

Hôtel de Ville (City Hall) [5]: The Geneva Convention, establishing the neutrality of battlefield medical facilities, was signed in 1864 in this 16th-century Renaissance building.

Institut et Musée Voltaire: One of the most important and influential men in the history of thought, Voltaire retired to this beautiful home he called "Les Delices" in 1775, only to leave three years later when his unorthodox views brought him into conflict with the Calvinist leaders in Geneva. His furniture and manuscripts are on view.

Jet d'eau (Water Fountain): From March through September, the world's tallest spume of water shoots out of this landmark fountain located in front of the Quai Gustave Ador.

Jean-Jacques Rousseau Museum, The Public and University Library, Salle Lullin, Promenade des Bastions: Native-son Rousseau suffered the indignity of seeing his books burned in one of Geneva's public squares; his manuscripts, letters, and death mask are on display.

Monument de la Réformation, Rue de la Croix-Rouge: This striking monument stands in a park under the old city ramparts. It commemorates the four main leaders of the Protestant Reformation—Calvin, Knox, de Beze, and Farel.

Musée d'Art et d'Histoire [7], 2 Rue Charles-Galland: Medieval sculpture and furniture are found in the archaeological section of this distinguished museum; there is also a fine arts section.

Musée de l'Horlogerie

(Watch Museum), 15 Rte. de Malagnou: A charming town house is filled with superb examples of the watchmakers' art, a specialty of Geneva.

Musée d'Instruments Anciens de Musique, 23 Rue Lefort: You don't have to be a soloist to appreciate the fine old fiddles and pianofortes in this charming museum. If you're lucky, a visiting musician may be on hand to demonstrate how they actually sound.

Palais des Nations, Av. de la Paix: Once the palace of the League of Nations, this complex now houses the European section of the United Nations and two museums, while surrounding buildings headquarter *The World Health Organization,* the *International Red Cross,* and the *International Labor Office.*

Place Neuve [3]: In the center of the square is an equestrian statue of General Dufour, the Swiss Liberator. Clustered around it are the *Musée Rath,* which

Geneva Attractions:
1. Pont du Mont-Blanc
2. Pont des Bergues
3. Place Neuve
4. University
5. City Hall
6. Cathédrale Saint-Pierre
7. Musée d'Art et d'Histoire

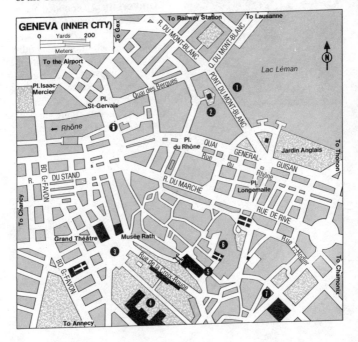

GENEVA (INNER CITY)

houses various temporary exhibits, the *Grand Théâtre*, Geneva's opera house modelled after the one in Paris, and the *Music Conservatory*.

Promenades on Lake Geneva: No visit to the city is complete without a walk along the promenades that line both sides of Lake Geneva and lead to several beautifully maintained parks. The *Quai du Mont-Blanc* offers a mag-

Rhône bridges

nificent view of the sail-strewn lake with the Alps behind and the Jet d'Eau fountain in the foreground; the monument is one to the duke of Brunswick. You can cross the lake on the *Pont du Mont-Blanc*, which leads to the lakeshore *Jardin Anglais* (English Gardens) and from there, along the *Quai Gustave Ador*, to *Parc de la Grange* with its stunning rose gardens and the adjacent *Parc des Eaux-Vives*. Alternatively, from the *Quai des Bergues*, take the *Pont des Bergues* to *Île Rousseau*, a charming little island with old trees and a statue of the philosopher.

University [4]: Founded in the 16th century by John Calvin, the university's library contains many treasures, including the 6th-century sermons of St. Augustine, written on papyrus, and original manuscripts by Rousseau. If the fire-and-brimstone era of Calvinism interests you, there's a *Museum of the Reformation* here.

Glasgow

Once the "Second City of the British Empire," Glasgow is one of the world's largest industrial centers and Scotland's biggest metropolis, with a population of some 800,000 (1.7 million, including its sprawling suburbs). The image of gritty, industrial Glasgow, however, has been replaced by that of a rich cultural center, with a plethora of museums, parks, theaters, festivals, shops, and significant architecture that now brings this grand Victorian city the admiration—and tourist trade—it rightly deserves. Foremost among its drawing points are the numerous buildings and designs of proto-modern architect Charles Rennie Mackintosh (1868–1928) scattered throughout the city; the Burrell Collection, which has been called "one of the most remarkable assemblages of works of art ever brought together by one man;" the ubiquitous expanses of green parks and colorful flower gardens; and, most of all, the welcoming warmth and charm of the Glaswegians, considered the friendliest of Scots.

History

There are traces of a prehistoric village on the site, but Glasgow did not really start to develop until around A.D. 550, when the British missionary St. Mungo (also known as St. Kentigern) founded a religious community on the banks of the River Clyde. The settlement subsisted quietly for centuries, but by the late Middle Ages, the town had grown into a major commercial center in western Scotland. In 1350, the first stone bridge over the Clyde was built. The university was founded in 1451, and a year later, Glasgow—the name derives from the Celtic *glas ghu,* or "green glen"—was designated a royal burgh. The city thrived as a market center, but did not grow significantly until the Scottish and English crowns were united (1603).

The 18th century proved an important time for Glasgow because of growing trade with the Americas. Fortunes were made on tobacco, rum, sugar, and other products that came into Europe through Glasgow's port; native coal, wool, and herrings were exported, too. The American Revolution brought an end to much of the trade with the New World. By this time, however, the Clyde had been dredged and made deeper, which helped the cotton-manufacturing, coal-mining, iron-founding, and shipbuilding industries to develop and thrive in the 19th century. Glasgow was again a prosperous city in the Victorian age; the Industrial Revolution transformed it into a huge, steaming metropolis with abundant natural resources and a large, willing work force. All the while, the city—as well as its waterways—widened its boundaries, eventually encompassing over 156 square km. (60 square miles). Handsome, new buildings sprouted up, and architect/designer Charles Rennie Mackintosh and other exponents of the exuberant Glasgow Style created a vibrant, artistic climate in the city that was admired and emulated all over the Continent.

In the early 20th century, the largely working-class city of Glasgow became a hub of union activity and agitation (today the Labour and Socialist parties still claim numerous adherents). The Depression badly hurt both heavy industry and shipbuilding—a situation exacerbated by the German bombing of shipyards during World War II; the two are still important factors in the city's economy today—but so are various other enterprises, from engineering to textiles. Since the 1960s, Glasgow has not only rediscovered its rich Victorian/Art Nouveau architecture, designs, and heritage, but it has become a significant cultural center as well, with major museums and other venues as prime drawing cards for residents and visitors alike.

Attractions

The Barras, between London Road and Gallowgate: This vibrant weekend flea market, which bills itself as the world's biggest open-air market, provides a big slice of East End Glaswegian life. Its vendors sell just about anything, from bona-fide antiques to bootleg cassette tapes.

Botanic Gardens, Great Western Road at Queen Margaret Drive: An orchid collection, palm trees, and a winter garden are features of this lovely 17-hectare (42-acre) park, first planted in 1817.

**The Burrell Collection, 2060 Pollokshaws Road, Pollok Country Park: Opened by Queen Elizabeth in 1983, this magnificent museum was a gift to the city from Sir William Burrell, a Glaswegian shipowner who, after selling his last fleet to the British during World War I, devoted his life to collecting art. The collec-

tion is diverse and excellent; more than 8,000 pieces represent a wide range of periods, cultures, materials, and techniques. Medieval architectural elements are nicely incorporated into the contemporary building, as are many examples from its huge holdings (some 700 in all) of stained glass. Among the classical treasures is the marble Warwick Vase, a second-century Roman masterpiece. The Oriental collection is huge, including Chinese porcelain, Persian carpets, and Japanese prints. The strongest fine-art holdings are late medieval-early Renaissance works and 18th- and 19th-century French; there is also a superb Rembrandt *Self-Portrait*. Three rooms replicate the interior of Burrell's house at Hutton Castle (near Berwick-on-Tweed).

Central Station [3]: Trains leaving and arriving here serve the south of Scotland, England, and Wales.

City Hall, Candleriggs: The Scottish National Symphony Orchestra calls this theater home, and the Scottish Chamber Orchestra performs here regularly.

George Square [1]: At the center of this busy square, which is the heart of present-day Glasgow, stands the tall *Walter Scott Memorial.* Nearby are monuments to Queen Victoria, Robert Burns, James Watt, and William Gladstone, among others, as are the City Chambers (1888) and main General Post Office. Fronting City Chambers is the moving *Cenotaph,* erected in 1924 to honor the soldiers who died during World War I.

Glasgow Cathedral [4], Castle Street: Standing majestically on a hill in Glasgow's oldest section, the Gothic cathedral is the only wholly medieval edifice of its kind in Scotland—and one of the most beautiful. Erected in the 12th and 13th centuries, it has an impressive, fan-shaped vault. It is said that a small wooden church was built on the site by the city's founder, St. Mungo, as early as 543; his tomb is in the cathedral's crypt. Behind it is the massive Necropolis, an old cemetery where many well-known Glaswegians are buried, including the reformer John Knox.

Glasgow Cross [6], intersection of Trongate, High Street, Gallowgate, and Saltmarket: The Mercat Cross is a modern copy (1929) of the original medieval

Glasgow Cathedral

market cross that once marked this crossroads. Until the Victorian age, the old cross was the heart of Glasgow, set in the so-called "Golden Acre" commercial area. The seven-story *Tolbooth Steeple* is in the middle of the street, a vestige of this once-elegant area.

Glasgow Green [8], along the River Clyde beginning at Saltmarket: This large park, the location of the *People's Palace* museum, was laid out in 1662.

Glasgow School of Art, 167 Renfrew Street: In 1896, Charles Rennie Mackintosh designed this impressive institution. It was finished in 1909 in a stunning combination of Scottish baronial and Art Nouveau styles. It still functions—and functions well—

as one of Britain's top art colleges, with its handsome library, large-windowed studios, and capacious public areas. Each of the façades is noticeably different: The east is traditional and medieval; the west bold and proto-modern; the north quite plain but for its lively wrought-iron details; and the south is fortresslike with a sheer surface.

Hunterian Art Gallery, University of Glasgow, 82 Hillhead Street: This relatively new museum (1980) displays works from its immense collection of paintings, sculpture, and prints belonging to the university, as well as four reconstructed rooms from Charles Rennie Mackintosh's Southpark Avenue house, and numerous other pieces by the Glasgow Four (as Mackintosh, his wife Margaret Macdonald, her sister Frances, and Frances's husband Herbert MacNair were known). There is a significant collection of works by and once belonging to Whistler—second only to that of the Freer Gallery in Washington, D.C. (the American-born artist was awarded an honorary degree by the university in 1903). Among the other major artists represented are Rembrandt, Chardin, Stubbs, Turner, Fantin-Latour, Pissarro, and modern painters R. B. Kitaj, Richard Hamilton, and Bridget Riley. The print collection is also superb, with works by Schongauer, Mantegna, and Pieter Brueghel the Elder (his only known print).

**Kelvingrove Art Gallery and Museum, Kelvingrove Park: This impressive collection—founded in part with moneys made from the 1888 International Exhibition in Glasgow—opened in 1902 with the lofty aim of being a comprehensive museum covering art, crafts, history, geology, zoology, and other assorted disciplines. Also known as the Glasgow Art Gallery, it still displays a variety of art and artifacts, from Oriental armor to Scottish folk art, but the painting and sculpture make it one of the most important museums in Great Britain. Among the Italian masterpieces are works by Filippino Lippi, Giorgione, Correggio, Guardi, and Rosa, and the Flemish and Dutch schools are especially well represented, with paintings by Rubens, Van Dyck, Hobbema, and Ruisdael. Among the 19th-century European artworks displayed are canvases by Delacroix, Courbet, Fantin-Latour, Millet, and van Gogh—although the best-known work in the entire museum is probably Salvador Dali's dizzying *Christ of St. John of the Cross.* The British collection is especially strong; the Pre-Raphaelites, the "Glasgow Boys,". and Colorists featured. Whistler's *Portrait of Thomas Carlyle: Arrangement in Grey and Black No. 2* is a gem.

Kelvingrove Park [9]: This lovely park, through which the River Kelvin meanders, is home to the city's Art Gallery and Museum as well as the *University of Glasgow.* The park has facilities for open-air concerts seating 4,500 people.

**Museum of Transport, Kelvin Hall, Bunhouse Road: Located just south of Kelvingrove Park, this collection illustrates the history of transportation. Among the many modes of transport on display are locomotives, tramcars, automobiles, ships, bicycles, and horse-drawn carts.

People's Palace, in Glasgow Green (enter by Morris Place): Two collections are housed in this greenhouselike structure, the *Old Glasgow Museum*—concerned mainly with the city's domestic heritage—and the *People's Palace Museum,* covering the history and evolution of the city from 1175 to the present.

Pollok House, 2060 Pollokshaws Road, Pollok Country Park: This 18th-century neo-Palladian furnished house has a fairly modest interior comprising many small rooms. Its greatest treasures are on its walls: paintings collected by Sir William Stirling-Maxwell, who acquired masterpieces of the Spanish

Glasgow Attractions:
1. George Square
2. Queen Street Station
3. Central Station
4. Glasgow Cathedral
5. Provand's Lordship
6. Glasgow Cross
7. St. Enoch Square
8. Glasgow Green
9. Kelvingrove Park

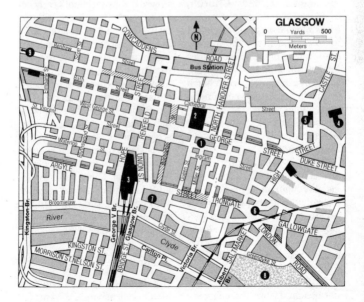

School—El Greco, Goya, Murillo, and others—as well as a group of unusual Blake temperas and works by Mengs, Hogarth, and others.

Provand's Lordship [5], 3 Castle Street: Glasgow's oldest house was built in 1471 for the priest in charge of the almshouse known as St. Nicholas Hospital. Today it serves as a museum featuring antique Scottish furniture, historical paintings (including one of Mary Queen of Scots—who may have lived in the house for a short time in 1567—attributed by some experts to Holbein), and Flemish tapestries and petit-point.

Queen Street Station [2]: This railroad station serves the north and east.

Queen's Cross Church, 870 Garscube Road: Native son Mackintosh designed this church in 1897, and it now houses the headquarters of the active Charles Rennie Mackintosh Society. Inspired by a medieval parish church he saw in Somerset—but punctuated with bold Mackintosh touches—Queen's Cross was the architect's only ecclesiastical commission.

Sauchiehall Street: Scots for "alley of willows," this thriving thoroughfare, with its many restaurants and shops, is partly a pedestrians-only precinct. A highlight of the street is the *Room de Luxe* at number 217, the recently restored gem of Miss Cranston's Willow Tea Rooms, which Charles Rennie Mackintosh finished in 1904. Tea can once again be taken here—almost exactly as it was at the turn of the century—amid high-backed chairs, leaded-glass windows, soft grey carpeting, and served in willow-motif crockery.

Theatre Royal, Hope Street: Lovingly restored to its Victorian splendor in the mid-1970s, the theater is home to the Scottish Opera and Scottish Ballet.

University of Glasgow, University Avenue: The university was founded in 1451 under papal order. *Gilmorehill Building*—an outstanding example of Scottish Gothic Revival architecture designed by Sir George Gilbert Scott in 1864 (and completed by his son John in the 1880s)—is its principal structure. The Reformation slowed down the school's early development, but the institution thrived in the 18th century, with faculty members that included economist Adam Smith and scientist James Watt. In the 19th century, its medical school pioneered antiseptic surgery under Lord Lister. Besides being the location of the *Hunterian Art Gallery* (see separate entry), the university displays archaeological and geological specimens in the *Hunterian Museum* (in Gilmorehill Building); both were named after the 18th-century surgeon William Hunter, who donated his diverse collections to the school.

Excursions

Hill House, Upper Colquhoun Street, Helensburgh, 37 km. (23 miles) northwest of Glasgow, accessible via train from Central Station: Charles Rennie Mackintosh designed this handsome sandstone home for publisher W. W. Blackie in 1902. Today, it is beautifully restored and well worth a visit, not only for the house itself—in the Scottish baronial tradition—but for its landscaping, interior design, and furnishings as well (all Mackintosh's work).

*Isle of Arran, some 60 km. (35 miles) southwest of Glasgow, accessible via ferry from Ardrossan: A wonderful vacation island, Arran boasts mountains, hills, beaches, lochs, and interesting flora. A hike up the largest island peak, Goat Fell, begins at *Brodick Castle,* a 15th-century building set in lovely gardens (Brodick town is also the ferry-landing point from the mainland). More remote and less touristy is the idyllic village of *Lochranza,* at the isle's northern tip; good seaside or inland walks abound nearby. The southern part of Arran is less rugged and has more rolling hills and sandy beaches; try the walk to *Glenashdale Falls* from Whiting Bay.

Kyles of Bute, some 40 km. (25 miles) west of Glasgow: The Kyles of Bute is a curving channel of water north of the Island of Bute, and accessible from Central Station to Gourock or Wemyss Bay; thence via ferry to the seaside resorts and yachting centers of Dunoon, Rothesay, or Tighnabruaich.

The Trossachs, beginning some 50 km. (31 miles) north of Glasgow: The rolling hills and peaceful lochs of the Trossachs provide an excellent introduction to the Scottish Highlands. Immortalized by Sir Walter Scott and terrorized by the outlaw Rob Roy MacGregor (1671–1734), the Trossachs are best explored from the village of Aberfoyle. The sparkling lochs Venachar, Katrine, and Achray lie in wooded valleys, surrounded by beautiful mountains; excursion boats operate daily on Loch Katrine (setting of Scott's *The Lady of the Lake*).

Granada

While the rest of Europe was languishing in the Dark Ages, Granada was the locale of a flourishing Arab culture that centered around the magnificent Alhambra palace. The Alhambra—one of the great sights of the world—draws most visitors to Granada, but the rest of the city can exert an equally intoxicating charm. Granada's Arab past is still palpable despite the Renaissance and Baroque redesigning and redecoration of former Moorish buildings. The distinctive *cármenes,* or private villas, perched on the streets of the hilly Albaicín area, breathe an air of quiet mystery from their fragrant patio gardens. In the evening, gypsies perform the flamenco from their cave-homes in the Sacromonte. Granada's location, with the snowy peaks of the Sierra Nevadas rising around it and the Costa del Sol only a short drive south, makes it an ideal headquarters for touring the region.

History

The Romans and the Visigoths both ruled Granada, but, in 711, it was captured by the Arabs and remained under their rule for over seven hundred years. The steep hill where the Alhambra is located was fortified as early as 720, and there was a citadel built in the middle of the ninth century.

Dynasty followed dynasty until 1238, when General Mohammed Banalahamar entered the city, had himself crowned king, and founded the Nasrid dynasty. Granada began to flourish, and was soon the richest city on the Iberian Peninsula. The earlier citadel was expanded to include the royal residence; the Alhambra, with the Generalife and fragrant fountained gardens, took on the distinctive look visitors see today.

Internal disputes and quarrels among factions of the ruling family led to its downfall in the 15th century. Boabdil was crowned king in 1485; after many battles, he was forced to hand Granada over to the Catholic monarchs Ferdinand and Isabella in 1492, ending the Moorish rule of Spain. Ferdinand and Isabella are buried in the flamboyant Gothic Royal Chapel.

Their grandson, the Hapsburg Charles V, commissioned the city's massive cathedral, which was not completed until 1667. Under Charles, Granada experienced new growth. A Moorish rebellion was suppressed in 1569, at which time the last of the once-mighty Moors were expelled from the city.

Attractions

***Alhambra** *(See Alhambra map for the following points of interest):* Puerta de las Granadas (Gate of Pomegranates [1], the entrance to the wooded park surrounding the Alhambra, dates from the 16th century and is decorated with three open pomegranates—the symbol of the city of Granada—and the Hapsburg coat of arms of Charles V. The Latin inscription on the *Pilar de Carlos V* (Charles Fountain) [2] states that the Hapsburg Emperor is also the king of Spain.

The Moorish *Puerta de la Justicia* [3] dates from 1348 and consists of a high horseshoe arch with an outstretched hand of Fatima carved in stone. The five fingers of the hand symbolize the five basic tenets of the Koran: fasting, almsgiving, praying, maintaining faith in the unity of God, and making a pilgrimage to Mecca.

Wine was once sold near the

Alhambra

14th–15th-century *Puerta del Vino* [4]. The *Alcazaba* [5] was built on top of the walls and fortifications of the old citadel. Its impressive defense tower, the *Torre de la Vela* [6], is now a landmark of the city; it provides a beautiful panoramic view.

The unfinished *Palacio Carlos V* [11], begun in 1526, was considered the most important building of the High Spanish Renaissance. The *Museo de Bellas Artes* (Fine Arts Museum), located on the upper story, provides a good overview of painting in Granada.

Erected on the site of an earlier Moorish mosque, the *Church of Santa Maria* [12] houses an 18th-century statue of the Virgin Mary called the *Virgen de las Augustias.*

The *Monastery of San Francesco* [27] was founded at the end of the 15th century and built over the ruins of a 14th-century Moorish palace.

Standing on the hill nearest the Alhambra Palace [10] is the white *Generalife* [28], former summer residence and garden of the caliphs; it is filled with roses, jasmine, yews, and cypress. During late June and July, the *Festival International de Musica y Danza* is held here.

South of the Alhambra is the *Torres Bermejas* (Fort of Red Towers) [29], laid out in the 13th century to protect the large Jewish district of Granada.

Alhambra Palace [10]. *(See Alhambra Palace map for the following points of interest.)* To the left, in front of the entrance to the palace, stands the *Torre de Machuca* [A], a residential tower with a nine-arched gallery. The seats of the Moorish main guard and the secretariat of the royal audience chamber were located in the *Jardín de Machuca* [B], while court magistrates heard grievances and issued decrees from the *Sala del Mexuar* [C], a hall later used as a church. An old Islamic prayer niche can be seen in the east wall of the small *Oratorium* [D]. One side of the beautiful inner courtyard known as the *Patio del Mexuar* [E] is dominated by the *Cuarto Dorado* (Golden Room) [F], which served as a private reception hall. The patio's southern façade is actually the exterior wall of the *Serallo* [G], where envoys of foreign monarchs and princes were received: It is covered with magnificent stucco ornamentation, arabesques, ceramics, and wood carving.

The slightly raised central vault of the north wall of the *Patio de los Arrayanes* (Myrtle Court) [H] is embellished with elaborate capitals; beautiful blue *azulejos* (tiles) from the 16th century decorate the bottom portion.

The ceiling of the *Sala de la Barca* [I], which served as a vestibule for the throne room, is shaped like an inverted ship's hull. Beyond is the *Throne Room* [J], also known as the *Salon de Embajadores* (Hall of Ambassadors), the most important room in the Alhambra. Once luxuriously furnished, the hall is now empty,

which helps to show off the elaborate wall decorations; the stucco was inlaid with gold and silver leaf to prismatically reflect the sunlight that pours through stained-glass windows. Small, tiled chambers are found in the thick walls of the *Torre de Comares* [K].

Continuing past a wing added during the reign of Charles V, you enter the renowned *Courtyard of Lions* [M], circled by a magnificent columned gallery whose surrounding rooms once held the pasha's harem. One of the rooms, the *Sala de los Mozárabes* [L], has a partially preserved Renaissance

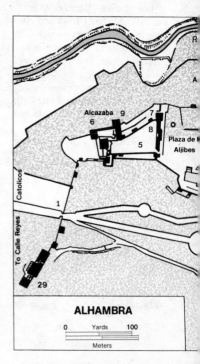

ALHAMBRA

0   Yards   100

Meters

ceiling. Crudely carved tenth-century lions surround the famous *Fountain of the Lions* in the center of the courtyard. The Courtyard of the Lions borders the *Sala de los Reyes* [N] to the east, with wall and ceiling decorations from the 15th century, and the *Sala de los Aben-*

Alhambra Attractions:

 1. Puerta de las Granadas
 2. Pilar de Carlos V
 3. Puerta de la Justicia
 4. Puerta del Vino
 5. Alcazaba
 6. Torre de la Vela
 7. Torre del Homenaje
 8. Torre Quebrada
 9. Torre de las Armas
10. Alhambra Palace
11. Palace of Charles V
12. Church of Santa Maria
13. Baths of Calle Real
14. Torre de las Damas

15. Torre de la Picas
16. Torre del Cadi
17. Torre de la Cautiva
18. Torre de las Infantas
19. Torre del final de la Carrera
20. Torre del Agua
21. Torre de Juan de Arce
22. Torre de Baltasar de la Cruz
23. Puerta de Siete Suelas
24. Torre del Capitán
25. Torre de la Bruja
26. Torre de las Cabezas
27. Monastery of San Francesco
28. Generalife
29. Torres Bermejas

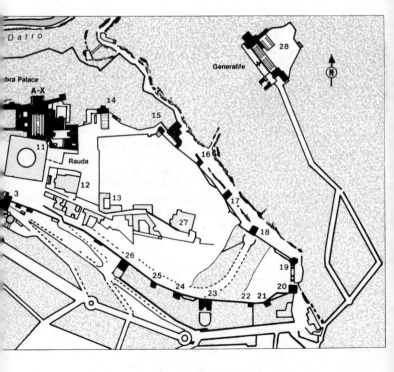

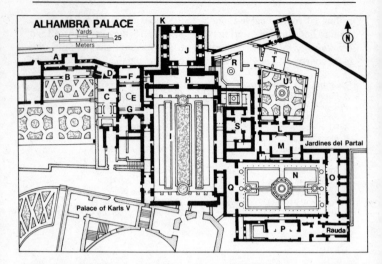

ALHAMBRA PALACE

Yards
0 ——————— 25
Meters

Palace of Karls V

Jardines del Partal

Rauda

cerrajes [O] to the south, where Boabdil, last of the Moorish rulers of Spain, supposedly had each member of his family murdered in order to secure the throne for himself. To the east of this hall is the *Rauda* [P], or royal cemetery: When Boabdil was forced from Spain by Ferdinand and Isabella, he had the remains of his ancestors removed from their graves here so that they would not remain in foreign soil.

The richly decorated *Sala de las dos Hermanas* (Hall of the Two Sisters) [Q] was the residence of the sultanas. The last hall in the harem area is the *Sala de los Ajimeces* [R].

One of the gems of the Alhambra is the *Mirador de Lindaraja*, [S] whose arched windows face the Darro Valley and the Albaicin.

American writer Washington Irving lived in the area that once encompassed the six *sitting rooms of Charles V* [T] and wrote his *Tales of the Alhambra* here in 1829.

A corridor with columns capped by extraordinarily beautiful capitals—no two alike—leads to the 16th-century suite of rooms Charles V commissioned for himself and his royal household. The *Peinador de la Reina* [U] was the boudoir of Charles's queen, Elizabeth, and is decorated with Italian Renaissance frescoes depicting heroic scenes from the life of her husband.

The *Patio de la Reja* [V] was named for the iron gate *(reja)* that was installed here. The *Jardín de Lindaraja* [W] was laid out as a pleasure garden for Charles V. At its south end there is an entrance to the *Sala de los Secretos*, a "whispering gallery."

From the gallery, singers and

women of the harem entertained the bathers in the *Baños Reales* (Royal Baths) [X], now restored to their original design.

See Granada map for the following points of interest:

Alcaicería [7]: The former market and silk bazaar from the Moorish period now offers local arts and crafts and a plethora of brass and silver items in its many tempting shops.

Casa del Castril [35]: The *Museum of Archaeology,* with prehistoric and classical collections, and the *Museum of Fine Arts,* with a noteworthy collection of paintings, share this beautiful Renaissance building with a Plateresque portal dating from 1539.

Casa del Chapiz [38]: Built in the 16th century over the ruins of a Moorish palace, this distinctive house has an especially lovely patio, as well as arcades and gardens with small ponds and canals.

Casa de los Tiros [10]: This 16th-century Moorish manor house, built around a patio, is home to the *Office of Tourism;* a small museum devoted to the art of Granada is also here.

Castillo Bibataubin [17]: In the mid-18th century, this former Arab fortress was transformed into a barracks, and now serves as the seat of the provincial government. There is a monument in the square to Mariana Pineda, a national heroine.

*Cathedral of Santa Maria de la Encarnacion [3]: Frequently called the most beautiful church building of the Spanish Renaissance, this enormous cathedral was begun under Charles V but not completed until 1667. It is richly decorated with marble sculptures and paintings (including some by El Greco), 16th-century stained glass, and monumental bronze statues of the twelve apostles. Connected to the right side aisle is the ****Capilla Real** (Royal Chapel), containing the tombs of Ferdinand and Isabella. The *sacristy* contains Ferdinand's sword, Isabella's crown and scepter, and Dutch paintings by Memling, van der Weyden, and others.

Corral del Carbon [8]: This caravansary from the Moorish period was originally a stockyard and later used as lodgings for merchants; it derived its name ("coal yard") during the reign of Ferdinand and Isabella, when it was a hostel for coal miners.

Hospital San Juan de Dios [24]: Founded in 1552, the hospital boasts a beautiful early-17th-century portal, an old fountain, and a two-story Renaissance arcade in the courtyard. A Baroque church, added in the 18th century, contains splendid decorations and relics of the saint.

La Madraza [2]: Once the Arab university, this palace was redesigned in the late 15th century and later became Granada's first city hall.

Monasterio de la Cartuja [26]: The 18th-century Baroque sacristy of this Carthusian monastery is often called the "Christian

Granada Attractions:

1. Gran Via de Colon/Calle Reyes Catolicos
2. La Madraza
3. Cathedral of Santa Maria de la Encarnaciòn
4. Capilla Real
5. Sagrario
6. Palace of the Archbishop
7. Alcaicería
8. Corral del Carbòn
9. Carmelite Convent
10. Casa de los Tiros
11. Santa Catalina de Sena
12. San Cedilio
13. Casa de los Griones
14. Santo Domingo
15. Santiago
16. San Matias
17. Castillo Bibataubín
18. Teatro Cervantes
19. Nuestra Señora de las Angustias
20. University
21. Santos Justos y Pastor
22. Colegio Mayor San Bartolomé y Santiago
23. San Jerònimo
24. Hospital San Juan de Dios
25. Hospital Real
26. Monasterio de la Cartuja
27. San Cristòbal
28. Mirador de San Christòbal
29. Real Chancilleria
30. San José
31. Santa Ana
32. Arab Baths
33. Santa Catalina de Zafra
34. San Pedro y San Pablo
35. Casa del Castril
36. San Juan de los Reyes
37. Cuesta de los Chinos
38. Casa del Chapiz
39. San Miguel el Alto
40. El Salvador
41. San Nicolas
42. Santa Isabel la Real
43. San Miguel el Bajo
44. Daralhorra
45. Puerta Monaita
46. Arco Elvira

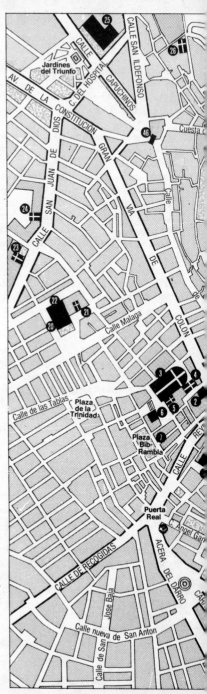

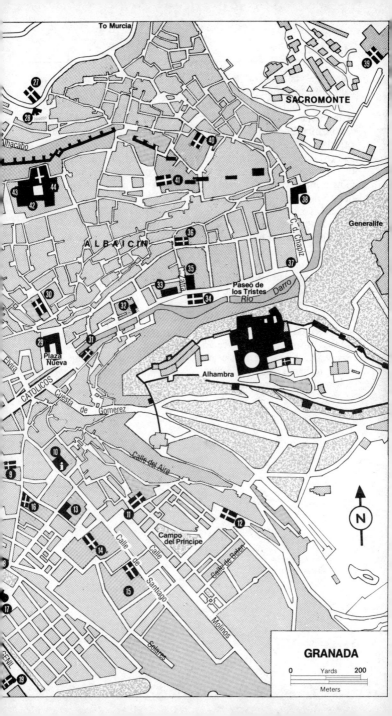

Alhambra" because of its abundant ornamentation and stucco work, some of it based on ancient Aztec models.

Nuestra Señora de las Angustias [19]: Built between 1664 and 1671, this church is graced by two splendid bell towers and contains a much-venerated statue of the "Señora de las Angustias," Granada's patron saint.

Sacromonte (Sacred Mountain): The religious history of this mountain dates back to the early Christian era. At the top is the former Benedictine monastery of *Sacro Monte,* dating from the 17th century. Gypsies living in the caves will perform (for a hefty load of silver) the *flamenco* and the *zambra,* a spirited folk dance accompanied by guitar music and clapping hands. Be forewarned, however, that there are usually better shows in the city, and you may find yourself at risk here—exercise caution.

**San Jeronimo [23]: Founded toward the end of the 15th century as the first ecclesiastical building after the victory over the Moors, this fine Renaissance church has a magnificent inner courtyard. Gonzalo Fernandez de Cordoba (1453–1515), an Andalusian national hero known as "El Gran Capitán" who fought in the wars against the Moors, is buried in the *Capilla Mayor,* which contains a splendid 16th-century altar.

San Nicolas [41]: This Gothic church, built at the beginning of the 16th century, has a beautiful high altar and fine Flemish tapestries. There is a marvelous view of the Alhambra from the church square.

Hamburg

The second-largest city and most important port in Germany, Hamburg is a mixture of proud, old prosperity and hustling new commerce. Located some 60 miles from the North Sea on the mouth of the Elbe River, this rich and perennially busy harbor city has become the country's media center, which guarantees an up-to-the-minute sophistication and a wide-ranging cultural menu. There's lots of old German decorum mixed in with a newer surface glitz and glitter . . . and then there's the notorious Reeperbahn. After dark in Europe's most famous red-light area, a coarser, lustier side of Hamburg emerges. Severely damaged in World War II, the city has been rebuilding ever since—and not always with the happiest results. Yet, the glass-and-steel anonymity of the new city is offset by the pockets of old Hamburg that still remain. A brisk, pervasive maritime atmosphere, aided by the presence in the center of the city of the Alster, an enormous lake, and many canals, gives the entire city its own distinctive flavor.

History

Traces of a permanent settlement date back some 6,000 years, but the Hamburg area has been inhabited for at least 15,000 years. From the beginning, it was a center of maritime trade.

Charlemagne founded the city of "Hammaburg" in 810, and it was soon elevated to an archbishopric. Vikings conquered the young settlement not long afterwards, and burned it to the ground. Two hundred years later, the city was fortified, and by 1189, the first port was built and granted special privileges by Frederick Barbarossa.

Hamburg entered into a trading partnership with nearby Lubeck in the mid-13th century. The move eventually resulted in the founding of the immensely powerful Hanseatic League, which dominated trading in the North Sea and the Baltic during the Middle Ages. As a result, Hamburg became extremely wealthy. The city, ruled by Denmark for several hundred years, was recognized as a Free Imperial City in 1768; it declared itself a sovereign and "Free Hanseatic City" in 1806, a title it retains to this day. After a brief period of French domination, Hamburg became a member of the German Confederation in 1815. The 19th century was a period of continued prosperity, as demonstrated by the fine houses built by wealthy burghers that characterize waterfront sections of the city.

In the period of a few days in 1945, half of the ancient city of Hamburg was destroyed by Allied bombs. Four years later, the city became a state of the Federal Republic of Germany and took as its official title The Free and Hanseatic City of Hamburg.

Attractions

Alster: Much of Hamburg's charm comes from two lakes, the smaller *Binnenalster* (Inner Alster) and the large *Aussenalster* (Outer Alster) that formed with the damming of the Alster River; cruises leave from Jungfernstieg, the southern promenade of Binnenalster, from April through October.

Bismarckdenkmal (Bismarck Memorial) [30]: This monument to the warmongering Prussian, known as the "Iron Chancellor," is an interesting, although somewhat creepy reminder of Germany's troubled past.

Börse (Stock Exchange) [9]: The oldest stock exchange in Germany was established in 1558; upstairs is Hamburg's Chamber of Commerce, founded in 1665.

Botanisch Garten: You don't

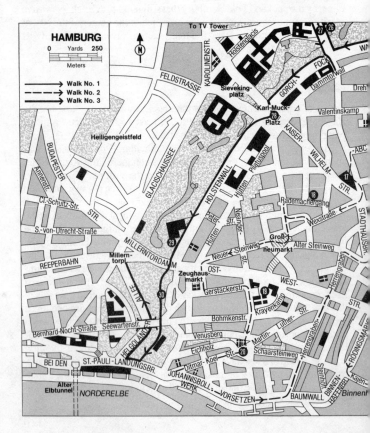

Hamburg Attractions:
1. Central Train Station
2. German Playhouse
3. Museum of Applied Arts
4. Mônckebergstrabe
5. St. Jacob's Church
6. Thalia Theater
7. St. Peter's Church
8. City Hall
9. Stock Exchange
10. Trostbrücke
11. St. Nicholas' Tower
12. St. Katherine's Church
13. Chile House
14. Old Post Office
15. Gänsemarkt
16. Hamburg State Opera
17. Axel Springer Publishing House
18. Hummel Memorial
19. St. Michael's Church
20. Schaarmarkt
21. Gôrtz'sches Palace
22. Deichtorplatz
23. Municipal Art Gallery
24. Lombard Bridge
25. Jungfernstieg
26. Institute for Applied Botany of the University of Hamburg
27. Planten un Blomen
27a. Heinrich Hertz Tower
28. Karl-Muck-Platz
29. Hamburg Historical Museum
30. Bismarck Memorial

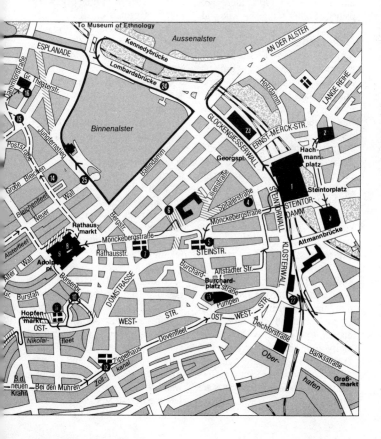

need a green thumb or a degree in botany to appreciate the towering palm trees in the splendid Palm House or the slightly sinister Amazonian waterlilies in the Victoriahaus; the gardens themselves were laid out in 1821.

Fischmarkt (Fish Market): On Sunday mornings this riverside area near the St. Pauli Landungsbrucken is a favorite haunt of Hamburgers looking for an early breakfast of raw herring; if you're not a fresh-fish type, there are plenty of other things for sale and lots of good people-watching.

Gänsemarkt (Goose Market Square) [15]: In 1677, the first opera house in Germany was built on this market square where geese once honked and buyers haggled over prices. The event is commemorated by the late 19th-century Lessing Memorial.

Jungfernstieg (Maidens' Path) [25]: The oldest of the three promenades on the Binnenalster (Inner Alster Lake), it was laid out in the 17th century; by 1842, it had become an elegant shopping street. On a dock jutting into the lake is the popular *Alsterpavillon* café and restaurant.

**Kunsthalle (Municipal Art Gallery) [23]: This domed hall next to the main train station contains an extraordinary collection of paintings and sculpture, from ancient to modern, with an especially good selection of 19th- and 20th-century German painting; all the northern European masters from the 14th century onwards are represented.

*Museum für Hamburgische Geschichte (Hamburg Historical Museum) [29]: Pieces from destroyed Hamburg buildings have been incorporated into the walls of this museum, which provides an overview of the city's history and culture and features an especially good collection of model ships.

***Museum für Kunst und Gewerbe (Museum of Applied Arts) [3]: Fabulous gold and silver work from the Middle Ages, as well as German clocks, Renaissance furniture, and superb examples of art nouveau (known in Germany as *Jugendstil*) are on display.

Oevelgönne: Running east and west between Elbchaussee and the bank of the Elb River, this charming 19th-century district breathes a Biedermeyer air and is filled with beautiful old captains' houses and several good restaurants.

*Planten un Blomen (Plants and Flowers) [27]: Hamburg's most famous park is filled with gorgeous displays of flowering plants and, on summer nights, features a popular "dancing fountain."

Rathaus (City Hall) [8]: This massive late-19th century public building in neo-Renaissance style features a heavily opulent interior that bears testament to Hamburg's rich, ostentatious past. The planners of the building and its surrounding area of canals and lake were consciously trying to emulate the Piazza San Marco in Ven-

View of the Rathaus

ice, and the town hall itself is built on wooden pilings sunk into the unstable ground of the old Alster marsh.

Reeperbahn: Named after the ropemakers who once inhabited this district, the Reeperbahn is now Hamburg's nighttime home of raunch, sleaze, and sex—in any form you want.

Sankt-Jacobi-Kirche (St. Jacob's Church) [5]: Almost completely rebuilt after the war, the church was originally constructed in the 13th century, and contains several medieval altars.

Sankt-Katharinen-Kirche (St. Catherine's Church) [12]: The original church, destroyed in the war, was built between 1380 and 1425; a Dutch Baroque tower was added later.

**Sankt-Michaelis-Kirche (St. Michael's Church) [9]: Morning and evening, the watchman blows his trumpet from the green-topped spire of this beautiful landmark Baroque church; from the same spot you can see an outstanding panorama of the city.

Sankt-Nikolai-Turm (St. Nicholas' Tower) [11]: All that remains of Gilbert Scott's mid-19th century imitation of the Cologne cathedral is this blackened ruin, now a memorial to the victims of Nazi persecution.

Sankt-Petri-Kirche (St. Peter's Church) [7]: The present church was built in the mid-19th century on the foundations of the original 14th-century church, one of Hamburg's oldest, and offers a splendid view from the tower.

Thalia Theater [6]: A German theater with an illustrious past, the Thalia was founded in 1843, although the present building on Gerhardt-Hauptmann-Platz dates from 1912 and was rebuilt after the war.

Excursions

Blankenese: You can actually walk the 13 km. (8 miles) from Hamburg to this pleasant village on the Elbe River by following the north bank of the river, or you can easily take the S-Bahn train from downtown. Although a suburb, Blankenese has retained the charm and character of an old fishing village, filled with narrow lanes and the retirement cottages of fishermen and sea captains.

Helsinki

Probably no other city in Europe—perhaps the world—is as environmentally aware as Helsinki. This very modern Finnish capital city is a wonder of tangy sea-air, ultra-modern and severely neoclassical buildings, and giant parks—all of which demonstrate a purity of design and integrity of principle. Life here is lived on a human, uncrowded scale, in a bracing way that respects nature and thereby celebrates the human spirit. In the summer, it's a city of the Midnight Sun, and in the winter a place where the Northern Lights play in the clear, dark skies. To experience life as the Finns in Helsinki do, set aside some time to spend in an authentic Finnish sauna—an exhilarating experience that shouldn't be missed.

History

Unlike most capital cities in Europe, Helsinki is relatively new—it's only 400 years old. Finland was ruled by Sweden at that time, and the Swedish king, Gustav Vasa, was responsible for having four separate Finnish towns relocate on the River Vantaa, where it emptied into a bay on the Baltic Sea. These four settlements combined to form Helsinki.

For three centuries, Helsinki struggled to survive as a trading town while Turku, to the west, flourished as the country's capital and seat of culture. But in 1812—when Finland was no longer ruled by the Swedes, but by Russia—Czar Alexander decided to move the country's political center closer to Russia. Helsinki was selected as the new capital.

Just before this, however, a raging fire had destroyed most of the city, a tragic event that was put to good advantage. The architect Carl Ludvig Engel was brought from Germany to redesign the new capital city, and left behind some of the finest remaining examples of neoclassical architecture in the world. In the 20th century, Helsinki was the home of the National Romantic style of architecture created by such pioneering architects as Alvar Aalto; the city contains several brilliant examples of this building style.

Independence from Russia was obtained in 1917, but both the Russian and Swedish presence linger in Helsinki: of the two major cathedrals, one is Lutheran while the other is Orthodox, replete with onion domes. Helsinki has, in the meantime, gone on to establish itself as a model of Finnish design and planning.

Attractions

Art Museum of the Ateneum
[2]: The country's most significant art collection is housed here and presents an excellent overview of Finnish art and sculpture.

Finnish Opera House [18]:

The Finnish National Opera performs here during the winter season.

Finlandia Hall [12]: One of the last projects of the esteemed Finnish architect Alvar Aalto, this striking building set in Hesperia Park houses concert and congress halls. The *National Museum,* with its extensive prehistoric and ethnological collections, and an example of the Finnish National Romantic style espoused by Saarinen, is just across the street. In the park on the east side of Mannerheimintie you'll find the *Helsinki City Museum* [11].

Kauppatori (Market Square) [4]: In the center of this bustling, harbor-side square, the quickest pulsepoint of the city, is a much loved city landmark: the early 20th-century *Havis Amanda Fountain,* showing the young girl Havis Amanda, symbol of Helsinki, emerging from the ocean. Across the street and overlooking the harbor at the beginning of Pohjoisesplanadi is the *Presidentinlinna* (Presidential Palace), at one time the imperial palace of the ruling Russian czar; next to it is the broad façade of the *City Hall* [5].

Korkeasaari Zoo [21]: A large island reached by ferry is home to the world's northernmost zoo, which includes the rare and endangered white snow leopard. In good weather, you can enjoy lunch and a seaward view of Helsinki from the open-air café here.

Linnanmäki [16]: This enormous pleasure park is far more than a collection of heart-stopping rides, although there are plenty of those. It's also an outdoor institution, a place for strolling—with cafés, restaurants, a dancing pavilion and theaters—proceeds from all of which go to children's charities.

Mannerheim Museum [19]: The beloved Finnish patriot and hero Marshal Mannerheim once lived in this old wooden house, which has been made into a museum in his honor.

Market Hall, Eteläranta Street: Sumptuous displays of everything from fresh fish to reindeer filets make this old brick hall on the western shore of the South Harbor worth a visit.

Military Cemetery [14]: Final resting place for Finnish and German soldiers killed in World War II and the much-revered Finnish national hero, Field Marshal Mannerheim.

National Theater [1]: Just north of Eliel Saarinen's *train station,* built in the National Romantic style of the 20th century and

Finlandia Hall

National Theater

decorated with enormous red-granite sculptures, is the Finnish National Theater. It was completed in 1902 for the presentation of plays in the native Finnish tongue.

Observation Hill [20]: There are few better outdoor spots for a panoramic view of city and harbor; the late 19th-century bronze sculpture is called *"The Shipwrecked Mariners."*

Olympic Stadium [15]: The stadium was completed in 1938 for the Olympic Games of 1940—which, because of World War II, were never held; the stadium finally hosted the games in 1952.

Parliament House [8]: This building with a colonnaded façade was built between 1927 and 1931.

Senaatintori (Senate Square) [7]: Surrounded by three important buildings, this graceful square is an example of Engel's redesign of Helsinki when it was chosen to be the country's new capital. West of the square is Engel's building for *Helsinki University*, with its adjacent library, built between

1828 and 1832. The square's north side is dominated by the domed *Tuomiokirkko* (Lutheran Cathedral), completed in 1852, with a late 19th-century statue of Czar Alexander II. The third building in the square is the *State Council Building*. The modern *Senaati Shopping Center* provides year-round activity on the south side of the square.

Seurasaari (Open Air Museum) [17]: For a vivid picture of Finnish life as it was lived earlier in the century, stroll around this pleasant, open-air museum; its reconstructed farm and manor houses were transferred here from other parts of the country.

Sibelius Park [13]: The great Finnish composer Jean Sibelius, whose symphonies and tone-poem "Finlandia" are known

Helsinki Attractions:
1. National Theater
2. Art Museum of the Ateneum
3. Swedish Theater
4. Kauppatori
5. City Hall
6. Uspenski Cathedral
7. Senaatorintori
8. Parliament House
9. Temppeliaukio
10. National Museum
11. City Museum
12. Finlandia Hall
13. Sibelius Park
14. Military Cemetery
15. Olympic Stadium
16. Linnanmäki
17. Seurasaari
18. Finnish Opera House
19. Mannerheim Museum
20. Observation Hill
21. Korkeasaari Zoo
22. Suomenlinna Sveaborg

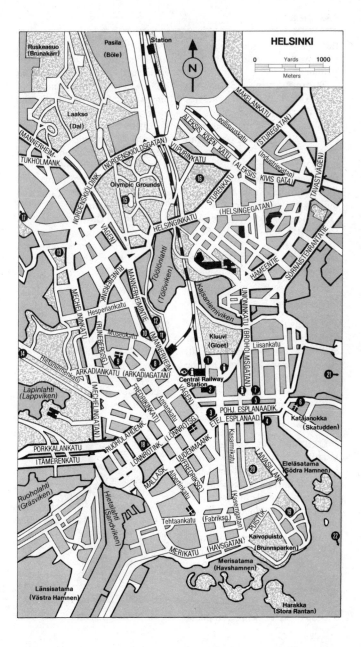

throughout the world, is honored here with a statue by Eila Hiltunen.

Suomenlinna Sveaborg [22]: There are frequent ferries from the marketplace to this fortress island, with its wonderful collection of gardens, parks, and museums. The early summer air is heady with French lilacs imported from Versailles, and there's a famous restaurant called *Walhalla* built in the old fort near King's Gate. The island's *Nordic Arts Center* is a showplace for Scandinavian art.

Swedish Theater [3]: A reminder that a different country

and a different language once ruled Finland, this circular theater is located at the junction of Helsinki's main artery and shopping street, Mannerheimintie, and the Esplanade.

Temppeliaukio (Rock Church) [9]: This must-see example of modern Finnish architecture was carved out of solid rock and topped with a copper dome with inset glass strips by Timo and Tuomo Suomalainen.

Uspenski Cathedral [6]: An impressive Orthodox structure with gilded onion domes and a rich interior, the red-brick cathedral was built in 1868.

Excursions

The sights listed here are located in the borough of Espoo, on the far end of what was once Laajalahti Bay, but is now a lake thanks to the construction of new roads. The trip is especially interesting for students of architecture and planning.

Otaniemi Technical University: On the way to Tapiola you'll pass by this Alvar Aalto-designed university building, an important example of modern architecture. The "Dipoli" building shouldn't be missed.

Tapiola: Designed by Aalto in the 1950s as a utopian and radical garden suburb—a kind of open-ended experiment in living in communal harmony with nature—Tapiola today has about 17,000 or so residents who main-

tain their own newspaper, libraries, and outdoor, glass-enclosed swimming pool.

On the island of **Kuusisaari** at the south end of the lake, connected to the mainland by bridges, is the *Didrichsen Art Gallery,* with

Tapiola

paintings, modern sculpture, pre-Columbian, and Chinese art. In **Leppavaara** at the north end of the lake, you'll find the *Gallen-Kallela Museum,* the palatial workshop of an important Finnish artist, Akeli Gallen-Kallela (1865–1931).

Istanbul

Istanbul is a fascinating East-West hybrid—an exotic mixture of Christian domes and Muslim minarets, of dusty bazaars and romantic seraglios, of glittering mosaics and sparkling seas. Standing upon the continents of Europe and Asia, erstwhile Byzantium and Constantinople is not only Turkey's largest and most crowded city (with a population of some six million), but it is also its biggest harbor, economic hub, and cultural and intellectual center. Ankara may have been declared the capital of the Turkish Republic in 1923, but from its scenic vantage point on the strait of Bosporus, Istanbul remains the heart and soul of two lost empires and their present-day descendants. The repository of the country's richest art treasures, loveliest buildings, and deepest traditions, as well as the location of its most dramatic battles and dazzling triumphs, Istanbul is an unforgettable mecca of superlative attractions.

History

Archaeological evidence points to a late Mycenaean (13th-century B.C.) settlement on the site of present-day Istanbul, although the city's history did not really start until 667 B.C. Tradition recounts that Byzas the Megarian founded a town on a spit of land—today's Saray Burnu—and named it Byzantium. In the centuries that followed, it became a hub of commerce and trade, albeit one that was repeatedly attacked, destroyed, and ruled by Persians, Greeks, Romans, and others.

In A.D. 330, Constantine the Great declared Byzantium the capital of the Roman Empire. Accordingly, the city was girded with a protective wall, and the emperor set about rebuilding and expanding so-called New Rome (Nova Roma) or, as it was popularly known, Constantinople. The first Church of Hagia Sophia (Holy Wisdom) was erected at this time (and finished under Constantine's son, Constantius, in 360), and great works of art were brought in from all over the empire. After the western territories were lost to the barbarians, the Eastern Roman Empire continued the old empire's traditions. The city blossomed under Emperor Justinian: During his long rule (527–65), Constantinople became the greatest and grandest city on earth, with the new Hagia Sophia, dedicated in 537, as its glistening crown. Justinian's generals—foremost among them, Belisarius—regained past territories, and the empire grew and prospered. After 565, however, lost battles and hostile invaders ruined the empire—until Heraclius came into power in 660. His reign is considered the start of the heroic age of the Byzantine Empire (which lasted until the death of Basil in 1025).

After Basil's demise, the empire began a decline. A large section of Asia Minor was lost to the Seljuk Turks after they defeated the Byzantine army at the battle of Manzikert (1071). The political intentions of the Byzantine emperors—who tried to achieve an agreement with the Seljuk Turks—were seriously interrupted by the Crusades. During the Fourth Crusade in the early 13th century, Constantinople was sacked by Christian armies, and in 1204, the Latin Empire was founded. The Venetians and Count Baldwin of Flanders were awarded the city. It was not until 1261 that the Byzantine emperor, Michael VIII, was able to recapture Constantinople.

In the 14th century, the Ottomans, powerful successors to the Seljuk Turks in Asia Minor, crossed the Dardanelles to expand their influence toward Europe; they conquered almost all of the Balkans. When the isolation of Constantinople became more and more threatening, however, the Mongol Tamerlane's victory over the Ottomans at Ankara in 1402 brought some relief. But half a century later, the Turks had recovered from this defeat and besieged the city once more. The last Byzantine emperor, Constantine XI Dragases, tried vainly to enlist European aid and even encourage unity with Rome in order to free the city; Nonetheless, May 29, 1453, spelled the end of the Byzantine Empire when the Ottoman Sultan Mehmet II stormed the city. Thereafter, it became known as Istanbul (a corruption of the Greek *eis ton polis,* or "to the city"), and for centuries was the capital of a huge Muslim empire that stretched from the Austrian border to the Persian Gulf.

The Ottoman Empire reached its peak during the long reign of Suleiman the Magnificent (1520–1566). The city's most renowned Ottoman structures date from this period into the 17th century. Although reform along Western lines was creeping in, the Sultan's power slowly began to crumble during the next century. In the 1800s, the Ottoman Empire was on its last, weak legs; not only were hungry foreign armies standing outside the city walls, but interior rebellions were being staged as well.

At the end of World War I, Istanbul was occupied by the Allies, and Sultan Mehmet VI became one of their puppets. A war of national liberation took place, and Atatürk became the first President of the Turkish Republic. In late 1923, Ankara replaced Istanbul as the capital of the new nation. With the removal of foreign embassies to Ankara, Istanbul—no longer an empire's capital, after nearly two millennia—lost some of its cosmopolitan aura. It also experienced a huge increase in population, notably poor Anatolians looking for work. Tumble-down slum housing came to dominate parts of this once-imperial city. Still, Istanbul retains much of its ancient, medieval, and sultanate splendors, despite being a sprawling, overcrowded metropolis with its inevitable share of modern urban problems.

Attractions

Aqueduct of Valens: Built by the Roman Emperor Valens in A.D. 368—and often rebuilt in the Byzantine and Ottoman eras—the massive conduit was originally about 1,000 meters (3,300 feet) long. A truly grand structure with its two rooms of arcades, the aqueduct was in use until the late 19th century.

At Meydaní [6]: The old Hippodrome (ca. A.D. 200), one of Byzantine Constantinople's best-known monuments, once occupied the site known today as *At Meydaní,* or "Square of Horses." Around the square are the Mosque of Sultan Ahmet I (the Blue Mosque); the 25-meter- (82-foot-) high pink-granite Egyptian Obelisk (dating from the 15th century B.C. and brought from Egypt in the fourth century A.D.); the Serpentine Column, comprising three intertwined bronze snakes and originally a trophy base at Delphi commemorating the Greek victory over the Persians at Plataea (479 B.C.); and the Stone Obelisk, made of small limestone blocks and restored in the tenth century A.D. (Crusaders removed the gilt-bronze plaques that once covered the monument and melted them down).

Beyazidiye (see *Mosque of Sultan Beyazit II*)

Blue Mosque (see *Mosque of Sultan Ahmet I*)

Bosporus: The narrow strait of Bosporus, approximately 30 km. (18 miles) long, is best seen by boat (ferries leave from the Galata Bridge). The historically significant passage served as a thoroughfare even in ancient times (the legendary Argonauts are said to have used it), and Persians, Crusaders, and Turks crossed it in their conquests. The longest suspension bridge in Europe connects with Asia at Ortaköy—68 meters (224 feet) high and 1,074 meters (3,544 feet) long. At the narrowest point of the Bosporus stands a spectacular sight: the romantic *Rumeli Hisarí* fortress, built by Mehmet II in 1452; on the opposite shore is the smaller medieval fortress of *Anadolu Hisarí,* rebuilt by Mehmet II at the same time.

Cannon Gate [11]: The word *topkapí* means "gate of the cannon." The armies guarding the harbor entrance were installed at this sea-wall gate, located at *Topkapí Sarayí,* along with two massive cannons.

Church of the Pantocrator (see *Molla Zeyrek Camii*)

*Church of St. Savior in Chora [13], Nester Sokagi: After Hagia Sophia, the former St. Savior—now *Kariye Camii*—is Istanbul's most interesting Byzantine church. Built during Justinian's reign and restored several times afterwards, it contains outstanding mosaics and frescoes. The mosaics depict, among other subjects, the lives of Christ and the Virgin, and the wall paintings feature scenes of the Resurrection, Last Judgment, and prefigurations of Mary in the Old Testament.

Church of St. Irene *(Hagia Eirene)*, entrance at Bab-í Hümayün, the Imperial Gate leading to the First Court of *Topkapí Sarayí:* One of Istanbul's oldest structures, St. Irene was once Constantinople's main church. The original fourth-century building was destroyed many times, and the present basilica-plan structure dates largely from Justinian's time. The church later served as an arsenal and antiquities storehouse for the Turks.

Church of Saints Sergius and Bacchus [9], off Küçük Aya Sofya Caddesi: The church, dedicated to two Roman soldiers martyred for their Christianity, was begun in Justinian's time. It became a Muslim place of worship in the 16th century, and is called the Mosque of Little Hagia Sophia in Turkish, because of its supposed similarity to the great church (in actuality, it was built before Hagia Sophia).

Çinili Köşkü, in the lower gardens of *Topkapí Sarayí:* This is one of Istanbul's oldest secular buildings; it was finished in 1472 (as a pavilion for Mehmet II and a respite from the palace) and restored in the 1590s. Its name, which means "Tiled Kiosk," refers to the faience covering its interior and exterior walls. Today it is a museum with displays of ceramics, including outstanding examples of Iznik ware and tiles (among them a *mihrab* and fountain).

Column of Constantine, Yeniçeriler Caddesi and Vezirhani Caddesi: In 330, Constantine the Great erected what is known today as the "Hooped Column" or "Burnt Column;" atop it once stood an equestrian statue of the emperor (a hurricane toppled it in 1105). A mix of Christian and polytheistic relics, including the sunrays of Apollo's crown and the nails of Christ's Passion, were buried beneath it. The original fifth-century iron hoops that held the porphyry column together have been replaced.

*Dolmabahçe Sarayí [35], on the Bosporus shore between Tophane and Beşiktaş: Sultan Ahmet I had a wooden garden pavilion set up on this site in the 17th century. The present, somewhat pretentious, marble palace dates from the 19th century and was built for the Sultan Abdül Mecit I, who moved here from *Topkapí Sarayí* in 1853. Atatürk used it as his presidential residence when visiting Istanbul, and he died here

Dolmabahçe Sarayí

in 1938. The palace, now used for grand official occasions, has over 200 rooms, including a throne hall, bath, and art gallery.

Egyptian Market, Eminönü Square: Established around 1660, the market originally sold spices, herbs, and other merchandise from Egypt. Today's *Mísír Çarşísí* is a restored jumble of shops offering spices, dyes, and assorted goods.

Eski Imaret Camii [19], Küçük Mektep Sokagi: The old Byzantine St. Savior Pantepoptes (All-Seeing Christ), with its 12-sided dome and decorative brickwork, was built in the 11th century by the Empress Anna Delessena (who co-ruled with her son, Alexius I Comnenus, for some 20 years). It became a mosque in the 15th century; it was then used as a kitchen and dining hall, and it is now a Koran school with a dormitory.

Fatih Camii (see *Mosque of the Conqueror*)

Fethiye Camii (see *Pammakaristos Church*)

Fountain of Ahmet III [2], Ishak Paşa Caddesi (opposite rear gate of Hagia Sophia): This elaborate square structure, whose roof is topped by five small domes, is a superb example of Turkish rococo architecture and one of Istanbul's finest fountains.

Galata Bridge [27]: The hub of hectic day-to-day life in Istanbul, the span connects old Stamboul with more modern Galata, crossing the Golden Horn 1 km. (one half-mile) above the spot where it meets the Bosporus. The squares at either end—Karaköy in Galata, Eminönü in Stamboul—are crowded with fishmongers, restaurants, and tourists. The lower level of the bridge has many cafés, teahouses, eating places, and commuters waiting for ferries.

Galata Tower [32], Kulesi Sokagi and Galip Dede Caddesi: The most visible landmark on the skyline this side of the Golden Horn, the present-day tower was built on the site of a sixth-century turret by the Genoese in 1348, when it was called the Tower of Christ. A restaurant and nightclub today perch atop its peak, and you can see a wonderful view of the city.

*Great Bazaar [30]: The *Kapalí Çarşí,* or "Covered Bazaar," is one of the world's largest and most picturesque markets, a dizzying maze of rugs, jewelry, clothes, and every other product imaginable. Don't miss the great domed hall, Old Bedestan, where some of the loveliest objects are sold. This is a place to wander, have a Turkish coffee, bargain with vendors, and lose yourself in the exotic mass.

Great Cemetery [41], entrance at Gündöğümü Caddesi: The vast cemetery *(Mezarlík)* of Karaca Ahmet—the largest burial place in the Moslem world—is named after a 14th-century warrior whose remains (and those of his horse) are said to rest here.

Gül Camii (see *Rose Mosque*)

***Hagia Sophia [1]: One of

the most extraordinary buildings in all the world, the Church of Holy Wisdom is the jewel of the Golden Age of the Byzantine Empire. Constantine the Great built a simple basilica on the site in the fourth century, but subsequent fires caused his successor Justinian to rebuild the church. After earthquake damage in the ninth and tenth centuries, Basil II ordered extensive reconstruction, but Crusaders mercilessly sacked it in 1204. The Byzantine age ended in 1453 when Constantinople fell to the Turks and Mehmet II transformed the church into a mosque. Although the mosaics were painted over, the inner structure remained unchanged. In 1935, Atatürk declared *Ayasofya* (as it's called in Turkish) a museum.

Hours can be spent exploring this repository of Christian and Muslim treasures, but try to linger over the huge bronze-sheathed doors leading to the narthex (from Justinian's church) and on the lunette over the door. This tenth-century mosaic panel depicts Justinian on the left (holding a model of Hagia Sophia) and Constantine the Great on the right, with a model of the city. The narthex itself, a vestibule of the old Christian basilica, has marble panels and vaults inlaid with well-preserved gold mosaics. The main nave is dominated by the famous soaring dome; its base is formed by a narrow row of 40 windows and its height exceeds that of a 15-story building. Unfortunately, lit-

Hagia Sophia

tle is left of the Byzantine-era frescoes.

The conversion of Hagia Sophia into a mosque necessitated the removal of the altar and many other Christian articles. The apse contained a *mihrab* (a niche facing Mecca). A *mimber* (a throne for readings) was set up to the right, and a latticework Sultan's loge was added to the left of the apse in 1849. Other additions made in the 19th century include green wooden discs bearing the names of Allah, Mohammed, and the first four caliphs (rendered in beautiful calligraphy), which were suspended from the piers at gallery level.

Unique to Hagia Sophia are its "Weeping Column," covered with bronze plates and always wet, and the "Cold Window," through which you can feel a cool breeze, even on the hottest of days.

Hippodrome (see *At Meydaní*)

Iskele Camii [38], Iskele Meydaní, Üsküdar: The ferry-landing point of Üsküdar is dominated by the *Iskele Camii,* the imposing 1547–1548 mosque built by the architect Sinan for Mihrimah Sultan, Suleiman's daughter (she commissioned another mosque of Sinan, near the Sixth Hill in 1562).

Kariye Camii (see *Church of St. Savior in Chora*)

Kíz Kulesi [37], on a tiny island off Üsküdar (accessible via boat hired at Üsküdar ferry landing): Also known as Leander's Tower or the Maiden's Tower, this quaint 18th-century structure is one of Istanbul's best-known (but least-visited) landmarks. Today it serves as a naval inspection station.

Little Hagia Sophia (see *Church of Saints Sergius and Bacchus*)

Molla Zeyrek Camii [20], off Atatürk Boulevard: Three adjoining churches comprise the *Molla Zeyrek Camii,* built in the 12th century as the Church of the Pantocrator by John II Comnenus and his Hungarian wife Irene. The emperors of the Comnenus and Paleologus dynasties are buried in the mortuary chapel, which is dedicated to St. Michael.

Mosaic Museum, Torun Sokagi: This museum near the Blue Mosque is more like an archaeological site. It displays the remains from the Great Palace of Byzantium on the Marmara coast (originally built by Constantine the Great).

Mosque of the Conqueror [18], Akdeniz Caddesi, off Fevzi Paşa Caddesi: Known in Turkish as *Faith Camii,* this huge mosque complex is located on the site of the Church of the Holy Apostles. Mehmet the Conqueror replaced the crumbling Byzantine structure with the first Mosque of Mehmet Fatih—for years the largest in the Ottoman Empire—but this was utterly destroyed by an earthquake and replaced with the present mosque (1766–1771) by Mustafa II. Within the complex are a hospice, library, caravansary, baths, and mausolea of great interest.

Mosque of Eyüp [31], Camii Kabir Caddesi, Eyüp (northwest of the old town, off the banks of the Golden Horn): Eyüp Ansari was the Prophet Mohammed's standard-bearer and his shrine is the holiest Moslem site in Istanbul. It was here that the Sultans were girded with the Sword of Osman (a coronation-like ritual). The present-day mosque dates from around 1800 (except for the minarets, which are early 18th century), while the original mosque—the supposed site of Eyüp's tomb—is ca. 1458. The cemetery on the mosque's north side is worth a visit.

Mosque of Mihrimah (see *Iskele Camii*)

Mosque of the Prince [22], Şehzadebaşí Caddesi: The *Şehzade Camii* mosque complex was built between 1544 and 1548 by Suleiman the Magnificent and dedicated to his eldest son, Prince Mehmet, who died of smallpox in 1543. Sinan was its architect, and it was his first imperial commission to build a mosque on a massive scale. Don't miss the tomb of young Mehmet, covered almost entirely with colorful Iznik tiles that liken it to a garden paradise.

Mosque of Rüstem Paşa

[26], Kutucular Caddesi: Built in 1561 for the husband of Mihrimah, Suleiman the Magnificent's daughter, this small but lovely mosque is famous for its Iznik tiles, sheathing not only the interior but also the façade of the porch.

Mosque of Şemsi Paşa

[39], Şemsi Paşa Caddesi, Üsküdar: Built on a spit of land jutting out into the Bosporus, this small, simple mosque of shiny white stone was designed by Sinan for the Vizier Şemsi Paşa in 1580; a handsome green grille separates his mausoleum from the mosque itself.

Mosque of Sultan Ahmet I

[7], east of At Meydaní: The so-called Blue Mosque was completed after eight years in 1616, a year before Ahmet I's untimely death at age 27. It is the only Istanbul mosque with six minarets (the Sultan had to donate a seventh to the mosque of the Ka'aba in Mecca to restore its dominant position). Its popular name comes from the multitude of blue and green tiles covering the inside walls and pillars.

Mosque of Sultan Beyazit II

[23], Beyazit Square: Constructed in the early years of the 16th century, the Beyazit Mosque is the earliest remaining example of great imperial mosques of Istan-

bul; its construction heralded two centuries of classical Ottoman architecture.

Mosque of Sultan Selim I

[16], Yavuz Selim Caddesi: Built by Suleiman the Magnificent in memory of his father, *Selimiye Camii* (as it's known in Turkish) was completed in 1522. The shallow-domed mosque, with a cluster of smaller domes on both sides, commands a magnificent view from its location on the apex of the Fifth Hill; its courtyard is especially lovely.

*Mosque of Sultan Suleiman

[25], between Mimar Sinan Caddesi and Tiryaki Çarşisi: The great court architect Sinan designed and built the *Süleymaniye*—one of Istanbul's most famous mosques—from 1550 to 1557. Considered by many the finest example of Moslem architecture in the city, the mosque has a brightly lit, colorful interior due to its 138 stained-glass windows, which are decorated with floral designs, and calligraphy-enhanced faience panels. Outside are the mausolea of Suleiman and his wife Roxelana to the east, and, to the north, the tomb of the architect Sinan (d. 1588). A huge *imaret* (public kitchen) in the complex, just west of the courtyard, houses the *Museum of Turkish and Islamic Antiquities.* Pottery, glass, carpets, metalwork, jewelry, musical instruments, calligraphy, Persian miniatures and books (including 8th- and 9th-century Korans) are on display.

Municipal Museum [21],

Atatürk Boulevard: Located at the foot of the Aqueduct of Valens, the museum is housed in a former Koran school, or *madrasah*, built during Mohammed II's rule. On display are relics of old Stamboul, from vintage musical instruments and marionettes to priestly vestments and Turkish handicrafts.

Museum of the Ancient Orient, in the lower gardens of *Topkapí Sarayí:* Twelve rooms house works of art and archaeological finds unearthed at sites throughout the Middle East; the Sumerian, Babylonian, Egyptian, Hittite, Assyrian, and Aramaic cultures are among those represented.

Museum of Archaeology [4], in the lower gardens of *Topkapí Sarayí:* The late 19th-century museum posesses a superb collection of Greek, Roman, and Byzantine antiquities, including the fourth-century B.C. Sarcophagus of Alexander (with relief scenes of the emperor hunting and fighting), Archaic funerary stelae, Attic vases, statues of the Roman Emperors, and a pair of large marble pedestals from the old Hippodrome.

Museum of the Conqueror (see *Çinili Köşkü*)

Palace of Blachernae, Dervişzade Sokagi: Although only a few lonely towers and vaults are extant, the site of the imperial residence from the twilight of Byzantine rule (11th to 15th centuries) is still a beautiful spot.

Palace of Ibrahim Paşa [8], west side of At Meydaní: Collec-

tions of Turkish and Moslem art can be viewed in the recently restored, 16th-century palace of Ibrahim Paşa, a Greek who converted to Islam and became a confidant of Suleiman the Magnificent (he married the Sultan's sister, Hadice, in 1524).

Palace of the Porphyrogenitus (see *Tekfur Saray*)

Pammakaristos Church [15], Fethiyekapísí Sokagi: Known to locals as *Fethiye Camii,* the church of the "Joyous Mother of God" is a large Byzantine structure comprising a 13th-century principal church, a sepulchral chapel built on the Greek-cross plan around 1315 (with lovely mosaics), and a triple arcade of slightly later date. Converted into a mosque in 1596, its Moslem name means "Mosque of the Conquest" and commemorates the taking of Azerbaijan and Georgia.

Pantepoptes Cloister (see *Eski Imaret Camii*)

Rose Mosque [17], off Abdül Ezel Pasa Caddesi: Its name in Turkish is *Gül Camii,* the "Mosque of the Roses," a title referring to the garlands that decorated its interior when the Turks stormed the city in the 15th century. Although moved by the display, the Turks seized the church and used it as a naval storehouse before it was heavily altered to become a mosque with minaret.

Selimiye Barracks [42], Kavak Iskele Caddesi and Çeşme Kebir Caddesi, Üsküdar: The massive 19th-century barracks are perhaps best-known for being the location of Florence Nightingale's hospital during the Crimean War. They are once again military housing, and you can apply to the officer in charge to see Nightingale's former quarters; there is also a small museum devoted to the "Lady with the Lamp" in the northeast turret.

Taksim Square [33]: The hub of the new city of Istanbul (north of Galata), the square is dominated by a memorial to those killed in the War of Independence; a huge expanse of lovely gardens stretches north.

Tekfur Saray [14], along the ramparts of the old Palace of Blachernae: Along with the Blachernae Palace, which once stood nearby, *Tekfur Saray* ("Palace of the Sovereign") served as a residence for Byzantium's last rulers. Dating to the late 13th and early 14th centuries, the three-story building has a façade with elaborate geometric designs in white marble and red brick.

Tiled Pavilion (see *Çinili Köşkü*)

***Topkapí Sarayí [3], main entrance through Bab-í Hümayün: For over 400 years, Ottoman Sultans and the members of their court had their imperial residence on this spot. Mehmet II ("The Conqueror") initially built a complex on the Third Hill (the Old Palace, or *Eski Saray*) in 1453, but a few years later he had a new residence erected on the First Hill, on the site of ancient Byzantium's acropolis. Its name, *Topkapí* (or

Cannon Gate), came from the main sea gate of the wall that Mehmet had built to encircle his new palace—a twin-towered gateway (destroyed in the 19th century) flanked by two massive cannons.

Istanbul Attractions:
1. Hagia Sophia
2. Fountain of Ahmet III
3. Topkapi Sarayí
4. Museum of Archaeology
5. Yerebatan Cistern
6. At Meydani
7. Mosque of Sultan Ahmet I
8. Palace of Ibrahim Pasa
9. Little Hagia Sophia
10. Yediküle
11. Canon Gate
12. Mihrimah Sultan Camii
13. Church St. Savior in Chora
14. Tekfur Saray
15. Pammakaristos Church
16. Mosque of Sultan Selim I
17. Rose Mosque
18. Mosque of the Conqueror
19. Eskilmaret Camii
20. Molla Zeyrek Camii
21. Municipal Museum
22. Mosque of the Prince
23. Mosque of Beyazit II
24. University
25. Mosque of Sultan Süleiman
26. Mosque of Rüstem Pasa
27. Galata Bridge
28. New Mosque
29. Sirkeçi Train Station
30. Large Bazaar
31. Mosque of Eyüp
32. Galata Tower
33. Taksim Square
34. Mosque of Dolmabahçe
35. Dolmabahçe Sarayí
36. Mosque of Nusretiye
37. Kíz Kulesi
38. Iskele Camii
39. Mosque of Semsi-Pasa
40. Mosque of Yeni Valide
41. Great Cemetery
42. Selimiye Barracks
43. Haydarpasa

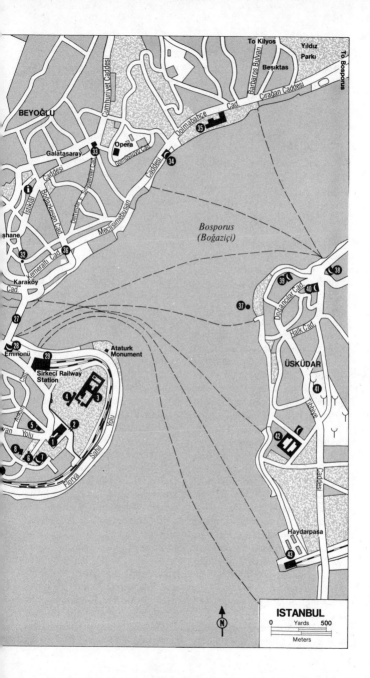

Besides its immense historical and architectural significance, *Topkapí Sarayí* displays in its many buildings outstanding collections of arms and armor, jewelry, textiles, ceramics, calligraphy, miniatures, and countless fine- and decorative-art objects once owned by the Sultans, their families, and their court. Surrounding a large courtyard to the southwest of the seraglio proper are the *Museum of Archaeology,* the *Museum of the Ancient Orient,* and *Çinili Köşkü* (see separate entries). Within the *Topkapí Sarayí* complex itself are the Divan and adjacent Inner Treasury (displaying, among other objects, clocks, arms, and armor) and, directly across the Second Court, there is the Porcelain Collection (in the old kitchens). The *Bab-üs Saadet,* or Gate of Felicity, leads to the once-private Third Court, where the Throne Room, Treasury, Pavilion of the Holy Mantle, and assorted educational buildings are located. Costumes and various imperial and religious treasures—including precious thrones and jewels—are on view in the four rooms of the Treasury. Just beyond the Third Court is an exhibition of exquisite Turkish and Persian miniatures. The Fourth Court, largely a garden, is scattered with several pavilions, as well as a fountain-centered marble pool and the 17th-century *Baghdad Köşkü,* a kiosk honoring Murat IV's conquest of that city.

The Harem, a busy hodgepodge of chambers, gardens, courtyards, stairways, and passages, was created over the centuries by continually adding onto the original, late 16th-century permanent structures. The most magnificent rooms are the salon and bedroom of Murat III, Ahmet I's library, and Ahmet III's dining room, but the more modest living quarters of black eunuchs and female servants also make fascinating viewing.

University of Istanbul [24], Beyazit Square and environs: Istanbul's oldest and biggest center of higher learning, the university was founded in the 15th century. It gradually increased in size and schools until a decline in the final years of the Ottoman Empire. Reformed after the founding of the Turkish Republic, the university now thrives. In its garden is the 50-meter- (165-foot-) high white-marble Tower of Beyazit, from which you can see a superb panoramic view of the city and the surrounding lands and waters.

Üsküdar: Formerly called Chrysopolis and then Scudari, this Anatolian suburb of Istanbul lies opposite the mouth of the Golden Horn, and is accessible by ferry (boats also leave from Galata Bridge). Among its sights are the 16th-century *Iskele Camii;* a fountain of Ahmet III (1726); the Mosque of Şemşi Paşa; the "Tiled Mosque" (*Çinili Camí*), built in 1640 by the mother of Murat IV, and *Atik Valide Camii,* the huge, late 16th-century complex by Sinan commanding the view of Üsküdar (some of its buildings are now used as a prison, although the mosque and other structures can be visited).

Yediküle [10], ramparts at southwestern part of the old town, toward Sea of Marmara: This "Fortress of the Seven Towers" is located where the sea wall and Byzantine land walls meet. The "castle" developed out of a triumphal arch, the so-called Golden Gate, built by Theodosius the Great. In the 14th century, a fortress was built by Emperor John VI Cantacuzenos; after the Moslem conquest that structure was expanded by Mehmet II and fortified by successive leaders. Numerous prisoners have been confined here over the centuries (several of whom left behind carved signatures in the stone).

Yerebatan Cistern [5], entrance at Yerebatan Caddesi: Occupying an underground area over 140 meters (460 feet) long and 70 meters (230 feet) wide, the cistern—also known as *Yerebatan Saray*—was constructed in the sixth century by Justinian to store water for the Great Palace and other structures on the First Hill (later it served *Topkapí Sarayí*). Its ceiling rests on 336 massive columns with Corinthian capitals.

Zeyrek Camii (see *Molla Zeyrek Camii*)

Leipzig

Known for centuries as a meeting place for trade between East and West, Leipzig has also won renown for its cultural traditions. During the 18th century, the boys' choir of St. Thomas' Church, still singing today, was led by Johann Sebastian Bach for many years. Richard Wagner, composer of the "Ring Cycle," was born and spent his student days here, as did Goethe. The musical tradition of the city continues today in the new *Gewandhaus* concert hall with its resident orchestra, founded in 1781, and the renowned School of Music. Leipzig is also the center of East Germany's printing industry and its fur trade. Like Dresden, the city was repeatedly bombed in World War II and reduced to rubble, but painstaking restoration has successfully revived many of Leipzig's most treasured buildings. With its many good restaurants, interesting cafés, and taverns, the city offers a special ambience not always found in East Germany.

History

Situated on ancient trading routes, the city became known in the Middle Ages for its enormous trade fairs, which attracted buyers and sellers from all over Europe. These important fairs were officially recognized by the Emperor Maximilian in the 15th century; this same period also saw the founding of the University of Leipzig.

Leipzig became the locus of an impressive cultural boom in the 18th and 19th centuries, and served as creative home to Johann Sebastian Bach, who composed his music here and conducted the Thomaner Boys' Choir from 1723–1750. The University and Conservatory of Music drew the likes of Goethe and Richard Wagner.

The decisive Battle of the Nations took place in Leipzig in 1813, and witnessed the defeat of Napoleon's army by the combined forces of Austria, Prussia, Russia, and Sweden. The first long-distance rail line in Germany, running between Leipzig and Dresden, opened in 1831.

A little over a hundred years later, the city was virtually leveled by Allied bombs dropped during World War II. After the war ended, Leipzig was absorbed into the new Communist Republic of East Germany, whose boundaries were defined in 1948.

Leipzig still hosts its twice-yearly Fair, when East and West meet over business, and has become a busy regional capital and the second largest city in the country.

Attractions

Alte Börse (Old Stock Exchange) [7]: Built in an early Baroque style, the stock exchange dates from the 17th century.

*Altes Rathaus (Old Town Hall) [1]: The completely restored, 16th-century Renaissance city hall, sited on the 12th-century *marketplace,* is an architectural landmark of Leipzig; it also acts as home to the *City Museum.* A gateway in the town hall leads to the city's most famous square, *Nasch Market.*

Alte Waage [4]: Another example of the meticulous restoration that has gone on in Leipzig, this Renaissance building dates from 1555 and is now headquarters of the East German National Travel Bureau.

Auerbachs Keller (Auerbach's Restaurant) [3]: This historic 16th-century inn located just off the market square was a favorite haunt of Goethe, who later used it as the place where his Faust met the Devil.

Barthels Hof [5]: Laid out in 1523 and then redesigned to suit Baroque tastes in the mid-18th century, these are the only fairgrounds that remain from old Leipzig.

Deutsche Bücherei (German Library) [17]: The library collects every work printed in ‣German, making it the largest German-language library in the world.

Grassi Museum [15]: Applied arts are the focus here, with arts and crafts, musical instruments, and an ethnology of German art forming the various collections.

Karl-Marx-Platz: The new center of Leipzig is dominated by the tall buildings of *Karl Marx University* and the cubistic *Neues Gewandhaus* (New Concert Hall) [12], completed in 1981 and home of Leipzig's internationally famous Gewandhaus Orchestra. The *Opera House,* built between 1956 and 1960, sits on the northern side of the square.

*Museum der Bildenden Kunst (Museum of Fine Arts) [19]: European paintings from the 17th to the 20th century are found here, arranged according to period, country, and genre.

Nikolaikirche (Church of Saint Nicholas) [11]: Founded in the 12th century, the church reveals a variety of building styles, from Gothic to neoclassical. Across from the church is the *Alte Nikolaischule* (Old Saint Nicholas' School), first built in 1568.

Thomaskirche (Church of Saint Thomas) [9]: Bach was buried and Wagner was baptized in this famous 15th-century church. It still echoes on Friday evenings and Sunday mornings with motets sung by the famous Thomaner Boys' Choir, once directed by Bach, who also acted as church organist.

Völkerschlachtdenkmal (Monument to the Battle of the Na-

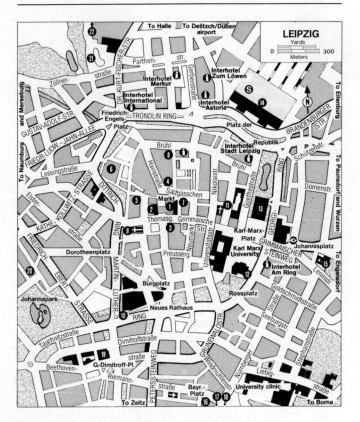

LEIPZIG

Yards
0   300
Meters

Leipzig Attractions:
1. Old City Hall
2. Central Office of Fairs and
   Conventions
3. Auerbachs Keller
4. Alte Waage
5. Barthels Hof
6. Zum Kafeebaum (café)
7. Old Stock Exchange
8. Romanus House
9. Church of St. Thomas
10. New City Hall
11. Church of St. Nicholas
12. New Concert Hall
13. Opera House
14. Central Train Station
15. Grassi Museum
16. Bayrischer Bahnhof (Train Station)
17. German Library
18. Monument to the Battle of the
    Nations
19. Museum of Fine Arts
20. German Technical College for
    Physical Culture and Sport
21. Zoo
22. Gohliser Château

tions) [18]: A view of Leipzig from its heights is the only worthwhile feature of this unattractive early-19th century monument commemorating the victory of the German, Russian, Prussian, and Swedish troops over Napoleon's army.

Zoo [21]: Lions, bears, and Siberian tigers are among the animals successfully bred here for export to other zoos around the world.

"Zum Kaffeebaum" [6]: One of Leipzig's most famous historic restaurants, "Zum Kaffeebaum" has been serving patrons—the composer Robert Schumann among them—since 1725.

Leningrad

Few cities in the world can equal Leningrad for sheer architectural beauty and wealth of artistic treasure. Leningrad has been a witness to a host of extraordinary personages—from Peter the Great to Lenin—and events—from the fabled excesses of the Russian imperial court to the revolutionary storming of the Winter Palace and the 900-day siege of the city in World War II. All of these have combined to give the city a remarkable, almost legendary atmosphere. Leningrad remains the undisputed cultural capital of the Soviet Union, and is unsurpassed for the quality of its museums (such as the Hermitage) and artistic life. Visitors are often surprised by the city's Western European look, characterized by monumental squares, baroque and neoclassical buildings (often beautifully painted in pastel colors), and the hundreds of fanciful bridges (this is a city built on islands). The European appearance is no accident: Peter the Great, the city's founder, wanted to create a Russian "window on Europe." When the White Nights come to banish darkness entirely for a few weeks each summer, Leningrad takes on a glow that truly makes it seem like a rejoicing, enchanted survivor.

History

Leningrad is a mere youngster by European standards. The city was founded in 1703 by Peter the Great, who had just defeated Sweden and built a fortress to ensure that there would be no future invasions. Strategically located on the mouth of the Neva River close to the Baltic Sea, the site was important for trade between Europe and Asia.

Peter moved the capital from Moscow to St. Petersburg, as the city was then called, within nine years of its founding. The new capital was meant to rival other European cities, and, to achieve this end, Western architects were called in to plan and design each stage of development. Government buildings, palaces, and cathedrals were built with the slave labor of tens of thousands of prisoners of war and serfs. Catherine the Great, who ruled towards the end of the 18th century, continued the tradition of bringing in French and Italian architects to design most of the great palaces, some of which she gave as gifts to her lovers.

Many of Russia's greatest artists, writers, and composers lived and worked in St. Petersburg, including Pushkin, Dostoevski, Tchaikovsky, and Gogol. The consummate artistry of dancers like Anna Pavlova and Nijinsky held Petersburg audiences in thrall. This was the city of Fabergé, of jewelled balls, and of lavish extravagance of all kinds. It was also a city where a huge underclass of dispirited serfs lived in appalling conditions in hovels around the aristocratic palaces.

Discontent had been simmering beneath the city's aristocratic façade for decades when the first revolutionary stirrings were unleashed in 1825. A group of young officers—nobles by birth—joined with 3,000 soldiers and sailors to force Czar Nicholas I to renounce the throne. They were unsuccessful, and the revolutionaries were summarily executed. Organized workers' movements took up the cause and, in 1895, Lenin formed the "Combat Union to Free the Working Class," out of which grew the new Revolutionary Party of the Proletariat.

A city-wide strike took place in 1905, and some 140,000 workers marched to the Winter Palace to present their grievances. The Tsar gave orders to his troops to fire into the crowd. Thousands of people were killed on the day that history records as "Bloody Sunday."

The days of the Czarist Russian Empire were nearly over. The First World War pushed the country to the very edge of economic and political catastrophe, and, in 1917, Nicholas II abdicated. A Civil Provisional Government was founded in the city, which then became known as Petrograd. On October 25th of that year, under Lenin's leadership, the Bolshevist Central Committee seized control, and the Great Socialist Revolution replaced the Russian Empire with the Union of Soviet Socialist Republics. The following year, the government left Petrograd to reestablish itself in Moscow.

After Lenin's death in 1924, Petrograd was renamed in his honor—Leningrad. Monumental tragedy struck again in 1941 when Hitler's armies entered Russia and began a siege of Leningrad that lasted 900 days. In the course of the three-year siege, some 650,000 citizens died of starvation, and thousands more were killed in air-raid attacks.

After the war, intrepid Leningrad rose again. Today it is home to some five million people, all of whom display pride in their city's historic and cultural legacy.

Attractions

**Admiralty (Admiralteiystvo) [20]: Baroque and Classical styles are united in this splendid building, constructed between 1806 and 1823 on the site of the city's first wharf and shipyard. The lavish sculptures symbolize Russia's maritime power, and the gilded spire acts as a city landmark.

Alexander Nevsky Monastery (Aleksandr Nevskaya Lavra) [30]: Founded in 1710 by Peter the Great on the site of a great 13th-century victory by Prince Alexander Nevsky, this important complex was one of the four most important monasteries in pre-Revolutionary Russia. It consists of ten churches, four cemeteries, a seminary, and a *Museum of Urban Sculpture* (located in the Church of the Annunciation). *Holy Trinity Cathedral* is one of the few churches still operating in the country. Music-lovers may wish to pay their respects to Tchaikovsky, Mussorgsky, Rimsky-Korsakov, and Rachmaninov—all of whom rest in the *Tikvinsky necropolis.*

Botanical Gardens (Botanitschesky Sad) [37]: One of the largest herbariums in the world is located in the northern section of the gardens.

*Central Lenin Museum (Musei W. I. Lenin), Chalturina Ulitsa 5/I [23]: A multitude of exhibits trace the life and activities of the founder of the Communist Party and the creator of the Soviet State. In the vestibule stands the armored car from which Lenin spoke to the workers after his return from exile in 1917.

Central Naval Museum (Tsentralny Voenno-Morskoi Musei) [6]: Housed in the former Stock Exchange building, the museum has more than 150,000 ship models.

*Cottage of Peter the Great (Domik Petra Pervogo) [3]: When Peter the Great was supervising the construction of his new capital in 1703, he lived in this two-room cabin, whose logs were painted to look like bricks; Catherine II erected its protective stone enclosure.

*Cruiser Aurora (Creiser Avrora) [4]: The *Aurora* was an important base of support for the Bolshevists. In 1917, the cruiser sailed up the Neva River and fired its cannon once: This was the signal for the Bolshevists to storm the Winter Palace.

Decembrist Square (Plo-

Cruiser *Aurora*

szhad Dekabristov) [18]: This square was named for the officers who pressed for reforms in 1825 and were rewarded with death or exile for their efforts. It is the home of the amazing **Monument to Peter the Great,* shown astride a rearing horse that is trampling a serpent (symbolizing his Swedish opponents). The monument inscription reads: To Peter the First from Catherine the Second, 1782. The largest church in the city, ****Saint Isaac's Cathedral** (Isakijewsky Sobor) [19], now a museum, stands in the southern part of the square. It took over 40 years to build this richly adorned monument, with its gilded dome and lavish interior of marble and malachite.

Field of Mars (Marsowo Polye) [24]: An eternal flame burns in the *Memorial to the Victims of the Revolution* in these 19th-century military parade grounds.

Finland Station (Finljandsky Wokzal) [27]: A bronze *Monu-*

St. Isaac's Cathedral

ment to Lenin commemorates his arrival here in 1917 after ten years in exile.

Great Mosque (Metschet), Revolution Square: Commissioned by a mistress of Nicholas II and built in 1912, this is the only mosque in the city.

***Hermitage Museum (see *Winter Palace*).

Institute of Coal, Iron, and Steel (Gornyj Institut) [9]: An impressive Doric colonnade imparts grandeur to this museum that's on the agenda of all Russian schoolchildren.

Kirov Islands (Kirowskije Ostrowa): Three islands in the Neva delta—*Island of the Cross, Yelagin Island,* and the *Island of the Workers*—are known collectively as the Kirov Islands. They were once filled with the country homes of the aristocracy, some of which still stand. After the Revolution in 1917, the islands became a popular recreation area. The *Kirov Culture and Recreation Park* [36] was laid out on Yelagin, and is

dominated by Carlo Rossi's first commission—a palace for Alexander I built in the 1820s.

Lenin Park: Both the *Zoo and the *Planetarium* are located in this crescent-shaped park enclosed by Gorky Prospekt.

Museum of the Great Socialist October Revolution (Musei Welikoj Oktjabrskoy Sotsialistitschekoy Rewoljutsii) [2]: The museum, whose exhibits illustrate the history of the revolutionary movement in Russia, is housed in the early 20th-century villa once owned by the ballerina Mathilda Kshessinskaya, Nicholas II's mistress.

National University of Leningrad (Leningradsky Gosudarstvenny Universitet) [8]: Over 20,000 students attend classes in this complex of 12 identical buildings completed in 1741.

**Nevsky Prospekt: A forest path that was enlarged and made into a "Great Perspective Road" in 1783, became the most fashionable avenue in the city. About 5 km. (3 miles) long, the Nevsky, as it's called by residents, is lined with structures ranging from 18th-century Baroque palaces to postwar examples of Soviet urban development, including museums, theaters, shops, and cafés.

***Peter and Paul Fortress (Petropavlovskaya Krepost) [1]: The first structure built by Peter the Great in 1703, the fortress eventually became a prison for opponents of the czarist regime: these included Peter the Great's own son, who died under torture,

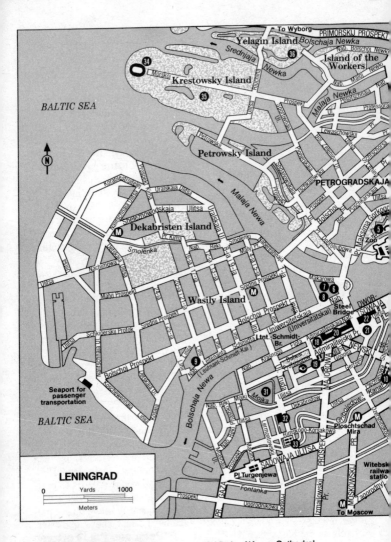

Leningrad Attractions:
1. Peter and Paul Fortress
2. Museum of the Revolution
3. Cottage of Peter the Great
4. Cruiser *Aurora*
5. Artillery Museum
6. Central Naval Museum
7. Pushkin House
8. University of Leningrad
9. Institute of Coal, Iron, and Steel
10. Virgin of Kasan Cathedral
11. Square of the Arts
12. Russian Museum
13. Comedy Theater
14. National Library
15. Ostrovsky Square
16. Pushkin Theater
17. Moscow Railway Station
18. Decembrist Square
19. St. Isaac's Cathedral

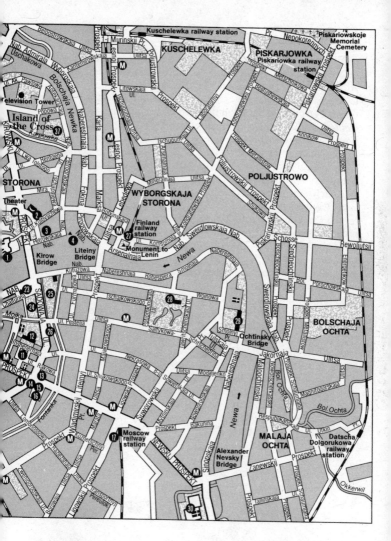

and the great writer Dostoevski before he was exiled to Siberia. All the Russian czars from Peter I to Alexander III (with the exception of Peter II) are buried in the *Cathedral of Saints Peter and Paul* (Petropavlovsky Sabor) [B], with its thin golden spire, located in the center of the fortress. *Peter's Gate* (Petrovsky Vorota) [A] is a triumphal arch erected in 1718. The small English ship with which Peter the Great learned to sail was once docked in the *Boat House* (Botnyj Domik) [C]. The *Mint* (Monetnyj Dwor) [D], where gold, silver, and copper coins were manufactured, dates from 1806; behind it, on the west wall of the fortress, is the *Trubetskoy Bastion* [E]. *Neva Gate* (Nevskaya Vorota) [F], at the fortress's south wall, was also known as the Gate of Death because criminals were led through it before being executed. A cannon shot is fired here every day at noon. Russian armaments from the 15th century to the present day are housed in the *Central Artillery Museum* (Tsentralnj Woyennoistoritschesky Musei Artillerii) [G].

Pushkin House (Institut Russky Literaturi—Puschkinsky Dom) [7]: Lovers of Russian literature will find manuscripts, letters, and archival materials from almost every Russian writer of the 18th and 19th centuries here.

*Pushkin Memorial Museum (Musei Kvartira Pushkina), 12 Moyka: The famous poet and writer *(Eugene Onegin),* mortally wounded in an 1837 duel, lived and died in this three-story house.

Pushkin Theater [16]: Six Corinthian columns decorate the front of this Empire-style theater, once known as the Alexandra. It faces Nevsky Prospekt and forms part of **Ostrovsky Square* (Ostrowskogo Ploschtschad) [15], one of the many masterful compositions designed by the architect Carlo Rossi. A *Monument to Catherine the Great* rises above the square in the center of a large gar-

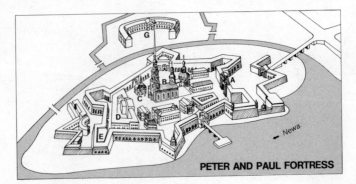

PETER AND PAUL FORTRESS

den. The street behind the theater, named *Rossi Ulitsa* in honor of the ubiquitous architect, is the location of the *Theatre Museum* and the *Waganowa Ballet School*. Pavlova and Nijinsky once studied here.

**Saint Nicholas of the Mariners Cathedral (Nikolsky Morskoy Sobor) [33]: An example of Russian Baroque, the cathedral features a magnificent interior colonnade.

**Smolny Monastery and Institute (Smolny Monastyr) [29]: One of Leningrad's most important historical complexes, the cathedral and convent of the monastery were built by Czarina Elizabeth. The institute, a school for young ladies of the nobility, was founded during the reign of Catherine the Great. In 1917, Lenin assumed the leadership of the Bolshevist revolution here; he lived and worked in a room that is now a museum.

Square of the Arts [11]: In the middle of this enormous architectural complex stands **Michael Palace (Mikhailovsky Dvorets), designed by Carlo Rossi and completed in 1825 for Grand Duke Michael, the youngest son of the Emperor Paul. The neoclassical palace, is a fine example of an aristocrat's town estate. It now houses the ****Museum of Russian Art* (Gosudarstvenni Russky Musei) [12], whose vast holdings encompass an unsurpassed collection of 12th-century icons, oils from the 17th through the 19th centuries, and examples of more

recent Soviet Realism. Every culture in the USSR is represented in the east wing's **Ethnographic Museum*.

**Summer Garden (Letny Sad) [25]: This popular and attractive park, filled with fine statuary, was laid out in a regular, geometric French style in the early 18th century. The two-story ***Summer Palace of Peter I* (Dvorets-Musei Petra I), painted primrose yellow and built in the Dutch style for Peter the Great, is located on the banks of the Kutuzov Embankment.

Taurida Palace (Tavritscheksky Dvorets) [28]: Built at the command of Catherine the Great between 1783 and 1789 for her lover, Potemkin, who conquered the Crimea and earned the title Prince of Tauria, the palace is a superb example of neoclassicism and has opulent interiors. The czarist Parliament met here from 1906 to 1917, after which the palace became a working and meeting place for revolutionary factions.

Virgin of Kasan Cathedral (Kazansky Sobor) [10]: Constructed between 1801 and 1811, the cathedral's enormous dome was modeled after St. Peter's in Rome. The cathedral was the first building to use cast iron as a structural element in architecture. It now houses the *Museum of Religion and Atheism*.

***Winter Palace (Zimnniy Dvorets) [22]: The Italian architect Rastrelli designed this grandiose, 18th-century Baroque palace as a home for the czars and czarinas of imperial Russia, a line that extended from Peter the Great's daughter Elizabeth to the last members of the Romanoff dynasty, who were executed at the time of the Revolution. The luxurious interiors, decorated with marble, jasper, rare woods and precious jewels, now act as a dazzling setting for the world-famous ***Hermitage Museum,* one of the greatest collections of art in the world. Housed in the Winter Palace and four adjacent buildings, the Hermitage has seven major collections, and includes Rembrandts, Titians, da Vincis, Raphaels, Impressionist and post-Impressionist works, as well as antiquities. A special tour of the *Gold Treasure Room* will let you see the fabulous jewels of Catherine the Great and a collection of Scythian gold. ***Palace Square* (Dvortsovaya Ploschtschad) [21], located between the Winter Palace and the Admiralty Building, was the stage for the major events that led to the overthrow of the czarist regime and the foundation of the Soviet Union. It was here that Czar Nicholas II gave orders to his army to fire on the hundreds of thousands of people who had marched to the palace to deliver a petition for reform in 1905. The "Great Socialist October Revolution" also began here in 1917, when the revolutionaries stormed the palace. The pink granite *Column of Alexander* (Aleksandrowskaya Kolonna), erected in 1834, stands in the center of the square.

Excursions

Petrodvorets (Peter's Court), about 32 km. (20 miles) southwest of Leningrad (leave the city by Stacek Prospekt or, in summer, take the hydrofoil down the Neva River to the Gulf of Finland): This 300-acre park and palace is located on the southern shore of the Gulf of Finland. Its construction was supervised by Peter the Great and meant to outshine Versailles. The terraced landscape, filled with small palaces, pavilions, and an amazing system of fountains, slopes down to the sea. The **Great Palace,* located between the Upper and Lower Parks, was begun in 1714 and completely redesigned by Rastrelli a few decades later. The **Great Cascade,* best viewed from the large terrace in front of the palace, abounds with gilded statues and decorative sculpture, bas-reliefs, two cascading staircases, 64 fountains, and a magnificent grotto. Its centerpiece is the awe-inspiring *Samson Fountain,* in which a geyser of water spews from the open mouth of a lion whose jaws Samson is prying apart.

Pushkin, 22 km. (14 miles) south of Leningrad along Moscow Prospekt, train service from Vitebsky Station with buses and taxis available at Pushkin: *Yekaterinsky Palace,* named for Catherine I, the wife of Peter the Great, is located in a 1,482-acre park. The palace, built in the 18th century, has an unusual aqua façade decorated with gold and white; part of it is now a museum. Another museum here is dedicated to the poet and writer Alexander Pushkin, for whom the village was named on the centenary of his death. Less than 3 km. (2 miles) from Pushkin is *Pavlovsk,* site of a beautifully restored palace that was a gift from Catherine the Great to her son Paul in 1777. Once used for hunting, the palace grounds today form one of the largest landscaped parks in Europe.

Lisbon

No other capital city in Europe retains as much Old World charm as Lisbon. You won't find anonymous fast-food restaurants or ubiquitous cash machines here—instead, you'll stroll down broad, 18th-century boulevards accented by mosaics, savor dishes made with fresh seafood caught in the nearby Atlantic, climb steep, cobblestone streets to visit ancient churches and modern museums, and wander through a fascinating medieval quarter where the avenues are so narrow you must walk single-file. All the while, you'll notice the drenching sunshine that creates a warm glow around the buildings painted with pastel colors and roofed with clay tiles. The closest that hilly Lisbon comes to technological wizardry is the series of charming old elevators and cable cars that ascend to the highest parts of the city, including the first elevator designed by Eiffel. Lisbon shook off a stultifying dictatorship in 1974, and is working hard to enter the modern world; but before it catches up, you'll be able to experience a city where the old Moorish influence can still be seen and felt. Here, the brooding guitar-accompanied songs called *fado* echo the soul of this ancient, fascinating city.

History

Lisbon, thanks to its location on the Tagus (or Tejo) River only 8 km. (5 miles) from the Atlantic Ocean, has been an important port since the days of the seafaring Phoenicians—over 3,000 years ago. Its natural harbor and location also attracted every band of marauding conquerors known to the ancient world: Greeks, Carthaginians, Romans, Visigoths, and finally the Moors, who made it their stronghold in 716 and occupied the city until 1255. The Moorish influence can still be seen in the architecture of the oldest sections of Lisbon.

A city of sea trade and exploration, Lisbon became one of the greatest of maritime powers in the Middle Ages, rivaling Genoa and outstripping Venice. Great explorers like Vasco da Gama set out from its harbor to find new trade routes and revenues.

Although the Spanish seized control of Lisbon after conquering the Moors, the Portuguese threw off Spanish domination in 1640 and ushered in a second "Golden Age." The city—the westernmost capital in Europe—was sufficiently isolated, however, so that it was barely influenced by the artistic and social currents that swept through the rest of Europe. The Renaissance hardly left a mark on Lisbon (neither did the Reformation nor even the Industrial Revolution).

On All Saints' Day (November 1) in 1755, a violent earthquake and tidal wave shook Lisbon to its foundations, killing some 60,000 people and reducing the entire city to rubble—with the exception of the old Moorish quarter called the Alfama. As a result, the historic sections of the city are dominated by 18th-century planning and proportions.

Lisbon remained the capital of a sizeable colonial empire until fairly recently. After the Portuguese king abdicated in 1910, a republic was proclaimed under the dictatorship of Antonio Salazar, who kept the city and country under strict rein. Lisbon remained much like a small town, but the revolution of 1974 forced dramatic changes when a democratically inspired junta gained control of the country. In the years of transition to a parliamentary form of government, Lisbon was inundated by refugees from Angola, its last major colonial holding. The city was sliding into a physical decline. More recently, however, Lisbon has been able to solve its most pressing social problems and has experienced a renewed vitality—all of which is reflected in the city today.

Attractions

**Alfama: is in the oldest section of Lisbon. One of the most intriguing and colorful locales in all of Europe, it's characterized by cobbled, shoulder-wide streets lit by wrought-iron lamps, vigorous fishwives *(varinas)* who trundle up the hill with baskets of the day's catch balanced on their heads, mysterious, winding, back alleys and stairs, balconies bright with geraniums and noisy canaries, hole-in-the-wall taverns decorated with garlands of garlic and peppers, and intimate restaurants where, late at night, you can listen to the distinctive Portuguese songs called *fado*. Some of the buildings here are Moorish, while others are medieval.

*Avenida da Liberdade [4]: Lisbon's answer to the Champs-Élysées, this splendid, busy avenue, lined with flowers and trees, stretches from the Baixa area near the river to Parque Eduardo VII.

Basilica da Estrela, Largo da Estrela: A famous landmark of the city, this Baroque church with its enormous stone dome was built in the late 18th century; beautiful marbles were used in the interior. Facing the church across the square are the *Estrela Gardens* and, beyond them, the *English*

Alfama

Cemetery, where the novelist Henry Fielding was laid to rest.

**Castelo de São Jorge (St. George's Castle) [11]: Perched on one of Lisbon's highest hills and providing spectacular views of the city, the ten-towered castle was originally built in the fifth century by the Visigoths and later revamped. White peacocks strut in the gardens of the Arabic palace used by the kings of Portugal from the 14th to the 16th centuries.

Cathedral (Sé) [9]: As much a fortress as a church, the cathedral of Lisbon was damaged in two earthquakes. It combines an original 12th-century, Romanesque-style façade with Gothic and Baroque elements in its interior.

Largo de Sant Luzia [10]: Lisbon offers several *miradouros* or observation terraces throughout the city, and from this one, atop the Moorish town wall, you have a view down over the steep valleys of the ancient Alfama section. The **Museum of Decorative Art,** featuring a series of authentically decorated Portuguese rooms, is housed in the Azurara palace in the *Largo das Portas do Sol,* on the northwest side of Largo de Sant Luzia.

Largo do Salvador [12]: Walk east from here along the *Rua Guilherme Braga* and you'll come to the *Largo de Santo Estevao,* where another panoramic view of the old town and harbor unfolds. Close to the *Santo Estevao church* is the small flower market called *Patio das Flores;* the surrounding houses are decorated with azulejos tiles.

**Gulbenkian Museum [6]: The superb pre-modern collection includes numerous Old Masters as well as several French Impressionist works; there are also Islamic art works, Chinese vases, Japanese lacquer work, and an enormous collection of ancient coins.

**Museum of Ancient Art (Museu Nacional de Arte Antiga) [13]: Partially housed in a former palace, the multifaceted collection here includes German, Dutch, Italian, and Spanish paintings, as well as many examples of Portuguese work.

Nossa Senhora de Conçeicao Velha [8]: First built in 1520, this church was reconstructed after the earthquake of 1755.

Ponte Vinte e Cinco de Abril (25th of April Bridge) [14]: One of the longest suspension bridges in Europe was named for the day when Salazar's dictatorship was overthrown in 1974. On the southern shore of the Tagus

Lisbon Attractions:
1. Praça do Comércio
2. Praça Dom Pedro IV
3. Praça dos Restauradores
4. Avenida da Liberdade
5. Praça Marquês de Pombal
6. Gulbenkian Museum
7. Zoo
8. Nossa Senhora da Conceiçao Velha
9. Cathedral
10. Largo de Santa Luzia
11. Castelo de Sao Jorge
12. Largo de Salvador
13. Museum of Ancient Art
14. Ponte Vinte e Cinco de Abril
15. Museu dos Coches
16. Mostiero dos Jeronimos
17. Torre de Belém

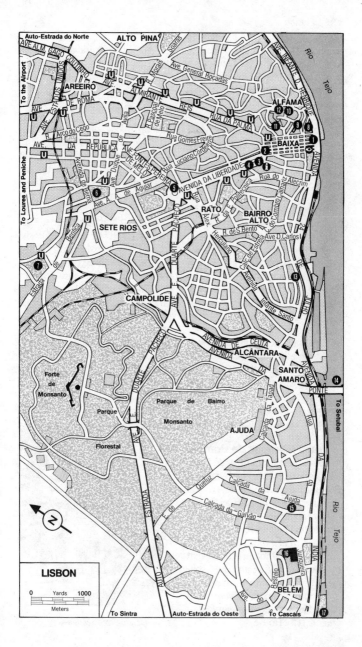

River is the enormous statue of *Christo Rei* (Christ the King) with a marvelous view from the top.

Praça do Comércio [1]: Formerly the site of Manuel I's royal palace, which was dramatically washed away by the 1755 tidal wave, the square is now framed on three sides by 18th-century, arcaded buildings. An equestrian statue of King José stands in the center.

*Praça Dom Pedro IV [2]: Cafés and restaurants line Lisbon's main square, the *Rossio;* the area is inlaid with black and white mosaic work, with fountains and a columnar monument to King Pedro IV. To the north is the neoclassical *National Theater.* The ruins of the *Convento do Carmo* stand above the southwest corner of the square; next to them is one of the street elevators that ascend to the higher parts of the city.

Praça dos Restauradores [3]: An obelisk commemorates the people who rebelled against the Spanish and restored Portugal's independence in 1640.

Praça Marquês de Pombal [5]: A memorial statue of de Pombal, a progressive, 18th-century Portuguese politician, overlooks the lower town of Baxtia; he had the area rebuilt after the earthquake. Just behind it stretches the beautiful *Parque Eduardo VII,* created in 1904 for an official visit by the King of England; rare species of plants thrive in its two greenhouses, one an *Estufa Fria* (Cool House), the other an *Estufa Quente* (Hot House).

Zoo [7]: Originally a royal park, Lisbon's zoo is one of the loveliest in Europe.

Lisbon Belém

Several major attractions are located in the suburb of Belém, which lies along the Tagus River about 7 km. (4 miles) west of the city center. Buses and trams leave regularly from the Praça do Comercio.

Museu Nacional dos Coches (Coach Museum) [15]: The idea of traveling in luxury gains new meaning once you've seen the three golden Baroque coaches made in Rome in 1716; dozens of other coaches make up this fascinating museum housed in the east wing of the *Paço de Belém,* once a royal castle and now the residence of the Portuguese president.

Hieronymite Monastery

***Mosteiro dos Jeronimos** (Hieronymite Monastery) [16]: A magnificent example of the late Gothic Portuguese architecture known as Manueline, the monastery was begun in the first years of the 16th century by King Manuel I, who wanted to give thanks for Vasco da Gama's successful voyage to India (and the revenue from spices that resulted). The great explorer, who set sail in 1497 from the Tagus just across from the monastery, is buried here, as are the Portuguese kings. The **Claustro* (Cloister) is renowned for the beauty of its slender columns and vaulting. An *Ethnological Museum* and *Naval Museum* are now housed in the former monastery.

Tower of Belém

*Torre de Belém** (Tower of Belém) [17]: Another superb piece of Manueline architecture and a landmark symbol of the city, the quadrangular tower was originally built between 1515 and 1521 on an island in the Tagus River, which has since changed its course. On a terrace atop the tower stands a statue of Our Lady of Safe Homecoming, seen from afar by returning seamen.

Excursions

Estoril (25 km.; 16 miles west) and **Cascais** (31 km.; 20 miles west), both easily reached by train from Lisbon's Cais do Sodre station, are international beach resorts with hotels, racing, gambling casinos, and seafood restaurants. Estoril became famous during the Second World War when it was filled with spies for both sides; Portugal itself was neutral.

Sintra (32 km.; 20 miles northwest), which you can reach by train from Lisbon's Rossio station, is one of the oldest towns in Portugal and once served as the summer residence for royalty. The *Paço Real* (Royal Palace), entered by a drawbridge, sits in a 500-acre park that is both an arboretum and a botanical garden. There is also a 16th-century Capuchin monastery and the 19th century *Castelo da Pena*, built in a mixture of styles.

London

London is a world center in many respects—culturally, ethnically, politically, and economically. Boasting a long, rich history, outstanding art and architecture, and a colorful and cosmopolitan population, the sprawling city on the Thames has managed to retain an atmosphere that's good-natured, comfortable, and, for the most part, user-friendly—a rarity for such a teeming metropolis. You'll find an abundance of museums, monuments, and historic byways and buildings that trace this city's heritage from the Middle Ages to the Swinging Sixties. A wide variety of neighborhoods can be explored—from ebullient Camden and romantic Chelsea to the resurrected Docklands and posh Mayfair—and you can still travel to most areas by red, double-decker bus. Only in London do Cockney vendors hawk their wares, enthusiastic buskers (of both classical and rock persuasions) enliven Tube (subway) stations, and royalty make public bows and not-so-private scandals: These are but a small segment of the nearly seven million who live in the square-mile "City" proper and the surrounding 32 boroughs (11 million if you consider the ever-growing suburbs). It's no wonder that this city of countless contrasts is one of the world's top tourist meccas: Its theater excels, its shops and stalls entice, its parks seem ever green, its palaces shine, its pubs overflow with easy chat and pints of bitter, and its list of attractions is endless.

History

A Celtic settlement was located on the site of present-day London as early as the pre-Roman period. The name of the city is probably derived from the Celtic *Llyn-Din,* which later became Londinium in Latin. The vicinity was described by the Roman historian Tacitus as a "flourishing trade community." In A.D. 43, invading Romans built the first bridge over the Thames, and by the end of the next century, the area encompassing today's City of London was enclosed within a fortification wall. Around 450, some four decades after the Roman legions had withdrawn from Britannia, the Angles, Saxons, and Jutes began to take possession of the land. The Benedictine monk Augustine came to Britain as a missionary in 596. Two hundred years later, under Anglo-Saxon rule, London became a royal residence for the first time. During the ninth century, the city was plundered several times by invading Vikings; in 884, Alfred the Great, King of Wessex and overlord of England, made London the capital of his empire. Alfred had defeated the Danes and encouraged the learning of English, but less than two centuries later, the Danish king Canute conquered England (1016–1035).

William I (the Conqueror), Duke of Normandy, conquered the Anglo-Saxon king Harold II in the Battle of Hastings and became the first English king to be crowned in Westminster Abbey; he ruled from 1066 to 1087. In 1191, the people elected Henry Fitz Aylwin London's first Lord Mayor, proof of the power of the crafts guilds in this growing port city that thrived on commerce and trade. In 1215, the privileges of the City of London were established with the signing of the Magna Carta, thus enabling the citizens to elect their own Lord Mayor (even though the choice had to be confirmed by the king). Under the powerful guilds of the 15th century, London experienced an incredible period of rapid prosperity. The city became one of the largest, wealthiest, and most powerful in all of Europe.

During the reign of Henry VIII (1509–1547), England broke away from Rome and set up its own Church of England. Blood was shed over religious loyalties during these years and those of Mary I (1553–1558), whose fierce devotion to Roman Catholicism provoked a purge of non-Catholics and earned her the nickname "Bloody Mary." The rule of Anglican Elizabeth I (1558–1603) witnessed the flourishing of the arts and sciences in London. Theaters on the south bank of the Thames (the Swan, the Rose, and the Globe) produced the plays of the period's great dramatists, with Shakespeare at its crest. With James I (1603–1625), the House of Stuart ascended the English throne. His quarrels with the Puritans, who were heavily represented in the House of Commons, led to the Gunpowder Plot of 1605—a vain attempt by the Catholics, led by Guy Fawkes, to blow up the king and Parliament. Charles I (ruled 1626–1649), ignoring the demands of Parliament, disbanded the House of Commons, and the country was wracked by civil war. He was executed in front of Whitehall Palace and the Republic was proclaimed, with Oliver Cromwell residing in the palace as Lord Protector (1649–1658).

Meanwhile, the City of London had grown to nearly half a million residents in the 17th century, and it began to experience its share of urban ills: overcrowding, crime, poverty, and filth. Epidemics spread throughout the population, and a catastrophic disaster occurred in 1666: The Great Fire of London raged for four days, leaving approximately four-fifths of the city in ashes. Planning and rebuilding commenced, with larger markets, wider streets, stone (not wood) structures, and various other urban improvements. Despite its disasters, the new London quickly reclaimed its prominent position in Britain and Europe, and by 1801—the year of the first official census—its population swelled to over one million and its boundaries had been extended to include rural hamlets and villages once far outside the city limits.

During the long reign of Queen Victoria (1837–1901), London experienced another period of phenomenal growth and prosperity, becoming, in turn, the cultural, intellectual, and commercial hub of Europe. At the same time, however, the Industrial Revolution contributed to a spate of big-city troubles—slums, starvation, and child labor abuses among them. In the 20th century, the city was victimized twice by foreign invaders. During World War II, London was heavily bombed by the Germans, causing over 30,000 deaths and untold damage, especially in the City, where nearly all the churches and civil buildings were badly hit. But by 1950, London had revived and rebuilt itself—with prosperity again the end product of this pattern. Two years later, a new monarch, Elizabeth II, ascended the throne in a flurry of pomp.

The London of the past thirty years has continued to grow and thrive for the most part. Although its city politics are no longer centralized since the Greater London Council was disbanded in 1986, it is still a city of great power, wealth, culture, tenacity, and diversity. To many it reigns supreme in the arts, especially the theater, and its economic, commercial, and financial sectors are of world importance.

Attractions

Albert Memorial [21], Kensington Gore, SW7: Opposite the concert hall also bearing his name, this High Victorian monument was designed by Sir George Gilbert Scott as a memorial to the Prince Regent after the Great Exhibition at the Crystal Palace in Hyde Park in 1851.

Apsley House [17], 149 Piccadilly: The gifted neoclassical architect Robert Adam designed this elegant house in the late 18th century; it served as the Duke of Wellington's town residence. Today it houses the Wellington Museum, displaying a wealth of objects relating to the Duke (whose equestrian statue stands across the way, in Hyde Park Corner).

Bank of England [35], Threadneedle St., EC2: The outer walls designed by Sir John Soane in the late 18th century still stand, although the massive structure—

which holds the country's gold reserves—was rebuilt in the 1920s.

Banqueting House [4], Whitehall, SW1: Inigo Jones designed this Palladian-style building, one of the few remaining structures of the old Whitehall Palace. Rubens painted the allegorical ceiling canvases in the great hall in the 1630s, and Oliver Cromwell later held his parliaments here.

Barbican Arts Centre, London Wall, EC2: A concert hall, museum, and theatres comprise this 1982 cultural enclave near the City, built around and named after remains of the old London Wall.

Bethnal Green Museum, Cambridge Heath Rd., E2: A diverse collection of dolls and dollhouses, toys and games, costumes, and textiles is on display in this 1872 red-brick structure, initially set up for the benefit of the East End's poor residents.

Bloomsbury, WC1: Virginia Woolf and her set made the area famous, and Bloomsbury still retains some of its Edwardian elegance. The British Museum, University of London, and countless academic and publishing offices are located here.

***British Museum [48], Great Russell St., WC1: One of the world's greatest repositories of art and artifacts, the sprawling British Museum displays room after room of priceless treasures, most famous among them the Elgin Marbles (sculptures from the Parthenon in Athens), the Rosetta Stone, and the Portland Vase, a superb example of early Roman glass. The *British Library,* presently in the museum but scheduled to move into its own new building within the next few years, displays the Magna Carta, the Lindisfarne Gospels, and other outstanding manuscripts and books; it was here Karl Marx researched and wrote *Das Kapital.*

British Telecom Tower (Post Office) [55], Howland St., W1: Once London's tallest structure (surpassed by the NatWest Bank's high-rise in the City), the 1966 tower is still an imposing landmark in this sprawling metropolis.

*Buckingham Palace [11], St. James's Park, SW1: The London residence of the British sovereign since Victoria ascended the throne in 1837, this impressive,

Buckingham Palace

early 18th-century pile—rebuilt by Nash in 1825 and refaced with Portland stone in 1913—is closed to the public, except for the Queen's Gallery and the Royal Mews. Changing of the Guard takes place daily at 11:30 A.M. In front of the palace is the *Victoria Memorial,* depicting the monarch seated amid various allegorical figures.

Camden Lock, Chalk Farm Rd. at Regent's Canal, NW6: A lively weekend market brings thousands to this area, where bric-a-brac, crafts, bootleg cassettes, and punk haircuts, among other sundries, can be bought. Boat rides on and walks along the canal are popular pastimes, but the people-watching alone is worth the trip.

Camden Passage, off Islington High St., N1: Every Wednesday morning and all-day Saturday, antique hunters flock to this charming market, a hodgepodge of temporary stalls and permanent shops tucked in around and about the Passage; some good restaurants are also located in the area.

Carnaby Street, W1: Although lined with slightly tacky souvenir shops and T-shirt boutiques, the pedestrians-only street made famous in London's Swinging Sixties still merits a stroll for its memories of the era.

Central Criminal Court [31], Old Bailey, EC4: Located on the site of the old Newgate Prison, the Old Bailey, as it's more commonly called, has 23 courtrooms where criminal justice is meted out. The Goddess of Justice, sitting atop the court's dome, is famous for *not* wearing a blindfold.

Charing Cross Road, W2: New and used books are sold up and down the road; the gigantic *Foyle's,* at numbers 119–125, has to be seen to be believed.

Chelsea, SW3: Once the haunt of artists, writers, and assorted aesthetes (and the birthplace of the miniskirt), this lively neighborhood, tucked between the Thames and Knightsbridge-Kensington, features trendy boutiques, lovely restaurants, and tempting antiques shops. Its hub is the King's Road, but for a true feel for the area, veer off the beaten track (and away from the ever-milling throng).

Chinatown, environs Gerrard St., W1: Chinese restaurants, food markets, video shops, and gift shops abound in this fairly small but bustling Soho enclave.

Courtauld Institute Galleries, Strand, WC2: The Courtauld's collection of French Impressionists is dazzling, but so are its holdings of Old Masters. (Note: The Courtauld is scheduled to open in its new location at Somerset House in May 1990.)

Covent Garden [26], WC2: Centering on the wrought-iron stalls from the old Flower Market, Covent Garden is a bustling mass of stall-holders, restaurants, shops, and tourists. Two museums are in the area as well, the London Transport Museum and the V & A's Theatre Museum.

Design Museum, Butlers Wharf, Shad Thames, SE1: The newly opened Thames-side museum displays a wealth of 20th-century products, from vintage typewriters and up-to-the-minute computers (some of which you can operate), to Bakelite radios and portable Sony Walkman stereos.

Docklands, east of Tower Bridge along the Thames: In past centuries, this was the busiest harbor area in the world. It is now in the midst of massive urban redevelopment with many newspapers relocating here, immense building and renovating projects, and people moving in. The next decade should markedly change this area in terms of its skyline, populace, and flavor. Take the Docklands Light Railway from Tower Bridge to the Isle of Dogs or elsewhere for an above-ground glimpse of this old East End neighborhood-turned-building-site.

Downing Street, SW1: The most famous resident lives at number 10—the British Prime Minister—on this street of 17th-century residences built by Sir George Downing.

East End: In London's East

End, an area steeped in history, pubs, markets, and authentic Londoners speaking in heavy Cockney accents (sometimes in rhyme), you can eat a bagel for breakfast, have a curry for lunch, and snack on jellied eel from a seafood stall. You'll also come upon some of London's most beautiful old churches and other buildings, tucked between 1960s council housing and tumble-down warehouses. It's best to visit on a Sunday, when the Petticoat Lane and Brick Lane markets are in full swing, brimming over with colorful vendors and gullible buyers.

Freud Museum, 20 Maresfield Gardens, NW3: After fleeing his native Vienna, the eminent psychoanalyst lived and practiced at this location; many of his possessions are on view, including his impressive antiquities collection.

Geffrye Museum, Kingsland Rd., E2: This gem of a museum, hidden among ugly high-rise council houses, deserves a visit. Located in a charming group of 18th-century almshouses, the Geffrye displays a series of English period rooms, from an Elizabethan paneled room to a 1930s lounge.

Gray's Inn [51], Holborn, WC1: An Inn of the Court since the 14th century, Gray's Inn has a lovely garden (open to outsiders only at lunchtime on weekdays). Heavily damaged by German bombs, the brick edifices underwent extensive reconstruction.

Greenwich, SE10: A visit to the home of the *Cutty Sark,* the Royal Naval College, Old Royal Observatory, and National Maritime Museum (see separate entry) is well worth it. The area also teems with charming gift and antiques shops, restaurants, and cafés. A foot tunnel takes you across the Thames to the Isle of Dogs in the Docklands area.

Guildhall [36], Aldermansbury, off Gresham St., EC2: This 15th-century structure (with an 18th-century, neo-Gothic façade and still later restorations) often hosts grand ceremonies, which take place in its Great Hall. The seat of the City government, Guildhall is also the location of a *Clock Museum* that displays some 700 timepieces from five centuries. Parts of its 15th-century crypt are extant, as is a lovely window from the same period.

H.M.S. Belfast, Symons Wharf, Vine Lane, SE1: The biggest cruiser ever built for the Royal Navy is now a permanently berthed museum. It served from World War II to the 1960's.

Hampstead Heath, NW3: One of London's loveliest, most rural parks, with hills, paths, and ponds. The surrounding "village" is worth meandering through as well, with its shops, restaurants, and handsome houses along quiet, tree-lined lanes. Try to visit *Fenton House* in Hampstead Grove, a late 17th-century, red-brick building with a collection of musical instruments, Chinese and European porcelain, and other decorative arts.

Harrods, Knightsbridge, SW1: A world-class mecca for shoppers, Harrods is a one-stop

London Attractions:

1. Trafalgar Square
2. National Gallery
3. St. Martin's in the Fields
4. Banqueting House
5. Horse Guards
6. Houses of Parliament and Westminster Hall
7. Westminster Abbey
8. Tate Gallery
9. Victoria Station
10. Westminster Cathedral
11. Buckingham Palace
12. Green Park
13. St. James's Park
14. St. James's Palace
15. Admiralty Arch
16. Piccadilly Circus
17. Apsley House
18. Hyde Park
19. Marble Arch
20. Kensington Palace
21. Albert Memorial
22. Royal Albert Hall
23. Science Museum
24. Natural History Museum
25. Victoria and Albert Museum
26. Covent Garden
27. St. Mary le Strand
28. St. Clement Danes
29. Law Courts
30. The Temple

LONDON

0   Yards   500

Meters

emporium. Don't miss the Food Halls, beautifully tiled and temptingly stocked.

Hayward Gallery [43], South Bank Arts Centre: The Hayward, which hosts a wide variety of temporary exhibitions, is a significant component of the massive South Banks complex.

Highgate Cemetery, Swains Lane, N6: The older part of this immense, largely overgrown burial ground was set out in the Tudor Gothic style; it is well worth seeing on a guided tour (you're not allowed to see it on your own), not only for the Victorian gravestones and mausoleums, but for the flora as well. Karl Marx's grave is dominated by an imposing bust (and always surrounded by curious or respectful visitors).

Hogarth's House, Hogarth Lane, Great West Rd., W4: This 17th-century house was the eminent engraver's country retreat; numerous relics and works of art are on view.

Horniman Museum, 100 London Rd., SE23: An eccentric turn-of-the-century Art Nouveau structure houses an eclectic collection of ethnographic objects, natural history specimens, musical instruments, and more.

***Horse Guards** [5], Whitehall, SW1: A mounted military presence stands at attention in front of this barrack of the royal cavalry. The guards change weekdays at 11:00 A.M., Sundays at 10:00 A.M.

***Houses of Parliament** [6], Parliament Sq., SW1: An impressive, Victorian spread—occu-pying some 20 hectares (8 acres) on the site of the 11th-century palace of Edward the Confessor—the Houses of Parliament stand majestically on the Thames. The clock tower's 13-ton bell, *Big Ben,* rings on the hour. Sir Charles Barry's neo-Gothic design was completed in 1857. At the opposite end is the *Jewel Tower* (Old Palace Yard), built in 1366 and once the treasury house for the jewels and gold of Edward III.

Hyde Park [18], W1: A lovely expanse that meets Kensington Gardens to the west, Hyde Park is the shining emerald of London's stretches of green. You can row on the Serpentine, ride horseback along Rotten Row, and catch an earful at Speaker's Corner. A royal park since 1536, Hyde Park was also the site of the Great Exhibition of 1851.

Imperial War Museum [45], Lambeth Rd., SE1: Located in a former asylum, this museum contains weapons, vehicles, uniforms, photographs, models, paintings, and other assorted relics pertaining to battles that have involved the British and Commonwealth forces since 1914.

Kensington Palace [20], Kensington Gardens, W8: William III built this palace, which was later reconstructed by Christopher Wren and William Kent. Queen Victoria was born here, and the Prince of Wales and his family reside here. Some of its State Apartments are open to visitors. *Kensington High Street,* to the west, is a popular London shopping area, with many of the country's more bizarre fashion designers selling their wares in the Hyper Hyper market at number 26.

Kenwood House, Hampstead Lane, NW3: A lovely Robert Adam house situated among handsome gardens on Hampstead Heath, Kenwood's Iveagh Bequest collection includes paintings by Rembrandt, Reynolds, Gainsborough, and Vermeer, as well as furniture and decorative arts.

Kew Gardens (see *Royal Botanic Gardens*)

Knightsbridge, SW1: This posh shopping area is dominated by Harrods, its rival department store Harvey Nichols, designer boutiques, and *nouvelle-cuisine* and exotic restaurants. Perpendicular to Knightsbridge (the street) is Sloane Street, which continues south to Sloane Square and is dotted with more of the same chic storefronts. Off the main shopping routes are charming residential streets and squares.

Lambeth Palace [46], Lambeth Palace Rd., SE1: For some 700 years the palace has been the residence of the Archbishop of Canterbury; the present living quarters date from the early Victorian era, although two late 15th-century towers are extant.

Law Courts [29], Strand, WC2: An immense Victorian Gothic-Revival structure, the Royal Courts of Justice comprise over a thousand rooms adjoined by several miles of corridors.

Leighton House, 12 Holland Park Rd., W14: The eminent Victorian painter, Lord Leighton, lived in this Kensington house, designed in 1866. Its walls are covered with his own paintings and those of his contemporaries. The Arab Hall is a splendid pseudo-Moorish fantasy with lovely tile designs by Walter Crane and William De Morgan.

Lincoln's Inn [50], WC2: This tree-shaded Inn of the Court, entered through the Henry VIII Gateway, features lovely red-brick structures. The Old Hall dates from 1506; the New Hall and library (London's largest legal library) are from 1845.

Lloyd's of London, Lime St., EC3: Arguably London's most famous (some say infamous) new building, Richard Rogers' postmodern structure is an interesting jumble of glass, pipes, steel, and exposed structural elements.

London Dungeon [58], 28 Tooley St., SE1: Notorious crimes and their perpetrators feature in displays at this unusual museum, as well as instruments of torture, the horrors of the Plague, and other such macabre subjects.

London Transport Museum, Covent Garden, WC2: The background and evolution of the city's transportation are surveyed through vintage trams, buses, railroad cars, and posters and advertisements.

London Zoo, Regent's Park, NW1: From the Moonlight Hall of nocturnal creatures to the modernist Penguin Pool, the London Zoo is one of the world's most comprehensive. Its setting in Regent's Park, which was laid out in the early 1800s by John Nash, is one of the most handsome in the country.

*Madame Tussaud's [54], Marylebone Rd., NW1: First established in 1833 (but on another site) by the Swiss sculptress whose name it bears, this repository of wax effigies has grown to include a cast of heroes, villains, rock musicians, politicians, and hundreds of others, as well as a Chamber of Horrors and a recreation of the Battle of Trafalgar. Next door is the ever-popular **Planetarium,** with permanent exhibits as well as laser displays (set to classical and rock music) Wednesday through Sunday evenings.

Mansion House [33], Bank, EC4: This 18th-century building, with a Corinthian portico and Egyptian Hall, is the official residence of the Lord Mayor of the City of London.

Marble Hill House, Richmond Rd., Twickenham: George II built this Palladian villa overlooking the Thames for his mistress, the Countess of Suffolk, in the early 18th century. Later, Mrs. Fitzherbert, George IV's "secret" wife, dwelled here.

Mayfair, W1: This elegant neighborhood of brownstone town houses, exclusive shops, expensive hotels, auctioneers, and charming squares nestles between Hyde Park and the West End.

The Monument [39], Monument St., EC3: Christopher Wren designed this fluted Doric column of Portland stone to commemorate the Great Fire of 1666. A climb up the 311 steps is rewarded with a spectacular view of the City and beyond.

*Museum of London [37], London Wall, EC2: London's heritage, from prehistoric times to the present, is covered in this museum. Its displays include the Lord Mayor's Coach, a vintage barbershop, and assorted archaeological artifacts, paintings, sculptures, costumes, and toys.

Museum of Mankind, 6 Burlington Gardens, W1: Spectacular bronzes from Benin are among the ethnographic and "primitive" objects displayed in this museum, located behind the Royal Academy.

Museum of the Moving Image, South Bank Arts Centre, SE1: This recently opened museum celebrates British, Hollywood, and other international cinema. It boasts a variety of "hands-on" displays, as well as vintage costumes, props, cameras, projectors, and live actors playing the roles of ushers and aspiring starlets.

***National Gallery [2], Trafalgar Sq., WC2: A world-class art institution, the National Gallery possesses a dazzling, comprehensive collection of British and European paintings, from Italian Renaissance masterpieces (by da Vinci, Botticelli, Mantegna, and others), to French Impressionist and Post-Impressionist works (Monet, Manet, Seurat, Degas); also, outstanding works by van Eyck, Rembrandt, Vermeer, Claude, and Velázquez.

National Maritime Museum, Romney Rd., Greenwich, SE10: Thousands of models, paintings, costumes, navigational instruments, and weapons tell the story of Britain's rich maritime history in this immense museum, which incorporates Inigo Jones's Queen's House and the Old Royal Observatory.

National Portrait Gallery, 2 St. Martin's Pl., W1: Located behind the National Gallery, this collection of historical portraits—dating from the ninth century to the present—includes paintings, sculptures, prints, and photographs of illustrious (and sometimes notorious) Britons.

National Theatre [44], South Bank Arts Centre, SE1: Three theaters actually comprise this complex: the Olivier, the Lyttleton, and the Cottesloe; the famed National Theatre Company is based here.

Natural History Museum [24], Cromwell Rd., SW7: From fossils to meteorites, this massive museum displays huge collections of animal, vegetable, and mineral specimens. Especially interesting are the dinosaur skeletons, the semiprecious stone collection, and a 3.5-ton iron meteorite found in Australia in 1854.

"Old Bailey" (see *Central Criminal Court*)

Oxford Street, W1: London's most popular thoroughfare for shoppers, Oxford Street stretches between Tottenham Court Road at the east end and Marble Arch at the west. It is home to Selfridge's,

John Lewis, Debenhams, C & A, and countless small boutiques and fast-food joints (as well as movie theaters and the Virgin Megastore, with records, cassettes, CDs, etc.).

Petticoat Lane Market, environs Middlesex St., E1: Set aside a Sunday morning, if you can, to explore this expansive and colorful East End market. You probably won't be too tempted to buy, but the people—vendors and "punters" (buyers) alike—provide value for your time.

Piccadilly Circus [16], W1: The noisy, neon-lighted heart of London's West End, Piccadilly Circus is a motorist's—and pedestrian's—nightmare, but that doesn't seem to keep either away, no matter what the time of the day or night. Don't miss Alfred Gilbert's statue of *Eros,* part of a memorial fountain to Lord Shaftesbury. You may want to pop into the *Criterion Brasserie* for a coffee and look at the gold mosaics.

Portobello Road Market, W11: Perhaps London's best-known antiques market (Saturday only), Portobello is a long stretch of sidewalk vendors and permanent stalls and shops. Don't expect great bargains, though, just lively atmosphere (the farther west you go, towards Notting Hill Gate, the funkier it gets) and plenty of fruit, vegetable, and junk dealers.

Regent's Park [53], NW1: John Nash designed this park in the early 19th century, although it was part of Henry VIII's hunting forest three centuries before. Regent's Canal, the London Zoo, Queen Mary's rose garden, and a lake for boating are just some of its attractions.

Royal Academy of Arts, Burlington House, Piccadilly, W1: From May to July a huge summer art show covers its walls with amateur and professional works, but the Royal Academy hosts major temporary exhibitions the rest of the year.

**Royal Albert Hall [22], Kensington Gore, SW7: Built in 1871, this massive, glass-domed concert hall, hosts classical, rock, jazz, pop, and other concerts, including the summertime "Proms."

Royal Botanic Gardens, Kew Rd., Richmond: More popularly known as Kew Gardens, these 750 hectares (300 acres) of trees, shrubs, and herbaceous plants feature Orchid, Palm, and Succulent houses, as well as a lake with an aquatic garden and park. The gardens were originally private, laid out by Princess Augusta in 1759.

Royal Exchange [34], Threadneedle St. and Cornhill, EC3: The present Victorian structure is the third on this spot; the 1564 market for craftsmen and merchants burned down in the Great Fire of 1666 and its replacement was also destroyed by fire in the 1830s. The murals inside depict the history of London. At noon, 3:00, and 6:00 P.M. the carillon plays British, Canadian, and Australian tunes.

Royal Festival Hall [42],

South Bank Arts Centre, SE1: The 3,000-seat theater, part of the massive South Bank complex, was originally built for the 1951 Festival of Britain.

Royal Mews [59], Buckingham Palace Rd., SW1: This coach house contains various state coaches, including the Gold State Coach, which has been used for coronations since the 18th century, royal sleighs, Edward VII's 1901 Daimler, and the see-through Glass Coach used by royal brides.

St. Bartholomew the Great [57], West Smithfield, EC1: London's oldest parish church, St. Bartholomew's was founded in 1123 as an Augustinian priory.

St. Clement Danes [28], Strand, WC2: Christopher Wren rebuilt this ninth-century church in 1681. Badly damaged in World War II, it was reconstructed and reconsecrated in 1958. Today it is the principal house of worship of the Royal Air Force.

St. James's Palace [14], Pall Mall, SW1: Holbein painted the ceiling of the Chapel Royal in this 1532 mansion. Built for Henry VIII, the palace is closed to visitors but for its chapel.

St. James's Park [13], SW1: Along with Palace Gardens and *Green Park* [12], St. James's combines to form a huge expanse of green in the heart of the city. It was a swamp until Henry VIII drained it and turned into a refuge for the royal deer. Later, Charles II brought waterfowl to its lake. Today St. James's resident pelicans are among London's best-loved avian specimens.

St. Martin-in-the-Fields [3], Trafalgar Sq., WC2: Wren's student, James Gibbs, built this neoclassical church in 1726; Nell Gwynne, the mistress of Charles II, is buried here.

**St. Paul's Cathedral [32], Ludgate Hill, EC4: Christopher Wren designed this huge Baroque church (built from 1675 to 1710) as a replacement for a Gothic structure that stood on the site and was destroyed in the Great Fire. Its harmonious proportions and great dome set the standard that many churches attempted to follow; even today, while surrounded by a sea of largely undistinguished modern structures, St. Paul's remains an imposing edifice. You can enjoy superb views of London from the Stone Gallery and the dome's Golden Ball. Its massive crypt is worth a visit to see the tombs of the Duke of Wellington, Lord Nelson, and the great architect Wren himself; its wooden stalls, carved by

St. Paul's Cathedral

the master Grinling Gibbons, are outstanding.

Science Museum [23], Exhibition Rd., SW7: The fascinating history of science, industry, and technology is presented in this museum, via various instruments, machines, models, and prototypes (including Galileo's telescope, Alexander Graham Bell's first telephone, and assorted space modules).

Sir John Soane's Museum, 13 Lincoln's Inn Fields, WC2: Architect/connoisseur Soane designed his own house in 1812; it contains a fascinating and eclectic collection of antiquities, drawings, and paintings displayed in the same eccentric manner that Soane arranged. His use of space was imaginative and his taste in art especially good (the jewels of his collection are Hogarth's *The Rake's Progress* and *The Election* painting cycles).

Soho: Legitimate theaters, sleazy and first-run cinemas, fast-food joints and ethnic restaurants, pubs galore, bookshops, and a small Chinatown are among the occupants of this fast-paced area that radiates northward from Leicester Square to Oxford Street, and borders Charing Cross Road and Regent Street.

South Bank Arts Centre, SE1: This massive cultural complex, on the south bank of the Thames, houses various theaters, concert halls, the Hayward Gallery, the National Film Theatre, and the newly opened Museum of the Moving Image (MOMI).

*Southwark Cathedral[41], Borough High St., SE1: This heavily restored church was originally a 13th-century priory; its tower dates from ca. 1520.

Stock Exchange, Throgmorton St., EC2: Located in a tall city building, the busy London Stock Exchange has a Visitors' Gallery from which you can watch 2,000-plus soberly dressed men and women perform their frantic task.

**Tate Gallery [8], Millbank, SW1: British painting from the 18th century to the present is displayed in this excellent museum, as well as international modern art from 1880, with fine works by Picasso, Chagall, Pollock, Degas, and many others. The pre-Raphaelites are also well represented, as are Constable and Blake. Hundreds of works by J.M. W. Turner are on view in the new post-modern *Clore Gallery* extension.

The Temple [30], EC4: The two Inns of the Court—the Inner Temple and the Middle Temple—comprising the lawyers' district known as The Temple—are both entered via a 1685 gatehouse in Middle Temple Lane. The early Gothic Temple Church (rebuilt by Wren in 1682), late 16th-century Middle Temple Hall, and a charming cluster of courtyards, narrow lanes, and brick buildings can be seen.

Tower Bridge, SE1: The twin towers of this 1894 neo-Gothic drawbridge are world famous. A glass-enclosed walkway above the Thames provides panoramic views of the city, as well as an interesting display of the span's history.

***Tower of London [40], Tower Hill, EC3: One of London's best-known and oldest historic sites, the Tower was built by William the Conqueror and served as his fortress. Later it was used as a prison, with the 1078 White Tower and subsequent keeps holding such famous prisoners as Sir Walter Raleigh and Princess Elizabeth I. The Gun Wharf, Crown Jewels, Traitors Gate, Chapel of St. John (a superb example of Norman architecture), and the Yeoman Warders, or Beefeaters (whose distinctive costume dates from the reign of Henry VII), are among the tower's many attractions.

Trafalgar Square [1], WC2: The 52-meter- (170-foot-) high Nelson Column, a granite pillar topped by a statue of the famous admiral, dominates this busy crossroads, guarded by a quartet of giant lions (designed by Sir Edwin Landseer in 1858) at its base. Pigeons and tourists abound; all-night city buses operate from here, so the square is swarming with people at all hours.

**Victoria and Albert Museum [25], Cromwell Rd., SW7: This Victorian pile, founded as the South Kensington Museum, displays a huge collection of fine and decorative arts. Of special interest are tapestry cartoons painted by Raphael ca. 1515 that depict the life of St. Peter; a former dining room designed by William Morris and others; a plethora of plaster casts of famous classical statuary; a costume gallery; extensive Oriental art works; sculptures by Donatello, Bernini, Canova, and Rodin, and paintings and watercolors by Gainsborough, Constable, Turner, Delacroix, Degas, and others.

Wallace Collection [56], Hertford House, Manchester Sq., W1: The 4th Marquess of Hertford and his grandson, Sir Richard Wallace, put together this impressive collection of paintings, sculpture, armor, and applied arts in the 19th century. The French 18th-century furniture, porcelain, gold boxes, and rococo paintings are outstanding, and there are superb works from the Dutch, Flemish, and Spanish schools.

The West End, W1: This busy central district teems with shops (from Oxford Street and the bookstores of Charing Cross Road to posh Fortnum & Mason and charming Liberty of London), entertainment (cinemas, music venues, and theaters), eateries, and just about any other diversion a tourist (or native) can imagine.

***Westminster Abbey [7], Broad Sanctuary, SW1: Originally a Benedictine monastery founded by Edward the Confessor in 1065 (and one of the few houses of worship to escape Henry VIII's wrath), the abbey is crowded with the tombs of royalty and writers (among the latter are Chaucer, Tennyson, Dickens, and Hardy). The Gothic building mainly dates

Westminster Abbey

from the 13th and 14th centuries, though both Christopher Wren and Nicholas Hawksmoor contributed to its design in the 17th and 18th centuries, respectively. Don't miss the Coronation Throne (dating from 1300 and still used by new monarchs), the medieval treasures in the Henry VII Chapel, and the various English Baroque statues scattered throughout.

Westminster Cathedral [10], Ashley Pl., SW1: The seat of Britain's Roman Catholic cardinal, the neo-Byzantine cathedral was finished in 1903. Its interior is magnificently embellished with marble and mosaics, and its tower commands wonderful city views. Eric Gill sculpted the lovely bas-relief Stations of the Cross.

William Morris Gallery, Forest Rd., Walthamstow, E17: Located in a boyhood home of the great Arts & Crafts Movement designer/socialist/writer, the gallery has a permanent display of furniture and other decorative-art objects by Morris and his contemporaries, as well as paintings and printed books. Interesting temporary exhibitions on Morris, his family, and his associates are mounted regularly.

Excursions

**Hampton Court Palace, East Moseley, Surrey: Cardinal Wolsey began building this palace in 1514, but it was seized and made into a royal residence in 1525, which it continued to be until 1760. Superb wooden carvings by Grinling Gibbons, Italian paintings, beautiful gardens, and the ghosts of two of Henry VIII's wives—this was the monarch's favorite country home—are part of the palace.

***Windsor Castle, Windsor, Berkshire: Located in the 1,943-hectare (4,800-acre) Great Park, the castle first housed royalty some 900 years ago. Superb portraits (by Holbein, Van Dyck, and others) are displayed in the State Apartments, as well as Italian landscapes, Thomas Lawrence portraits, and royal dollhouses; there are masterworks by Leonardo da Vinci in the Print Room. St. George's Chapel, dating from the 15th and 16th centuries, is one of the finest examples of late Gothic architecture in Great Britain.

Luxembourg

The bustling city of Luxembourg, co-capital (with Brussels) of the European Economic Community, is perched high atop a huge bank of rock; within its confines lie a 21-km.- (13-mile-) maze of underground passages. At one time an impenetrable fortress, Luxembourg boasts a rich history which is essentially that of the entire Grand Duchy of the same name. The tunnels, casements, turrets, and spires that characterize the older environs of this city of 100,000 give it a fairy tale aura, whereas the ultra-modern, industrial and EEC-related structures on the Plateau de Kirchberg place it firmly in the 20th century.

History

In A.D. 963, Sigefroi, the young Count of Ardennes, built a small citadel over the ruins of a third-century Roman (later Frankish) fort. Luculinburh, as it was then known, was situated high on the Rocher du Bock, a cliff that dropped down to the valleys of the Alzette and Pétrusse rivers. The walled town grew steadily, and received its charter from Countess Ermesinda in 1244. Successive rulers expanded the mighty fortress considerably, so that by the late 15th century it comprised virtually the entire area that makes up the older sections of present-day Luxembourg. In 1684, the French occupied the city, and its fortifications were remodeled by the noted architect/military engineer Sébastien Vauban.

Over the centuries, "the Gibraltar of the North," a highly desirable strategic location, was under the rule of various countries; however, in 1815, the Congress of Vienna established the Grand Duchy of Luxembourg, with the city of Luxembourg as its capital. In 1839, under William I of the Netherlands, the Grand Duchy became nominally independent (true independence came about in 1867, when the Prussian garrison stationed in the city finally left). The fortifications came down, and within three years these defenses were transformed into handsome boulevards.

In the 20th century, the German leaders chose to ignore Luxembourg's neutrality during both world wars, and occupied both the city and Grand Duchy. The early 1950s witnessed the further rise of the hilltop city of Luxembourg, as it became home to various European political and financial institutions, among them the Court of Justice, Investment Bank, Monetary Fund, and European Economic Community.

Attractions

*Casemates de la Pétrusse
[2], entrance at Place de la Constitution: Carved within the solid rock of the shore cliffs by the Spanish in 1674, these casemates are stacked five stories high.

In the casemates

Casemates du Bock [12], Rocher du Bock: With canon niches hollowed out of walls of steep rock, these casemates (1737–1746) are particularly fascinating. During excavations in 1963, the ruins of an ancient tower were discovered just in time to be dedicated as a "Thousand-Year Memorial" to the founding of the fortress in 963.

*Cathédrale Nôtre-Dame de Luxembourg [3], Boulevard Franklin Roosevelt: Designed as a Jesuit church in the Gothic manner by Jean de Blocq (1613–1618), the cathedral boasts an exceptional Renaissance portal. Of interest inside are the broad choir, the unusual strapwork decoration on the huge nave pillars, and the crypt, which contains the sarcophagus of John the Blind. He was nearly sightless when he fell to the British fighting for the French at Crécy in 1346 (two ministers had to lead him into the battlefield).

Cimetière Militaire Américain, 5 km. (3 miles) east at Hamm: The grave of General George S. Patton, Jr., commander of the 3rd U.S. Army, is here, as are those of 5,000 American soldiers killed in World War II.

Église Saint-Michel, Marché aux Poissons: This church, situated in Luxembourg's oldest square, was consecrated in 987 as the castle chapel. Although rebuilt in the 17th century, it still retains a few Romanesque windows.

European Center, Plateau de Kirchberg: A huge, 22-story glass-and-steel tower dominates the complex, which is surrounded by an array of modern buildings that house political institutions.

Marché aux Poissons [6]: Located on an old Roman crossroads and subsequently the nucleus of the town that sprouted up around the castle, the *Fish Market* still has some quaint old houses clustered around it.

Musée de l'Etat, Marché aux Poissons: Housed in the former governor's residence, Luxembourg's National Museum displays a rich mixture of art works as well as archaeological, mineralogical, and zoological specimens. Especially strong are its collections of arms and armor and Gallo-Roman objects. Paintings include works by Jacob Jordaens, Pieter Brueghel the Younger, and Lucas Cranach the Elder.

Palais Grand-Ducal [5], Rue de l'Eau: Though it was renovated and enlarged between 1891 and 1894, the palace, which originally served as the city hall, still has some sections dating back to the Renaissance. Guards march 40 measured steps back and forth in front of the modest structure, whose interior is largely in the Italian Renaissance style.

Place d'Armes [7]: During the summer months, this square, surrounded by cafés and restaurants, is used as an outdoor theater for concerts. A tourist information

Luxembourg Attractions:
1. Pont Adolphe
2. Petrusse Casemates
3. Nôtre-Dame Cathedral
4. Wilhelm's Square
5. Palais Grand-Ducal
6. Fish Market
7. Parade Square
8. City Park
9. Rond Point
10. Pont Grand-Duchesse Charlotte
11. Trois Glands
12. Casemates du Bock
13. Palace Bridge

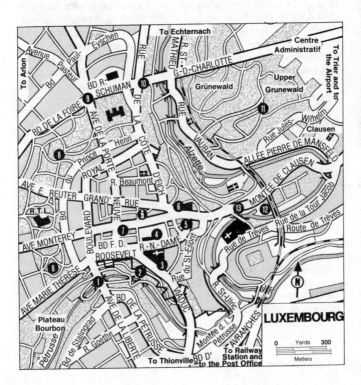

center is here, as well as a model of the old citadel.

Place Guillaume [4]: In the center of this market square stands an equestrian statue of its namesake, William II, King of the Netherlands and Grand-Duke of Luxembourg. The *Hôtel de Ville* (City Hall) was built here between 1830 and 1838.

Pont Adolphe [1], off Place de la Constitution: The wide Avenue de la Liberté (with its high-rise hotels and office buildings) leads from the train station through the Lower City, ending at Pont Adolphe, the "New Bridge" of 1903. The dramatic structure overlooks a gorge; under the bridge, the small Pétrusse River flows through parklike gardens, and atop it there's a fine view of the Upper City.

Pont du Château [13]: This bridge offers a beautiful vista that includes the *Citadelle du Saint-Esprit* (built by Vauban on the site of an old convent) and the *Spanish Towers,* among other sights.

Pont Grand-Duchesse Charlotte [10]: Linking the old city to the new European Center complex, the bridge spans the valley of the Alzette River; it measures 85 meters (279 feet) high, 230 meters (754 feet) wide, and 355 meters (1,164 feet) long. The bridge is the newest (1966) and largest of the hundred some bridges and five large viaducts that define Luxembourg's skyline. (The oldest, the *Portcullis Bridge* of the "Meierchen" sentry walk, dates from 1390.)

Promenade de la Corniche: Extending like eaves along the cliffs of the Upper City, the pedestrians-only promenade offers beautiful views and a lovely walk to the Rocher du Bock.

Rond-Point Robert Schuman [9]: The Rue Robert Schuman extends east of this intersection; both are named after the Luxembourg-born statesman (1886–1963), whose program to pool Europe's coal and steel industry was a prelude of sorts to the Common Market. A striking steel-girded memorial to Schuman can be seen on the wide thoroughfare, as well as the *Théâtre Municipal,* an interesting contemporary building (1966).

Spanish Towers: These three sentinel's outposts cling like swallows' nests to the crown of the fortification wall. They date from around 1400, and were part of the ramparts that protected the Plateau du Rham.

Trois Glands [11], Plateau de Kirchberg: With the European Center as a contemporary backdrop, this trio of rotund gunpowder towers dates from Luxembourg's Austrian era (1732).

Madrid

Madrid, the capital of Spain and its largest city, is appropriately situated in the country's geographical center—this also makes it the hub of rail, road, and flight communications. It sits on a high plateau amid a rather featureless countryside, although you don't have to travel far to find more beautiful landscapes.

Despite an automatic association in nearly everyone's mind of Madrid and the Prado Museum (which is certainly a marvel), there is much else in the city to delight, refresh, and illuminate, not the least of which is the lively street life. Activity hardly diminishes as the evening goes on, for Madrilenos don't even think of having dinner until quite late. Hunger at the end of a heavy day of sight-seeing can be delectably assuaged in the tapas bars everywhere.

As compelling as the bustle in the streets is, look up from the sidewalk level; there's a special sort of entertainment in the upper structures of buildings along the main avenues. At times, the enthusiastic, 19th-century architectural extravagance, with a Spanish accent, can stop you in your tracks. Palatial buildings abound; it's very easy to mistake a certain grand edifice in the center for the Royal Palace, when, in fact, it is merely the Central Post Office! Grandly conceived structures can be seen everywhere in this otherwise down-to-earth city.

History

Madrid's Royal Palace is located on the site of what was a small, 9th-century Moorish fortress town called Majrit. This district, with its narrow, winding alleys, still bears the reminiscent name of Moreria. In the early years of the 12th century, the fortress was seized by King Alfonso VI, and by 1239, Ferdinand IV had made it one of his official residences. In 1561, Philip II moved his court from Toledo to the palace—formerly the Moorish Alcazar—and made the city the capital of his empire.

The city expanded significantly during the reigns of Philip IV (1621–1665) and Charles III (1759–1788). Among their contributions were the creation of the Parque del Retiro and the Plaza Mayor, the establishment of the botanical garden, the construction of the splendid avenues Paseo del Prado, de la Castellana, and others, and the Puerto de Alcala.

Spanish history was marked by a revolt of the citizens against General Murat in 1808. Desperate street fights in which more than 1,000 lives were lost led to the Peninsular War against France. Goya's painting of this subject hangs in the Prado.

During the Spanish Civil War, the city was occupied by Nationalist troops from November 1936 to March 1939, but the damage done during those years is no longer visible.

Attractions

The **Biblioteca Nacional y Museo Arqueologico** (National Library and Museum of Archaeology) [30], built in Classical style in the late 19th century, incorporates the National Library, a modern art collection (entrance from Calle Serrano), and the National Archaeological Museum. The museum offers much more than archaeological finds; there are Egyptian, Greek, and Roman artifacts, a magnificent anthology of Iberian art over the centuries, and a pottery collection of considerable note. Particularly notable features include the famous *Dama de Elche* sculpture, dating from between the third and fifth centuries B.C., and the reproduction of the *Altamira Ice Age caves* from the Santander province (in the garden), showing marvelous wall paintings.

In the *Jardines del Descubrimiento* [32] of the National Library are a monument to Christopher Columbus and several other heroic sculptures commemorating the discovery (discubrimiento) of America.

Below the *Plaza de Colon* is a cultural center; on its west side is the **Museo de Cera Colon,** a wax museum considered to be one of the best on the Continent. It not only displays historic and royal figures, but also many representations of contemporary interest and popularity.

The vast ***Casa de Campo,** once royal property, is now a popular amusement park, complete with a zoo and a boating lake. There are likely to be a great many Madrilenos enjoying the facilities, especially on weekends. You can ascend to the zoo by cable car.

The **Centro de Arte Reina Sofia** [38], formerly the Hospital de San Carlos, has been the city's largest art and culture venue, primarily for provocative temporary exhibitions, since 1986.

Convento de las Descalzas Reales [23]: The Renaissance palace of Emperor Charles V was converted into a convent in 1559. Originally it bore the name of the religious order meaning "Royal Barefoot Sisters," a misnomer given its members: Most of the sisters were aristocratic ladies who, on entering the order, brought their valuable dowries, in addition to the generous contributions made by their wealthy families to the convent coffers. Among the gifts are the many precious art objects that lent the convent its museumlike character. The convent is now maintained by the Franciscan order.

A superb staircase leads into the upper gallery of the cloister, which opens into splendidly decorated chapels, each founded by a royal sister. Of particular note are the tapestries based on designs by Rubens; there are also many paintings by other famous masters.

The small church of **Ermite de San Antonio de la Florida** [25], built in the last decade of the 18th century, was decorated with Goya's delightful perspective paintings around the central cupola. Goya is buried here.

The *Real Museo Academia de Bellas Artes de San Fernando (Fine Arts Museum) [28]: A vast assemblage of art works are presented behind its classical façade, despite the transfer of many of its holdings to the Prado in the early part of the 20th century.

The *Museo Carralbo [24] (entrance Calle Ventura Rodriguez 17) has a private collection in this former palace. Its small but choice collection of paintings also include many examples that are of more decorative or historical interest.

The ***Museo del Prado [36] is known throughout the world simply as *The Prado*. The neoclassical building, designed originally to house a natural history museum and science academy, opened as an art museum in 1819. Its collections, originally belonged to Charles V, and have grown to represent one of the most valuable, complete, and rewarding holdings in the world. The core of the collection is the works of Spain's greatest painters, principally Goya and Velásquez among them; in general, its offering of European art is one that no art lover should miss.

Not far from the Prado, the **Cason del Buen Retiro,** once a 17th-century ballroom, now exhibits paintings and sculptures of the 19th century. Picasso's *Guernica,* together with his preliminary sketches, have also been displayed here.

The more intimate **Museo Romantico** [19] contains an

Madrid Attractions:
1. Palacio Real
2. Catedral Nuestra Señora de la Almudena
3. Plaza de la Villa
4. Capilla del Obispo
5. San Francisco el Grande
6. Catedral San Isidro Labrador
7. Plaza Mayor
8. Puerta del Sol
9. Plaza de Santa Cruz
10. Plaza del Angel
11. Casa de Lope de Vega
12. Palacio de las Cortes Españolas
13. Convento de la Encarnaciòn
14. Plaza de España
15. Church and Monastery de las Comendadoras
16. Montserrat
17. Church and Monastery Salesas Reales
18. Museo Municipal
19. Museum Romántico
20. San Antòn
21. San Antonio de los Alemanes
22. San Plácido
23. Convento de las Descalzas Reales
24. Museo Cerralbo
25. Ermita de San Antonio de la Florida
26. Estaciòn Teleférico
27. Plaza de la Cibeles
28. Museo Academia de Bellas Artes
29. Puerta de Alcalá
30. Biblioteca Nacional y Museo Arqueològico
31. Santa Bárbara
32. Jardines del Descubrimiento
33. Plaza Cánovas del Castillo
34. Museo del Prado
35. San Jerònimo el Real
36. Museo Etnològico
37. Royal Tapestry Factory
38. Centro de Arte Reina Sofia
39. Rastro (Flea-Market)
40. Glorieta de la Puerta de Toledo
41. Puente de Segovia

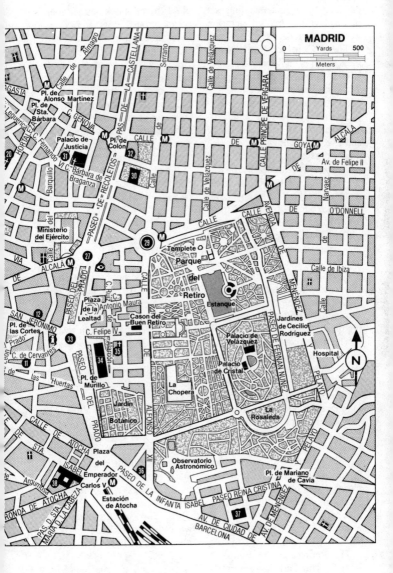

engaging and undemanding set of displays illustrating Victorian taste in art and decor.

The ****Palacio Real** (Royal Palace) [1] is an impressive, opulent, 18th-century edifice of granite and limestone, comprising several specialist museums. The four tremendous wings of the palace surround an inner courtyard, and two more wings frame a second courtyard, the *Plaza de Armes.* It was designed by the Baroque architect Filippo Juvarra, and built by King Philip on the site of the old burned-out Moorish *Alcazar* (palace). Although the palace no longer serves as a royal residence, it is used for official government functions as well as a museum. Its 2,800 magnificent salons are richly furnished; they are notable for their many works of art, including a fine Tiepolo ceiling fresco.

The **Plaza de Oriente** (1841), just outside the Palace, is lined with statues of Spanish kings, queens, and warriors. It has always served as an important meeting place for political gatherings.

The very attractive and popular **Parque del Retiro** has a long history, but was not opened to the public until the 19th century. Although nicely situated to provide a pleasant breather after a tour of the Prado, its shaded paths, greenery, rose gardens, ponds, boating lake, and cafés make it a desirable refuge at any time.

The Retiro may be compared with Central Park in New York; there is always an event taking place here—book fairs, sports competitions, dog shows, parades, and musical and theatrical entertainment. In the *Palacio de Cristal,* an impressive glass building on the grounds, you can see temporary art exhibitions.

From the Prado, it is a very short way to the **Plaza Canovas del Castillo** [33], a junction of several streets. The main street, the Carrera San Jeronimo, leads to the old town, the Plaza Mayor, and the Royal Palace. Note the plaza's 18th-century Neptune Fountain.

The **Plaza de España** [14] lies north of the Palace on the border of Old Madrid. It is dominated by two skyscrapers, the *Torre de Madrid* and the *Edificio de España,* as well as the luxury *Hotel Plaza,* from which a 25th-floor restaurant offers an admirable panorama of the city. The two, tall buildings dwarf the *Cervantes Memorial,* which depicts the author and his two best-known characters, Don Quixote and Sancho Panza.

The ***Plaza de la Ville** [3] is one of the most interesting in Old Madrid. The Baroque *City Hall* (Ayuniamento) is here, with its towers, beautiful interior (particularly the staircase), a salon filled with paintings (including a Goya), and a frescoed chapel. The restored *Torre de los Lujánes* is where the French king, Francis I, is said to have been imprisoned in 1525.

The grand and spacious **Plaza Mayor** [7], defined on all sides by romantically arcaded buildings, was laid out and inaugurated at the beginning of the 17th century. Since that time, it has been the setting for public events of various sorts, from sentencings and executions during the Inquisition, to religious, political, theatrical, and social celebrations. Bullfights, too, took place here at one time. An equestrian statue of King Philip III, for whom the plaza was built, stands in its center.

The **Puerto del Sol** [8], with streets fanning out from it like sun rays, was named for an earlier city gate, the Gate of the Sun; it lies at the very heart of the old city. It was once the scene of insurrections, principally against the French, in 1808. With so many streets coming together, it is not exactly a peaceful junction, but the area is all the more exciting as a result.

San Francesco el Grande [5]: Completed in 1785, this is a grandiloquently large and heavily decorated church—rather than a lovely one. Its great dome is imposing, and its Goya chapel one of the greatest attractions of its interior. The painting depicts St. Bernardino of Siena preaching before the King of Aragon.

Excursions

***El Escorial, in the village of San Lorenzo de El Escorial, 50 km. (30 miles) from Madrid, is a city in itself, in which there are a church, a library, a monastery dedicated to St. Lawrence, a palace, and a royal mausoleum. After his victory over the French in the battle of San Quentin, Philip II fulfilled his father's wish by beginning construction on his mauseoleum in 1563. The first architect was Juan Bautista de Toledo, who had worked in Rome with Michelangelo. Toledo's pupil, the great Renaissance architect Juan de Herrera, succeeded him and completed the enormous project in 1584.

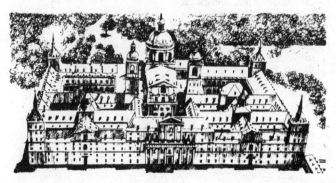

El Escorial

The vast, severely rectangular structure has high towers at its corners, and endless courtyards, chambers, apartments, chapels, cloisters, and galleries.

The *Patio de los Reyes* (Kings' Courtyard), together with the *Church,* constitute the central axis of the whole structure. To its left is the monastic college; to the right stands the monastery proper. Statues of the Kings of Judah decorate the façade of the church, which has two bell towers.

Some of the opulent Italian paintings in the *Coro Bajo,* the central hall shaped like a Greek cross, have a character somewhat at odds with the austere architecture. Luca Giordana's paintings hang in the central nave, and most of the statues are by Pompeo Leoni, who died in Madrid in 1608. Groups of statues depict emperors with their wives, sisters, and daughters.

To the right of the church is the *Patio de los Evangelistas,* an ambulatory with chapter houses, the so-called Old Church, and the sacristies, which now house a museum. At the Antisacristia, a stairway descends to the *Crypt,* which lies directly below the Capilla Mayor (high altar); this has been extended into the *Panteon de los Infantes* (Princes' Pantheon), containing the graves of princes and princesses, and into the octagonal *Panteon de los Reyes* (Royal Pantheon), where most of Spain's kings and queens since Charles V have been buried.

To the left of the church is the *Palacio,* the former royal palace. The entrance is in the middle of the north wing. Several royal apartments, in particular the *Palacio de Verano* (Summer Palace), surround the church apse; these chambers now compose the *Nuevos Museos* (New Museums), housing the Escorial's most precious paintings.

The apartments of the Bourbon kings, decorated with 300 tapestries, are notable, as well as the *Sala de Batallas,* lined with huge paintings of battles.

Marseille

An earthy Mediterranean atmosphere pervades France's oldest city and largest commercial seaport. Marseille is a gritty, noisy, down-to-earth place that just happens to be beautifully situated on a series of hills overlooking a broad bay in the Gulf of Lyon. Although you can't exactly call Marseille charming, it does exude a kind of raw vitality and fascination that are unmistakable and exciting. The city has a number of worthwhile sights to see and, between stops, gourmands will want to try a bowl of bouillabaisse, the pungent fish stew invented in Marseille.

History

The Phoenicians settled this area even before the Greeks, who founded a city here in 600 B.C. Commanding a natural and important trade route on the Rhône, the city prospered from a very early date, establishing commercial ties through Europe and as far as the west coast of Africa.

An alliance with Rome helped to establish Marseille as a seat of learning—praised as such by Tacitus and Cicero—and eventually it became the last outpost of Greek learning in the West. Later, however, Marseille sided with Pompey, Julius Caesar's political adversary; when Pompey was defeated in battle, Caesar took revenge on the city by demolishing its fortifications and reducing its stature to that of a provincial town.

Marseille began to prosper again during the Middle Ages when it was a departure point and supply depot for the thousands of crusaders traveling East to fight the Infidel. By the beginning of the 13th century, it had formed a republic around what is today the Vieux Port.

The discovery of the Americas, and the consequent shifting of trade to the Atlantic ports of Bordeaux and La Rochelle, caused a major economic setback for Marseille. The city languished until a period of prosperity helped to revive it in the 17th century—a short-lived triumph, since the plague of 1720 then wiped out half of the city's 80,000 inhabitants.

Sixty years later, the remaining population enthusiastically participated in the events of the French Revolution—so enthusiastically, in fact, that their patriotic song became known as *La Marseillaise,* and is now the French national anthem.

After the French conquests in North Africa and the opening of the Suez Canal in 1869, Marseille became the "port of the empire." Its harbors were later extended to accommodate the huge ocean liners entering the Mediterranean. The city and harbor suffered extensive damage during World War II. Since the war, Marseille once again has become a powerful center of shipping and industry.

Attractions

Arc de Triomphe [3]: The patriotic sculptures decorating Marseille's triumphal arch, completed in 1832, commemorate France's struggles under the First Republic and First Empire.

*Basilique-Nôtre-Dame-de-la-Garde [4]: Dominating the city and the bay, this landmark pilgrim church is designed in a neo-Byzantine style popular in the mid-19th century, and has a bell tower crowned with a gilded statue of Saint Mary. From the terrace, there's a fabulous view of Marseille's port and docks, with Cap Croisette visible to the south and the Estaque Peninsula to the northwest.

Basilique Saint-Victor (Basilica of Saint Victor) [1]: Marseille's oldest church was built in the 11th century on the site of an earlier one and is named after a third-century Roman officer who died a martyr in Marseille. The remains of the older church can be seen in the subterranean crypt and **catacombs.*

Cathedrale Sainte-Marie Majeur [2]: Also known as the New Cathedral, Saint Mary's was built in a ponderous, 19th-century style with alternating layers of white and dark green limestone. Next to it stands the *Old Cathedral,* a Provençal structure built in the 12th century, from whose west terrace you can look out over the New Port and the port train station.

Hôtel de Ville (Town Hall),

Quai du Port: This Baroque building, completed in 1683, was one of the few buildings spared when the Germans demolished the picturesque old port quarter of Marseille in 1943.

La Cité Radieuse, Boulevard Michelet (about 1.5 km. or just over a mile from the Rond Point): Anyone interested in architecture will want to see Le Corbusier's controversial *Unité d'Habitation,* a residential complex built on concrete piles between 1947 and 1952 as part of a larger and unfinished community. The complex, which created an international sensation when it opened, is now considered a landmark in the history of modern French architecture.

*Musée d'Archéologie Borély, Avenue Clot-Bey: An 18th-century château houses the collections which include some of the finest Egyptian antiquities in Europe as well as Greek, Etruscan, and Roman finds.

Musée des Beaux-Arts (Fine Arts Museum), Boulevard Philpon: Housed in the north wing of the Palais Longchamp, the museum is especially noted for its excellent *Daumier Room* on the top floor, which has numerous portraits and lithographs by the famous caricaturist Honoré Daumier, who was born in Marseille in 1808.

Musée des Docks Romains [6]: The museum displays the *in situ* ruins of the ancient Greco-Roman harbor and docks, first discovered when the Germans blew up the old port area of the city in 1943; there is also a Roman warehouse and various objects salvaged from ancient shipwrecks along the coast. In the adjacent **Musée du Vieux-Marseille** [5], there are exhibitions of 18th-century, provincial furniture and old Christmas crèches.

Promenade de Corniche: Also known as Corniche J.F. Kennedy, this road, which begins southeast of *Parc du Pharo,* follows the coast as far as *Cap Croisette* (some 9 km./5.5 miles away), and offers constantly changing vistas of the sea and offshore islands.

Vieux Port (Old Port), Quai des Belges: At the end of the famous boulevard *La Canebière,* which divides the rich and poor

sections of Marseille, lies the old port city and the port itself. Marseille's only harbor until 1844, the Vieux Port forms a long rectangle, at the end of which is a narrow outlet to the sea guarded by two 17th-century forts—Saint-Nicholas on the south side and Saint-Jean on the north. The forts were used by the collaborationist Vichy government (1940–1944) to imprison Allied airmen forced down over France. Recently renovated, the surrounding area is now a pedestrian zone filled with boutiques, bookstores, cafés, and restaurants.

Marseille Attractions:
1. Basilique Saint-Victor
2. Cathédrale Sainte-María Majeur
3. Arc de Triomphe
4. Basilique Notre-Dame-de-la-Garde
5. Musée du Vieux-Marseille
6. Musée des Docks Romains

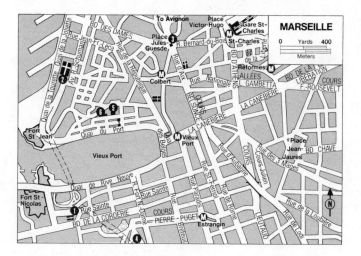

Excursions

Château d'If, 30 minutes by motorboat from the Vieux Port: Tiny If is the most popular of the islands off the coast of Marseille, and is the setting for the Château d'If built by Francois I in 1524 to protect Marseille from the Spaniards. It gained popularity when Alexandre Dumas set his novel *The Count of Monte Cristo* here; the fortress was later converted to a prison where Huguenot (Protestant) prisoners were incarcerated before being condemned as galley slaves.

Milan

Unlike so many other Italian cities, Milan is not a place where ancient ruins or marvels of Baroque architecture predominate the scene. Milan is Italy's equivalent of New York—the country's most important center for business and trade, contemporary culture, fashion and design. In short, it's thoroughly sophisticated and dedicated to money. Although there's lots to see and do, the treasures here don't always reveal themselves immediately and must be sought out. Except for it's spectacular cathedral, the city—rebuilt after heavy bombing in World War II—is not always in and of itself particularly beautiful. It does, however, have the kind of life and energy that characterize a major modern metropolis.

History

Milan was a Celtic settlement until the Romans conquered it in 222 B.C. It was an early center of Christianity, which was officially recognized as a religion in the 4th century when Constantine the Great issued his Edict of Milan. By the early Middle Ages, Milan had been overrun by Attila the Hun, the Franks, and the Burgundians.

For centuries afterwards, the city was dominated by a series of now-legendary families, particularly the Visconti and the Sforzas. Ludovico il Moro Sforza (1451–1508) was a powerful patron of the arts who brought Leonardo da Vinci and Bramante, among others, to work in Milan.

The French invaded and seized control of the city in the 16th century, but were ousted by the Austrians in 1713. A French-Austrian tug-of-war ensued, with Napoleon proclaiming Milan the capital of his Cisalpine Republic, and the Austrians returning after Napoleon was defeated.

The Milanese themselves finally rebelled and claimed their independence in 1848, throwing their support to King Victor Emmanuel of Savoy, who eventually became king of a united Italy. In the Second World War, the city lost countless architectural and artistic treasures in bombing attacks. Another gruesome spectacle took place in 1945 when Mussolini, his mistress Clara Petracci, and several other Fascist leaders were shot by Italian Partisans and strung up by the heels in the Piazza del Duomo.

Attractions

Arco della Pace (Arch of Peace) [10]: First built in honor of Napoleon, this neoclassical triumphal arch in the park behind the Sforza castle was modelled after one in Rome to mark the beginning of Napoleon's Simplon Road through the Alps to France.

Castello Sforzesco (Sforza Castle) [9]: The Sforzas eventually succeeded the Viscontis; in 1405, Duke Francesco commissioned a new family castle to be built right over the old Visconti pile. Today, its restored rooms house the *Museo d'Arte Antica* (Museum of Antique Art), featuring Michaelangelo's unfinished Rondanini Pietà, among other treasures. Behind the castle is the large and pleasant *Parco Sempione,* a welcome oasis of green.

Cimitero Monumentale (Cemetery) [11]: Sometimes described as a museum of funerary art, this large necropolis exerts an odd fascination.

***Duomo (Cathedral): Undoubtedly the greatest site and true glory of the city, the massive cathedral of Milan was begun under a Visconti in the 14th century and completed over the course of the centuries in a Gothic style. Lombard art and noteworthy mon-

Milan Attractions:
1. Cathedral
2. Palazzo Reale
3. Palace of the Archbishop
4. Galleria Vittorio Emanuele
5. Teatro alla Scala
6. Museo Poldi Pezzoli
7. Pinacoteca di Brera
8. Museo Civico di Storia Naturale
9. Castello Sforzesco
10. Arco della Pace
11. Cimitero Monumentale
12. Santa Maria della Grazie
13. Museo Nazionale della Scienza e della Tecnica
14. Sant'Ambrogio
15. San Lorenzo Maggiore
16. Sant'Eustorgio
17. San Babila
18. San Satiro
19. Palazzo Ambrosiana
20. Piazza Mercanti

uments fill the interior. No visit is complete without a special trip to the roof, where you can look out over the piazza and climb among the intricately carved finials.

Galleria Vittorio Emanuele [4]: In front and to one side of the cathedral, leading to La Scala, is this famous glass-roofed Milanese landmark—*the* place to stroll, window-shop, see and be seen; the intense sport of people-watching is a daily ritual at several cafés and restaurants here.

Museo Nazionale della Scienza e della Tecnica (National Museum of Science and Technology) [13]: Extensive collections in several areas of this museum may be of interest to the scientifically minded.

Museo Poldi Pezzoli (Pezzo-Poldi Museum) [6]: Once the home and private art collection of a Milanese nobleman, the museum is especially noteworthy for

Duomo

MILAN

0 Yards 400

Meters

its paintings by such masters as Piero della Francesca, Bellini, Guardi, Tiepolo, and Brueghel.

Palazzo Reale [2]: A neoclassical building from the late 18th century, the palace now houses the *Museo del Duomo* (Cathedral Museum) and the *Civico Museo d'Arte Contemporanea* (Museum of Contemporary Art). Behind the palazzo, at Piazza Fontana, you'll find the *Palace of the*

Archbishop [3], the oldest section of which dates from 1170.

**Palazzo dell'Ambrosiana [19]: The palazzo, dating from 1618, contains a remarkable series of masterpieces in oil by artists like Raphael, Leonardo, Caravaggio, and Titian in its *Pinacoteca* (picture gallery). Its world-famous *Biblioteca* (library) is stocked with precious manuscripts, including one by Virgil.

***Palazzo e Pinacoteca di Brera (Brera Palace and Art Gallery) [7]: One of the most important picture collections in Italy, with a special emphasis on Venetian and Lombard work, fills room after room of this 17th-century palace. Highlights include a Caravaggio, a Raffaello, and Mantegna's powerful *Dead Christ*.

San Lorenzo Maggiore [15]: A striking assemblage of 16 ancient Roman columns in front serves as a reminder that the original church here dated from the fourth century; you'll find fragments of wall mosaics from that same period inside.

San Satiro [14]: The architect Bramante, who helped create St. Peter's in Rome, designed this treasure of early Renaissance architecture.

*Sant'Ambrogio [14]: This early church, with its distinctive peaked gable, originally dates from the 4th century and was later rebuilt as a Romanesque basilica. A side chapel leads to the ancient

Sant'Ambrogio

San Vittore in Ciel d'Oro (Basilica Fausta), one of the oldest churches in Italy.

Sant'Eustorgio [16]: A pure Lombard style characterizes the façade of this 13th-century reconstruction of a 4th-century church.

*Santa Maria delle Grazie [12]: Magnificent 15th-century frescoes decorate the interior of this church, which was started in Gothic and completed in Renaissance style. In the Dominican monastery next door you'll find Leonardo's famous *Cenacolo* (Last Supper).

Teatro alla Scala [5]: Italy's most famous and demanding opera house, where perfect acoustics reveal every twinkle and edge in a singer's voice. The opera season tends to sell out instantly, but try to get seats for one of the other musical events held here—an experience you won't forget.

Moscow

Moscow has always been considered the heart of Russia, and it is here that the monuments of Soviet power and culture are seen at their most grand and grandiose. The capital of the Soviet Union is one of the largest cities in the world, both in size and population (over 8 million), and it's a melting pot of all the ethnically diverse groups that comprise the Union of Soviet Socialist Republics. The great sights of Moscow range from 15th-century cathedrals with onion domes and ancient icons to the mighty fortress known as the Kremlin to Lenin's Tomb in Red Square. Though you'll need to reserve tickets well in advance, an opera or ballet performance at the Bolshoi, or an evening at the famed Moscow Circus—where laughter and excitement break down the barriers of language and ideology—are memorable experiences. The outward character of Moscow, so often viewed as stiff, regimented, and unfailingly propagandist, is slowly changing in the wake of *glasnost* and *perestroika*. You may be surprised at the cleanliness of Moscow—it's just one example of the intense civic pride the Muscovites feel towards their city.

History

Moscow was officially noted for the first time in 1147; less than ten years later, the first wooden fortress was erected by Prince Juri Dolgoruki. In the 13th century, the city was captured by a Tartar-Mongolian descendant of Genghis Khan. The Great Khan of the Golden Horde ruled the area as a province for 250 years. In this subservient capacity, it became the capital of a principality.

Appointed Grand Duke by the Great Khan, Ivan Kalita transferred his residence to Moscow in 1328 and walled in his *kremlin* (fortress) with oak beams. A new stone wall was added in 1368, which later withstood sieges by the Great Khan. Hostilities between the Muscovites and the Tartars continued up until about 1400, although Crimean Tartars destroyed the Kremlin walls as late as 1571.

Between 1462 and 1505, Ivan III, calling himself Grand Duke of Moscow and all of Russia, expanded the boundaries of the Russian state, which he called Moscovia. Aware of the Renaissance in Western Europe, Ivan brought architects and artists from the west, and from other culturally rich Russian cities, to work in Moscow. The legendary Ivan the Terrible (1547–1584) was the first to have himself crowned Czar of all Russians.

After destruction by Tartars and Poles in the 16th century, Moscow grew steadily and established itself as the most powerful city in Russia.

In 1714, however, Peter I (called Peter the Great), one of a long line of Romanov czars, moved the country's capital from Moscow to St. Petersburg. Moscow remained the headquarters of the Russian Orthodox Church, and the czars returned for their coronations, which were held in the Uspensky (Assumption) Cathedral in the Kremlin.

A university and the city's major theaters were established in the 18th and 19th centuries. As the city spread beyond the walls of the Kremlin, the ring of protective fortress monasteries and convents that had helped to protect Moscow in times past were gradually assimilated into the newer parts of the city. The armies of Napoleon could not conquer Moscow in 1812, yet devastating fires raged, consuming almost three-quarters of the city. In 1825, Alexander I assembled a special commission to reconstruct Moscow, and this resulted in the building of the Bolshoi Theater and several other lavish, imperial-style structures.

Following the success of the 1917 Revolution, Russia's Bolshevik government moved its headquarters to Moscow and the Kremlin again became the seat of Russian power. Since that time, the city has undergone major urban changes, as new office blocks and skyscrapers were built, streets widened, and older areas of the city were demolished. The population doubled between 1926 and 1939. Despite formidable forces, the Nazis were unable to conquer Moscow in the Second World War.

Today, Moscow stands in the center of Mikhail Gorbachev's bold plans for restructuring the moribund Soviet economy (long lines and shortages of basic goods characterize life for the average Muscovite) and democratizing, in some respects, the monolithic Communist party structure.

Attractions

*Andrei Rublyov Museum [43]: Andrei Rublyov (1360–1430) is considered the most important Russian painter of the Middle Ages. Several of his icons, along with those painted by Theophanes the Greek and Daniel Tschorny, are housed within the former Andronikov monastery, founded in the 14th century.

*Bolshoi Theater [11]: The famed Bolshoi Opera and Ballet company perform in this impressive neoclassical theater rebuilt in its present form in the mid-19th century. Tickets are hard to come by, so reserve well in advance of your visit.

Borodino Panorama [35]: A cylindrical building erected in 1962 on the 150th anniversary of the Battle of Borodino houses enormous canvases depicting this decisive battle against Napoleon in 1812.

Chekhov Museum [27]: The life and work of the great dramatist Anton Chekhov is commemorated in this house, where he lived from 1886 to 1890.

Don Monastery [44]: Founded in 1591 after the final

victory over the Tartars, the monastery was named for the much-revered image of the Holy Virgin of Don; today the *Museum of Architecture* is housed here.

Gorky Park [33]: One of Moscow's most popular spots, although recently it's developed a reputation as a place of petty crime, Gorky Park was built in 1928 on the right bank of the Moskva River. Several imperial and private gardens were taken over to make the park, which features cafés, a beer hall, an open-air theater, and two giant ferris wheels.

Museum of History

House of the Soviet Army [29]: The building, which dates from 1802, was known in pre-Revolutionary days as the Institute for Young Aristocratic Women.

Kremlin (see below).

*Lenin Library [7]: One of Moscow's most attractive buildings, the library was built in the late 18th century as the home of a wealthy family; the older section sits behind a newer one, erected in 1940.

*Museum of History [4]: Moscow's oldest museum was completed in 1883 and is dedicated to the origin and history of the Russian peoples from their beginnings through the end of the 19th century. A renovation program has shifted many of the exhibits to various annexes, but the museum still contains many uniquely fascinating collections, including ancient furnishings, birch-bark scrolls from the 10th century, the robes of Ivan the Terrible, and the bed Napoleon abandoned when he left Russia.

***New Maiden Convent (Novodevichy Monastyr) [20]: After the Kremlin, this 16th-century convent, once part of a protective ring of fortified convents and monasteries, is the most historically important building complex in Moscow. Boris Godunov was proclaimed czar here in 1598; about a hundred years later, the sister of Peter the Great, Sophia, was imprisoned in the convent for promoting rebellion against her brother; and scores of unwanted noble ladies ended their days in rooms here. *Smolensk Cathedral* is now a museum of 16th- and 17th-century Russian applied arts, and the whole complex is a branch of the Museum of History. Numerous Russian greats are buried in a cemetery to the south of the convent: Gogol, Chekhov, Prokofiev, Scriabin, and Krushchev, among them.

Kremlin Attractions:
1. Borovitsky Tower
2. Water Tower
3. Annunciation Tower
4. Secret Passage Tower
5. First Unnamed Tower
6. Second Unnamed Tower
7. Peter's Tower
8. Beklemischev Tower
9. Konstantin-Jelena Tower
10. Nabat Tower
11. Tower of the Czar
12. Spassky (Savior) Tower
13. Senate Tower
14. Nicholas Tower
15. Corner Arsenal Tower
16. Central Arsenal Tower
17. Troitskaya (Trinity) Tower
18. Bridge to the Kutafja Tower
19. Kutafya Tower
20. Commandant Tower
21. Armaments Tower
22. Kremlin Wall
23. Cathedral Square
24. Church of the Twelve Apostles
25. Cathedral of the Annunciation (Blagoveshchensky)
26. Uspensky Cathedral (Cathedral of the Assumption)
27. Palace of Facets (Granovitaya Palace)
28. Cathedral of Michael the Archangel
29. Ivan the Great Belltower
30. Terjem Palace
31. Kremlin Palace Churches
32. Patriarchal Palace
33. Pleasure Palace
34. Arsenal
35. USSR Supreme Council
36. Lenin Statue
37. Kremlin Palace
38. Armory (Oruzheinaya Palata)
39. Czar Puschka
40. Czar Bell
41. Cannons
42. Cannons
43. Palace of Congress
44. Tomb of the Unknown Soldier

New Monastery of the Savior (Novospassky Monastyr) [32]: Behind the beautiful brick wall are five churches from the mid-15th century and a bell tower.

Ostankino Palace Museum [40]: The estate belonged to Count Sheremetyev, but it was his 210,000 serfs who created this marvelous timber palace in the 18th century—embellishing it with superb parquet floors, tiled stoves and fireplaces, painted ceilings, and delicately carved portals, doors, columns, and cornices. On the grounds of the estate is the ****Exhibition of Economic Achievement** [41], a kind of cultural theme park where various aspects of Soviet life are delineated in exhibits ranging from agriculture and science to culture and industry. There's much to see and do: A zoo, a circus, theaters, restaurants, and cafés fill the grounds. Outside the North Gate is Vera Mukhina's immense steel statue called "Worker and Farm

Exhibition of Economic Achievement

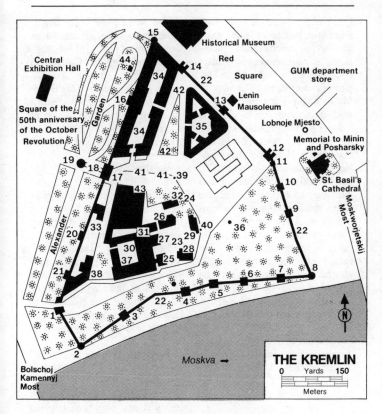

Central Exhibition Hall

Historical Museum

Red Square

GUM department store

Square of the 50th anniversary of the October Revolution

Garden

Lenin Mausoleum

Lobnoje Mjesto

Memorial to Minin and Posharsky

St. Basil's Cathedral

Alexander

Moskworjetskij Most

THE KREMLIN

0   Yards   150

Meters

Moskva →

Bolschoj Kamennyj Most

N

Woman," exhibited at the Paris World's Fair of 1937, and another huge monument commemorating Soviet space exploration.

Pushkin House (Museum) [19]: Memorabilia and documents pertaining to the life, work, and personality of the great Russian poet are on display.

**Pushkin Museum of the Visual Arts [16]: Because this is primarily a teaching museum, there are many copies mixed in with original works of art, but the originals tend towards the magnificent and the copies are convincing: The painting collection contains works by Botticelli, Perugino, Canaletto, Tiepolo, Veronese, El Greco, Rubens, Rembrandt, Brueghel, Fragonard, and a whole shimmering host of Impressionists.

***Red Square: Since the time of Ivan III (15th century), Red Square has been a place for assemblies, seasonal markets, political, and religious events. It was here that the Tartars assaulted the Kremlin, patriarchs and czars marched in ceremonious processions, state enemies were executed, and, today, May Day parades are held. The **Lenin Mausoleum** [2]: Lenin is venerated in Russia much like the wonder-working saints of old, and his embalmed body lies in this mausoleum of red porphyry and black granite dating from 1930 and located on Red Square. Lines are long, so expect a minimum wait of half an hour, and remember, cameras are not allowed inside. Escorted groups are generally given precedence. (For further information on the founder of the Soviet state, visit the comprehensive **Central Lenin Museum** [10], where his life is documented and his personal belongings are shown.) Several prominent Soviet heroes and one American (John Reed, who wrote *Ten Days That Shook the World*), are buried in the Kremlin wall behind the mausoleum. On the east side of Red Square is the largest department store in the Soviet Union, called *GUM* [3] for short.

**Saint Basil's Cathedral [5]: Ivan the Terrible commissioned the construction of this unusual church to celebrate his victory over the Tartar Khan of Kazan in the 16th century. Nine churches in all comprise the complex.

Tolstoy Museum [18]: The author of *War and Peace* and *Anna Karenina* lived here with his family from 1872 to 1901, and sixteen rooms from that period have been preserved as a museum.

***Tretyakov Gallery [24]: Moscow's finest art gallery provides a comprehensive overview of Russian painting, displaying everything from rare mosaics and icons to contemporary work—only the Constructivists have been omitted.

***Kremlin (*See the map of the Kremlin for the following points of interest*):

The political heart of the Soviet Union is this roughly pentagonal complex surrounded by massive, red-brick walls punctuated by 21 towers, five of which have gates and illuminate giant red stars at night. The whole complex takes up about 70 acres and was built on a hill overlooking the Moskva River. Within this amazing historical compendium you'll find Moscow's greatest architectural treasures, spanning the centuries from pre-czarist Russia to the Russia of the Soviet state.

When you enter from Red

Lenin Mausoleum

Moscow: Saint Basil's Cathedral

Munich: Chinese tower in the English Garden

Paris: Eiffel Tower

Prague: Hradčany

Rome: Spanish Steps and Church of Trinità dei Monti

Stockholm: Church of Riddarholm

Vienna: Saint Stephan's Cathedral

Zurich: Grossmünster in the Old City

Square through the *Spassky Tower*
[12], the building of the *Presidency of the Supreme Soviet of the
Soviet Union* is on your right. The
triangular neoclassical building
behind this with a Russian flag flying over its green dome is the seat
of the Soviet government. An
enormous bronze cannon cast in
1586 and known as *Czar Puschka*
[39] stands to one side of Kalyayev
Square. Across the lawn to the
west is the 17th-century *Church of
the Twelve Apostles* [24], which
served as the Russian Patriarch's
private church, and the adjacent
Patriarchal Palace [32], where he
lived. The two buildings now
serve as the *Museum of the Art and
Culture of the 17th Century.*

Cathedral Square [23]: The ancient center of the Kremlin is surrounded by three large cathedrals
(see below) built in old Russian
style, the enormous golden-domed *Ivan the Great Bell Tower*
[29], dating from about 1600, and
the 15th-century *Palace of Facets*
(Granovitaya Palace) [27], the
oldest of Moscow's public buildings.

***Uspensky (Assumption) Cathedral* [26]: With its limestone
walls and five gilded onion domes,
it is the largest cathedral on the
square. It was built in the 15th century by the Italian architect Fiorovanti, and is filled with rare icons
and original frescoes. The coronations of the czars took place here
and it was also their private
church.

Cathedral of Michael the Archangel (Arkhangelsky) [28]: Char-

Moscow Attractions:
1. Tower of the Savior
2. Lenin Mausoleum
3. GUM
4. Museum of History
5. St. Basil's Cathedral
6. Great Palace of the Kremlin
7. Lenin Library
8. Riding School Building
9. Intourist Center
10. Central Lenin Museum
11. Bolshoi Theater
12. City Hall
13. Polytechnic Museum
14. Museum of the History and
Reconstruction of Moscow
15. Medical Academy
16. Pushkin Museum of the
Visual Arts
17. Open-Air Swimming Pool
"Moscow"
18. Tolstoy Museum
19. Pushkin House (Museum)
20. New Maiden Convent (Novodevichy
Monastyr)
21. Permanent Architectural Exhibition
of the SU
22. Luzhniki Sport Center
23. New Lomonosov University
24. Tretyakov Gallery
25. Planetarium
26. Zoological Garden
27. Chekhov Museum
28. Byelorussian Train Station
29. House of the Soviet Army
30. Komsomol Square
31. Museum of the Art and Culture of
the Orient
32. New Monastery of the Savior
33. Gorky Park
34. Gorki Museum
35. Kiev Train Station/Borodino
Panorama
36. Peter's Palace
37. Church of the Mother of God of
Tichwin
38. Sputnik Memorial
39. Botanical Garden of the Academy
of Sciences
40. Ostankino Palace Museum
41. Exhibition of Economic
Achievement
42. Sokolniki Park
43. Andrey Rublyov Museum
44. Don Monastery

acterized by five silver domes, this early-16th-century cathedral has been the burial place of every Russian czar from Ivan Kalita to Peter the Great (the one exception is Boris Godunov). A 15-meter- (43-foot-) high carved wooden iconostasis contains an icon of the Archangel attributed to Andrei Rublyov, and there are restored medieval murals.

Cathedral of the Annunciation (Blagoveshchensky) [25]: This remarkable monument, once a private chapel of the czars, stands beside the Grand Kremlin Palace. Begun in the 14th century, it was rebuilt during the reign of Ivan the Terrible, when six new gilded cupolas were added. The stone portals date from the 16th century and are particularly fine. Inside you'll find a beautiful iconostasis with icons by Andrei Rublyov, important frescoes painted in 1508, and a floor of polished agate jasper, a gift of the Shah of Persia.

Grand Kremlin Palace [37]:

The imperial family once used this 19th-century, yellow-and-white-walled palace as their Moscow residence; today it acts as a government building where the Supreme Soviets of the USSR and the Supreme Soviets of the Russian Federation (Parliament) meet.

Palace of Congresses [43]: The newest addition to the Kremlin is this glass-and-aluminum building completed in 1967. It contains a concert hall where opera, ballet, and concerts are performed, and its hundreds of different rooms are used for official functions of all kinds.

Armory [38]: Czarist treasures and royal frou-frou of all kinds (Fabergé eggs, imperial carriages, ball gowns) fill the display cases of this museum located beside the Grand Kremlin Palace. A special highlight, for which advance arrangement must be made, is the *Diamond Fund,* where Catherine II's diamond-studded crown and scepter may be seen.

Munich

Beer and *gemütlichkeit* flow freely in Munich, as a visit to any of the city's crowded *Hofbräuhausern* will immediately testify. The Bavarian character of Munich makes it softer, friendlier, and more lighthearted than any other city in Germany—a place of easygoing charm and considerable ambience. It's also the southern cultural capital of the Federal Republic, as well as the home of the renowned Bavarian State Opera, dozens of theaters, concert halls, and art museums of the highest caliber. Munich wears its sophistication with a smile for most of the year—but the city can get downright raucous during its two major festivals: the *Oktoberfest* and the pre-Lenten *Fasching,* when anything can and usually does happen. Although Munich was greatly damaged in the last war, it rebuilt and restored itself with a Baroque exuberance that matches the personality of the city.

History

The city developed along the Isar River, which flows down from the nearby Bavarian Alps to eventually empty into the Danube. In the ninth century, Benedictine monks—*Münichen* in High German—founded a monastery in the area. The city named *München* was founded in 1158 by Henry the Lion, who had been given this part of Bavaria by the Emperor Friedrich Barbarossa. Henry was eventually ousted and was replaced by a line of Palatine princes, the Wittelsbachs, who ruled Munich from the 12th century until the end of World War I.

During the 17th century, Munich was briefly occupied by both Swedish and Spanish troops; then the omnipresent Napoleon marched into the city in 1805, bestowing the title of king on the Wittelsbach line.

Munich's fortunes rose with the accession of the Bavarian King Ludwig I, whose goal was to make the city one of the most beautiful in Europe. Many of Munich's most prominent buildings date from his reign, which ended in 1848, when his affair with a Spanish dancer named Lola Montez lead to his abdication during a civil revolution. Ludwig II, his 18-year-old grandson—later known as the "Dream King" and "Mad Ludwig"—assumed the throne in 1864. It was he who ordered the construction of three now-famous castles and supported the composer Richard Wagner. Unhappily, he was declared mentally incompetent and stripped of his powers; he eventually died by drowning at the age of 40.

The last remaining Wittelsbach, King Ludwig III, was overthrown by revolutionaries after Germany's defeat in World War I, at which time Bavaria declared itself a republic. Munich then became an early center of the Nazi movement, and it was here that Hitler and his National Socialists tried to seize power in 1923 during the Beer Garden Putsch. By 1933, the Nazis had expelled the last legitimately elected town council and become the capital of the Nazi movement. Mussolini, Chamberlain, and Daladier came to Munich in 1938 to meet with Hitler and agree to his demands to annex the Sudetenland.

Bombing raids in World War II destroyed much of old Munich, but the city was rebuilt with an astute regard for historical accuracy. The 1972 Olympic Games, held in Munich, were the tragic backdrop for the terrorist kidnapping and murder of Israeli athletes.

Attractions

***Alte Pinakothek** (Old Picture Gallery) [33]: An outstanding collection of paintings—including Dutch and Flemish works from the 14th to the 18th century, important Dürers, and some marvelous canvases by Rubens—is on display in this early 19th-century museum. It was built in 1836 to house the collections of Ludwig I.

Alter Hof (Old Court) [18]: In 1255, Ludwig the Strong commissioned the construction of this castle, which became the imperial residence of Ludwig the Bavarian when he was crowned Kaiser of Germany in 1328.

***Asamkirche** [13]: The endlessly swirling roulades of rich decoration in this late Baroque church, designed and built by the Asam brothers in the 18th century, are exhilarating to some and vulgar to others; either way, it's worth a visit to make up your own mind.

Augustinerkirche [6]: This former church and monastery of the Augustinian order was built in the late 13th century and is now the home of the rather specialized *Deutsches Jagdmuseum* (German Hunting Museum).

****Bayrisches National-museum** (Bavarian National Museum) [39]: Look no further if you want an introduction to Bavarian culture: Art and historical exhibits from the Middle Ages through the 19th century form the basis for the museum, but there is also an enormous arts and crafts collection and a charming collection of Christmas nativity scenes.

Damenstiftskirche [3]: One of Munich's most beautiful Baroque churches, it was completed in 1735 and decorated by the Asam brothers; it was restored after it was utterly destroyed in the last war.

***Deutsches Museum** (German Museum), Isarinsel (Ludwigsbrucke): A U-boat from 1906, antique locomotives, a planetarium, mining exhibits in simulated caverns . . . the largest technical museum in the world offers enough of the unusual to keep you (and the kids) occupied for hours.

Englischer Garten (English

Garden) [38]: A favorite spot for strolling, nude sunbathing, bike riding, and beer drinking (the beer garden at the Chinese Pagoda is one of Munich's largest), this lovely, landscaped park is one of Europe's oldest, dating from the 18th century.

**Frauenkirche (Cathedral of Our Lady) [7]: A distinctive Munich landmark with its two, tall towers capped by onion domes, the cathedral contains some rare, Gothic, stained-glass windows, religious art, and the tombs of the Wittelsbach line.

Friedensengel (Angel of Peace) [41]: A 19th-century, Florentine-style garden and terrace are a monument to peace.

*Glyptothek [32]: Ancient Greek and Roman sculptures are exhibited in the halls of this early 19th-century museum designed by Carl von Fischer.

**Haus der Kunst (House of Art) [37]: Built during the Hitler-era—which makes it something of a curiosity in itself—the building's west wing houses the **Staatsgalerie Moderner Kunst (State Gallery of Modern Art), dedicated to the sort of work the Third Reich would no doubt have found decadent and consigned to the flames.

Heiliggeistkirche (Church of the Holy Ghost) [16]: One of the oldest buildings in Munich, the Gothic church and adjacent hospital were completed in 1392. The interior received its Baroque embellishments some 400 years later.

*Hofbräuhaus [17]: To see

Munich Attractions:
1. Karlsplatz
2. Bürgersaalkirche (Municipal Hall Church)
3. Damenstiftkirche
4. The Old Academy
5. Michaelskirche (Church of Saint Michael)
6. Church of the Augustinians
7. Frauenkirche
8. Marienplatz
9. New City Hall
10. Old City Hall
11. Dreifaltigkeitskirche (Church of the Holy Trinity)
12. Promenadenplatz
13. Asam Church
14. City Museum
15. Peterskirche (St. Peter's Church)
16. Heiliggeistkirche (Church of the Holy Spirit)
17. Hofbräuhaus
18. Alter Hof (Old Court)
19. Münzhof
20. Max-Joseph-Platz
21. National Theater
22. Residenz
23. Odeonsplatz
24. Feldherrnhalle (General's Hall)
25. Theatinerkirche
26. Library
27. Ludwigskirche
28. University
29. Siegestor
30. Wittelsbacherplatz
31. Karolinenplatz
32. Königsplatz (Glyptothek)
33. Old and New Pinakothek (Picture Gallery)
34. City Gallery
35. Hofgarten (Royal Gardens)
36. Palace of Prince Carl
37. Haus der Kunst (Museum of Modern Art)
38. The English Garden
39. Bavarian National Museum
40. Schackgalerie
41. Friedensengel (Angel of Peace)
42. "Bavaria" (statue)

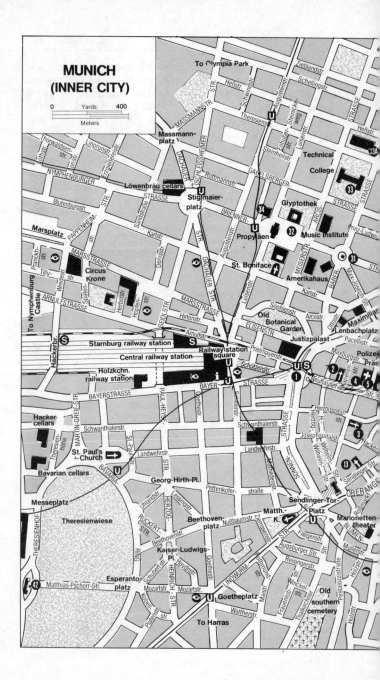

SCHWABING

Chinese Tower

Monopteros

Adalbertstr.
Akademiestr.
Blutenstr.
Lurkenstr.
Adalbertstr.
29
Theresienstr.
Schellingstr.
28
27
26
Schönfeldstr.
Turkenstr.
Amalienstr.
MÜLLER-RING
VON-DER-TANN-STRASSE
Glückstr.
Jägerstr.
Fursten-
str.
Finken-
str.
30
Galerie-
36
PRINZREGENTEN-
37
38
Salvator-
platz
23
35
HOFGARTEN
39
40
41
Salvatorstr.
25
24
22
12
Maffeistr.
Perusa-
20
21
MARSTALLSTRASSE
KARL-SEITZ-STRASSE
OETTINGER STRASSE
STRASSE
Lerchenfeldstr.
Liebigstr.
Sankt-Anna-
str.
Isar
WILDENMAYR-
Schrammerstr.
19
Platz
MAXIMILIANSTR.
Rob.-Koch-Str.
Gewurzmuhlstr.
STERN-
STR.
Reitmorstr.
Kaufingerstr.
Burkleinstr.
18
9
DIENERSTR.
Museum of
Ethnology
Monument to
Maximilian II
Maximilianeum
10
17
Maximilians-
brücke
Rosental
15
16
Tal
Marienstr.
WIMMER-R.
Mariannen-
platz
N
kobs-Platz
14
Outdoor
market
Westenriedertr.
Valentin-Mus.
Isartor-
platz
FRAUENSTRASSE
Thierschstr.
STEINSDORF-
Rumfordstr.
Buttermelcherstr.
Aventinstr.
Baaderpl.
ZWEIBRÜCKENSTR.
Ludwigs-
brücke
INNERE WIENER-STRASSE
Preysingstraße
CORNELIUS-
STR.
Reichenbach-
Kohlstr.
Gärtner-
platz
Baaderplatz
Congress Hall
GASTEIG
Center of
Culture
Kellerstr.
Theater am
Gärtnerplatz
ERHARDTSTR.
HAID-
HAUSEN
FRAUNHOFERSTRASSE
Klenze-
str.
Baaderstr.
MITTELSBACHERSTR.
German Museum
Zeppelin-
straße
Paulaner-
platz
Hochstr.
Rosenheimer Platz
Isar
Quellenstr.
Luften-
str.
Scheltinger-
str.

Hofbräuhaus

Neues Rathaus

what life in the beer capital of the world can be like, take a seat in this enormous hall: overworked fräuleins bring your beer in steins; fresh pretzels and radishes are sold; and you can eat, drink, dance, and be merry.

Karlsplatz [1]: The locals call this square "Stachus" and go underneath it to shop; if subterranean boutiques don't appeal to you, try Hertie's department store across the square.

*Marienplatz [8]: This bustling square, the urban heart of Munich, takes its name from the 17th-century, gilded statue of the Virgin, which acts as a centerpiece. The north side of the square is taken up by the ornate **Neues Rathaus** (New City Hall) [9], completed in 1908 with a much-loved **Glockenspiel* in its tower: At 11 A.M. and 5 P.M., a contingent of figures, some dancing, some jousting, make their circuit. At 9 P.M., the "Münchner Kindel" (Child of Munich) is taken off to bed by an angel. On the east side of the square sits the medieval **Altes Rathaus** (Old City Hall) [10], destroyed in the war and restored using the original plan.

*Max-Joseph-Platz [20]: In the center of this 19th-century, cobblestoned square stands a bronze monument erected by Ludwig I to honor his father, Maximilian I Joseph. To everyone's surprise, a 21-year-old novice named Carl von Fischer won the royal commission to design the stately **Nationaltheater** [21], that faces the square. It was completed in 1818, then rebuilt after damage from a fire and World War II; today it is the home of the highly esteemed Bavarian State Opera. Also on the square is the entrance to the **Residenz** [22], the royal palace of the Wittelsbachs, where you can see state rooms and royal suites in a variety of historical styles—Renaissance to neoclassical—as well as the *Schatzkammer,* or treasury. Mozart's opera *Ideomeneo* premiered in the sumptuously rococo *Cuvillies Theater.*

*Michaelskirche [5]: The Jesuits built this spacious, barrelvaulted, white-stucco, Renaissance church—one of the finest in Germany—as a preaching hall. Napoleon's stepson, Eugène de Beauharnais, rests in a large neoclassical tomb designed by Thorvaldsen, and Ludwig II is buried in the vault.

***Neue Pinakothek (New Picture Gallery) [33a]: Ludwig I assigned many building projects in Munich, and commissioned the Neue Pinakothek to house his "modern" collections, which still reside here. The building itself was completely rebuilt after the war.

*Odeonsplatz [23]: While still Crown Prince, Ludwig I commissioned Leo von Klenze to design and build this square and many of the other buildings extending down to Theresienstrasse. The **Feldherrnhalle** (General's Hall) [24] was inspired by the Florentine Loggia dei Lanzi. Italian influences can also be discerned in the handsome façade of the **Theatinerkirche** [25], built in the mid-17th century for the Theatine monks (the façade, with its twin domes, came a century

later); the interior, mostly a pristine white, contains paintings by Tintoretto.

*Olympiapark, Petuelring: The 1972 Olympic Summer Games were held in this sports and recreation complex, which includes swimming pools (where U.S. athlete Mark Spitz won his five gold medals), tracks, and the *Olympic Stadium* with its remarkable roof. At the top of the *Olympia Tower,* there is an observation deck and a revolving restaurant.

Peterskirche [15]: The reconstructed spire of this 14th-century church is a Munich landmark and offers a grand view out over the city towards the Lower Alps. Many of the interior treasures—including the high altar—were hidden during World War II and thus escaped the destruction that consumed so much of the city.

*Schackgalerie [40]: This interesting collection of 19th-century paintings belonged to Adolf Schack, a Prussian official, who bequeathed them to Kaiser Wilhelm II. The Kaiser had the Schackgalerie built in the early years of the 20th century to house them.

***Schloss Nymphenburg: Located just west of the city limits, the palace—the former summer residence of the kings of Bavaria—stands in an enormous park filled with lakes, hunting lodges, pleasure palaces, and gardens. Baroque and rococo embellishments abound.

Schwabing: This famous dis-

Schloss Nymphenburg

trict, once the city's artistic and intellectual center and today a kind of Bavarian Greenwich Village, lies north of the University of Munich. Over 200 restaurants (many of them ethnic), lots of cafés, boutiques, discos, and an endless street scene make Schwabing a great place to wander in the evening hours.

Siegestor (Victory Gate) [29]: Ludwig I commissioned this gate, based on the Arch of Constantine in Rome, to commemorate the Bavarian army.

**Staatliche Antikensammlungen (State Antiquities Collection) [32]: You'll find superb attic vases, among other noteworthy treasures, in this Corinthian-style hall built between 1838 and 1848.

*Städtische Galerie (City Gallery) [34]: Paintings by the German Romantics and *Der Blaue Reiter* expressionist group highlight this collection housed in the late-19th-century villa of the painter Franz von Lenbach.

Stadtmuseum (City Museum) [14]: This late 15th-century building contains an intriguing hodgepodge of city museums and collections, ranging from a *Museum of Photography* to a remarkable collection of puppets and an exhibition of interior decoration in Munich.

*Viktualienmarkt (Food Market): Cheese, wine, fruit, sausages, sauerkraut—you name it, it's here from Monday through Saturday in this fabulous open-air market.

Villa Stuck, Prinzregentenstrasse 60: Devotees of Art Nouveau, called *Jugendstil* in Germany, will not want to miss this superb example of a house decorated entirely in this distinctive fin-de-siècle style. It contains several galleries.

Oslo

Like most of his countrymen, King Gustav V of Norway enjoys cross-country skiing, and is sometimes seen leaving his Oslo home—the Royal Palace—for a brisk trek along one of the many wooded trails in this Nordic capital city. Oslo, as the king would be the first to admit, is a city for nature-lovers. Those who love brisk air, white snow, the summer midnight sun, panoramic vistas of fjords, and the salty exhilaration that goes with a maritime port city will find Oslo just what the Vikings ordered. Located on the edge of a fjord, the city's topography of wooded hills and vast expanses of water ensures its status as one of the most beautiful of the Scandinavian cities. Be forewarned, however: It's also one of the most expensive cities in the world.

History

Indications are that the Oslo area was settled as long as 7,000 years ago, but in 1050, it was Viking King Harold Hårdråde who founded the trading town that became today's city. Later in the 11th century, the settlement became a regional ecclesiastical center and a massive cathedral was built, only the stones of which remain today.

Under King Håakon V Magnusson (1299–1319), Oslo was officially decreed the capital of Norway, and the mighty Akershus Castle—a symbol of royal power—was built. Harder times followed: The dread Black Death arrived in 1349, killing off most of the inhabitants; Norway united with Denmark, Oslo thus lost its capital status; and the wood-built town finally burnt to the ground in 1624 after repeated fires.

The ruling king of Norway and Denmark, Christian V, wanted a new capital to be built, and changed the ancient name from Oslo to one he liked better: Christiana. It was Christian who laid out the main streets of his new city as you find them today.

Separated from Denmark during the Napoleonic wars, Norway was realigned with Sweden, and ruled by Swedish-Norwegian kings until 1905. In 1925, the city's ancient name, Oslo, was put back into use.

Now a constitutional monarchy with parliamentary government, Norway's capital is a place where women have begun to make significant inroads in governmental policy—eight women are members of the female prime minister's cabinet.

Oslo has been home and battleground for such great artists as the playwright Henrik Ibsen and the Expressionist painter Edvard Munch. And, as might be expected in a hilly city where even the king skis after work, it was in the neighborhood of Oslo that the sport of ski-jumping was introduced to the world in 1879.

Attractions

*Akerhus Castle and Fortress (*Akershus Festning og Slott*) [2]: An important relic of medieval Norway, the castle and fortress were built around 1300 by King Håakon V and then redesigned in the 17th century in Renaissance style to suit the more modern taste of King Christian IV.

Aker Brygge: A favorite downtown meeting place, full of lively bars, cafés, shops and restaurants, this waterside development is a Viking version of Fisherman's Wharf.

Cathedral (Domkirken) [3]: Since its construction in the late 17th century, Oslo's cathedral has been through two major restorations; only the pulpit and altarpiece remain from 1699. Artists of the 20th century have also left their mark here: Emanuel Vigeland created the stained glass, Dagfinn Werenskiold made the bronze doors, and Hugo Lous Mohr painted the ceiling decorations.

City Hall (Rådhus) [1]: Sitting in a large square directly on the harbor, this two-towered Oslo landmark with its notable Art Deco interior was built in the 1930s.

Frogner Park: Located in the west of the city, the park acts as an outdoor museum for the massive metal and stone sculptures—650 in all—of the Norwegian sculptor Gustav Vigeland. Vigeland was given carte blanche by the city for this project; he took on nothing less than the entire cycle of human life as his subject, and worked on his creation from 1921 to 1943. A stadium and the *city museum* are also located on the grounds of the park.

Gamle Aker Kirke, Akersbakken 26: The oldest building in Oslo, dating from 1100, it still serves as a parish church.

Harbor: Oslo's lively waterfront is always full of incoming and outgoing vessels, and they're even more fun to watch when accompanied by a snack of fresh, tiny shrimp sold fresh from the boats of local fishermen.

Holmenkollen Ski Jump, take the "Holmenkollenbanen" train from the National Theater to Holmenkollen train station: As you stand in the observation tower, try to imagine yourself sailing off the edge of this giant landmark ski jump, built for the 1952 Winter Olympics and one of the world's highest; if the thought makes your legs wobbly, take the elevator back down to the intriguing *Ski Museum* carved in the rock face at the base of the jump. There you can see the preserved tip of a ski some 2,500 years old, among other things.

Kon-Tiki Museet (Kon-Tiki Museum): In 1947, Thor Heyerdahl crossed the oceans from Peru to Polynesia in the fragile balsa raft known as *Kon-Tiki,* exhibited here with Heyerdahl's *Ra II,* made from papyrus and sailed across the Atlantic in 1970. More examples of the Norwegian skill in sea exploration are on display in the nearby ***Norwegian Maritime Museum** (Norsk Sjofartsmuseum), which features two ships used for early polar expeditions.

Munch Museet (Munch Museum), Toyen Gate 53: Famous for the modern *angst* of his tortured Expressionist paintings, the Norwegian artist Edvard Munch bequeathed his entire collection of oils, drawings, and prints to the city. Here's a rare chance to see much of this brilliant artist's work assembled in one place.

National Gallery (Nasjonalgalleriet) [8]: Norwegian artists are given prominence here, but there is a good international collection and some particularly fine works by the French Impressionists.

*Norsk Folkemuseum (Norwegian Folk Museum), Museumveien 10: Close to the Viking Ship Museum lies this highly interest-

Oslo Attractions:
1. Town Hall
2. Akerhus
3. Cathedral
4. Parliament Building
5. Government Offices
6. Deichmanske Library
7. Arts and Craft Museum
8. National Gallery
9. History Museum
10. University
11. National Theater
12. Oalnu Palace

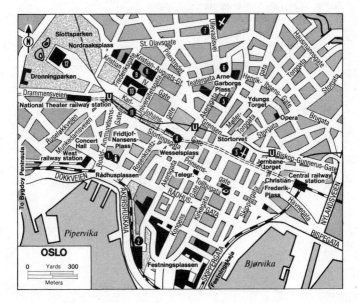

ing, open-air museum with historic buildings from all over Norway, including a distinctive wooden stave church from 1200 and the last apartment of the playwright Henrik Ibsen.

Royal Palace (Slottet) [12]: The changing of the guards take place at 1:30 P.M. and you can visit the undeniably lovely gardens, but you can't get into the palace itself unless you have a personal invitation.

Ruin Park (Minneparken), Oslo Gate at Bispegata: Excavations from medieval Oslo, including the foundation stones from the old St. Hallvard Cathedral, may be seen in this city park.

Sonja Henie–Niels Onstad Art Center (Sonja Henie–Niels Onstads Kunstsenter): Sonia Henie, the Norwegian skating champion who went on to star in the rinks of Hollywood, donated her important collection of 20th-century art to this museum.

Tryvannstarnet, Holmenkollen suburban rail line to Voksenkollen: The highest observation tower in Scandinavia is located atop Tryvann Hill in the outskirts of the city and features a buffet lunch and, after 3 P.M., a bar.

*Viking Ship House (Vikingskiphuset), Huk Aveny 35.: Don't miss this museum which contains three restored Viking longships, remarkable for their sophisticated simplicity of design; on ships such as these, the bodies of dead Viking kings and queens sailed out for a watery burial with all their treasures.

Paris

Paris, the City of Light; Paris, the City of Art; Paris, the City of Love—
everyone thinks of Paris in his own special way. It's been written about,
sung about, sighed over, and celebrated in a hundred different ways.
What makes this city so irresistible and endlessly fascinating? For one
thing, the physical beauty of Paris is incomparable; this is a world capital
where strolling is still a pleasure, and where delicate filigree details
haven't been mutilated or defaced. It's a city of great architectural splendor, where city planning has for the most part been sensitive to the needs
of those fortunates who live here. Consequently, it's a city that works *for*
people instead of against them. And, of course, it's a world center for the
arts and for science, and continues to set the pace in taste and fashion. In
Paris you'll find the greatest (and most modern) museums in the world,
the showrooms of the most famous designers, the best restaurants, the
most avant-garde (and the most classical) theater . . . add to this its evocative history and the dozens of major historical sights to be seen—Nôtre-
Dame, the Louvre, Sainte Chapelle, Napoleon's tomb, to name but a
few—and you begin to understand why, as the saying goes, *"Paris, c' est
la France."* Paris *is* France, in all its chic, sophisticated, fascinating
glory.

History

In 52 B.C., one of Julius Caesar's lieutenants seized the river fort of the
Gallic Parisii tribe on the ancient site of what is now the Île de la Cité and
began a new settlement. By the first decade of the sixth century, Paris had
its name and was the capital ruled by Clovis, King of the Franks. The city
remained in Merovingian hands for nearly 250 years.

Frequent Norman raids terrorized Paris until the Normans were defeated towards the end of the 9th century, after which time the monarchy
in France became established with the Capetians. Several of Paris' greatest monuments and institutions were begun, completed, or established
during the Capetian reign (987–1328), including Nôtre-Dame cathedral, the first fortress of the Louvre, the University of Paris (one of Europe's greatest medieval centers of learning), the Sorbonne, Sainte
Chapelle, and the basilica of St. Denis, just outside the city, which was
the prototype for the new Gothic style of architecture.

Paris, and all of France, entered a chaotic period under the Valois
kings. War with England was a constant factor; Paris was captured by the
English king, Henry V, and remained in English hands from 1420 to
1453.

François I (1515–1547), a great patron of the arts, helped to introduce the Italian Renaissance to France and began the reconstruction of the Louvre. For 30 years, however, Paris was the scene of murderous conflicts between Catholics and Protestants, culminating in the St. Bartholomew's Day Massacre in 1572, when 3,000 Huguenots were murdered in the city.

The size, influence, and architectural magnificence of Paris grew steadily during the 17th century, known as "Le Grand Siècle." Louis XIV, the "Sun King," built Versailles, Les Invalides, the Louvre colonnade, and the Comédie Française. He also abolished the important office of the mayor of Paris and tightened the grip of the monarchy by placing Paris under the rule of the state.

Paris was the scene of one of the great turning points in French and world history when, on July 14, 1789, a mob stormed the Bastille and set in motion the events leading up to the French Revolution. During the Reign of Terror, nearly 3,000 people were executed in Paris alone, many of them on guillotines set up on the Place de la Concorde.

With the advent of Napoleon, who appointed himself First Consul of France in 1799, Paris entered into a new period of material expansion and prosperity; the city was terrorized, however, by the excesses of Napoleon's secret police. In 1804, Napoleon had himself crowned emperor in Nôtre-Dame cathedral. Paris was captured by the invading allied armies in 1814, and the Bourbon monarchy was restored, only to be ousted again in 1830 during the July Revolution in Paris. Modernization began in Paris with the opening of the first French railway line and gas lighting.

The "Citizen King," Louis Philippe, spent a fortune upgrading the city. Beginning in 1853, the architect Baron Haussmann transformed Paris from a large medieval town to the most modern city in the world by creating the Grands Boulevards and 20 great squares. The famous and extravagant Paris Opéra was built in this period. In 1889, Paris was host to the World Exhibition, whose symbol was the cast-iron tower by Gustave Eiffel.

The first Metro line opened in 1900. In the early years of the 20th century, Paris became the art and expatriate capital of the world, home to dozens of famous painters and writers. Relatively little damage was done to the city in the two wars of this century, although Paris was occupied by the Germans in the Second World War. The city was rocked by student riots in 1968, and more recently, it has been troubled with terrorist bombings and kidnappings.

Postwar Paris has seen the addition of several controversial buildings and urban renovation projects, including the skyscrapers of La Défense, The Tour Montparnasse, the Pompidou Center, and the Forum des Halles. The most recent controversy revolves around I. M. Pei's new glass pyramid, which has been built in the courtyard of the Louvre.

Attractions

*Arc de Triomphe [17]: Napoleon ordered the construction of this impressive arch in 1806 to commemorate his victories and honor his troops. *The Tomb of the Unknown Soldier* lies beneath it and there is an observation deck above that offers a beautiful view of Paris and the famous ***Avenue des Champs-Élysées,** the main avenue (one of 12) leading to the arch. The Champs-Élysées (Elysian Fields), no longer the fashionable and exclusive promenade it was in the 19th century, is now devoted to showrooms, cinemas, cafés, and various airline and tourist offices.

***Centre Georges Pompidou: Known as *Beaubourg* after the surrounding area, this huge cultural center with its naked, inside-out architecture created an enormous controversy when it opened in 1977. The building signaled a new age in public building projects. In addition to a library, two theaters, a music research center, and a gallery for industrial design, it contains the *Musée National d'Art Moderne* with works by such renowned moderns as Dufy, Matisse, Utrillo, Picasso, Braque, Chagall, Modigliani, and many others.

***Eiffel Tower (Tour Eiffel) [25]: Called "The Queen of Paris" by Jean Cocteau, the most famous landmark of the city was built as a temporary structure for the Paris World Fair of 1889. It provides glorious panoramas of the City of Light from several different viewing platforms, as well as a restaurant, nightclub, post office, and bank.

Forum des Halles: Just northeast of the Louvre, the old Central Market of Paris, Les Halles (as it's also called) is now a trendy, popular area filled with boutiques, galleries, restaurants, and food stands.

Hôtel Carnavalet [9]: The one-time residence of that superb, 17th-century letter-writer Madame de Sevigne is now a pleasant and informative municipal museum *(Musée Carnavalet)* that illustrates the history of Paris from the 15th to the 19th centuries.

*Hôtel de Cluny [18]: Built by the Burgundian abbots of Cluny in the late 15th century, it is the oldest Gothic residential structure in Paris. It is also home to the *Musée de Cluny,* with its magnificent collection of medieval art, in-

Hôtel de Cluny

cluding the nearly 500-year-old *Lady and the Unicorn* tapestry.

Hôtel de Ville (City Hall) [10]: Noted for the fin-de-siècle extravagance of its interior, this 19th-century, Renaissance-style building stands on the site of two earlier city halls. It is the office of the mayor of the city of Paris and assembly place for the 109 councils of the city.

***Hôtel des Invalides [29]: A beautiful architectural complex built for aging, wounded, and pensioned soldiers, it contains a 17th-century masterpiece of Baroque architecture, the *Dôme des Invalides* (Church of the Invalides), in which rests *Napoleon's Tomb,* carved from red porphyry. The former emperor of France is encased within six coffins of different materials. Across the cobbled *Cour d'Honneur* (Court of Honor) is the *Musée de l'Armée,* the largest military museum in the world, whose Napoleonic collection is particularly interesting: You'll find his personal equipment and furniture, his death mask, and even his white horse—stuffed, of course.

Île Saint-Louis: This island in the Seine, "behind" Nôtre-Dame cathedral and with a view of its famous flying buttresses, has retained much of its 17th-century charm.

Institut de France [6]: The 40 members of the Academie Française, called "The Immortals" and charged with preserving the French language from impure influences, meet under the large gold dome of this 17th-century palace.

***Louvre [5]: Now entered through a new—and controversial—glass pyramid, the Louvre, a royal palace for over three centuries, is one of the richest museums in the world and can exhaust the most dedicated art-lover. Masterpiece follows masterpiece here, but most visitors make a point of at least seeing the *Winged Victory,* the *Venus de Milo,* the *Mona Lisa* by Leonardo da Vinci, and the breathtaking 137-carat "Regent" diamond in the *Galerie d'Apollon.* From the courtyard you can see—through the triumphal *Arc du Carousel* erected by Napoleon—straight down to the distant Arc de Triomphe. The **Tuileries Gardens,* beginning just west of the arch, were designed in the 17th century by André Lenôtre as part of the Palace of the Tuileres, which was destroyed by the Commune in 1871. You can stroll through the dappled sunlight and past the fountains and sculpture to the ****Place de la Concorde** [24], the largest and arguably most beautiful square in Paris, designed in the 18th century during the reign of Louis XV. In the center is the pink granite **obelisk* from Luxor, more than 3,000 years old, surrounded by fountains and sculptures. During the Revolution, the guillotine was kept busy here day and night.

Madeleine [15]: The Grands Boulevards which encircle the entire inner city begin at this church, built in 1806 by Napoleon in the form of a Greek temple. Originally intended to serve as a pantheon for the army, it was consecrated as a church in 1842.

Marché aux Puces [26]: Paris' oldest flea market, with lots of bric-a-brac and some occasional treasures, is held every Saturday, Sunday, and Monday.

**Montmartre [36]: This old Parisian artist and Bohemian quarter on top of *La Butte,* with its narrow streets, steep stairs climbing the hillside, and Impressionist atmosphere remains one of the most picturesque sections of the city (although it's not nearly so authentically boisterous today as it once was). Montmartre's central square is *Place du Tertre,* which used to be the center of a wine growers' village; the last surviving vineyard in Paris is next to the *Musée de Montmartre* (17 Rue St.-Vincent). You may wish to pay your respects to some of the several notables buried in the *Cim-*

Place du Tertre

itière Montmartre—they include Jacques Offenbach, Hector Berlioz, Heinrich Heine, and Stendahl.

Musée des Arts Africains et Océaniens [32]: A rather specialized collection of art and artifacts from former French colonies is on display here.

**Musée d'Orsay, 1 Rue de Bellechasse: Paris' newest museum, located in a former train station, sparks a lively reaction from everyone who visits it. On display in its upper stories are all the major Impressionist works that were formerly housed in the Jeu de Paume, including masterpieces by Monet, Manet, Renoir, Degas, Toulouse-Lautrec, and van Gogh; the entry level acts as a kind of boulevard for sculpture, and small exhibits off to the side deal mostly with other applied arts of the 19th century.

*Musée Picasso, 5 Rue de Thorigny: A large part of Picasso's private collection, including works by Braque, Cézanne, and Rousseau, is housed in the 17th-century Hôtel du Sale; examples of the Spanish artist's own *ouevre* lean heavily on more recent works.

*Musée Rodin [33]: You'll find the great sculptor's most famous work, "The Thinker," in the garden of this beautiful 18th-century residence, while other rooms are graced with powerful works like "The Gates of Hell," "The Kiss," "The Shadow," and "Eve."

***Nôtre-Dame [2]: Construction on the mighty and monu-

Paris Attractions:

1. Pont Neuf
2. Nôtre-Dame
3. Palais de Justice
4. Saint-Germain-de l'Auxerrois
5. Louvre
6. Institut de France
7. Place de la Bastille
8. Place des Vosges
9. Hôtel Carnavalet
10. Hôtel de Ville
11. Théâtre-Français
12. National Library
13. Stock Exchange
14. Opéra
15. Madeleine
16. Palais-Bourbon
17. Arc de Triomphe
18. Hôtel de Cluny
19. Sorbonne
20. Panthéon
21. St.-Etienne-du-Mont
22. Jardin des Plantes
23. Palais du Luxembourg
24. Place de la Concorde
25. Eiffel Tower
26. Marché aux Puces
27. Porte Maillot
28. Père Lachaise
29. Napoleon's Tomb
30. Place Vendôme
31. Palais Chaillot
32. Musée des Arts Africains et Océaniens
33. Rodin Museum
34. Montparnasse
35. Saint-Germain-des-Prés
36. Montmartre
37. Sacré-Coeur

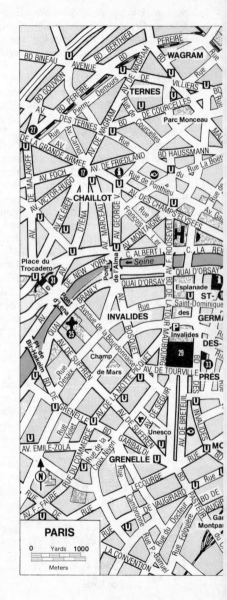

Nôtre-Dame

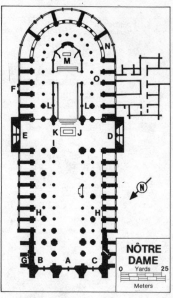

NÔTRE
DAME

0 Yards 25

Meters

mental cathedral of Paris began in 1163, and the building is one of the finest examples of Gothic architecture in the world. A superb, 13th-century *rose window* acts as a focal point in the third level of the exterior façade, below which are the main portal [A], called the *Portal of the Last Judgment*, created between 1220 and 1230; the left portal [B], known as the *Portal of the Virgin* for its image of the Virgin Mary with Child; and the right portal [C], named the *Portal of St. Anna*. *St. Stephen's Portal* [D] was begun in the mid-13th century and illustrates the saint's martyrdom. *Cathedral Square Portal* [E], dating from 1250, once led from the cathedral into the former monastery, while the *Red Portal* [F] is characterized by elaborate sculptures of plants and animals. At the foot of the north tower you'll find the entrance [G] to the tower, which should by no means be missed, although it's a long, steep climb: At the top you'll stand cheek-by-jowl with the cathedral's famous gargoyles and have a stunning view of the city. The cathedral's *outer naves* [H] are lined with chapels. The best interior view of the magnificent rose windows, one red, one blue, both created in 1270, is from the *transept* [I]. The much-revered statue of *Nôtre-Dame de Paris* (Our Lady of Paris) [J] dates from about 1300; across from it stands an 18th-century statue of *St. Denis* [K]. The *choir stalls* [L] were carved between 1300 and 1351; through an iron rood screen you can glimpse the *altar* [M] and, behind it, a Pietà donated by Louis XIV. A macabre image of the dead Count d'Harcourt rising from his grave is found in a *side chapel* [N]. Precious religious objects are on view in the *treasury* [O].

Opéra [14]: The grand and heavily opulent manner of the Second Empire can be seen in this flamboyant structure, covered with gilded sculptural decoration outside and Chagall frescoes on the auditorium ceiling within. The Paris Opéra has moved to its new home on Place Bastille, but performances of dance and music will continue to be held here. Behind the Opéra on Boulevard Haussmann you'll find the Art Nouveau department store called *Galeries Lafayette*, constructed between 1904 and 1906.

Palais-Bourbon [16]: The seat of the Chambre des Deputes, or French Parliament, was built in 1722 by a daughter of Louis XIV; from here you can look across the river and the Place de la Concorde to the church of the Madeleine, whose Classical façade echoes the one of the Palais.

Palais de Chaillot [31]: Built for the 1937 World's Fair, its Classical-style wings house four museums—*Musée de la Marine* (Maritime); *Musée de l'Homme*—(Ethnography); *Musée des Monuments Françaises;* and *Musée de Cinema* (Film)—with a terrace between. The magnificent view of the Eiffel Tower and Champ-de-Mars takes the breath away and inevitably sets your mind to dreaming.

**Palais de Justice [3]: For centuries, this massive complex was the center of the city's govern-

Conciergerie

ment. The *Conciergerie, once an apartment of the royal caretaker, eventually became a state prison and held some very famous victims of the guillotine during the Revolution—Marie Antoinette among them—whose cells you can visit today. The word masterpiece hardly does justice to the 13th-century ***Sainte-Chapelle, whose famous stained-glass windows, relating familiar Biblical stories, glow with luminous intensity.

Palais du Luxembourg [23]: A checkered history is attached to this 17th-century palace, commissioned by Marie de Médicis and built in Florentine style to remind her of her home: After her exile and death, the palace became a monastery, a prison, and a German military headquarters before finally becoming the home of the French Senate. Behind the palace stretches one of the most beautiful gardens in Paris, filled with statues of French writers and artists, the 17th-century *Medici Fountain,* and an Orangerie.

*Panthéon [20]: In 1791, this former church, with its enormous dome and Greek portico, was transformed into a temple to honor the greatest men in France; the likes of Voltaire, Rousseau, Zola, and Victor Hugo are buried here. The church of *Saint-Étienne du Mont* [21], whose façade has three gables one on top of the other, is located behind the Pantheon.

Père-Lachaise Cemetery [28]: The largest cemetery in Paris is an oddly fascinating place to visit; celebrated tombstones include those of Chopin, Balzac, Bizet, Sarah Bernhardt, Oscar Wilde, Molière, and Colette.

Place de la Bastille [7]: At the outbreak of the French Revolution on July 14, 1789, the Bastille—now demarcated by white stones—was stormed by the angry citizens of Paris. Thanks to the recent construction of the new theatre for the Paris Opéra here, the entire area has become gentrified.

Place des Vosges [8]: This distinguished square of 17th- and 18th-century mansions with arcades and steep roofs was once the most fashionable address for the aristocracy and later housed such notable Parisians as Victor Hugo (No. 6). A copy of an equestrian statue of Louis XIII sits in the center of the square, and you can see the initials of Henry IV on the south side on the *Pavillon du Roi.*

**Place Vendôme [30]: A

Place Vendôme

magnificent reminder of the "Grand Siècle" of Louis XIV, Place Vendôme, with its arcades and beautiful proportions, was designed by Jules Hardouin-Mansart and completed in the last year of the 17th century. It remains the appropriately aloof setting for exclusive shops, banks, and the most famous hotel in the world, the Ritz.

Pont Neuf [1]: The "New Bridge" with its frieze of masks is actually the oldest (constructed 1578–1607) bridge in Paris and connects the Île de la Cité with the two banks of the Seine.

Porte Maillot [27]: In this modern district in the west of the city you'll find the *Palais de Congres,* completed in 1974, and the *Tour du Concorde,* with its well-known observation deck and restaurant.

**Sacré-Coeur [37]: Perched high atop Montmartre, Sacré-Coeur is a highly visible and popular landmark of Paris, despite its heavy and undistinguished architecture. There is a memorable panoramic view of the city from the square in front of the church or from the dome.

*Sorbonne [19]: The famous university, with its long, distinguished, and turbulent history, was founded in 1253 as a theological seminary but the present structure dates from the turn of the century.

St.-Germain-des-Prés [35]: There are considerable Romanesque remains in this, the oldest church in Paris, which has undergone several transformations over the centuries. Across from the church are two famous cafés, the *Deux-Magots* and the *Café de Flore,* one-time hangouts for Paris' artists, writers, and philosophers.

Théatre-Français [11]: Home of the prestigious and classically oriented *Comédie-Française,* founded by Molière, the theater was built in the late 18th century. Extending northeast from the theater is the delightful *Palais Royal,* built for Cardinal Richelieu in the early 17th century, with shops and restaurants on the gallery level and an intriguing post-modern forecourt.

Prague

Golden Prague, as the capital of Czechoslovakia is called, is the art and architectural treasure house of Central Europe. It's a city of slender Gothic spires and sumptuous Baroque details, of ancient medieval streets and mighty hilltop fortresses. Built on seven hills, with the majestic Vltava River flowing through it, Prague is actually five historic cities in one; the five, each with its own distinctive personality, were officially incorporated in 1784. Because it was one of the few major cities to escape wartime damage and thus remains architecturally intact, exploring its numerous nooks and crannies with their accretion of historical styles is an especially rewarding experience. After you've visited its most important sites, Prague remains a city to discover on your own. Wander at will (it's perfectly safe, even after dark). It will repay your interest by yielding up one delightful detail after another.

History

Prague's history is one of foreign domination and local resistance. It's also the history of five royal towns which finally became incorporated into one in the 18th century. Ninth century settlements were located at the foot of two castles—Hradčany and Vyšehrad—on opposite sides of the River Vltava. These two ancient strongholds eventually became the homes of the kings of Bohemia. What is known today as the Old Town was originally a small market center, and the Lesser Quarter grew up on the opposite bank of the river. The New Town was founded by Charles IV in the 14th century.

For a brief period under Charles IV (Karel IV), the city became the seat of the Holy Roman Empire, and, as such, the capital of western Europe. The distinctive Gothic look of much of Prague—although it's often overlaid by later Renaissance and Baroque additions—dates from this period in the 14th century.

In the early years of the 15th century, Prague was the home and pulpit for John Huss, a revolutionary preacher who thundered against the excesses of the Catholic church and advocated a Czech national spirit that would eventually engulf and destroy the strong German influences at work in the city. Huss, still much revered by the Czechs, was burned at the stake in 1415 and his death ushered in the religious Hussite wars.

The Austrian Hapsburg dynasty under Ferdinand I took over Prague in 1526, increasing tensions between the ruling house and the citizenry. The attempts of the Hapsburgs to Germanicize their country and bring back Catholicism led to Czech resistance. The Thirty Years' War—which resulted in a Central European bloodbath—was ignited when two

Czech government officials were hurled from the windows of Prague Castle by the Austrians in 1618. After the Czech defeat, Hapsburg nobles confiscated lands and estates, and under Maria Theresa, the Austrian Empress, German was made the official language. Prague at this time became a city of the Baroque, and a musical capital of Europe. Mozart, whose opera *Don Giovanni* premiered in Prague, claimed that no one understood him better than the Praguers.

The Republic of Czechoslovakia was not born until 1918, when the Austro-Hungarian empire collapsed, and then had a tragically short life. Between the wars, Prague remained a cultural center and Central Europe's commercial center, but Hitler's troops occupied the country from 1939 until 1945, when the citizens of Prague rose up to liberate their city. The Soviets arrived a few days later.

The first postwar government under Benes contained a Socialist majority, but hard-line Communists ousted him in 1948. Since then, Czech dissidents have made repeated attempts for political freedom. In the "Prague Spring" of 1968, liberalizing measures were squashed by the Soviet Army. However, reform movements in late 1989 have led to the fall of hard-line Communism as the Soviets vow to take a less active role in their satellite countries' politics.

Attractions

Bethlehem Chapel (Betlémská kaple) [16]: Praguers hold the 15th-century preacher John Huss in such high esteem that, in the 1950s, they entirely rebuilt this chapel, where he preached from 1402 until 1415. (It had been demolished in the 18th century.)

Carolinium [17]: Charles IV, King of Bohemia and Moravia, and the Holy Roman Emperor, made Prague the capital of his empire and was responsible for the construction and restoration of several major buildings in the 14th century. The Carolinium, with its beautiful Gothic bay window, was the original building of Charles University, which he founded in 1348. Next to it is the historic *Tyl Theater* (Tylovo divadlo), which saw the premiere of Mozart's opera *Don Giovanni* in 1787.

Charles Bridge (Karluv most) [12]: This wonderfully picturesque stone bridge spanning the Vlatava River between the Old Town and the Lesser Town is the oldest in Prague (14th century), and is lined with Baroque statues.

Church of the Loretto [7]: A famous pilgrimage church, the Baroque Loretto derives its name from the town in Italy to which the Virgin Mary's house was miraculously transported to save it from desecration at the hands of the Infidel. In the treasure vault is the eye-opening "Sun of Prague," a monstrance set with 6,222 diamonds.

*Church of Saint Nicholas

Charles Bridge

[9]: The largest Baroque church in Prague, built by the architect Christoph Dientzenhofer and his son Kilian Ignaz (responsible for many of the city's Baroque structures), was completed in 1755 and is graced by an enormous ceiling fresco.

***Hradčany/Prague Castle** (Hrad) [1]: This enormous complex, built like a Chinese puzzle box around a series of interior courtyards, has (in one form or another) been in existence for over a thousand years. The earliest settlement of Prague grew up around the great *Castle Square* (Hradčanské náměstí) in front of it. Charles IV was responsible for the rebuilding and refurbishing of the castle in the 14th century, and additions were made in different styles over the course of later cen-

turies. Today it is the seat of the Czech government.

Three impressive palaces are grouped around Castle Square. On the south is the *Schwarzenberg Palace,* one of the most beautiful Renaissance buildings in Bohemia; its façade is enlivened by Italianate sgraffito. The *Archbishop's Palace,* to the north, dates from the mid-16th century and was later rebuilt, most recently during the 18th-century reign of Empress Maria Theresa of Austria. Enter the left gateway of the archbishop's palace to reach the former *Sternberg Palace,* which now houses the treasures of the *National Gallery* (Narodni galerie) [6]. The remarkable collections here include works by artists such as Dürer, Cranach, Veronese, Tintoretto, El Greco, Holbein, Brueghel, Rembrandt, and Rubens. If 19th- and 20th-century French art is your passion, you'll find an enormous variety here— every important French artist from the period is represented.

In the third courtyard within Prague Castle, you come to the remarkable *St. Vitus's Cathedral* (Katedrála sv. Vita) [2]. Recently restored, it took over 600 years to complete and acts as a history book of architéctural styles, although Gothic predominates. Several Bohemian kings are buried in the cathedral, including Charles IV and Good King Wenceslas, whose chapel sparkles with semiprecious stones. At the right end of the cathedral courtyard is the splendid late-Gothic *Wladislaw's*

St. Vitus's Cathedral

Hall. Beyond is the oldest of all the palace buildings, *Saint George's Church and Monastery* [3], wearing Baroque dress over a Romanesque foundation. It has a marvelous collection of Bohemian art. *Golden Lane* (Zlatá ulička) [4], behind the church, takes its name from the medieval legends of alchemists who turned lead into gold. This tiny and utterly charming little lane is filled with bookstores and antique and souvenir shops—quite a different appearance from the street as Franz Kafka knew it: The great writer lived briefly at number 24. At the end of the street is the 15th-century *Daliborka tower,* where you have a lovely view as you make your way down the *Old Palace Steps* towards the river. Alternatively, you can head northeast to the *Belevedere* [5], a Renaissance pleasure palace built for Queen Anna in the 16th century; there are charming Renaissance gardens and a "Singing Fountain."

Knights of the Cross Square (Krizornické náměstí) [13]: Situated at one end of the Charles Bridge, this square is one

Golden Lane

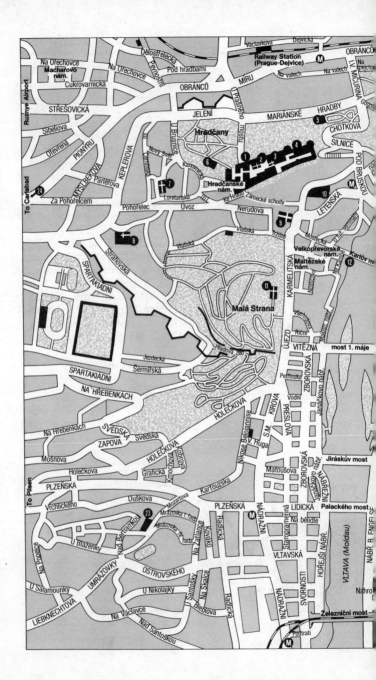

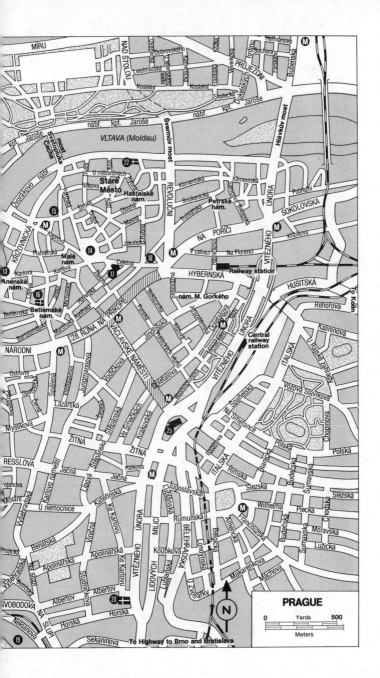

of the finest in Central Europe. A 19th-century memorial to Charles IV stands in front of the Baroque *church of Saint Frances,* and the Jesuit *church of Saint Salvador* boasts an impressive dome fresco of "The Final Judgment" dating from 1722. Next to it stands the former Jesuit theological college known as the *Clementinium* which today contains a major portion of the State Libraries. One end of the bridge is dominated by the beautiful, 14th-century *Old Town Bridge Tower.* Music-lovers may wish to visit the nearby *Smetana Museum* at Novotneho lavka, with its exhibits on the life of the composer "Ma Vlast."

*Old Jewish Quarter [15]: The ancient buildings of this fascinating district, one of the oldest Jewish ghettos in Europe, are now part of the State Jewish Museum, housed in several former synagogues. One of Prague's finest examples of early Gothic architecture is the *New-Old Synagogue* (Staronova synagoga), built around 1270 and still used—it is the oldest surviving synagogue in Europe. Artifacts from Jewish life and religious culture are found in the *High Synagogue* and the *Maisel Synagogue;* on the walls of the *Pinkas Synagogue* are inscribed the names of the 77,000 Jews from the city and country who were murdered by the Nazis. The *Old Jewish Cemetery* (Stary zidovsky hrbitov) is at one end of the Pinkas Synagogue. An amazing sight, it contains layer upon layer of gravestones—over 12,000 of them that date from the 15th through the 18th centuries.

Old Town Square (Staromestské náměstí) [14]: The lively hub of Prague's Old Town, recently scrubbed up and restored, is lined with patrician houses and surrounded by several important buildings. In the center of the square is a statue of the religious and nationalist leader John Huss, who was burned at the stake in 1415. **Old Town Hall** has been rebuilt many times since it was founded in the 14th century, and features a 15th century council chamber where Prague's city government still gathers. Every hour you'll see a crowd staring up at the 15th-century *astronomical clock* in the town hall's tower, waiting for the appearance in two windows of the mechanical figures of Christ and the apostles—but it's a figure of Death, standing below, that actually strikes the hours. The Gothic *Tyn Church,* across from the town hall, has an impressive

Astronomical clock

Gothic exterior, while the interior is aswirl with Baroque additions. In the northwest corner is the 18th-century *church of Saint Nicholas.*

Our Lady of Victories (Chram Panny Marie Vitezny) [11]: The first Baroque building in Prague, the church is also known as the Church of the Infant of Prague because it is the home of a famous wax effigy of the Infant Christ dating from the Spanish Renaissance.

Powder Tower (Prašna brana) [18]: Gunpowder was once stored in this 15th-century gate to Old Town, where the Kings of Bohemia set out on their coronation routes; there is a good view from the top.

*Saint Agnes Cloister (Klaster svat Anezky) [22]: Two collections from the National Gallery—"Czechoslovakian Painting of the 19th and 20th Centuries" and "Applied Arts of the 19th Century"—are on display in a restored portion of this early Gothic convent established in 1234 by Agnes, a sister of King Vaclav (Wenceslas) I.

*Strahov Monastery (Strahovsky klaster) [8]: Impressive Baroque halls house the *Cloister Library* and the *Museum of National Literature* in this former monastery located high above Petrin Hill. Mozart played on the enormous organ in the *Church of the Assumption.* The gardens offer a wonderful view of the city.

Villa Bertramka [23]: Mozart visited this house on several occasions between 1787 and 1791, and completed his last opera *Don Giovanni* here; the villa now houses a *Mozart Museum.*

Vyšehrad [19]: One of the original settlements of Prague was here, nestled close to Vysehrad castle (now in ruins) high on the cliffs overlooking the Vltava River. Next to the *Church of Saints Peter and Paul* is a cemetery where several notable Czechs are buried, Smetana and Dvořák among them. At the end of Horska Street you come to *Charles' Square* [20], with a domed building dedicated by Charlemagne in 1377.

Wallenstein Palace [10]: Built between 1623 and 1630 in an early Baroque style, the palace is noted for its charming stuccowork and ceiling frescoes.

Wenceslas Square (Václavské náměstí): Prague's busy center is not really a square, but a broad avenue filled with hotels, restaurants, shops, cafés, and night spots. At one end sits the monumental ***National Museum** (Narodni muzeum) [25], built in the late 19th century, with an equestrian statue of Wenceslas. Legend says that he will return to lead the Czech people in their time of greatest need. At the other end is *Na příkopě*, once part of a moat protecting the Old Town and now a lively and elegant mall for pedestrians only.

Rome

Nowhere do you get a better sense of the vast, mysterious, chaotic, and unending turmoil of history than looking down into the Forum, with a distant palm tree silhouetted against the dying splendor of a Roman sunset. Rome—the name instantly conjures up ancient ruins and the names of the emperors who ruled the known world and then lost it. Rome, as the center of the old pagan world and then headquarters for the new Christian one, has seen it all. The city is a cradle of history, filled with tantalizing fragments and enormous reminders of times gone by. But the pleasure of Rome lies in the way modern life has adapted to and goes on against the theatrical backdrop of the city's awesome antiquities, Baroque churches, and Renaissance palaces. Rome is a city of color and light and noise; a place where life unfolds in cobbled piazzas, around splashing fountains, and at outdoor restaurants. Pilgrims still come from around the world to be blessed by the pope and to pray at St. Peter's, headquarters of the Roman Catholic Church. Rome can be a difficult city; opening times are confusing, everything closes down in the afternoon, there are endless strikes, and the traffic—well, it's killing. But then you turn a corner and enter Piazza Navona, or see the Pantheon for the first time, or drink the best cappuccino you've ever tasted . . . and all the irritations dissolve in appreciation for what is still one of the most seductive cities in the world.

History

According to tradition, Rome was founded on the Palatine hill by Romulus, its first king, in 753 B.C., at the meeting point of Latin, Sabine, and Etruscan territories. In its earliest period, it was ruled by seven legendary kings.

The kingdom was abolished, and Rome became a republic in 510 B.C. By this time, it was strong enough to conquer all the neighboring tribes, and the three Punic Wars ended with Rome's victory in 146 B.C. over Carthage, its mightiest rival. Aggressive and unceasing military campaigns expanded the size of Rome's dominions; under the reign of Trajan (A.D. 98–117), the Roman Empire included the entire known world. Rome, as headquarters of the Empire, grew steadily in size and importance and Roman architects, after the conquest of Greece, began to use Greek models for their own buildings.

The foundation of the Empire under Octavian (later Augustus) inaugurated a period of peace and prosperity for Rome. Augustus, in a vigorous building program, had many beautiful monuments and temples erected and older buildings restored. After a fire in A.D. 64, Nero began to rebuild Rome on a regular plan. Later emperors also left their mark on the city. The Colosseum was begun in A.D. 72 by Vespasian; Hadrian was responsible for the construction of the Pantheon and his mausoleum, which later became Castel Sant'Angelo; Caracalla's magnificent Baths were built in 217. Imperial Rome was a place of great splendor, filled with temples, monuments, fora, markets, palaces, and sumptuous villas—and equally great squalor, for the enormous underclass of Romans and slaves had to make do as best they could. The city had a population of over a million by the second century A.D.

Rome's decline as center of the temporal world began when Diocletian (284) divided the empire into two administrative units (the Western Empire and the Eastern Empire), and Constantine (330) moved the seat of government from Rome to Byzantium. When Christianity became the official state religion in 334, Rome began to change from a pagan city to a Christian one. The first basilica of St. Peter was consecrated in 326, and the building of other great basilicas and countless churches (sometimes incorporated into older pagan temples) began.

Barbarian tribes repeatedly sacked Rome in the fifth century, and in the seventh century, it came under the protection of the popes. Robert Guiscard, a Norman, devasted the city in 1084, but Rome continued to grow as an administrative center of the Church. By the 13th century, it had become capital of the Christian world. During the period of "Babylonian Captivity," however, when the popes moved from Rome to Avignon in France, the city was torn apart by rival factions. The return of the popes in 1378 led the way for the rebuilding and restoration of Rome.

A humanistic revival of the arts—the Renaissance—began in Florence, but soon reached Rome. During the next 250 years, beginning with Pope Julius II (1503–1513), who employed the talents of Bramante, Michelangelo, and Raphael, Rome was virtually transformed. The new St. Peter's was begun, countless magnificent palaces and churches were built, buildings were restored, and town planning was carried out on a major scale. The stylistic austerity of the Renaissance then evolved into the theatrical sweep and flow of the Baroque, whose presiding geniuses in Rome were the ubiquitous Bernini and the more introspective Borromini.

The French entered Rome in 1798 and proclaimed it a republic; by 1811, Napoleon was able to confer the title of King of Rome on his son. Until Napoleon's fall, Rome was the second capital of his French Empire.

Rome took an active part in Italy's next period of political turmoil. The nationalistic Risorgimento pitted the pope, who was in control of the Papal States, against the unification movement. The papal forces were defeated in 1860, King Victor Emmanuel II of Sardinia was declared King of Italy, and Rome, although still in the hands of the pope, was declared the capital of the new kingdom. Ten years later, the king entered the city and established his court at the Quirinal, while the pope retired to the Vatican. A great speculative building boom changed whole sections of the city at this time. Rome became a bureaucratic center of the new government.

The First World War had little direct effect on Rome, but immediately afterwards the Fascismo movement under Benito Mussolini grew in popularity. Mussolini's "March on Rome" took place in 1922, and King Victor Emmanuel III was forced to invite Mussolini to form a government. Italy entered the Second World War on the side of the Axis in 1940. The American Fifth Army entered Rome in 1944, Mussolini was killed in 1945, and Victor Emmanuel III abdicated a year later. A general election approved the establishment of a republic, and in 1946, the first of Italy's many presidents was elected.

In the 1950s and 1960s, Rome became known as "Hollywood on the Tiber" because of the number of movies filmed here; a now-legendary "dolce vita" became associated with it. Today's Rome, with a population of over three million, faces the same international problems of terrorism, crime, congestion, and pollution that are dreaded in all large cities.

Attractions

***Basilica di San Pietro
(Saint Peter's Basilica) [17]: See the special section on Saint Peter's and the Vatican below.

**Campidoglio (Capitoline Hill) [3]: Although the smallest of Rome's seven hills, the Capitoline played the most prominent role in ancient times because it was the religious and political center of the city. Michelangelo designed the beautifully harmonious square *(Piazza Campidoglio)* as you see it today, with the two **Musei Capitolini* (Capitoline Museums) facing each other and the *Palazzo Senatorio* between them. One ticket admits you to both museums. They are renowned for their collection of antique sculptures, including that famous symbol of Rome, the "Capitoline She-Wolf," the "Dying Gaul," and the "Capitoline Venus," as well as an important *Pinacoteca* (Picture Gallery) containing paintings from the 16th through the 18th centuries.

**Castel Sant'Angelo [15]: Originally built by the Emperor Hadrian in the second century as a family mausoleum, this dramatically imposing structure on the Tiber has been used over the centuries as a residence for kings and popes, a fortress, and a prison (Floria Tosca leaps to her death

Castel Sant'Angelo

from here in Puccini's opera *Tosca*). The museum within it displays art and ancient weapons, but it's the building itself that is fascinating and provides some memorable views.

***Colosseo (Coliseum) [6]: "Panem et circenses"—"Bread and Games"—were the demands of first-century Romans, so Vespasian appeased them with the construction of this enormous amphitheater which began in 72 A.D. Brutal and bloodthirsty spectacles of all kinds were held here—from gladiatorial combats to mock naval battles (the floor could be flooded) to fights pitting men against wild beasts and, of course, all of the various horrors devised at the expense of the early Christians. Overhead awnings provided comfort to the 55,000 spectators while perfumes masked the smell of blood. A short walk away is the imposing fourth-century **Arco di Costantino** (Arch of Constantine) [7], dedicated to the first emperor to accept Christianity.

**Fontana di Trevi (Trevi Fountain) [10]: The most famous of Rome's fountains, the Trevi is a splashy aquatic fantasy of gods, horses, and mythological creatures—If you turn your back to them and toss in a coin, they may put in a good word and bring you back to Rome someday.

***Forum Romanum (Roman Forum) [4]: See special section below.

*Galleria Nazionale d'Arte Moderna [30]: The work of Italian artists of the 19th and 20th centuries is featured in this museum on the north side of the splendid Villa Borghese park.

*Il Gesù: This sumptuous Baroque church for the Jesuit order contains the tomb of Saint Ignatius Loyola and is noteworthy for its lavish interior decoration.

Monumento Nazionale a Vittorio Emanuele I (Victor Emmanuel Monument) [2]: Called "The Wedding Cake" by ir-

Rome Attractions:
1. Palazzo Venezia
2. Victor Emmanuel Monument
3. Capitoline Hill
4. Roman Forum
5. Palatine Hill
6. Coliseum
7. Arch of Constantine
8. Spanish Steps
9. Trinità dei Monti
10. Trevi Fountain
11. Piazza Colonna
12. Piazza di Pietra
13. Pantheon
14. Piazza Navona
15. Castel Sant'Angelo
16. Saint Peter's Square
17. Saint Peter's Cathedral
18. Vatican Museums
19. Gianicolo
20. Stazione Termini
21. Santa Maria degli Angeli
22. Santa Maria Maggiore
23. San Pietro in Vincoli
24. San Giovanni in Laterano
25. Santa Croce
26. Baths of Caracalla
27. Porta San Paolo
28. San Paolo fuori le Mura
29. Villa Borghese
30. National Gallery of Modern Art
31. Villa Giulia
32. Pincio
33. Piazza del Popolo
34. Via Vittorio Veneto
35. Quirinale Palace
36. Porta San Sebastiano
37. "Domine quo vadis"

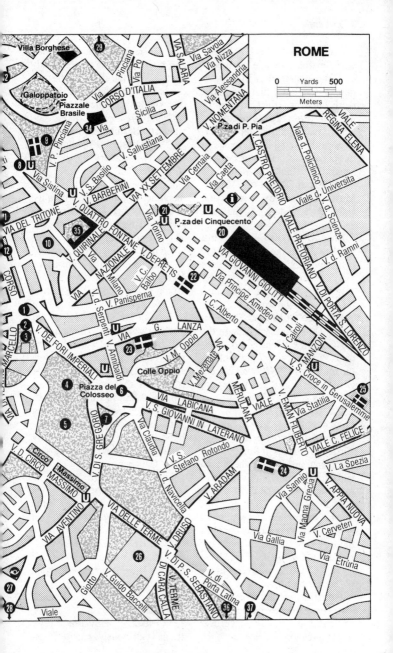

reverent Romans, this bombastic, white-marble monument was built to commemorate Italian unification under Italy's first king. Directly opposite is the 15th-century mass of ***Palazzo Venezia** [1], which once housed representatives of the Republic of Venice to the papal state and later became Mussolini's Roman headquarters.

***Musei Vaticani (Vatican Museums): See the special section below on St. Peter's and the Vatican.

Museo Nazionale di Villa Giulia [31]: If the art and culture of the ancient Etruscans fascinates you, head for this museum—quite simply, it is the best and most comprehensive in the world.

Palazzo Colonna: The enormous, 18th-century façade of the palace of the Colonna family dominates *Piazza Apostoli* and contains the impressive **Galleria Colonna* with works by Titian, Tintoretto, Veronese, among others.

Palazzo Farnese: Now the French Embassy, Palazzo Farnese is one of the most beautiful Renaissance palaces in Rome; it was completed in 1580 (Michelangelo had a hand in its design). The surrounding area is the heart of Renaissance Rome, and contains several other palaces, while just down the street is the site of one of the city's most colorful morning markets, **Campo dei Fiori* (Field of Flowers), filled with fresh produce and flowers.

Palazzo del Quirinale [35]: Two enormous marble sculptures of Castor and Pollux watch over the 16th-century palace, once the summer residence of the popes and now the home of the president. Across the street and next to the park is an architectural gem, the small Baroque church of ****Sant'Andrea al Quirinale**, designed by Bernini on an oval plan.

***Pantheon [13]: Rebuilt in the second century by the Emperor Hadrian, and one of the world's best-preserved ancient monuments, the massive nobility of this structure strikes a responsive chord in everyone who sees it. The interior dome with its open-holed roof (ocula) is the largest of its kind ever built and represents a high point of ancient engineering. To the left and down the street is the *Piazza della Minerva*, where in front of the ***church of Santa Maria sopra Minerva* a small obelisk sits atop an elephant by Bernini. The façade of the church is early Renaissance, but the interior is one of the few examples of Gothic design in Rome and contains many treasures, including 15th-century ***frescoes* by Filippo Lippi, **statue of Christ* by Michelangelo, and the tombs of Saint Catherine of Siena and the painter Fra Angelico.

*Piazza Colonna [11]: On the north side of the square is the 17th-century *Palazzo Chigi*, seat of the Italian Prime Minister; the ***Colonna di Marco Aurelio* (Column of Marcus Aurelius), erected around 180, depicts comic-book style, the emperor's campaigns against foreign tribes in ascending bas-reliefs.

***Piazza Navona [14]: Rome's gloriously beautiful piazza, laid out in the late 16th century on the site of Domitian's Circus, boasts three fountains, the most notable of which is Bernini's central **Fontana dei Fiumi** (Fountain of the Four Rivers), topped by an obelisk brought to Rome from Egypt in the first century. There are several restaurants and cafés here, perfect for people-watching, and lots of vendors selling jewelry and bad art. The vaulted *church of Sant'Agnese* was designed by Borromini and dates from the 17th century.

San Giovanni in Laterano [24]: The cathedral of Rome and the world is built on the site of a fourth century basilica founded by Constantine; the 13th-century **ambulatory** is particularly beautiful, and the whole interior is decorated with works of art. The oldest and highest Egyptian obelisk in Rome, dating from the reign of Pharoah Thutmosis III (1457–1428 B.C.), stands in the *Piazza San Giovanni in Laterano;* next to the cathedral is the octagonal **church of San Giovanni in Fonte,** the oldest baptismal church in the Christian world, with bronze doors dating from the second century and mosaics created between the fourth and seventh centuries. Directly across from the Lateran Palace in a 16th-century building designed by Fontana is the *Scala Santa* (Sacred Steps), said to be the same staircase ascended by Christ in the palace of Pontius Pilate.

San Paolo fuori le Mura (Saint Paul's Outside the Walls) [28]: One of the most important churches of the Christian world, it was first erected by Constantine on the site of the Apostle Paul's burial place and then replaced by a larger, fifth-century basilica that burned down in 1825 and was then completely rebuilt. The cloisters are among Rome's finest and most beautiful.

San Pietro in Vincoli [23]: Built to house the chains *(vincoli)* that bound Saint Peter after his arrest in Rome, this 15th-century church is the site of Michelangelo's majestic statue of **Moses,** originally meant to embellish the tomb of his patron, Julius II.

Santa Maria degli Angeli [21]: Michelangelo was commissioned to turn the ancient Baths of Diocletian—the largest public baths in Rome—into this monastic church. Next to it is the **Museo Nazionale Romano delle Terme di Diocleziano** (National Museum of the Diocletian Baths), which has a large collection of ancient art and antiquities.

Santa Maria Maggiore [22]: One of the four basilicas of Rome, it is a treasure trove of paintings, monuments, tombs of the popes, and contains the lavishly decorated *Cappella Sistina* (16th century) and **Cappella Paolina.**

Scalinata dell Trinità dei Monti (Spanish Steps) [8]: One of the most popular tourist spots in Rome, the 18th-century steps and the *Piazza di Spagna* in front of them are named for the Spanish Embassy, which has been here since 1647. At the base of the steps is the charming *Fontana* della Barcaccia, a ship-shaped fountain, and at the top is the 18th-century *church of San Trinità dei Monti* [9]. One of Rome's most exclusive shopping streets, *Via dei Condotti,* begins (or ends) at the piazza.

Terme di Caracalla (Baths of Caracalla) [26]: This enormous structure opened in 216 and once served up to 1,500 people, with a variety of steam baths and pools; grand operas are now performed here in the summer.

Via Appia Antica: The Old Appian Way opened in 312 B.C. to link Rome with southern Italy. It remains one of the most picturesque, moving, and historically rich areas of the city: Here are the great early Christian catacombs of Saint Calisstus, Saint Sebastian, and Domitilla, as well as the fortresslike *Tomb of Cecilia Metella* and the small church *Domine quo vadis* [37] where Peter is said to have met Christ after his crucifixion.

Villa Borghese: Rome's largest and most beautiful park was created for the private use of Cardinal Scipione Borghese in the early 17th century. His "villa" (a palace by most standards) now houses the outstanding collections of antiquities and Italian masterpieces (works by Raphael, Botticelli, Perugino, Correggio, Rubens, Cranach, Titian, and others) of the ****Museo Borghese [29].

***Forum Romanum (Roman Forum): Before it developed into the pulsing heart of the far-reaching Roman Empire, this was

nothing more than a swampy valley. Over the centuries, with the steady addition of magnificent temples and public buildings, it became the site of all aspects of the ancient city's public life—social, religious, administrative, judicial, and commercial. An aura of legend, excitement, and grandeur—as well as a hushed melancholy—hovers over these fragments of a lost empire, and you can wander among the ruins for hours without exhausting the accumulation of history scattered hereabouts.

The *Basilica Emilia* [A] was a second century B.C. money-changers' hall.

The Empire was governed from the *Curia* [B], where the Roman Senate convened.

According to legend, Romulus, one of the founders of Rome, is buried under the black marble pavement known as the *Lapis*

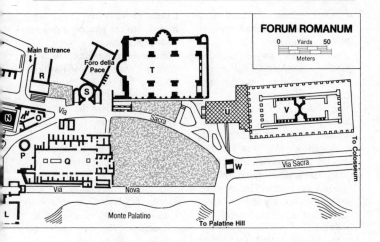

FORUM ROMANUM

0   Yards   50

Meters

Niger (Black Stone) [C], the oldest relic in the Forum.

Reliefs on the third-century **Arco di Settimo Severo* (Triumphal Arch of Septimius Severus) [D] depict the emperor's campaigns in the Orient.

Roman orators spoke from *Imperial Rostra* [E], whose north end contains the "Umbilicus Urbis," supposedly marking the exact center of the ancient city. To the left stood the *Miliarium Aureum* (Golden Milestone) [F], a marble block sheathed in bronze and set up by Augustus as the starting-point of all roads in the Empire.

One of the most ancient sanctuaries in the Forum is the *Tempio di Saturno* [G], dating from about 497 B.C. and used as the state treasury.

The newest monument in the Forum is the seventh-century *Colonna di Foca* (Phocas' Column)

[H], erected to honor the Byzantine emperor who presented the pope with the Pantheon, which was then converted into a Christian church.

The ancient pool known as the *Lacus Curtius* [I], now paved, was probably a remnant of the original swamp. It was sacred to the Romans, who considered it an entrance to the underworld. The surrounding area was the meeting place of the citizenry of Rome.

Built by Caesar around 50 B.C., the *Basilica Julia* [J], of which only the bases of the columns remain, was once the largest hall in the Forum.

Three superbly evocative Corinthian columns are all that is left of the ***Tempio di Castore e Polluce* (Temple of Castor and Pollux) [K], dating originally from about 484 B.C. and rebuilt several times, most notably in the time of Augustus. A square marble basin indicates the location of an ancient well and healing shrine known as the *Lacus Juturnae*.

Santa Maria Antiqua [L], built in 365, is the oldest Christian edifice in the Forum, and contains sixth-century frescoes.

In 33 B.C., two years after the defeat of Antony and Cleopatra at Actium, the *Arco di Agosto* (Arch of Augustus) [M] was erected, only the foundations of which remain. The adjacent *Tempio di Cesare* [N] was built soon after on the site where the body of Julius Caesar was burned on his funeral pyre in 44 B.C.

The Pontifex Maximus, highest priest in Rome, had the *Regia* [O] as his residence and official headquarters. Six, high-ranking priestesses, known as the Vestal Virgins, presided over the sacred hearth in their own *Tempio di Vesta* [P]; they lived in strict seclusion in the adjoining *Casa delle Vestali* [Q], guarding the eternal flame and watching over the Palladium, an image of Pallas Athena—and were buried alive if they broke their vows of virginity.

The pillared vestibule of the *Tempio di Antonio e Faustina* (Temple of Antonius Pius and Faustina) [R] still stands, although the entire complex was restructured in the 12th century as the *church of San Lorenzo in Miranda*. The gently sloping Via Sacra, the oldest street in Rome, leads to an ancient cemetery where archaeologists have dated finds back to the Iron Age, and on past the circular *Tempio di Romolo* (Temple of Romulus) [S], incorporated into the *church of Saints Cosimo and Damian*.

The towering remains of the *Basilica of Constantine* (or Basilica of Maxentius) [R], an enormous, triple-naved hall from the fourth century, are perhaps the most impressive ruins in the Forum; concerts are often held here in the summer. Next to the basilica was the double temple dedicated to Venus and Roma, the largest sanctuary in the city. In front of it is the *church of Santa Francesca Romana* [U] with its bell tower. The *Antiquarium Forense,* with archaeological finds from the excavations in the Forum, is located in the former convent.

Marking the end of the Via Sacra is the *Arco di Tito* (Arch of Titus) [W], the oldest triumphal arch in Rome, built to commemorate Titus' capture of Jerusalem in 70 A.D. From the Arch of Titus, a path branches off to the right and leads up toward the Palatine Hill (see below); from this path, another branches off to the right and leads up to the *Orti Farnesiani* (Farnese Gardens) and the *Terrace*, from which you have a view down over the entire Forum.

Palatino (Palatine Hill) [5]: This hill that rises in a plateau above the Forum, is where Rome really began. It's here that the city's most ancient relics are found. The Palatine was populated in prehistoric times, and later became the site of magnificent imperial palaces and villas whose ruins are incorporated into what is today a beautiful park filled with flowers and trees.

The *Farnese Gardens,* laid out in the 16th century, are located above the palace of Tiberius, of which little has been excavated. From here a vaulted subterranean passageway, the *Kryptoportikus,* leads to the so-called *Casa di Livia* (House of Livia), part of the palace of Augustus. The rooms surrounding the atrium have **wall paintings and floor mosaics,* and give some idea of what a Roman residence in the first decades of the new Christian era was like. Adjacent is an excavation area where the oldest section of Rome has been uncovered.

Built in 204 B.C., the *Tempio di Cibele* (Temple of the Sibyls) was consecrated to an Oriental cult of the Great Mother, or Magna Mater. Stairs lead to the oldest traces of settlement in Rome, Iron Age huts dating from the eighth century B.C.

To the east of the House of Livia are the impressive ruins of a basilica, chapel, and dining hall belonging to the *Domus Flavius;* next to them are the remains of the private residence of the emperor, the *Domus Augustana,* where a museum, the *Palatine Antiquarium,* exhibits material from the excavations.

Continuing to the southeast, you reach the *Ippodromo* (Stadium of Domitian), probably used for races and athletic contests commanded by the emperor. The colossal ruins of the thermal baths and the *Palace of Septimius Se-*

verus form the farthest boundaries of the Palatine.

***Saint Peter's Basilica/ Vatican: **Piazza San Pietro* (Saint Peter's Square) [16]: In 1667, the brilliant and ubiquitous Baroque architect Bernini completed this enormous oval "square," which is often thronged with crowds of pilgrims. Two curving colonnades, each with four rows of Doric columns and pillars, extend from St. Peter's Basilica and seem to embrace the piazza from both sides. A giant obelisk brought to Rome from Heliopolis in 37 A.D. stands in the center of the square.

***Basilica di San Pietro* (St. Peter's Basilica) [17]: The site has been a sacred place of pilgrimage from the earliest days of the Christian church, when a basilica was built at the place where St. Peter the Apostle was crucified and buried in 67 A.D. The present basilica was consecrated in the early 17th century and incorporates the work of several architects, including Bramante and Michelangelo. Grandiose and awesome, the interior is filled with hundreds of statues, monuments, mosaics, chapels, tombs, and grottoes.

Five entrances lead into Carlo Maderna's portico: On the right is Bernini's *statue of Constantine* [A] and on the left is an 18th-century equestrian *statue of Charlemagne* [B], who was crowned Emperor of the Holy Roman Empire in Old St. Peter's in the year 800.

Michelangelo's moving ***Pi-*

età, created when he was 25 years old, stands behind a protective plate of glass in the *Cappella della Pietà* [C].

Diagonally across from the Pietà, on the first pillar, is a *Memorial to Queen Christina of Sweden,* who disavowed Protestantism, gave up the throne of Sweden, and came to Rome in the 17th century. Across from here is Bernini's oval *Cappella San Nicola,* adjacent to the *Cappella di San Sebastiano* [E] with its mosaic that portrays the martyrdom of a favorite Catholic saint.

The *Cappella del SS. Sacramento* (Chapel of the Most Holy Sacrament) [F] is closed off by an impressive bronze screen de-signed by Borromini, a contemporary and sometime rival of Bernini; it was Bernini who created the gilded bronze tabernacle.

Michelangelo designed the *Cappella Gregoriana* [G].

At this point, you enter the right transept of the basilica and can see the enormous **dome,* with the words of Christ written in gold along its lower edge: "Tu es Petrus et super hanc petram edificabo ecclesiam meam et tibi dabo claves regni coelorum" ("You are Peter; upon this rock I shall build my church and I will give you the key to the kingdom of heaven.") Some of the most revered relics of the church are contained in the transept chapels: the lance of Saint

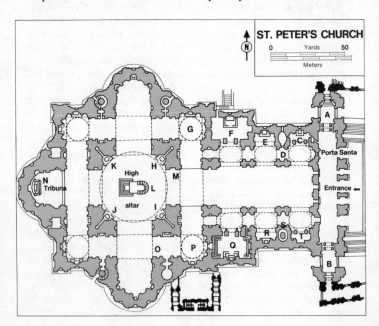

ST. PETER'S CHURCH

Longinus [H], who pierced the side of Christ as he hung on the cross; the head of Saint Andrew [I], the brother of Peter; the cloth used by Saint Veronica [J] to wipe the face of Christ on his way to Calvary; and a piece of the cross brought from Jerusalem by Constantine's mother, Saint Helena [K]. Against the Pillar of Longinus you'll find a fifth-century statue of the *Seated Peter* [M], whose foot is kissed by pilgrims. In front of the altar you can descend into the *Confessio* [L], site of St. Peter's tomb.

The central nave ends in the elevated *Tribuna,* a choir containing the **Cattedra Petri* [N], the wooden Chair of Peter. Huge bronze figures created by Bernini represent the four fathers of the church, and the group is flanked by two impressive tombs. On the right is the **Tomb of Pope Urban VIII,* also designed by Bernini, and on the left is the **Tomb of Pope Paul III,* a work by Giacomo della Porta.

The 19th-century *Tomb of Pius VIII* [O] is in the left aisle, as is the entrance to the sacristy and the *Tesoro di San Pietro* (Treasury). Pope Gregory the Great, canonized as a saint, lies entombed under the altar in the *Cappella Clementina* [P]; the adjacent tomb of Pope Pius VII is the work of the Danish neoclassical sculptor Thorwaldsen.

In the richly decorated *Cappella del Coro* (Choir Chapel) [Q] you'll find Antonio Pollaiuolo's bronze **tomb of Pope Innocent VIII,* a late-15th-century work that originally stood in the Old Saint Peter's. Passing through the ambulatory, you come to the *Cappella della Presentazione* [R] and the *Cappella Battistero* [T], with its baptismal font made from an ancient porphyry sarcophagus and a bronze cover fashioned by Carlo Fontana.

The Dome and the Roof: An elevator, and a spiral staircase [S] lead to the dome and roof of Saint Peter's. A trip up to the dome provides a breathtaking view over the high altar and into the vast space of the basilica, allowing you to see the mosaics covering the dome's interior walls at much closer range. From here you can go up to the roof of Saint Peter's—an unforgettable experience. From behind the balustrade with its colossal statues, you have a clear view out over Saint Peter's Square, down the Via della Conciliazione, and into Rome itself.

**Vatican Grottoes:* The *Sacre Grotte Vaticane* (Grottoes) can be entered from either the *Pillar of Longinus* [H] or the *Pillar of Andrew* [J]. Excavations under the ancient church, whose ceiling was about level with the floor of the present structure, have provided evidence for the existence of an ancient necropolis. Here lies Pollaiuolo's tomb of *Pope Sixtus IV* (1471–1484), who founded the Vatican Museum and commissioned the Sistine Chapel and the lavishly decorated tomb of Saint Peter, the *Cappella Clementina.*

***Vatican Museums* [18]: Part

of the largest palace in the world, the museums contain immense and valuable collections of art and scholarly works. The public entrance to the museums is around to the left from St. Peter's, along the wall of Vatican City. There is so much to see here that you can choose a timed route offered at the entrance, or wander at will through the endless salons and passages, stopping as your interest dictates. In addition to the various exhaustive museums (antiquities, Etruscan art, early Christian art, Egyptian art, Greek and Roman statuary, and picture gallery, to name a few) the following rooms are of particular interest:

The four chambers comprising the ***Stanze di Raffaello* (Rooms of Raphael) were commissioned by Julius II, the "Builder Pope," and Raphael worked on them until his death in 1520. Raphael is also responsible for the aptly-named *Logge di Raffaello:* He built the two-story structure according to designs by Bramante and then, with his students, painted the arcades of the upper story with scenes from the Old and New Testaments (work known today as the "Raphael Bible").

Admirers of Fra Angelico will want to visit the *Cappella di Niccolo V* with their 15th-century frescoes.

The ***Cappella Sistina* (Sistine Chapel), which has been undergoing a thorough cleaning and restoration for several years (financed by the Japanese), is decorated with a breathtaking series of wall and ceiling frescoes. Between 1481 and 1483, the greatest artists of the period worked here, including Botticelli, Ghirlandaio, Perugino, and Pinturicchio. Julius II commissioned Michelangelo to design and paint the ceiling frescoes in the early 16th century—a momentous feat that took 20 months of unending work and resulted in one of the unquestioned masterpieces of Western art.

Salzburg

Without a doubt, Salzburg is one of the prettiest cities in Europe, filled with charming Baroque churches and buildings that sit like dollops of whipped cream on the old and undeniably picturesque streets. The River Salzach divides the city: On one side, the city is dominated by a mighty fortress that was once the abode of the powerful archbishops of Salzburg, and on the other, by a mountain known as the Mönchsberg. The birthplace of Mozart, the world's best-known composer, Salzburg is especially renowned for its summer music festival, an international event that was formerly presided over by Herbert van Karajan. The special glory of Salzburg, its unique sense of harmony and charm, stems from the fact that it was spared serious wartime damage and has carefully preserved its fabric. Its architectural authenticity is only heightened by its pristine Alpine setting.

History

The ubiquitous Romans, colonizers par excellence, arrived around A.D. 40 and took over what had earlier been a gathering place for Alpine Celts. Christianity arrived in the fourth century in the person of Saint Maximus, who was responsible for the digging of catacombs under the Mönchsberg. About four centuries later, Saint Peter's Monastery was built in front of the catacombs, and cloisters were erected on another nearby peak. These buildings paved the way for Salzburg's future greatness as an ecclesiastical seat: In 798, the city became the see of the bishop-princes of Salzburg, who were so powerful that they had authority over every other bishop in the German-speaking world (Salzburg, at that time and up until the 18th century, was considered part of Germany).

Salzburg's landmark fortress, known as the Festung Hohensalzburg, was begun by an archbishop in the 11th century and eventually became a kind of German Vatican. The archbishops who resided there ruled over the religious and temporal life of what is today western Austria; they were, in fact, considered princes of the Holy Roman Empire. The Festung, continually expanded over the centuries, served another useful purpose as a place of refuge during the many wars that plagued the region. After the Reformation, however, the Roman Catholic archbishops forced large numbers of Protestants to leave the area.

Wolfgang Amadeus Mozart was born in Salzburg in 1756 and quit the city when he was 25. (He made a decisive break with the then-ruling archbishop and basically exiled himself to seek work elsewhere.) Although Mozart didn't achieve any measure of renown here during his lifetime, his birthplace is now regarded as something of a shrine; *the* summer musical event is called the Mozart Festival in his honor.

At the Congress of Vienna, which met to reapportion Europe after Napoleon's downfall, Salzburg—by now a city and a State in its own right—was ceded to Austria. Salzburg, thanks to a rare civilized gesture on the part of American and German generals meeting there in 1945, was spared the fate of so many European cities in the Second World War.

Attractions

*Dom (Cathedral) [10]: The Italian architect Solari designed this beautifully proportioned, 17th-century church, the earliest example of monumental Italian Baroque north of the Alps. Mozart was baptized in the ancient baptismal font, which came from an earlier Romanesque cathedral. During the Festival of Music and Drama, the square in front of the cathedral becomes the stage for performances of Hugo von Hofmannsthal's version of the old morality play "Everyman."

Festspielhaus (Festival Playhouse) [7]: Most of the musical events of Salzburg's annual Festival (the *Festspiel*) are heard in this impressive new complex built into the side of the Mönchsberg. The 17th-century Winter Riding School, where horses were stabled, has been incorporated into the larger complex and provides another performing space.

**Festung Hohensalzburg (Hohensalzburg Fortress) [16]: You can ride a funicular (or take the more exhilarating footpath that starts beside it) up to this completely preserved, mountaintop fortress, where the princely archbishops of Salzburg once sat and

ruled their surrounding domains. Work began in the 11th century and continued with rebuilding and additions for almost seven centuries. Original Gothic wood carving and coffered ceilings grace the rooms, the highlight of which is *Saint George's Chapel,* dating from 1501.

*Marionettentheater, Schwartzstrasse 24: For over 200 years, the family of Professor Herman Aicher, the theater's proprietor, have been making and

Salzburg Attractions:
1. City Hall
2. Mozart's Birthplace
3. Mönchsberg
4. Carolino-Augusteum Museum
5. Natural Science Museum
6. Pferdeschwemme
7. Festival Playhouse
8. Kollegienkirche
9. Franciscan Church
10. Cathedral
11. Residence Fountain
12. Glockenspiel Tower
13. Old Market
14. Kapitelschwemme
15. St. Peter's Abbey
16. Hohensalzburg Fortress
17. Nonnberg Convent
18. Schloss Mirabell
19. Kur- and Kongresshaus
20. Mozarteum
21. Makartplatz
22. Schloss Arenberg

performing with marionettes; the famous puppets perform here in their home theater from mid-April through September.

Mozarts Geburtshaus (Mozart's Birthplace) [2]: On January 27, 1756, one of the world's greatest musical geniuses was born in this house, which is now a museum.

Residenz: An elegant and impressive square called *Residenzplatz*—in the center of which sits the **Residenzbrunnen** (Residence Fountain) [11]—is the setting for this former episcopal residence, built in the 12th century and renovated in the 17th. A guided tour takes you through the staterooms, living quarters, offices, and reception rooms of the archbishops. In the same building

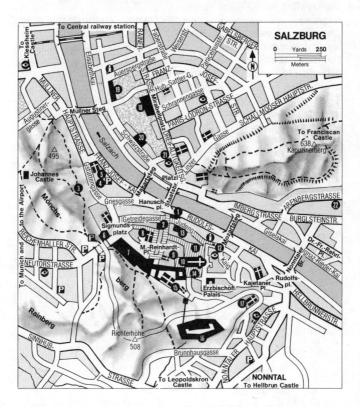

is the *Residenzgallerie,* with a noteworthy collection of paintings from the 16th to the 19th century. A sweet chiming peal of bells wafts out over the square at 7:00 A.M., 11:00 A.M., and 6:00 P.M. daily from the early 18th-century *Glockenspiel Tower.*

Schloss Mirabell [18]: Civil servants don't usually get to work in extravagant Baroque palaces, but in Salzburg, this is the home of the city's Registrar's Office. It's not unusual to see a just-married couple gliding down the cherub-covered staircase and foyer. The countless cherubs may be less angelic than they seem, for the palace was built by the archbishop Wolf Dietrich for his lover, Salome Alt. In the summer, chamber music concerts take place in a lavish Baroque hall upstairs.

Sebastianskirche, Linzergasse: Paracelsus, a famous physician and philosopher (1494–1541), is buried in the mid-18th-century church, while tombs of the Mozart family are found in the arcaded cemetery.

*Stiftskirche St. Peter (St. Peter's Abbey) [15]: Austria's oldest monastery was founded by Saint Rupert in the late seventh century; the church, dating from the 12th century, was redesigned in Rococo style in 1754. It contains the tomb of Mozart's sister Nannerl. A guided tour will take you through the third-century *catacombs* in the wall of the Mönchsberg, beside the ancient cemetery.

Excursions

Schloss Hellbrunn, about 5 km. (3 miles) from the city: If you've ever wondered what a *Lustschloss* (pleasure palace) really is, here's your chance to see one from the 17th century. Designed as an amusing getaway for the prince-bishops of Salzburg, it contains some splendid trompe l'oeil decorations, landscaped gardens, and the famous *Wasserspiele,* trick fountains hidden in unlikely spots (such as the table you're sitting at) which suddenly spurt water. There is also a well-designed *Tiergarten* (zoo), where the animals live in natural surroundings.

Seville

Seville, the capital of Andalusia, is one of Spain's loveliest and most distinctive cities. The city has an almost legendary appeal, which perhaps explains why it has been the setting for so many operas: Mozart's *Don Giovanni* and *The Marriage of Figaro*, Rossini's *Barber of Seville*, and Bizet's *Carmen* all take place in the streets, squares, white-washed houses, and factories of Seville. Religious emotions run high here during *Semana Santa* (Holy Week) and the *Feria* at the end of April—festivals that transform Seville into yet another stagelike setting as processions bearing opulently decorated holy images wind through the narrow streets and wild cheers rise from the bullring. Seville's ties to the New World—dating back to Christopher Columbus, who lies enshrined in the city's enormous cathedral—will be spotlighted in 1992 when the Andalusian capital hosts celebrations of the 500th anniversary of the discovery of America.

History

Like other cities in Andalusia, Seville was dominated by the Moors for many centuries, from their invasion of Spain from North Africa in the early eighth century until their expulsion in 1492. The Christian reconquest of Andalusia began in the 13th century, at which time Seville began to come into its own. The Castilian king Ferdinand III, later canonized and still revered, recovered the city from the Moors in 1248. The city retains a Moorish flavor, perhaps most evident in the Giralda, it's landmark bell tower that was once a minaret attached to a mosque.

Christopher Columbus was received by Queen Isabella in Seville after his second voyage to America. Over the next three centuries, Seville became the most important maritime city in the country; riches poured in from the New World trade, and the profits were used to embellish the city with Baroque palaces and churches with sumptuous interiors. The explorers Vespucci and Magellan set sail from Seville's Guadalquivir River.

In the 16th and 17th centuries, Seville was the home of the artists Velázquez and Murillo and the great writer Cervantes, who was twice jailed in Seville—small wonder that his immortal dreamer, Don Quijote, is born in a Sevillean prison.

Unfortunately, for all its picturesque beauty and cultural associations, Seville today has the highest unemployment in western Europe and has gained notoriety for its connections to the drug trafficking trade along Spain's southern coast. There has been a marked increase in petty crime here, and you are advised to be careful. Don't travel with large amounts of money and credit cards on your person, and don't leave valuables in a parked car.

Attractions

**Alcázar [4]: In the 14th century, Pedro the Cruel—so-called because he murdered his stepmother and four half-brothers—had this palace built on the site of a Moorish fortress, and lived here with his mistress Maria de Padilla. The work was done by *mudéjars,* Moors working under Christian masters; additions and embellishments were added later when the Catholic monarchs came to power. Rooms and patios of remarkable grace and beauty lie beyond the high, fortified walls, including the *Patio de las Doncellas,* where the earlier sultans received their yearly tribute of 100 virgins, and the *Salón de Embajadores,* where Charles V married Isabel of Portugal. A second and smaller palace built by Charles V, is reached through another patio—this one offering sublime views of Seville's landmark tower, the Giralda. Superb Flemish tapestries grace the Gothic hall of this palace. For a special treat, stroll in the calm, fragrant gardens where the fountains murmur and huge, lazy goldfish glide in a pool of waterlilies.

Barrio Santa Cruz [5]: This fascinating maze of narrow lanes and quiet squares clustered around the Alcázar and cathedral was once Seville's Jewish ghetto. It is now a gentrified area of private homes, old bars, and antique and ceramic shops. It's a place to meander, simply to enjoy the sight of whitewashed garden walls with wrought-iron lanterns and splashes of bougainvillea, the distinctive pot-bellied grilles that hide the windows of the houses, and glimpses of charming, private patios. The great Spanish painter

Seville Attractions:

Alcazar

Murillo once lived in this area and is buried in the Plaza Santa Cruz. The **Murillo Gardens** [7] (next to those of the Alcázar but separated from them by a wall), make for a pleasant rest stop.

Casa de las Dueñas [13]: Once the palace of the dukes of Alba, the structure exemplifies Mudejar and Plateresque detail; the inner courtyard, chapel, and several apartments may be visited.

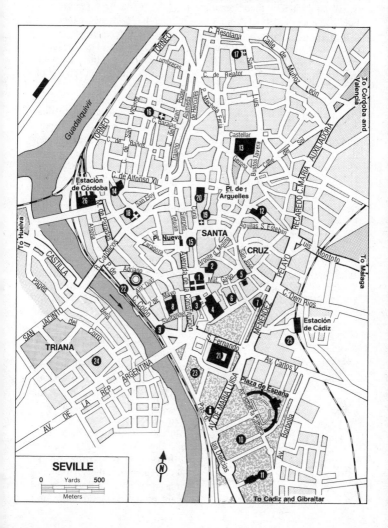

*Casa de Pilatos (House of Pilate) [12]: On his return from the Holy Land in the 16th century, the Duke of Tarifa decided to build a palace in the style of Pontius Pilate's residence. Actually, the palace is more Mudejar than Roman, but that doesn't detract from its charm; there's a huge patio, delicate stucco work, and, on the upper floor, works by Goya, Murillo, and Velázquez.

***Cathedral [1]: Built between 1402 and 1506 on the site of the main Arabian mosque, Seville's cathedral is the largest and most impressive Gothic edifice in the world—in fact, of Christian churches, only Saint Peter's in Rome and Saint Paul's in London are larger. The interior, though filled with ornate Baroque treasures and rich decoration, is curiously dark—even gloomy—but look for the splendid paintings by Murillo, Zurbarán, and Morales, the silver tomb of Saint Ferdinand in the Capilla Real, and Christopher Columbus's mausoleum. The cathedral bell tower, known as the *Giralda,* is a former Moorish minaret crowned by a massive statue of "Faith" that turns in the wind.

City Hall (Ayuntamiento) [15]: This stately, 16th-century building has sections richly decorated in the Plateresque style.

El Salvador [19]: Consecrated in 1712, this Baroque church was erected on the site of an earlier mosque and has a magnificent Rococo interior.

Hospital de los Venerables Sacerdotes [6]: Baroque predominates in the beautiful inner courtyard and church.

Hospital de La Caridad [8]: Miguel de Manara, better known as Don Juan, died in this Baroque almshouse after renouncing his lascivious ways and joining the brotherhood of the order, whose job it was to collect and bury the bodies of executed men. In addition to a portrait of the famous rake, there are two morbid paintings he commissioned which represent the Triumph of Death—not for the squeamish.

*Museo de Bellas Artes (Museum of Fine Arts) [14]: One entire room of this 17th-century former monastery is reserved for El Greco's famous painting of his son, known as "Portrait of a Painter." There are also works by Murillo, Zurbarán, Velázquez, and Goya.

Museum of Archaeology [11]: Finds from the surrounding area and the nearby Roman settlement of Italica predominate and

The Giralda

include statues of "Diana," "Venus," and "Hermes."

Parque de Maria Luisa [10]: The gardens of the palace of San Telmo were redesigned in 1929 when Seville hosted an Ibero-American exhibition; many buildings remain from that time, although they are now used as schools and consulates. The sunken gardens with pools and fountains and the beautiful *Plaza de America* provide a welcome respite from Seville's summer glare and heat.

San Lorenzo [16]: The church contains a beautiful high altar and the *Nuestro Padre Jesus del Gran Poder,* a much-venerated image of Christ by Juan de Mesa that dates from 1620.

Santa Maria Magdalena [18]: A former monastic church of the Dominican order, this is one of the most impressive Baroque structures in Seville; it contains sculptures, paintings by Zurbarán, and a remarkable Mudejar dome.

Torre del Oro (Tower of Gold) [9]: At one time this 18th-century tower, which rests on 12th-century Moorish foundations, was covered with gilded tiles; today it houses the *Museum of Navigation,* filled with reminders of Seville's important role in world seafaring and exploration.

Triana [24]: This suburb on the west bank of the Guadalquivir River has been Seville's pottery district for centuries; the famous, painted ceramic tiles known as *azulejos* are manufactured here.

Sofia

Ironically enough, a first impression of ancient Sofia may be that it looks relatively new. Late 19th-century planning accounts for the broad boulevards and spacious parks—so many parks, in fact, that Sofia is known as the greenest city in Europe. The city sits on a high plain ringed by mountains, the closest of which is Mount Vitosha, also considered a city park. As the economic, cultural, and political capital of Bulgaria—one of the easiest Soviet bloc countries to visit—Sofia offers a host of cultural and outdoor attractions. On the streets of Sofia you'll encounter a rich and architecturally diverse assortment of buildings that range from ancient Roman to modern Russian, many with a substantial Turkish overlay. The use of the Cyrillic alphabet on signs can be bewildering, so it's helpful to obtain a translation of the alphabet into English.

History

As early as the fifth century B.C., the Thracians—known for their magnificent gold work and who were later absorbed by the armies of Alexander the Great—laid the foundations for a settlement at the intersection of important trade routes and warm mineral springs. The first period of growth for the future city of Sofia began under the Romans, who established the city of Serdica and made it an important center of trade for the Roman Empire. It was put to the torch by Attila in 447, and rebuilt about a hundred years later by the Emperor Justinian.

Beginning in the seventh century, the Slavs, who came from the plains region around the Danube, forced the Romanized population to the south. Serdica became Sredet when the Bulgars took over the city in 809 and made it a pivotal point of the first Bulgarian empire. Christianity was adopted, and an important monastic tradition established; the Cyrillic alphabet, introduced by the monks, was the first Slavic alphabet.

During the late 14th century, the city was ruled for almost 500 years by the Turks. Although this did not detract from Sofia's importance, it did inspire the numerous uprisings that culminated in Russia's going to war against the Turks on Bulgaria's behalf. In 1879, Sofia became the capital of newly liberated Bulgaria.

Attractions

**Alexander Nevski Cathedral (Ploštad Alekssandar Nevski) [16]: With its overwhelming gold-leaf domes, this massive structure was built in the early part of this century in gratitude for the Russian liberation of Bulgaria from the rule of the Turks. Bulgarian and Russian artists worked together to create the cathedral. It is named after Alexander Nevski (1220–1263), patron saint of Alexander II—the "Czar of the Liberation." A crypt in the cathedral is filled with a superb collection of 12th- to 17th-century icons from various parts of Bulgaria.

Bathers' Mosque (Banja baši džamija) [5]: The enormous dome contrasts sharply with the slender minaret of this 16th-century, Turkish mosque. Its name comes from its proximity to the **Mineral Baths of Sofia** (Sofijskatabanja) [6], built in 1913. One block north on Georgi Dimitrov Street is the **Central Department Store** [7], with Roman ruins in the basement.

Church of Saint Petka the Saddler (Sveta Petka Samardžijska) [4]: Frescoes from the 15th through the 19th century decorate this church, built around 1400.

Church of Saint Nedelja (Sveta Nedélja) [1]: Erected toward the end of the 19th century on the site of much earlier churches, Saint Nedelja was the scene of a 1925 bombing attempt on the life of Czar Boris III.

Church of Saint Sophia (Sveta Sófija) [17]: Emperor Justinian had this sober little church—now overshadowed by the looming, dramatic majesty of Alexander Nevski Cathedral—built during the sixth century on the site of old church ruins. With its combination of Byzantine and Roman elements, it was transformed into a mosque by the Turks and then heavily damaged by earthquakes in the 19th century.

North of the Saint Sophia is the famous **National Opera House** [18], founded in 1909.

George Dimitrov Mausoleum [13]: The "Father of the Nation," Communist leader Georgi Dimitrov, died in 1949 and lies embalmed in a glass sarcophagus within the mausoleum; outside, a military guard clad in 19th-century costume changes every hour.

*Great Mosque (Bujuk džamija) [11]: A new dome covers this fascinating quadrangular remnant of Turkish-occupied Sofia; the former mosque now houses the *Museum of Archaeology,* but

Sofia Attractions:
1. Church of St. Nedélja
2. Church of St. George
3. National History Museum
4. Church of St. Petka the Saddler
5. Bathers' Mosque
6. Mineral Baths
7. Central Department Store
8. TSUM Department Store
9. Council of Ministers
10. Communist Party of Bulgaria
11. Great Mosque
12. National Gallery
13. Georgi Dimitrov Mausoleum
14. Natural History Museum
15. Church of St. Nicholas
16. Alexander Nevski Cathedral
17. Church of St. Sophia
18. National Opera House
19. Monument to the Liberators
20. Parliament
21. University
22. National Library
23. Monument to the Soviet Army
24. Obelisk
25. Universiade Sport Hall
26. Museum of the Bulgarian Revolutionary Movement
27. Dimitrov Museum
28. Dimitâr Blagoev Museum

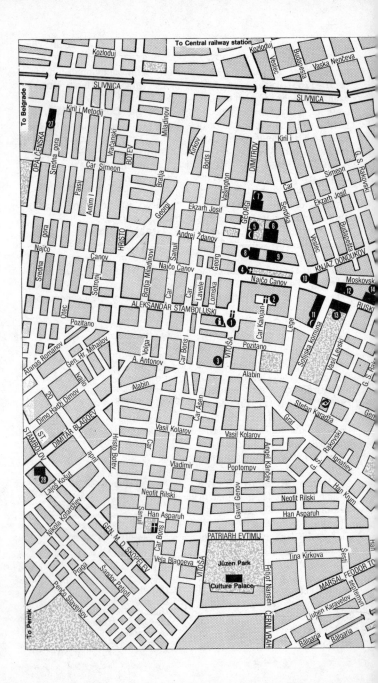

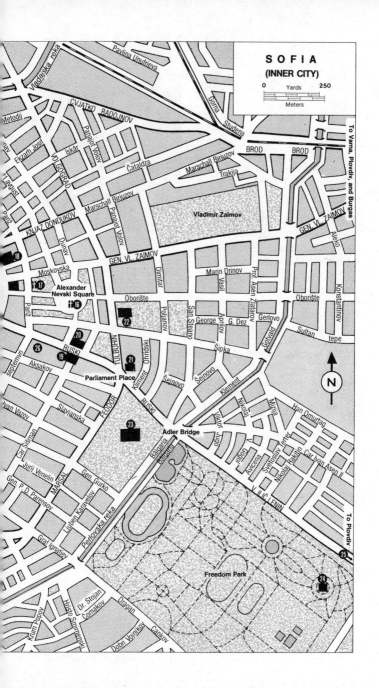

its best collections have been moved to the Natural History Museum.

Lenin Square: A number of newer buildings—none of them architecturally noteworthy—are found on this square dedicated to the Russian revolutionary: the *Sheraton-Balkan Hotel,* the *TSUM department store* [8]; the *House of the Council of Ministers* [9]; and the *House of the Communist Party of Bulgaria* [10]. South on Vitosha Boulevard stands the **Natural History Museum** [3], with a fabulous collection of treasures dating back as far as the fourth century B.C., including a set of gold Thracian vessels.

Monument to the Liberators [19]: An equestrian statue of Czar Alexander II, who liberated Bulgaria from the Turks, stands in front of the National Assembly building.

National Gallery [12]: Housed within the former royal palace on Boulevard Ruski, the

Church of St. George

main street of Sofia, the museum contains Bulgarian art of the last two centuries and a *Museum of Ethnography.*

Rotunda of the Church of Saint George (Sveti Georgi) [2]: This ancient building—not open to the public—was built in the fourth century as a Roman temple and later served as a Turkish mosque and a Christian church. East of the church are the substantial Roman ruins, including a paved street.

Stockholm

You may be astonished to see people fishing in the middle of downtown Stockholm, but there's a lot that's surprising about this Swedish capital—not the least of which is its sparkling cleanliness. Stockholm, the largest port on the Baltic Sea, is a city of islands, built where Lake Mälaren meets the Baltic; it derives much of its distinctive flavor from its maritime location. White steamer ferries ply the waters in and around the city, providing transport to the various islands. Stockholm is a city that counterbalances a royal past—Sweden maintains a constitutional monarchy, and one Swedish Royal Palace is here—with a thoroughly progressive modern commitment to high standards for all of society. The undeniably picturesque old center of the city, with its quiet squares and medieval streets, forms a striking contrast to "new" Stockholm, just minutes away.

History

Founded in 1252 by Birger Jarl, a powerful regent, Stockholm quickly became an important center of fishing and trade. Danish rule of what was then one strategically located island on the Baltic ended in 1523 when King Gustav Vasa entered the city and claimed it as his own.

Under Vasa's rule, Stockholm enjoyed a period of peaceful economic progress. A century later, King Gustavus Adolphus chose Stockholm as the official capital, and the city became a center of culture and learning.

The city grew, spreading out over a series of small, nearby islands. After a period of economic decline, Stockholm's fortunes rose again with the advent of the Industrial Revolution, at which time the business center moved north from today's *Gamla Stan* (Old Town).

Attractions

Church of Adolf Frederik [17]: This Italianate church with its interesting interior was built in 1774.

Church of Saint Clara [9]: You'll find this church with its small cemetery in the heart of Stockholm's newspaper district.

Gamla Stan (Old Town): Now connected to the mainland by five bridges, this island just south of the city center is the oldest section of Stockholm. It is filled with winding, medieval streets, small, quiet corners, and tempting shops of all kinds. The main square is dominated by Stockholm's 550-room **Stockholms Slott* (Royal Palace) [4], where a colorful changing-of-the-guard takes place at noon during the summer. You can visit the *State Apartments*, admire the *Royal Armory* [18], or ponder the Swedish crown jewels

Royal Palace

in the *Treasury*. Stockholm's cathedral, *Storkyrka* [5], is located behind the Royal Palace. Swedish kings have been crowned here since the 15th century. It was originally built in the 13th century and then rebuilt in the mid-18th. Look for the 15th-century wooden sculpture of Saint George and the Dragon in the cathedral's ornate interior.

Kaknäs Television Tower, Djurgården: You'll understand the island topography of Stockholm better with a bird's-eye view from this observation tower, the highest structure in Scandinavia.

Kungliga Dramatiska Teater (Royal Dramatic Theater) [13]: Everything from Ibsen to *Oklahoma!*, performed in Swedish by the best actors in the country.

Museum of National Antiquities and the **Royal Coin Cabinet,** Narvavägen 13–17: Don't let the names keep you away—there are silver and gold Viking treasures in the first museum, and the world's largest coin collection in the second.

**National Museum [11]: The most significant art collection in Sweden focuses primarily on paintings by Swedish and other European masters, including Rembrandt, Frans Hals, and Rubens.

Nordic Museum: Located on the northern peninsula of Skansen Island, this museum, with its holdings of furniture, national costumes, household artifacts, and tools, illustrates Swedish life through the centuries.

Riddarholm Church [1]: Built on the small island from which its name derives, this magnificent edifice was begun as a monastery in the 13th century, and is the final resting place for the Kings of Sweden.

*Riddarhus (House of the Nobility) [2]: The Riddarhus, built in the 17th century, is considered the most beautiful Baroque structure in Stockholm. Escutcheons from each of the Swedish noble families decorate its Hall of Knights.

Rosendal Palace: Home now to the *Karl Johans Museum,* this early-19th-century building was once a royal summer residence.

*Royal Army Museum [18]: The military-minded will enjoy the museum's collections of uniforms and weapons.

Royal Opera House [10]: International standards and top-notch productions prevail at the Swedish Opera, which performs in this turn-of-the-century building. Just behind the Opera is the small, Gothic *Church of Saint James,* with its beautiful portal.

Skansen: A prototype for all

Stockholm Attractions:
1. Church of Riddarholm
2. Riddarhus
3. Reichstag Building
4. Royal Palace
5. Storkyrka
6. Tyska Kyrka
7. Slussen
8. City Hall
9. Church of Saint Clara
10. Royal Opera House
11. National Museum
12. Skeppsholm
13. Royal Dramatic Theater
14. New Cultural House
15. Royal Towers
16. Concert Hall
17. Church of Adolf Frederik
18. Royal Army Museum
19. Strandväg

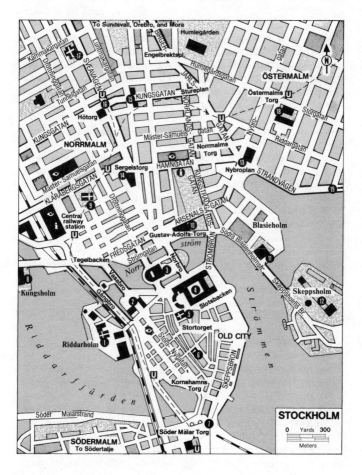

subsequent open-air museums, Skansen, now nearly a hundred years old, provides a lively, comprehensive overview of Swedish life through the ages. Besides the historic buildings brought here from all over the country, and the native handcraft demonstrations, you'll find a zoo and an excellent aquarium.

*Skeppsholm [12]: The island boasts a mid-19th-century church and two worthwhile museums. A large collection of modern Swedish and international art can be found in the *Moderna Museet* (Museum of Modern Art), housed in a former barracks. You can discover older treasures in ceramics, jade, wood, ivory, and lacquer from Japan, Korea, and India in the impressive *Ostasiatiska Museet* (Museum of Far Eastern Antiquities).

Stadshuset (City Hall) [8]: The subdued red-brick exterior of this colonnaded seat of city government, completed in 1923, is a model of architectural restraint— which makes the 19 million gilded tiles of the spectacular Golden Hall inside all the more eye-opening. You can get a great view over the city from the tower.

Steamers: Stockholm's fleet of turn-of-the-century steamships is moored opposite the Grand Hotel by the City Hall; they are still in service, and visitors should definitely make a steamer trip to one of the innumerable islands in the Swedish archipelago.

Strandväg [19]: Running along the southern shore of the mainland, this street leads to Djurgardsbrunnsvag and two adjacent museums, the *National Maritime Museum* and the *Museum of Technology*.

Tyska Kyrka (German Church) [6]: The impressive interior of this superb, mid-16th-century structure is embellished with gifts donated by German merchants.

*Wasavarvet (Wasa Dockyard): Docked at the large island of Djurgården, close to Skansen, this restored, 17th-century Swedish warship has become one of Stockholm's prime attractions. For all its intended ferocity, the *Wasa* never saw action because it sank on its maiden voyage. The *Gröna Lund Tivoli* amusement park, with terrifying roller coasters for the strong of heart and simpler pleasures for the rest of us, takes up the southwestern corner of Djurgården.

Excursions

Drottningholm Palace: Located 3 km. (1.5 miles) west of Stockholm on the island of Lovon, this 17th-century, French-style palace, with its splendid gardens, is now the residence of the royal family (and is open to visitors). On the grounds is the marvelously preserved Rococo *Drottningholms Slottsteater* (Court Theater), built in the 18th century to serve the court; original sets and machinery are still used in the summer performances of opera and ballet. You can reach Drottningholm by the steamer that departs from Klara Mälarstrand near City Hall, or take the subway to Brommaplan, where you'll find a Malarobus that stops at the palace grounds.

Gripsholm Castle: Sweden's most romantic castle is located on the southern shore of Lake Mälaren at Mariefred, about 64 km. (40 miles) from the city. The present building was erected by King Gustav Vasa in 1577, and houses the state portrait collection. The best way to travel to Gripsholm is on the coal-fired steamer *Mariefred,* which departs from Klara Mälarstrand near City Hall.

Skokloster Palace: Destination point for another extremely popular steamer trip, Skokloster dates from the mid-17th century and has some marvelous Gobelins tapestries. The boat leaves from the City Hall bridge and follows the "Royal Waterway" of Lake Mälaren, stopping at *Sigtuna,* Sweden's ancient capital.

Strasbourg

A flourishing metropolis of over 400,000, Strasbourg—only 4 km. (2.5 miles) from the Rhine and the German border—is the largest city in France's Alsace region, and also one of its busiest. Famous for its cuisine (notably its *pâté de foie gras*), its eminent university, its many museums, and its handsome cathedral, this river port is also the birthplace of France's national anthem, "La Marseillaise." Rouget de Lisle, a Rhine Army soldier, composed the patriotic song in 1792, which was quickly adopted by Marseille's citizens. Much of the charming old city survives, centering on the island of Ill; the Petite-France district is especially lovely, with the steeply, sloping roofs and decorated façades of its charming medieval "gingerbread houses." Strasbourg's Franco-Germanic history and cultural heritages are immensely rich—among many other famous figures, Gutenberg worked, John Calvin settled, and Goethe studied here—and today, as the home of the Council of Europe and the European Parliament, it is an important site of history-in-the-making.

History

In 15 B.C., the Romans built the garrison of Argentoratum, as Strasbourg was then known, on the site of an old Celtic fishing village. It was conquered by the Franks in the fifth century, when it was given the name of Strateburgum (meaning "city of the crossroads"). During the Merovingian dynasty, Strasbourg became the site of an episcopal see. In 842, the "Strasbourg Oath" was taken by the West Frankish king, Charles the Bald, and the East Frankish monarch, Louis I, thus affirming their alliance (their *Serment de Strasbourg* is the oldest written document in Old French). In the mid-13th century, the bishops' control of the city ended; a period of economic prosperity began in this free city of the Holy Roman Empire, governed democratically by a guild of citizens.

In the 14th century, Strasbourg was the center of German mysticism, and in the 1400s, it became the hotbed of humanism (and also the home of Johannes Gutenberg, who worked here from 1434 to 1444 perfecting the printing press). From 1518 on, the Reformation won ever greater support in the city; among others, John Calvin settled here in 1538. The university was also founded at this time (1566). On the whole, the 16th century was an era of economic prosperity for Strasbourg.

A period of decline began with the Peace of Westphalia (1648). The Alsace region fell completely under the control of France in 1681, when it was seized by Louis XIV. During the French Revolution (1789), the bishopric became secularized and the cathedral became the "Temple of Reason."

Completion of the canal and railroad lines in the 19th century brought economic recovery to the area. In 1871, Strasbourg became the capital of the new German state of Alsace-Lorraine, having surrendered to the Prussians in 1870 after a 50-day siege. In 1918, the beleaguered city once again belonged to France, and the establishment of an autonomous harbor in 1924 proved a major boost to its economy. In 1940, the Nazis annexed Alsace-Lorraine, but the city was liberated in November of 1944. After World War II, Strasbourg became the headquarters of the Council of Europe (1949) as well as an important industrial center, with its metallurgical factories, petroleum refineries, and food-processing plants. Today it is also the location of the European Parliament and the Court of Justice; and, as it was in Gutenberg's time, it is a major communications center as well.

Attractions

***Cathédrale Notre-Dame

[3], Place de la Cathédrale: This overpowering structure, one of the most beautiful Gothic cathedrals in France, dates from the 11th to 15th centuries (although a church stood on the site as early as A.D. 500). A Romanesque-style building was begun around 1010, but the nave was rebuilt in the 13th

Cathédrale Nôtre-Dame

century and construction of the present Gothic cathedral commenced. The red-sandstone west front (late 13th to mid-14th century) and the two towers up to the landing are by Erwin von Steinbach and his successors; they feature lovely tracery and elaborate statuary. Pay special attention to the figures on the three portals, including the highly expressive Wise and Foolish Virgins (at the right). Von Steinbach's work was continued by Ulrich von Ensingen from the late 14th to early 15th century; his daring tower is also decorated with statuary. Atop the tower is a pierced spire built from 1420 to 1439 by Johann Hültz of Cologne; on a clear day, the tower offers a magnificent view of the city and the Black Forest. The rose window is especially lovely, as is the rest of the stained glass in the cathedral. The 13th-century "Pillar of Angels," in the south transept, features seraphim trumpeting the Last Judgment. The late

Gothic stone pulpit was carved by Johann Hammerer in 1486. The Renaissance astronomical clock (reconstructed in 1842) sets numerous figures in motion every afternoon at 12:30.

Château des Rohan, Place du Château: A former episcopal palace (briefly home to the university in the 1870s), the château was built for the Cardinal de Rohan-Soubise in 1730–1742. Today it houses the *Musée des Beaux-Arts* (see below), as well as museums of archaeology and decorative arts.

*Maison Kammerzell, 16 Place de la Cathédrale: Strasbourg's beautiful half-timbered house—with its ornate, carved façade and interior murals—is now a popular restaurant. Its stone-ground floor dates to 1467, while its overhanging upper stories are late 16th century.

Musée Alsacien, 23–25 Quai Saint-Nicolas: Located in a 17th-century merchant's house, the museum is a rich repository of costumes, folk art, furniture, Jewish ritual objects, and assorted domestic utensils from the Alsace region.

Musée de l'Oeuvre Nôtre-Dame, Place du Château: In 1349, the Maison de l'Oeuvre Nôtre-Dame became the headquarters of the architects of the Cathédrale. Now it is a museum (restored in 1944), with some 40 rooms in its Gothic and German Renaissance wings displaying medieval and Renaissance art (including original statuary from the cathedral).

Musée des Beaux-Arts, 2 Place du Château: The lavish Rococo rooms of the *Château des Rohan* house this fine-arts museum. On view are works from the 14th through 19th centuries, representing the major European schools. Among the highlights are a Rubens sketch, Correggio's *Judith,* and works by Van Dyck, Goya, and Zurbarán. Dutch 17th-century landscapes abound, and the museum features a large, special collection of still lifes.

Musée Historique, Rue du Vieux-Marché-aux-Poissons: Located in the *Grande Boucherie* (1586–1588), the old meat-market building, the museum is devoted to the rich history of Strasbourg. It displays prints, early photographs, arms and armor, and assorted militariana.

Palais de l'Europe, Avenue de l'Europe: Opened in 1977, the nine-story, fortresslike "Palace of Europe" serves as the headquarters of the Council of Europe and the meeting place of the European Parliament.

*Parc de l'Orangerie, off Boulevard de l'Orangerie: Laid out in the early 19th century, this beautiful park includes an Orangery built for Empress Joséphine (since rebuilt after a 1968 fire).

La Petite-France, north of Rue Finkwiller and east of the Ponts Couverts (southwest of the main island of Ill): This cluster of medieval houses, located on small islands in the Ill, is especially charming. From the Quai de la Petite France, the *Ponts Couverts* (once-covered bridges that lost their roofs in 1784) cross the tributaries of the Ill; towers once belonging to the town's medieval fortifications are also nearby.

Place Broglie [10]: The *Hôtel de Ville,* or City Hall, (1730–1736; rebuilt in 1840) and the municipal theater, the *Opéra du Rhin* (1825; rebuilt 1870) are situated on this square, laid out in 1742 on the location of an old horse market. On the north side of the square is the *Banque de France,* where Rouget de Lisle first sang "La Marseillaise."

Place de la République [11]: This spacious square boasts an array of impressive public buildings, as well as a monument

honoring those killed in World War I. The *Palais du Rhin* (1883–1889), a neo-Renaissance pile built for the German Kaiser, is on the northwest side of the square; farther east are the handsome Art Nouveau *Municipal Baths,* designed by J. C. Ott (1908).

Strasbourg Attractions:
1. Place Kléber
2. Rue des Grandes-Arcades
3. Cathedral
4. Place du Château
5. Place du Corbeau
6. Saint Thomas
7. Rue du Bain-aux-Plantes
8. Saint-Pierre-le-Vieux
9. Grand' Rue
10. Place Broglie
11. Place de la République
12. Allée de la Robertsau

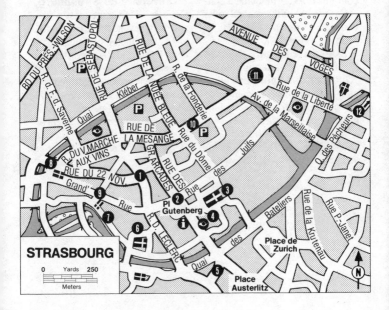

STRASBOURG

Place du Corbeau [5]: "Raven Square" is the site of the famous 14th-century *Hôtel du Corbeau,* an inn where such notable guests as Frederick the Great (in 1740) stopped for the night.

Place du Marché-aux-Cochons-de-Lait: Close by is the old meat market, or Grande Boucherie, today the *Musée Historique;* across the street is the old Customs House (Ancienne Douane), now the *Musée d'Art Moderne*—with works by Braque, Klee, Rodin, Renoir, Arp (a Strasbourg native), and others.

Place Kléber [1]: The hub of city traffic, this square was named after the famous general of the French Revolution, Jean-Baptiste Kléber, who was born in Strasbourg in 1753. A monument conceals the tomb of the general, who was assassinated by a Muslim fanatic in Cairo in 1800.

Rue du Bain-aux-Plantes [7]: This lane goes through the old ***Quartier des Tanneurs** (Tanning District), with its multitude of half-timbered houses, including those of *La Petite-France.*

Saint-Pierre-le-Vieux [8], Grand' Rue and Rue du 22 Novembre: In 1681, Old St. Peter,

with its austere 14th- and 15th-century façade, was divided into two separate churches, one Catholic (the choir), the other Protestant (the nave); the former part was renovated in the early 20th century.

Saint-Thomas [6], Place Saint-Thomas, off Rue des Serruriers: Built in the 13th and 14th centuries, this Protestant hall-church is best known for its tombs, the most elaborate being that of the French marshal Maurice of Saxony (1696–1750), which comprises an allegorical marble group by sculptor Jean-Baptiste Pigalle. Albert Schweitzer started a tradition of organ concerts here in 1908, commemorating the death of J. S. Bach.

Université de Strasbourg, Place de l'Université (east of the old town, beyond the Ill): Founded in 1621 by the Holy Roman Emperor Ferdinand II, the prestigious university is now divided into three autonomous, state-financed institutions: the *Université Louis Pasteur* (medical and related sciences), the *Université des Sciences Humaines,* and the *Université des Sciences Juridiques, Politiques et Sociales.*

Turin

Turin is traversed by the Po River and surrounded by a hilly landscape with a view of the Alps to the west. While it may be Italy's most important industrial city as well as the capital of the Piedmont region, Turin maintains an elegant French air. For many years, it was the home of the dukes of Savoy, who filled it with the Baroque churches and palaces that still characterize the old town. Strolling in the great arcaded squares of Turin is always a pleasure, and one of the city's biggest surprises is its great Egyptian Museum, which has no equal outside of Cairo.

History

The ancient Celtic settlement of Taurasia became an important military foothold under the Romans, who renamed the city Julia Augusta Taurinorum. In 218 B.C., it was seized by Hannibal and destroyed. A new city, founded in A.D. 65, was granted Roman civil rights under Julius Caesar.

After the fall of the Roman Empire, Turin was annexed by the Goths; it successively became a duchy of Lombard, a Frankish county, an independent episcopal city, and finally a free municipality. A period of great progress began with the rule of the house of Savoy: Turin became the seat of the court and the highest administrative offices, and the center of Italian politics.

In 1645, the city was rebuilt and expanded in Baroque style under Carlo Emanuele II. After a triumphant victory over the French in 1706—the battle in which Prince Eugene of Savoy distinguished himself—the Superga basilica, a landmark of the city, was built.

A few years after this decisive victory, the duchy of Savoy became a kingdom, with Turin as its capital. During the six-year Napoleonic occupation (1808–1814), Camillo Borghese, Napoleon's brother-in-law, made Turin his home.

After the restoration of the house of Savoy, efforts to form a united Italy began in Turin, that led to Victor Emmanuel II's assumption of the title "King of Italy" in 1861.

Attractions

*Basilica Maria Ausiliatrice [12]: Consecrated in 1868, this is considered one of the finest churches in Turin.

Mastio (Keep) [21]: The keep—all that remains of the original citadel, which was the scene of the French siege of Turin in 1706—now houses the *Artillery Museum*. The *Gallery of Modern Arts,* on nearby Via Magenta, is also worth a stop.

Castello del Valentino [19]: A French Renaissance-style palace, built between 1630 and 1660, it was the residential seat of Maria Christina of France, wife of Vittorio Amedeo I, and the scene of magnificent festivals. At the south end of the *Parco del Valentino* you'll find the modern *Palazzo Esposizioni*, built for the 1948 Turin automobile show. Car-buffs can indulge their motoring fantasies at the outstanding *Museo dell'Automobile,* on Corso Unità d'Italia, about 1 km. (a half-mile) farther south.

Castello e Borgo Medioevale [20]: This 19th-century replica of a medieval Piedmont village—replete with pinnacled castle—is a museum with antique weapons and armaments.

Duomo San Giovanni Battista (Cathedral of Saint John the Baptist) [9]: Turin's only Renaissance building, this monument to Tuscan gracefulness and order dates from the 15th century and contains the much-publicized (and rarely displayed) *Shroud of Turin* in the Baroque *Cappella della Santa Sindone.* A few steps away in Via Porta Palatina is the **Porta Palatina [10], one of the original Roman gates of the city wall erected by order of Augustus. During the Middle Ages, the towers were furnished with battlements; the later bronze statues are of Julius Caesar and Augustus. This entire area is an archaeological zone, and contains Roman ruins as well as 15th and 16th century houses.

Gran Madre de Dio (Holy Mother of God) [16]: Built in 1831 at the foot of the wooded **Monte dei Cappuccini** [18], this copy of the Roman Pantheon serves today as a memorial to those who died in the First World War. North of the church lies the **Zoo** [17], while on the mountain itself you'll have a magnificent view of the city. The interesting *Duca degli Abruzzi* (Mountain Museum) also is located here.

Mole Antonelliana [14]: Originally built as a synagogue, this unusual structure was once the highest masonry-constructed building in Europe. A tornado knocked down the spire in 1953, which was then replaced in aluminum; there's a great view from the summit.

Palazzo Carignano [3]: This Piedmontese, Baroque-style masterpiece by Guarini, built in 1679, was the birthplace of two kings, Carlo Alberto and Victor Emmanuel II. The first Italian Parliament (which proclaimed Rome the capital of Italy) met here in 1861. The *Museo Nazionale del Risorgimento Italiano* (National Museum of the Italian Unification Movement) is housed within the palace.

**Palazzo dell'Accademia delle Scienze (Palace of the Academy of Sciences) [4]: Built in 1679 by Guarini, Turin's most prominent architect, it houses two remarkable museums. If your tastes tend toward ancient marvels, head first for the magnificent *Museo Egizio* (Egyptian Museum), the most important collec-

Turin Attractions:
1. Stazione Porta Nuova
2. Piazza San Carlo
3. Palazzo Carignano
4. Palazzo dell'Accademia delle Scienze
5. Piazza Castello
6. San Lorenzo
7. Palazzo Reale
8. Palace Gardens
9. Cathedral
10. Porta Palatina
11. Sanctuario della Consolata
12. Basilica Maria Ausiliatrice
13. Piccola Casa della Divina Providenza
14. Mole Antonelliana
15. Piazza Vittorio Veneto
16. Gran Madre de Dio
17. Zoo
18. Monte dei Cappuccini
19. Castello del Valentino
20. Castello e Borgo Medioevale
21. Mastio (Keep)

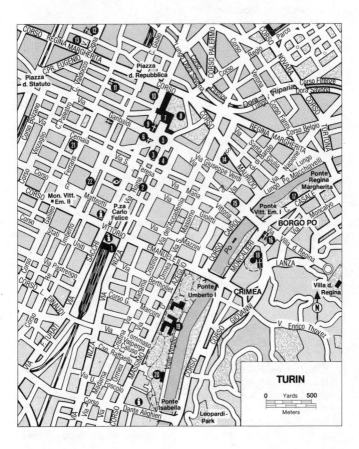

tion of Egyptian statuary, mummy caskets, and papyri in Europe. The *Galleria Sabauda* is given over to painting, and the walls are crowded with one major work after another: The various Italian schools are represented by Fra Angelico, Andrea del Sarto, Bronzino, Tintoretto, Veronese, and Tiepolo, while the Flemish and Dutch masters on display include Van Eyck, Memling, Rembrandt, Brueghel, and Van Dyck.

Palazzo Madama

*Palazzo Reale [7]: The sober façade of this 17th-century royal palace contrasts sharply with the sumptuous decoration of the interior. The so-called *Scissor Staircase,* devised by Filippo Juvara to lead from the second to the third floor, is an extraordinary architectural curiosity. The ground floor houses the *Royal Library,* with its collection of valuable drawings by artists such as Leonardo, Raphael, Tiepolo, and Rembrandt. One of the most extensive antique weapon collections in the world is located in the *Armenia Reale* (Main Gallery). The *Museo di Antichita* (Museum of Antiquity) features prehistoric and Roman artifacts. Behind the palazzo is the **Giardino Real** (Palace Gardens) [8], designed by the famous French landscape architect Le Nôtre in the last years of the 17th century.

Piazza Castello [5]: The War of Independence from Austria was declared in this historic square embellished with a number of statues. The 12th-century *******Palazzo Madama,* in the center of the

square, was made into a medieval castle in 1403, although its west façade was not begun until 1718. A triumphal staircase leads to the luxurious 17th-century halls designed as living quarters for the two Madama Reales who once lived here: Marie-Christine of France, the mother of Charles Emmanuel II, and Giovanna Batista, his widow. Today the palace houses the *Museo d'Arte Antica* (Museum of Ancient Art) and displays Romanesque and Gothic sculptures, wood carvings, and stained glass.

*Piazza San Carlo [2]: One of Italy's most beautiful and distinctive squares, Piazza San Carlo is surrounded by a series of 17th- and 18th-century arcades and luxurious shops. A bronze equestrian statue of Duke Emanuele Filiberto (1838) acts as a focal point in the center of this lively square.

Piazza Vittorio Veneto [15]: Laid out between 1825 and 1830 with a series of arcades, Turin's largest square opens onto the Po River, framing a lovely view of the green hills on the opposite bank.

Santuario della Consolata (Sanctuary of Peace) [11]: Comprised of two independent churches—the tenth-century Sant'Andrea and a Baroque basilica built by Guarini during the 17th century—the church is an important pilgrimage site because of a much-revered image of the Virgin Mary, said to be more than 1,400 years old. The massive Roman campanile of Sant'Andrea dates from the 11th century, making it the oldest medieval monument in the city.

Excursions

Basilica della Superga, 10 km. (6 miles) northeast of city center: From the suburb of *Sassi* you can take a cog railway up the Superga hill to the basilica, designed by the famous Turinese Baroque architect, Juvara. The basilica was built between 1714 and 1731 to commemorate a victory over the French, who laid siege to the city in 1706. The tombs of Sardinian kings and princes of the House of Savoy lie in the vaults. Above ground, you get a memorable view of the Alps from the terrace and dome.

Stupinigi, 10 km. (6 miles) southwest: The Baroque castle of Vittorio Amedeo II, built by Juvara between 1729 and 1733 as a royal hunting lodge, was decorated by the best-known artists of the Piedmont; it contains a *Museo dell'Ammobiliamento* (Museum of Interior Design). The palace has served as a country seat of Napoleon Bonaparte and a summer residence of Queen Margherita.

Venaria, 8 km. (5 miles) north: Completed in 1660, this hunting and pleasure palace of Carlo Emanuele II was rebuilt and embellished by Juvara after it suffered heavy damage by the French.

San Antonio di Ranverso, 18 km. (11 miles) west: One of the most interesting and important architectural monuments in the Piedmont is this abbey, founded in 1188 and continuously expanded until the end of the 15th century.

Valencia

Spain's third largest city is the capital of the Levante region of Spain and lies on the Rio Turia, which empties into the sea only 3 km. (1.5 miles) to the east. Although a decade of unrestrained and unimaginative building has transformed whole sections of Valencia into monotonous high-rise complexes, there remain sites of historical and artistic interest dating back to Roman times. Valencia is at its flamboyantly wild and colorful best during the March fiesta known as the *Fallas de San Jose,* when colossal papier-mâché effigies are paraded through the streets and burned.

History

Valencia was founded by the Greeks and later captured by the Carthaginians and the Romans. The conquering Visigoths, arriving in 413, were ousted three hundred years later by the Moors. Under the legendary leadership of El Cid, the city was recaptured in 1094, but was soon retaken by the Moors. It was not until 1238 that the Christians took permanent control. At the end of the 15th century another "holy war" was waged in the name of Catholic Spain, at which time the Moors were forced to become baptized as Christians or face permanent exile.

Valencia rose up against Napoleon and suffered extensive damage before its surrender to the French in 1812. During the civil war of this century, the city was the seat of the Popular Front party.

Attractions

*Alumdín [6]: The old market of medieval Valencia today houses the *Museum of Paleontology,* the most comprehensive of its kind in Europe.

Ayuntamiento (City Hall, also known as Palacio Consistorial) [25]: A palatial structure dating from the second half of the 18th century, it houses the Tourist Information Office and *Museo Històrico de la Ciudad* (City History Museum).

Casa Museo Jose Benlliure [45]: The house and gardens of the painter Jose Benlliure (1855–1937) have been made into a museum with many of his works, as well as those of his son, Benlliure Ortiz.

Castillo del Marqués de Dos Aguas [21]: The inspired dementia of Hipolito Rovira—who died insane in 1740—helps to explain the fantastic Rococo façade he designed for this unique palace, today home of the **Museo Nacional de Cerámica*. The collection here is definitely worth seeing.

*Cathedral [3]: Three portals—one Romanesque, one Gothic, and one Rococo—attest to the age and successive refurbishment of this 14th-century edifice; the interior, however, has been stripped of later decoration and restored to its original Gothic splendor. A painting of Saint Francis Borgia by Goya hangs in one of the side chapels, and in the *Capilla del Santo Cáliz* (Chapel of the Holy Chalice), there is the Grail rumored to have been used at the Last Supper but actually made at least 15 centuries after the event. Near the cathedral porch, where farmers have gathered since the 14th century to settle questions of local irrigation, stands the basilica of **Nuestra Señora de los Desamparados** [5]. There's a noteworthy view from the *Miguelete,* the cathedral's unfinished 15th-century bell tower.

Colegio del Patriarca [18]: Founded in the 16th century by the famous scholar San Juan de Ribera, the college—now a seminary—has an impressively severe Renaissance façade and patio, which is open to males only. Splendid Flemish tapestries decorate the ornate *Capilla de la Concepciòn;* paintings by Van der Weyden, El Greco, and Morales, among others, hang in rooms made into a museum. Next door is the 16th-century *church of Corpus Christi* with a beautiful high altar painting of "The Last Supper" by Ribalta, and San Juan de Ribera's tomb.

Jardin Botanico [41]: The oldest garden of its kind in Spain and one of the most important in Europe, it is well laid-out with exotic trees and bushes.

*Lonja de la Seda (Old Silk Exchange) [29]: This lovely Gothic building, dating from the 15th century, has a particularly fine inner courtyard called the *Patio de los Naranjos* (Orange Tree Courtyard).

*Museo de Bellas Artes (Museum of Fine Arts) [44]: One of Spain's finest art galleries, the museum's painting collection includes works by Spanish primitives and masters such as El Greco, Velázquez, Ribera, Murillo, Morales, and Goya; additional galleries are devoted to medieval, Renaissance, Romantic, and 20th-century works.

Museo de Prehistoria [48]: Remarkable collections of Iberian artifacts from the Paleolithic Age to the time of the Romans are on display.

Palacio de la Generalidad [34]: This Renaissance palace, the seat of Valencia's government, was built in the 15th and 16th centuries and contains impressive carved wooden ceilings and noteworthy frescoes in the *Salòn de Cortes* and *Sala Dorada*.

Plaza del Ayùntamiento [23]: With its fountain, shade trees, and surrounding shops, cafés, and entertainment district, this lovely square is full of life at all hours.

Plaza de Toros (Bull Fighting Arena) [28]: With 18,000 seats, this is one of the largest of Spain's bullfighting rings; there is an adjacent *Museo Taurino* (Bull Fighting Museum).

San Andrés (also known as San Juan de la Cruz) [20]: Built between 1602 and 1682, the church has a Baroque portal and a beautiful bell tower; many pictures by 16th- to 18th-century Valencian masters fill the interior, including a famous madonna known as the "Virgen de la Leche."

San Esteban [9]: Saint Vicente Ferrer, Valencia's patron saint, was baptized here, and in the 11th century the daughter of El Cid was married in this much-restored church.

San Juan del Mercado (also

Valencia Attractions:
1. Plaza de Zaragoza
2. Santa Catalina
3. Cathedral
4. Palace of the Archbishop
5. Nuestra Señora de los Desamparados
6. Almudín
7. San Salvador
8. Puente Trinidad
9. San Esteban
10. Iglesia del Templo
11. Palace of the Admiral of Aragòn
12. Santo Tomás
13. Birthplace of saint Vicente Ferrer
14. Glorieta
15. Palace of Justice
16. Santo Domingo
17. Puente del Real
18. Colegio del Partriarca
19. University
20. San Andrés (San Juan de la Cruz)
21. Castillo del Marqués de Dos Aguas
22. San Martín
23. Plaza del Ayùntamiento
24. Central Post Office and Telegraph Exchange
25. City Hall
26. Ateneo Mercantil
27. Main Train Station
28. Plaza de Toros
29. Lonja de la Seda
30. San Juan del Mercado
31. La Compañia
32. San Nicolás

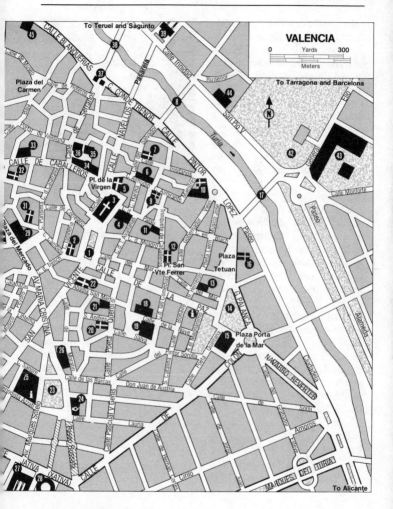

33. Palacio de Mercader
34. Palacio de la Generalidad
35. Palacio del Marqués de la Scala
36. Palacio de la Bailía (Juamandren)
37. Torres de los Serranos
38. Puenta de Serranos
39. Train Station Puenta de Madera
40. Torres de Quart

41. Botanical Gardens
42. Jardines del Real
43. Exhibition and Fair Grounds
44. Museo de Bellas Artes
45. Casa Museo Jose Benlliure
46. San Agustín
47. Hospital Provincial
48. Museum of Prehistory

known as the church of Los Santos Juanes) [30]: Originally built in the Gothic style of the 14th century, the church's interior later became Churrigueresque and a Baroque façade was added around 1700; the slender bell tower was added in 1705.

San Martin [22]: A portrait by Goya and a late-15th-century bronze equestrian statue of Saint Martin (above the portal) are among the numerous works of art found here.

San Nicolás [32]: This 15th-century Gothic church was later redesigned in Churriequesque style; there are frescoes by Vidal and altar retables of the 15th and 16th centuries. The ancient **Palacio de Mercader** [33] stands opposite the church.

Santo Domingo [16]: Saint Vincente Ferrer once lived in this Dominican monastery, whose church has an imposing neoclassical portal. Particularly noteworthy is the 16th-century tomb of Marshall Mendoza in the *Capilla de San Vicente Ferrer* and the Gothic hall of the monastery.

Santo Tomás [12]: A magnificent neoclassical façade and inte-

Torres de los Serranos

rior characterize this 18th-century church with a bell tower and octagonal dome. Inside there are numerous paintings by Vergara.

Torres de Quart [40]: This impressive gateway in the old city wall dates from the 15th century.

Torres de los Serranos (37): These mighty watch towers, erected in 1398 as an additional entrance to the city, were built on Roman foundation walls; there is a good view from the top.

University [19]: Established in 1498, the present building dates from the 18th century and houses a valuable library.

Venice

If any city may be said to cast an immediate spell, surely it's Venice, majestically known as *La Serenissima,* the Most Serene. The entire city is built on a human scale that has not surrendered to the blight of 20th century, high-rise buildings that dominate most urban skylines. Boats in one form or another—vaporetti, gondolas, water taxis—serve as the principal means of transport here. If you take a ride down the Grand Canal when the water and the ancient palace façades reflect the setting sun, the magic of this city on the Adriatic will become seductively obvious. Venice is intimate, mysterious, and bewilderingly complex. It's an island-city of canals, bridges, time-haunted squares, and slowly rotting palaces. The soft, languorous air of decay is unmistakable, yet it makes you treasure Venice even more, for you become infused with the city's timelessness.

History

An Illyrian tribe known as the Veneti occupied the area and formed a defensive alliance with Rome in the third century B.C. Several centuries later, the invading forces of Attila the Hun forced inhabitants from the mainland to seek refuge on the islands in the lagoon. These island communities eventually formed a naval confederation under the leadership of a doge (from the Latin *dux,* leader), and in 811, Venice became the seat of their government. The remains of the Evangelist Mark were brought to Venice soon after, and he was adopted as the patron saint of the Venetian Republic; his symbol, a lion, became the city's emblem.

Venice's location made it a primary trading center with the Orient, and by the tenth century, the Venetians had created an empire that extended all the way to Asia Minor. The city became so powerful and well-defended that, in 1502, it was able to withstand a combined assault by Emperor Maximilian I, Louis XII of France, Ferdinand of Aragon, and Pope Julius II.

The 15th and 16th centuries were a golden age for Venetian art and culture, when its character was most vividly expressed by such masters as Titian, Tintoretto, and Veronese; Works by all of these painters are on display throughout Venice today. Although aspects of the economic and political decline of the city were apparent as early as the 16th century, its culture managed to flourish, as the works of Tiepolo, Canaletto, Guardi, and Longhi make clear.

In 1797, the once mighty republic yielded to the strength of Napoleon's armies. Venice was subsequently ruled by Austria until 1866, when it was incorporated into the United Kingdom of Italy.

Attractions

***Accademia di Belle Arti

(Academy of Fine Arts) [18]: It's difficult to take in the richness of the paintings on display in the *Galleria* here in one visit, so try to make more than one trip; there are masterpieces by Titian, Tintoretto, Veronese, Canaletto, Guardi, and Bellini.

Ca' d'Oro (Golden House) [7]: This richly decorated Gothic palace on the Grand Canal was built in the 15th century. Its name derives from the façade, which was once covered with gilding. Within is the beautiful *Galleria Franchetti,* with sumptuous paintings by a host of Italian masters. Across the canal is the *Pescheria* (fish market) and *Erberia* (fruit and vegetable market) landing where fish and produce boats anchor late in the afternoon. Farther along the canal, just before the Rialto bridge, is the *main post office* [8], known as the *Fondaco dei Tedeschi* because German merchants once had their warehouses here.

Ca' Foscari [15]: With its openwork façade and numerous loggias, this 15th-century building—once the home of the deposed Doge Foscari—is a prime example of Venetian late-Gothic style.

Ca' Rezzonico [16]: To glimpse what life was like for a privileged few in the 18th century, you can enter the most opulent palace on the Grand Canal, now home of the *Museo del Settecento Veneziano,* with its collections of paintings, furniture, and objets d'art.

Chiesa del Redentore

(Church of the Redeemer), Campo Redentore, Giudecca Island: Architecture buffs should make a special point of visiting this perfectly proportioned, 16th-century church designed by Palladio.

Fondaco dei Turchi [4]: A Byzantine influence can be seen in this 13th-century palace, one of the oldest buildings in Venice, which was the residence of Emperor Frederick III from 1452 to 1469. It eventually became a warehouse for Turkish merchants.

Canal Grande: Venice's wide, watery, main thoroughfare winds in an "S" shape for more than 3 km. (2 miles) through the center of the city and offers a spectacular and unforgettable vision of more than 200 Gothic-Renaissance palaces that front onto it. If you're not inclined to fork over lots of lire for a gondola ride, you can catch the Vaporetto Line 1 just off the Piazzetta beside Saint Mark's: It runs the entire length of the Grand Canal, and makes frequent stops along the way.

La Fenice, Campo San Fantin 1977: Music-lovers should try to get a seat for the opera or any other musical event being held here; the gold and pink interior of this late-17th-century opera house exemplifies a certain kind of purely Venetian taste, and the acoustics are marvelous.

Palazzo Corner-Spinelli [11]: Built around 1500, the upper story of this palace on the

Grand Canal features a wealth of ornamentation, including double-arched windows; it is a masterpiece of early Venetian Renaissance architecture.

Palazzo Grassi [17]: Also called Palazzo Fiat because it was recently bought by the Agnelli family, this 18th-century, Classical palace is an art museum with year-round exhibitions as well as permanent displays of fine art, folk art, and antiquities.

Palazzo Pesaro [6]: Two museums, one devoted to modern art and the other to Oriental art, are housed in this magnificent Baroque palace completed in 1710.

Palazzo Véndramin-Calergi [5]: The composer Richard Wagner died in this late-15th-century palace in 1883; when cold weather sets in, the Municipal Casino takes up residence.

Peggy Guggenheim Museum, Grand Canal: Palazzo Venier dei Leoni, home of the late heiress and art-collector (who seems to have been married at one time or another to many of the artists represented), offers a sampling of some fine modern works and a chance to see the interior of a palazzo on the Grand Canal.

***Piazza di San Marco (Saint Mark's Square): One of the largest and most ravishing urban spaces in the world, Saint Mark's is the much-loved heart of Venice. It is enclosed by two, long, colonnaded palaces, a bell tower *(campanile),* and the stupendous cathedral (see below). In warm weather, two world-famous (and expensive) cafés, Florian and Quadri, set up tables outside, bands play, thousands of pigeons flap and flutter, and endless tourists mill around, happy just to gawk. The **Campanile** [24] in front of the cathedral is a restoration of a tenth-century bell tower

Piazza di San Marco

that collapsed in 1902; take the elevator up to the top for a superb panoramic view. Two 12th-century granite columns in the *piazzetta* connecting the square with the Grand Canal frame a view of the canal: The symbol of Venice, Saint Mark's lion, stands atop the east column, while Saint Theodore, atop the other, balances on a crocodile.

On the west side of the piazzetta stands the **Libreria Vecchia** [20], dating from the 16th century and with rooms and ceilings decorated by Titian, Veronese, Tintoretto and others. Two bronze figures known as "I Mori" (The Moors) appear with their hammers and strike the hours on the 15th-century **Torre dell'Orologio** (Clock Tower) [22], whose upper section has a beautiful mosaic of Saint Mark's lion on a blue, star-studded background. Napoleon ordered the wing between the two older palaces in Saint Mark's Square to be built, and today it houses the information office and the ***Museo Correr** [23], with 15th-century paintings and historical collections.

***Saint Mark's Cathedral (Basilica di San Marco) [25]: An edifice that truly merits the adjectives "exotic" and "fantastic," Saint Mark's is the crowning glory of the Venetian Republic and immediately invites awe. The present cathedral dates from the 11th century and stands on the site of two earlier churches built to house the remains of Saint Mark that were brought to Venice from Alex-

andria in 828. Five Byzantine domes echo the five Romanesque portals, above which stand replicas of the noble fourth-century B.C. *bronze horses* brought from Constantinople in 1204 (the originals are now in the basilica's *Museo Marciano* to protect them from damage caused by pollution). The darkly gleaming interior is filled with a feast of decoration, including extraordinary medieval mosaics, best seen from the galleries around the walls. Above the remains of Saint Mark rises the famous *Pala d'Oro* altarpiece, a masterpiece of Byzantine goldwork and inset with precious gems and enamels.

**Palazzo Ducale (Doges' Palace) [21]: Located next to Saint Mark's Cathedral, the former residence of the doges and seat of government for the Venetian Republic has creamy, pink-and-white, geometrically patterned

Palazzo Ducale

walls, pointed arches, and pierced rosettes; it dates from the 14th and 15th centuries. In the magnificent Renaissance courtyard, the *Scala dei Giganti* with colossal statues of Mars and Neptune, leads up to the *Scala d'Oro* (Golden Staircase) and the second floor *(piano nobile)* where the doges had their private apartments. Apartments throughout the palace, including state chambers, cabinet rooms, and council halls, contain some of the city's finest works. On the far side of the palace, in front of the entrance to the dungeons, a staircase leads to the legendary *Ponte dei Sospiri* (Bridge of Sighs), which spans a narrow canal and gives access to the New Prison.

Ponte di Rialto [9]: The most elaborate bridge in Venice and a landmark of the city was built in the late 16th century and crosses the Grand Canal with a single arch. The surrounding area is the business and shopping center of Venice, which provides an extremely animated and colorful scene.

San Salvatore [26]: This

Ponte di Rialto

church at the end of the Merceria, Venice's main shopping street, boasts two famous paintings by Titian—an *Annunciation* painted in 1566 and a *Glorification* from 1560.

Santa Maria della Salute [19]: In 1630, Longhena built this Baroque church with its impressive dome and noble air in thanksgiving for Venice having escaped the plague; the interior is graced with remarkable paintings by Titian and Tintoretto, and there is an altarpiece by Giordano.

*Santa Maria Gloriosa dei Frari [29]: Usually referred to as "I Frari," and one of the most beautiful churches in the city, it is notable for Titian's dizzying *Assumption* on the high altar, his *Madonna di Ca' Pescaro,* and a triptych by Giovanni Bellini; the tombs of Titian, the sculptor Antonio Canova, and several doges are here, as well.

Santi Giovanni e Paolo [27]: Located in the second most important square in Venice (the first being St. Mark's), this immense Dominican church with its unfinished façade was built between 1246 and 1430. It contains a famous 18th-century ceiling painting by Piazzetta as well as monumental tombs of many of the doges. In the piazza just south of the church you can't miss the dramatic **Colleoni Monument,** a 15th-century equestrian statue— one of the most important works of the Italian Renaissance— created by Verrocchio, the teacher of Leonardo da Vinci. The Renais-

Venice Attractions:
1. San Simeone Piccolo
2. Degli Scalzi
3. San Geremia
4. Fondaco dei Turchi
5. Palazzo Véndramin-Calergi
6. Palazzo Pesaro
7. Ca' d'Oro
8. Fondaco dei Tedeschi
9. Rialto Bridge
10. Municipio
11. Palazzo Corner-Spinelli
12. Palazzo Pisani
13. Palazzo Mocenigo
14. Palazzo Balbo
15. Ca' Foscari
16. Ca' Rezzonico
17. Palazzo Grassi
18. Accademia di Belle Arti
19. Santa Maria della Salute
20. Libreria Vecchia
21. Palazzo Ducale
22. Torre dell'Oorlogico
23. Museo Correr
24. Campanile
25. Saint Mark's Cathedral
26. San Salvatore
27. Santi Giovanni e Paolo
28. San Zaccaria
29. Santa Maria Gloriosa dei Frari
30. Scuola Grande di San Rocco

sance *Scuola di San Marco,* with trompe l'oeil panels on its lower façade, is adjacent to the church.

San Zaccaria [28]: The Renaissance façade of this church was completed in 1504, and its 13th-century campanile reveals Byzantine influence; both Gothic and Renaissance features are found within, as is the last work of Giovanni Bellini and paintings by Tintoretto.

Scuola Grande di San Rocco [30]: Lovers of Tintoretto will find some 56 of his canvases in this 16th-century edifice, one of six Venetian charitable confraternities active during the Renaissance period.

Excursions

Lido, 1.5 km. (1 mile) from Venice, Vaporetto Numbers 6 or 11 from Riva degli Schiavoni, or Number 2 from Piazzale Roma or Rialto: The Lido is known

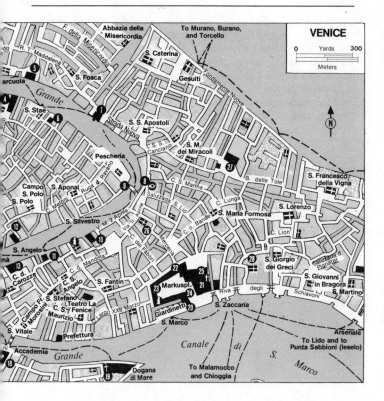

throughout the world for its sandy beaches and cosmopolitan atmosphere. The casino is open in the summer, and there are cabins and cabanas for bathers along the shore.

Murano, 15 minutes by steamer from Fondamenta Nuove: This lagoon island has been the center of the Venetian glass industry since the 13th century. You can watch glass being blown and molded at one of the factories and visit the *Museo Vetrario* to see

stunning examples of this Venetian art.

Burano, 30 minutes by steamer from Fondamenta Nuove: Fish and lace have been the staples of this island for centuries. Women here still make and sell lace, and there is a museum dedicated to the art. If you have time, eat at one of the restaurants specializing in fresh fish dishes.

Torcello: Perhaps the most romantic of the islands, Torcello was the main town of the lagoon from the seventh to the ninth centuries, but as Venice prospered, Torcello declined. *Santa Maria Assunta,* a seventh-century Byzantine cathedral (rebuilt in 1008), contains remarkable Byzantine mosaics and Greek columns. A pair of 14th-century palaces now serve as museums with collections of excavated and salvaged items from the island. The church of *Santa Fosca,* dating from the 11th century, has some noteworthy features, including regal columns with Byzantine capitals.

Vienna

Mention Vienna and a cluster of associations instantly arise: the waltz, which was invented here; sinfully rich pastries consumed by the Viennese with a delightful disregard for calories; and coffee houses, a home away from home for the locals. Oddly enough, the city's rather light-hearted reputation is contradicted at every turn by the sobering monumentality of many of its buildings and the serious formality of its population, a large percentage of which is middle-aged or elderly. Traditions die hard in Vienna, and a kind of gracious, old-fashioned *noblesse oblige* still clings to the city—perhaps inevitably, since it was the center of the vast Hapsburgian, Austro-Hungarian empire for over 600 years. Culturally, Vienna ranks among the greatest cities of the world: This is a place where music is sacred, theater revered, art deeply appreciated. It is, in fact, the music capital of Europe, home of the highly esteemed Vienna Philharmonic, the Vienna State Opera, and the Vienna Boys' Choir. Small wonder that composers like Beethoven, Mozart, Brahms, and Johann Strauss, the "Waltz King," were drawn here. The city's architecture is fascinating, filled with Gothic churches, Baroque palaces, towering monuments, early Secessionist buildings, and several important examples of Art Nouveau, called *Jugendstil*. Vienna was the city of Freud and Klimt—a place where, at the turn of the century, revolutionary ideas clashed with the fading traditionalist values of a population devoted to the court and the empire. Vienna's mix is particularly rich, and delights of all sorts make it a feast to be savored by all the senses.

History

Vienna's history extends back for centuries before it became a Roman outpost called Vindobona, where the emperor-philosopher Marcus Aurelius died. Two main trade and migration routes—one along the Danube River, the other a route from the Baltic down to the Adriatic—gave the site importance as far back as the Stone Age. The Romans arrived around 100 B.C. and left 600 years later; they established the wine-growing traditions that are still a distinctive feature of the outskirts of modern Vienna.

Vienna has been home to two major ruling families, the Babenbergs and the Hapsburgs. The Babenbergs, who appeared in the 12th century, turned Vienna into a cultural center and saw its first expansion; under Heinrich Jasomirgott, Vienna became the capital of Austria. They were succeeded by the Hapsburgs, whose reign began in 1278 and lasted into the 20th century. Under the Hapsburgs, Vienna became one of the great cities of the world and the headquarters for the enormous Austro-Hungarian empire.

In later centuries, the city was besieged by two deadly foes: the Turks and the Plague. (Many of the city's monuments are thanksgiving offerings for being spared from one or the other.) The Turks were finally defeated in 1683, allowing Vienna to spread its boundaries beyond the ancient walls that encircled it. The Turks left behind one legacy that has become an essential part of Viennese life: coffee. The first Viennese coffeehouse opened over 300 years ago.

A Baroque outpouring of churches, palaces, and monuments followed as Vienna entered a prosperous golden age under the forty-year reign (1740–1780) of Maria Theresa. The Empress's sixteen children included Marie-Antoinette (who became the ill-fated queen of France), and the empire extended its power and influence through royal marriage alliances. Mozart came to Vienna as a child prodigy and performed for the Empress at Schönbrunn palace.

Throughout the 18th and 19th centuries, Vienna became a mecca for composers and musicians. Haydn, Mozart, Beethoven, Schubert, Brahms, Mahler, and Joseph Strauss all worked or lived here. The city continues to maintain its pre-eminent reputation as the musical capital of Europe by offering an amazing array of symphony, opera, and chamber music concerts throughout the year.

Vienna became the center of Europe, even supplanting Paris, when Napoleon's empire collapsed in 1814. An international assembly—known as the Congress of Vienna—met to redraw the map of Europe; the period, known as the *Vormärz* (Before March), was one of glittering balls and constant entertainment. It lasted until the revolutionary days of March, 1848.

During the reign of Franz Joseph in the mid- to late-1800s, Vienna went through its next great surge of change. The ancient city walls were demolished and replaced by a wide, elegant avenue known as the Ring. Several massive buildings were constructed along it—among them, the Votive Church, the New University, the Burgtheater, the Town Hall, Parliament, and the buildings housing the Fine Arts and Natural History museums—each in a different period style, and embellished with parks and vistas. The waltz became king as ballrooms resounded to the strains of such compositions by Johann Strauss junior as "The Blue Danube" and "Tales from the Vienna Woods."

Around the turn of the century, Vienna witnessed another artistic and intellectual flowering, the legacy of which is several striking Art Nouveau buildings and the severe, functional style of architects like Adolf Loos and Joseph Olbrich. At this time, Freud was developing his theories, and Gustav Klimt was painting his sensual canvases.

A period of decline followed the end of the First World War, as the Hapsburg empire crumbled and a severe depression gripped the city. During World War II, Vienna was occupied by the Nazis and suffered bomb damage. Prosperity has returned in more recent years, and Vienna has become the world's "Third United Nations City," and headquarters for several international agencies.

Attractions

**Albertina [48]: Although it houses the world's greatest collection of graphic arts, only a fraction of the more than one million items are displayed at any one time; however, these always include exceptional examples of work—drawings, etchings, woodcuts, engravings—that date from the 14th to the 20th centuries.

Basilisk House (Basilisken-haus) [39]: Parts of this house date back to the 13th century when—legend has it—a fire-breathing basilisk (a small dragon) lived in the well, poisoning the water and turning anyone who ventured too close into stone. A baker's apprentice had the foresight to show the monster its own face in a mirror, at which point it turned itself into stone—perhaps like the one on the façade of the house.

**Belvedere [59]: Two palaces built for Prince Eugene of Savoy in the early years of the 18th century now contain two superb and very different collections of art. The Lower Belvedere houses the sumptuous *Museum of Baroque Art* with its highlight, the *Gold Room;* the *Austrian Gallery for 19th and 20th Century Art* is found in the Upper Belvedere: pride of place here goes to the sensuous work of Gustav Klimt.

*Burgtheater [77]: Considered one of the pre-eminent thea-

Upper Belvedere

ters of Austria and Germany, the Burg dates from the period of Vienna's new Ringstrasse. It was completed in the late 1880s; Klimt designed and painted the interior staircase frescoes.

Dreimäderlhaus [80]: When he wasn't composing lieder, Franz Schubert liked to court the ladies—three of whom were from the same family and lived here.

Figarohaus (Figaro House, or Mozart Memorial) [11]: Wolfgang Amadeus Mozart lived in this house for three years (1784–1787) and composed *The Marriage of Figaro* here; it is now a small museum.

Graben: A former Roman moat, the Graben has been a busy hub of Viennese life since the time of Maria Theresa; the most dramatic sight here is the Baroque **Plague Monument** (Pestsäule) [14], built by the Emperor Leopold I to fulfill a vow he made in 1679 when thousands of his subjects were dying every day.

Griechenbeisel (Greek pub) [43]: The signatures of former habitués—Beethoven and Johann Strauss among them—decorate the walls of this 15th-century wine pub.

*Historical Museum of the City of Vienna [60]: A profound view of Vienna from its prehistoric beginnings through the 20th century emerges during a tour of this museum; included are period rooms, including that of the famous architect Adolf Loos.

***Hofburg (Imperial Palace): A town within a castle, the Hofburg was the favorite residence of the Hapsburgs. Built and expanded over the centuries, its style ranges from Gothic to turn-of-the-century. Before you enter the palace from Michaelerplatz, have a look at the simple glass-and-brick *Loos Building* opposite the Hofburg's entrance: Completed in 1911, it's one of the earliest modern buildings in Europe. It so enraged Emperor Franz Joseph (whose windows in the Hofburg overlooked it), that he tried to have it demolished. Once in the Hofburg, you can visit the fascinating *imperial apartments,* including the exercise room of the Empress Elizabeth (who was stabbed to death in 1898 by an Italian anarchist). The fabulous Hapsburg crown jewels are on dis-

play in the ****Schatzkammer** (Treasury), and the famous Vienna Choir Boys sing at Sunday mass in the *Hofburgkapelle* (Court Chapel), although tickets are hard to come by. More museums—dedicated to weapons, ethnography, and musical instruments—are found in the *Neue Hofburg* (New Palace), whose sweeping, monumental façade was completed in 1913.

Hoher Markt (High Market) [33]: The oldest square in Vienna and originally part of Roman Vindobona. You can find the **Ankeruhr** (Anchor Clock) [34], here which tells time using figures from Austrian history that move across a scale; at noon, all the figures come out on parade.

Kapuzinerkirche (Church of the Capuchins) [46]: Three centuries of Hapsburgs lie entombed in the *Kaizergruft* (Imperial vault) of this simple, 17th-century church. An ornate, 18th-century fountain—the *Donner Brunnen*—stands in the center of the square in front; its figures represent the main rivers that flow into the Danube.

*Karlskirche (St. Charles's Church) [62]: Designed by Fischer von Erlach and completed by his son in 1737, the enormous, domed Karlskirche, with its two free-standing columns, is the most important Baroque church in Vienna and shows heavy Italian influence (the architect did his apprenticeship in Rome). The church was pledged by Emperor Karl VI in 1713 when the plague entered

Vienna, and is dedicated to Saint Charles Borromeo. Teeming frescoes by Rottmayr decorate the dome, and an oddly inappropriate sculpture by Henry Moore stands in front.

*Maria am Gestade [32]: An ornate "folded hands" spire, one of the most beautiful Gothic spires in existence, graces this church. It is located near the Danube Canal, and was originally built for fishermen.

Maria-Theresien Platz: Two enormous museums, both of them constructed as part of the Ringstrasse remodelling of the city, flank the sides of a square named for Vienna's favorite empress. The seated statue of Maria Theresa in the center is surrounded by some of the figures who helped to make her reign so memorable, Mozart and Beethoven among them.

The **Naturhistorisches Museum** (Natural History Museum) [68] contains some remarkable prehistoric relics on its ground floor, including the 20,000-year-old statuette of an earth goddess known as the "Venus of Willendorf." Across the way is the **Kunsthistorisches Museum** (Art History Museum) [69], whose incomparable collection of Old Masters make it one of the greatest museums in the world; paintings by Cranach, Tintoretto, Caravaggio, Canaletto, Rubens, Giorgione, and Velázquez line the seemingly endless rooms, but particularly noteworthy is the room of Brueghels.

Art History Museum

Michaelerkirche (Church of Saint Michael) [16]: The overall effect of this former parish church of the Hapsburgs is Gothic, but elements of just about every other historical period—Romanesque, Baroque, and neoclassical—are also in evidence. Some very old frescoes and carvings may be seen within. In the *Michaelerpassage,* on the right side of the church, there is a 16th-century, painted carving of the "Agony in the Garden."

Neues Rathaus (New City Hall) [78]: This stately neo-Gothic building, built between 1872 and 1883, contains the offices, archives, and library of the city. Monuments and statues of famous Viennese surround the building.

Osterreichisches Museum für angewandte Kunst (Austrian Museum of Applied Art) [52]: An extensive collection of European and Oriental applied art is on display in this museum, which was completed in 1871 using unhewn bricks and sgraffito.

Parliament [75]: Built in a heavy Grecian style during the Ringstrasse building boom of the 1870s and 1880s, the monumental Parliament building is the home of the legislative assembly of Austria.

Peterskirche (Church of Saint Peter) [15]: Johann Lukas von Hildebrandt designed this little gem of a church in 1730, and gave it one of the most theatrically flamboyant interiors you're ever likely to see; the Turkish tents outside of the city walls during the siege of Vienna provided inspiration for some of the decorative elements.

Prater: This popular amusement park, filled with rides, wine and beer gardens, and coffeehouses, served as an imperial hunting ground until 1766. The old ferris wheel, dating from 1897, is a symbol of Vienna and still provides one of the best views of the city.

Ringstrasse: When the old city walls were torn down by order of the Emperor Franz Joseph in 1858, they were replaced with a long boulevard that was to be lined with important civic buildings, monuments, gardens, and parks. Construction went on for about 30 years and changed the face of Vienna (Baron Haussmann was modernizing Paris at about the same time).

Ruprechtskirche (Church of Saint Rupert) [35]: Traditionally said to have been founded in 740, the church is the oldest in Vienna. Among its interesting features are an 11th-century nave and lower tower, and the 13th-century stained glass in the middle window of the choir.

***Schönbrunn Palace: A riot of Rococo decoration and a wealth of historical memories fills the imperial chambers of this beautiful Baroque palace built for the Hapsburgs between 1696 and 1713. It was the primary residence of Maria Theresa; her daughter, Marie Antoinette, grew up here, and Franz Joseph was born and died here. The obligatory guided tour takes you through about 45 of the palace's nearly 1,500 rooms, and includes the relatively simple apartments of Franz Joseph and his oft-absent Empress Elizabeth, and a series of rooms used by Maria Theresa and her enormous family (the Blue Chinese Drawing Room, the Vieux-Laque Room, the Porcelain Room, and the "Millions" Room).

Schönbrunn Palace

In a landscaped park behind the palace, is the colonnaded *Gloriette,* providing a glorious view of the city. The *Wagenburg* (Coach House) in front contains a magnificent assembly of imperial carriages, sleighs, and hearses.

Secession [65]: Josef Olbrich designed this important (and recently restored) Art Nouveau building in 1897–1898 as an exhibition space for artists; Gustav Klimt designed the metal doors.

Staatsoper (State Opera) [1]: Performances are inevitably sold out in what is considered to be one of the top opera houses in the world. It opened in 1869 with Mozart's *Don Giovanni,* was bombed to near extinction at the end of World War II, and rebuilt during the ensuing decade, when it reopened with a performance of Beethoven's *Fidelio* in 1955. If you should get lucky and obtain a ticket, you'll feel unobtrusive if you dress up—opera in Vienna is a very elegant affair, and carries with it a definite "attitude."

Stadtpark (City Park) [53]: Situated between the Ringstrasse and the Vienna River, the park is one of Vienna's most attractive and fashionable spots. A memorial to Johann Strauss, Vienna's "Waltz King," admirably captures the romantic essence of the music and the dance that still characterize the city.

***Stephansdom (Saint Stephan's Cathedral) [13]: The ornate and awesome spire of the cathedral—Austria's most venerable Gothic structure—towers over its surroundings and is set off by an intricately patterned tile roof unlike any other in Europe. Dating from the late 13th century, the soaring and heavily carved *Riesentor* (Giant Doorway) is the oldest section of the building. Although the cathedral was badly damaged in the last world war, its vast, dark interior still exudes a mysterious medieval atmosphere. A staircase in the south tower (called *Alte Steffl,* or Old Steve) leads to a fine view, or you can take an elevator in the north tower up to the *Pummerin,* the cathedral's 22-ton cast bell, where there's another

Vienna Attractions:
1. State Opera
2. Maltese Church
3. Stock im Eisen
4. Church of St. Ann
5. Former Convent of the Sisters of St. Ursula
6. Court Chamber Archives
7. Women's Convent of Savoy
8. Winter Palace of Prince Eugen
9. Franciscan Church
10. Teutonic Order Church
11. Figaro House
12. Archbishop's Palace
13. St. Stephan's Cathedral
14. Plague Monument
15. Church of St. Peter
16. Church of St. Michael
17. Offices of the Chancellor
18. Archives
19. Minoriten Church
20. Museum of Lower Austria
21. Landhaus (Federal Government Offices)
22. Church of the Scots
23. Kinsky Palace
24. Harrach Palace
25. Heidenschuss
26. The Church on the Courtyard
27. Fire Department
28. Clock Museum

good panorama. In the crypt you'll see the copper jars that contain the entrails of the Hapsburgs.

Theater an der Wien [66]: The director Emanuel Schikaneder, who wrote the libretto for Mozart's *The Magic Flute,* had this revered theater built in 1801. It's been in continual use ever since; Beethoven's opera *Fidelio* premiered here in 1805 and most of the operettas of Johann Strauss and Franz Lehar were first performed here as well. The *Papageno Gate* in Millokergasse was part of the original building and shows Schikaneder as Papageno. In front of the theater is the *Naschmarkt* (Market Place).

Uhrenmuseum (Clock Museum) [28]: The setting for this museum is a lovely Renaissance house dedicated to time in all its earthly manifestations—over 3,000 items going back to the 1440s and up to the digital present.

Universität [79]: The university was founded in 1365, making it the oldest German-speaking university in Europe; the New University Building was erected in Italian Renaissance-style between 1873 and 1883.

Votivkirche [81]: When the Emperor Franz Joseph narrowly escaped an assassination attempt in 1853, his brother had this neo-Gothic church built as a gesture of thanks that the Emperor's life was spared.

Volksgarten (People's Garden) [76]: Located next to the Hofburg, the gardens are famous for their roses and the *Theseus Temple,* completed in 1823.

Warsaw

That Warsaw not only exists, but *thrives* is a sign of the unquenchable spirit of the Poles. During the Second World War it suffered incomprehensible atrocities: The Nazis killed at least 200,000 people here and the city was reduced to a tragic pile of rubble and ashes by war's end. Warsaw rebuilt quickly under Communist rule after the devastation of the war, and, as a result, it often looks gray, Stalinesque, and not particularly beautiful. But there are restored pockets of beauty to seek out, and an unforgettable history lesson to be learned on its streets. Today, Warsaw is a city poised on the edge of a new experiment in democracy after forty years of Communist domination, and the streets seem to buzz with a new energy.

History

Warsaw has been invaded and fought over for much of its 900-year history. It was annexed by the kingdom of Poland in the 16th century, and soon after became the residence of Sigismund III Vasa, whose royal arrival signaled a tremendous growth in the building of new churches and palaces. Invading Swedes plundered the city in 1656, followed by the Russians, and the city was then acquired by Prussia. In 1806, Napoleon captured the city and formed the Duchy of Warsaw, but in 1813, the Russians took over again. Germans occupied the city during the First World War.

It was occupied again when Hitler's troops marched in to take it over in 1939. Hitler's order in 1943 was fanatically simple: Not one stone of Warsaw was to remain standing. The chilling finality of this command stemmed from the resistance the Nazis had encountered in Warsaw since their arrival. By 1940, mass executions were taking place, and a wall was built around the Jewish ghetto. Between 1940 and 1945 hundreds of thousands of Jews died as a result of epidemics, starvation, liquidation, and deportation. In 1943, the Jews fought a losing battle for their lives, and tens of thousands were killed; the ghetto was completely demolished in reprisal. Various underground groups joined forces the following year to mount another unsuccessful assault on the Nazis—an event remembered as the Warsaw Uprising. After this, Hitler's men began their all-out destruction of the city and its population. When the Russians entered Warsaw in 1945, fully 90 percent of the inner city had been destroyed.

Warsaw was rebuilt, but it never forgot the massive losses it incurred in the war. Today, memorial tablets and monuments throughout the city commemorate those who fell, and the reconstructed inner city provides at least a glimpse of what was destroyed.

Attractions

Barbican [4]: A red-brick defensive fortification in front of the Brama Nowomiejska city gate, the Barbican was built in the 16th century and then partially dismantled as the city grew. During the summer, artists exhibit their work along the restored city wall and the atmosphere of old Warsaw hovers around the neighboring lanes.

Church of Saint Anna [15]: Built in 1454 by Duchess Anna of Masuria, the interior and exterior of this church and bell tower combine elements of the late Baroque and the neoclassical.

Church and Monastery of the Capuchins (Kosciol i Klasztor Kapucynow) [8]: This Gothic edifice was built in 1692 under the direction of King Johann III Sobieski.

Church of the Holy Cross (Kosciol Sw. Krzyza) [20]: The heart of the great pianist and composer Frederic Chopin is interred in a pillar of this 17th-century Baroque church.

Dzershinski Square (Plac Dzierzynskiego) [10]: The square is named after and contains a memorial to the first Soviet Commissioner of the Interior, a Pole named Felix Dzershinski. The west side of the square is taken up by a massive neoclassical building complex restored to its original design and containing the *Treasury,* the *Office of the Prime Minister,* and the *Museum of the Revolution.*

*Krasinski Palace [7]: The most beautiful Baroque palace in Warsaw was built in 1682 according to the plans of a Dutch architect, Tylman van Gameran. It now houses the National Library.

Lazienki Palace [29]: Located in Warsaw's most beautiful park, this 18th-century palace (known as the Palace on the Water) was built for the last of the Polish kings and features an exqui-

Warsaw Attractions:
1. Palace Square
2. St. John's Cathedral
3. Old Town Marketplace
4. Barbican
5. New Town Marketplace
6. Kosciòl Najswietszej Marii Panny
7. Krasinski Palace
8. Capuchin Church and Monastery
9. Plac Teatralny
10. Dzershinski Square
11. Museum of Archaeology
12. Lenin Museum
13. Memorial to the Unknown Soldier
14. Plac Malachowskiego
15. Church of St. Anna
16. Kosciòl i Klasztor Karmelitòw
17. Radziwill Palace
18. Kosziòl Wizytek
19. University of Warsaw
20. Church of the Holy Cross
21. Staszic Palace
22. Ostrogski Palace
23. Syrena Memorial
24. House of the Party
25. National Museum
26. Plac Trzech Krzyzy
27. Sejm
28. Observatory
29. Lazienki Palace
30. Chopin Memorial
31. Belweder Palace
32. Kròlikarnia Palace
33. Mauzoleum Walki i Meczenstwa
34. Plac Konstytucji
35. Palace of Culture and Science
36. National Philharmonic
37. Memorial to Heroes of the Ghetto
38. Jubilee Stadium
39. Warsaw Citadel
40. Cemetery for Soviet Soldiers
41. Powazki Cemetery

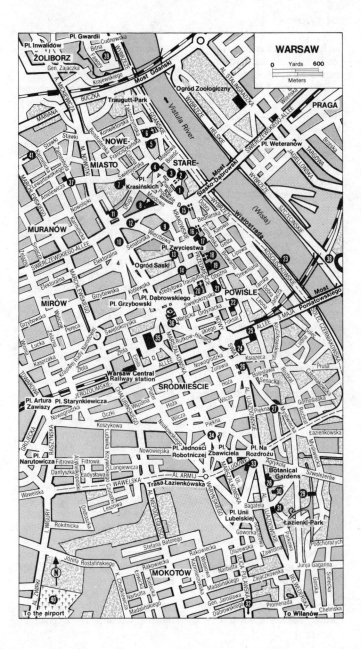

sitely restored interior. In the park you'll also find the **Chopin Memorial** [30], where concerts featuring the great Polish composer's music are given on Sunday afternoons throughout the summer. The official residence of the President of the State Council, **Belweder Palace** [31], sits nearby in its own adjacent park.

Lenin Museum [12]: The former Przebendowski palace, restored according to the original 18th-century plans, is now a museum dedicated to the Russian revolutionary Vladimir Ilyich Lenin.

Memorial to the Heroes of the Ghetto [37]: The memorial was unveiled on April 19, 1948, the fifth anniversary of the uprising of the Jews in the Warsaw ghetto; south of the memorial, on the grounds of the former Pawiak prison, a museum provides additional material relating to this heroic and tragic event.

Museum of Archaeology [11]: Treasures from the Stone, Bronze, Iron, and early Middle Ages fill the display cabinets of this intriguing museum.

**National Museum [25]: Despite heavy losses suffered during the war, this museum still has extensive collections of Roman, Greek, Egyptian, and Etruscan art, as well as magnificent works from the Gothic and Renaissance periods.

New Town Marketplace (Rynek Nowego Miasta) [5]: Completely destroyed during the war, this city district was painstakingly rebuilt in the mid 1950s according to original plans; it now features houses in the style of the 18th and early 19th centuries, complete with sgraffiti work and painted façades. The 17th-century *Church of the Sisters of the Sacrament* (Kosciol Sakramentek) on the east side of the square was founded by the wife of King Johann III Sobieski as a thanksgiving for the victory over the Turks near Vienna in 1683.

Old Town Marketplace (Rynek Starego Miasta) [3]: A center of activity in the city for over 600 years, the square is surrounded by reconstructed 17th- and 18th-century town houses with gabled roofs and colorful wall ornamentation.

Ostrogski Palace [22]: Another Baroque structure designed by the Dutch architect van Gameran, the Ostrogski palace was substantially restored after the Second World War and now acts as the headquarters for the Chopin Society.

Palace of Culture and Science [35]: A not-much-admired gift from the Soviet Union, this modern Stalinesque edifice was completed in 1955 and dominates the city's skyline; one good feature (the only one, according to most locals) is that the gallery on the 31st floor offers a wide panoramic view of Warsaw and the surrounding countryside.

Palace Square (Plac Zamkowy) [1]: In the center of the square stands the restored 17th-century *Column of King Sigismund* (Kolumna Zygmunta) crowned by a statue of Sigimund III (1587–1632), who made Warsaw his official residence in 1596. To the east stands the former *royal palace,* a complex that first belonged to the Masurian dukes in the 13th and 14th centuries, and served as the residence of Sigismund III from 1599 to 1619.

Radziwill Palace [17]: An equestrian statue of Stanislaw August Poniatowski, a favorite of Catherine the Great, stands in front of the palace. The structure was built in the 17th century and redesigned in 1819 in a neoclassical style. Today it is the seat of the Council of Ministers.

Saint John's Cathedral (Katedra Sw. Jana) [2]: The oldest church in Warsaw, several Polish kings were crowned here. It was originally built in the late 13th century, rebuilt several centuries later, and reconstructed again after severe damage in World War II.

Sejm [27]: This circular building dates from 1929, and is used for assemblies of the Polish parliament.

Syrena Memorial [23]: Syrena, a winged mermaid armed with a sword and shield, is the symbol of Warsaw, and her statue stands watch over the city from the Kosciusko embankment.

University of Warsaw [19]: Founded in 1818, the university was closed by the czarist government in 1832 and later reopened—however, all classes were taught in Russian. After the German occupation in 1915, the university again became a Polish institution and now has an enrollment of over 20,000 students. The *Academy of Fine Arts* is located in the Czapski Palace across from the university.

Warsaw Citadel [39]: The former stronghold of the czars, built in 1834, is now a military area off-limits to the public.

**Wilanow Palace: The former residence of King Johann III Sobieski, this important Baroque palace in south Warsaw was designed in the late 17th century; its interior has been partially restored and renovated. A unique *poster museum* has been installed in the former riding school.

Zurich

Described by some devotees as "The Garden City on the Lake," Zurich is the largest and most densely populated city in Switzerland, the capital of its canon, and one of the most important financial and industrial hubs of the country. It is also associated with notables of a more cultural cast, such as the psychiatrist Carl Jung, the writer James Joyce, and the composer Richard Wagner; its scientific and educational establishments are also well-respected. Although banks, modern businesses, elegant stores, and an often hectic volume of traffic give the city a distinctly metropolitan character, tranquility still prevails in the narrow lanes of the old quarter; there one finds a more appealing, "quaint" Zurich, with a less super-efficient and international atmosphere—one, we may add, notably free of industrial pollution and/or slums.

History

Zurich has a very long history of human occupation; it is pretty certain that as long ago as a thousand years B.C. Lindenhof Hill was occupied. In the middle of the first century A.D., the Romans built a fort on it that they called Turicum; they held onto it until the fifth century. In the eighth century, Charlemagne was credited with founding the church that later became known as the Grossmünster; in the next century, his grandson founded the other important church, known in its present form as the Fraumünster. By the 13th century, Zurich was part of the German Empire, and then joined the Swiss Federation in the mid-14th century. In the 16th century, it was in the forefront of the Reformation movement. After the disturbances of the French Revolution, Zurich expanded economically and culturally, and from that time on developed into the very impressive city it is today.

Attractions

The elegant tree-lined and vehicle-free shopping street, the **Bahnhofstrasse,** which leads south from the central railroad station to Burkliplatz on the lake, was created in 1864–1867 on the site of medieval defense walls. The lake frontage not only affords magnificent views of the Glarner and Urner Alps, but is delightfully enhanced by promenades and gardens, and bathing and boating facilities. From this location, streets and quais branch out into areas where entertainment and conference venues of every description serve inhabitants and visitors alike. One such is the **Congree Center** [9], with its conference and concert halls and restaurants.

By crossing the lakefront bridge over the Limmat River where it flows into the lake, you enter the oldest area of the city; splendid mansions and picturesque old guildhall façades line the narrow side streets. The **Fraumünster Church** [7] was built between the 12th and 15th centuries on the site of a ninth-century convent. The artistic surprises here are the stained-glass pictures by Marc Chagall in the five windows of the choir and in the rose window on the south transept wall. Modern frescoes graphically illustrate the founding of the convent, the Romanesque cloister wall of which now forms part of the adjoining Stadthaus.

The **Grossmünster** (Cathedral) [5] is Zurich's principal church, where its pastor, Ulrich Zwingli, first preached the principles of Reformation in 1519. This imposing Romanesque-Gothic structure also stands on the site of a convent that Charlemagne is said to have founded. A statue of him here attests to that legend.

The **Lindenhof** [8], an ancient lookout point on the flattened knoll of a moraine hill formed by the great Ice Age glaciers, provides a beautiful view of the Limmat River and the eastern section of the old town center.

The foundation for the imperial fort, **Pfalzburg,** was laid on the old Roman site during the time of the Carolingians, and later expanded. At the start of the 13th century, the fort crumbled, and its stones have been utilized in other

The Lindenhof

buildings. A monument here celebrates the Zurich women who heroically saved their city from the Austrians. The area round here is very attractive, and packed with restaurants.

The **Rietberg Museum** [10] houses several thousand examples of non-European art, including most of the famous Eduard von der Heydt collection. The examples of Chinese art are very fine.

Schipfe is a picturesque old lane which follows the banks of the Limmat River to the Rathausbrucke. Its historical character has been preserved, making it one of the city's landmarks. It was first mentioned in 1292, and there is later documentation of its loading docks and bath houses. Most of the present buildings along its length date from the 17th and 18th centuries; the most richly adorned structure is the Haus Zum Steinbockli (No. 45), next to an antique shop.

The **Schweizerisches Lan-**

desmuseum (National Museum of Switzerland) [2] contains the largest art and cultural collection relating to the country's history from prehistoric times to the 19th century.

St. Peter's Church, in the old part of the city, has an imposing tower, and its gigantic clock is the largest in Europe (another Zurich landmark). A clock has struck the time in the tower since 1366.

Zurich Attractions:
1. Hauptbahnhof (Main Train Station)
2. National Museum of Switzerland
3. City Hall
4. Wasserkirche
5. Grossmunster
6. Kunsthaus (Art Museum)
7. Fraumünster Church
8. Lindenhof
9. Congress Center
10. Rietberg Museum
11. Eidgenossische Technishe Hoschschule (Technical University)
12. University

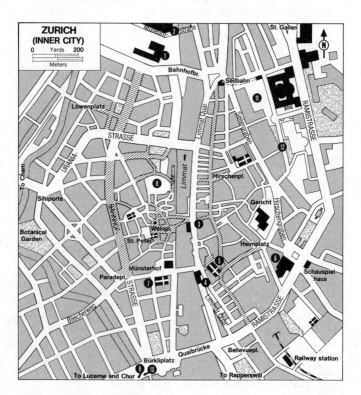

Practical Information

Time Zones. Britain, Ireland, and Portugal all operate on Greenwich Mean Time, which is five hours ahead of Eastern Standard Time. Therefore, if it is noon GMT, it is 7:00 A.M. in New York and Toronto, Canada, and 11:00 P.M. the previous evening in Sydney, Australia.

Western Europe functions on Central European Time, which is one hour ahead of Greenwich Mean Time. These countries include Czechoslovakia, East Germany, Hungary, Spain, and Yugoslavia. If it is noon in Central European Time, it is 6:00 A.M. in New York and Toronto, Canada, and 10:00 P.M. the previous evening in Sydney, Australia.

Eastern European countries, as well as Finland, Greece, Turkey, and the western portions of the Soviet Union, operate two hours ahead of GMT. Therefore, if it is noon in Athens, Greece, it is 5:00 A.M. in New York and Toronto, Canada, and 9:00 P.M. the previous evening in Sydney, Australia. Moscow operates three hours ahead of Greenwich Mean Time.

Daylight Savings Time goes into effect in the spring, when the clocks are set ahead one hour; standard time goes back into effect in the fall.

European communities use either a 12-hour or a 24-hour clock to categorize time; the 24-hour (military) clock is used to differentiate between the morning and evening hours. Therefore, midnight is expressed as 2400 hours; 1:00 A.M. is 0100 hours; noon is 1200 hours; 1:00 P.M. is 1300 hours, etc.

Passport and Visa Requirements. All United States, British, Canadian, and Australian citizens must carry a valid passport when traveling in Europe. To be on the safe side, make certain that the expiration date of your passport does not fall within six months of your traveling schedule. Bulgaria, Czechoslovakia, East Germany, Hungary, Romania, the Soviet Union, and Yugoslavia also require visas (valid for 30 or 60 days) for entrance into the country. France also requires a visa unless you are from a Common Market country. Extended visas may be obtained once you arrive at your destination. With the exception of the aforementioned countries, a valid passport is the only requirement for U.S. and British citizens traveling in Europe. Canadian and Australian visitors should check beforehand to find out if a visa is necessary.

Customs Returning from Europe. *U.S. citizens* returning from Europe may declare $400 worth of purchases duty-free; for the next $1,000, there is a 10% duty tax. For goods exceeding $1,400, the duty rates vary. Specific arrangements can be made to combine individual exports. You may also return with 200 cigarettes, 100 non-Cuban cigars, and one liter of alcohol. Another option is to mail packages under $50 duty-free, as long as they're not mailed to your own address. You can send only one package marked UNSOLICITED GIFT—VALUE UNDER $50 to each address during a 24-hour period. The U.S. has recently established the GSP, or Generalized System of Preferences, which allows a U.S. citizen to export particular items that exceed the $400 limit duty-free. A list can be obtained at a customs office.

Importation of many items is prohibited in the U.S. (e.g., certain species of plants, items made from tortoise shell, products made from endangered species, etc.). Such items will be confiscated by customs officials if you attempt to bring them into the U.S. The U.S. Customs Service publishes a pamphlet called "Know Before You Go" that details prohibited products. To receive it, write to: U.S. Customs Service, 6 World Trade Center, Customs Information, Room 201, New York, N.Y. 10048; tel. (212) 466-5550.

British subjects are permitted £32 of duty-free purchases, plus 200 cigarettes, 100 cigarillos, or 50 cigars (any equivalent of 250 grams of tobacco), one liter of alcohol over 22 percent proof, two liters under 22 percent proof, or two liters of table wine, and 50 grams of perfume.

Canadians may bring back duty-free purchases of $100, or $300 if you've been away seven days or more. This includes 200 cigarettes, 50 cigars, two pounds of tobacco, and 40 oz. of liquor. Packages marked UNSOLICITED GIFT—VALUE UNDER $40 may be mailed to Canada duty-free (one package during a 24-hour period).

Australian residents may return with $400 worth of duty-free purchases, 250 grams of tobacco, and one liter of alcohol.

If you travel with items from home that were manufactured abroad (i.e., cameras), carry all receipts with you so that you will not have to pay duty.

Clothing Sizes. Listed below are men's and women's standard clothing size equivalents for the U.S., Britain, and Europe.

		U.S.	U.K.	Europe
Chest	*Small*	34	34	87
	Medium	36	36	91
		38	38	97
	Large	40	40	102
		42	42	107
	Extra Large	44	44	112
		46	46	117
Collar		14	14	36
		14½	14½	37
		15	15	38

	U.S.	U.K.	Europe
	$15^{1}/_{2}$	$15^{1}/_{2}$	39
	16	16	41
	$16^{1}/_{2}$	$16^{1}/_{2}$	42
	17	17	43
Waist	24	24	61
	26	26	66
	28	28	71
	30	30	76
	32	32	80
	34	34	87
	36	36	91
	38	38	97
Men's Suits	34	34	44
	35	35	46
	36	36	48
	37	37	$49^{1}/_{2}$
	38	38	51
	39	39	$52^{1}/_{2}$
	40	40	54
	41	41	$55^{1}/_{2}$
	42	42	57
Men's Shoes	7	6	$39^{1}/_{2}$
	8	7	41
	9	8	42
	10	9	43
	11	10	$44^{1}/_{2}$
	12	11	46
	13	12	47
Men's Hats	$6^{3}/_{4}$	$6^{5}/_{8}$	54
	$6^{7}/_{8}$	$6^{3}/_{4}$	55
	7	$6^{7}/_{8}$	56
	$7^{1}/_{8}$	7	57
	$7^{1}/_{4}$	$7^{1}/_{8}$	58
	$7^{1}/_{2}$	$7^{3}/_{8}$	60
Women's Dresses	6	8	36
	8	10	38
	10	12	40
	12	14	42
	14	16	44
	16	18	46
	18	20	48
Women's Blouses and Sweaters	8	10	38
	10	12	40
	12	14	42
	14	16	44
	16	18	46
	18	20	48

	U.S.	U.K.	Europe
Women's Shoes	4½	3	35½
	5	3½	36
	5½	4	36½
	6	4½	37
	6½	5	37½
	7	5½	38
	7½	6	38½
	8	6½	39
	8½	7	39½
	9	7½	40
Children's Clothing	2	16	92
(One size larger for knitwear)	3	18	98
	4	20	104
	5	22	110
	6	24	116
	6X	26	122
Children's Shoes	8	7	24
	9	8	25
	10	9	27
	11	10	28
	12	11	29
	13	12	30
	1	13	32
	2	1	33
	3	2	34
	4½	3	36
	5½	4	37
	6½	5½	38½

Weight, Measure, Temperature Equivalents. Throughout the text, metric weights and measures are followed by U.S. equivalents in parenthesis; likewise, Fahrenheit degrees are provided for centigrade temperatures. The following table is a quick reference for U.S. and metric equivalents.

Metric Unit	U.S. Equivalent	U.S. Unit	Metric Equivalent
Length			**Length**
1 kilometer	0.6 miles	1 mile	1.6 kilometers
1 meter	1.09 yards	1 yard	0.9 meters
1 decimeter	0.3 feet	1 foot	3.04 decimeters
1 centimeter	0.39 inches	1 inch	2.5 centimeters
Weight			**Weight**
1 kilogram	2.2 pounds	1 pound	0.45 kilograms
1 gram	0.03 ounces	1 ounce	28.3 grams

Metric Unit	U.S. Equivalent	U.S. Unit	Metric Equivalent
Liquid Capacity		**Liquid Capacity**	
1 dekaliter	2.38 gallons	1 gallon	0.37 dekaliters
1 liter	1.05 quarts	1 quart	0.9 liters
1 liter	2.1 pints	1 pint	0.47 liters

(*Note: there are 5 British Imperial gallons to 6 U.S. gallons.*)

Dry Measure		**Dry Measure**	
1 liter	0.9 quarts	1 quart	1.1 liters
1 liter	1.8 pints	1 pint	0.55 liters

To convert centigrade (C°) to Fahrenheit (F°):
$C° \times 9 \div 5 + 32 = F°$.
To convert Fahrenheit to centigrade:
$F° - 32 \times 5 \div 9 = C°$.

General Sources of Information. The following is a listing of tourist offices listed by country.

Austria

Landesverkehrsamt
Mozartplatz 5
Salzburg
tel. 0662 4 15 61

Austrian National Tourist Office
Oesterreichische Fremden-
    verkehrewerbung
Margaretenstrasse 1
A-1040 Vienna
tel. 0222 58 86 60/0222 5 87 57
    24

Niederisterreich-Information
Heidenschluss 2
1010 Vienna
tel. 02223 63 31 14

Belgium

Brussels Tourist Information
Grand'Place
1000 Brussels
tel. 513 89 40

Rue Marchéaux Herbes 61
1000 Brussels
tel. 513 90 90

Bulgaria

Balkantourist
1 Vitošha
Sofia
tel. 43331

Czechoslovakia

Cedok (National Tourist Office)
Na Prikope 18
Prague 1
tel. 212 71 11

Denmark

Turistrad
Hans Christian Andersens Blvd.
    22
1553 Copenhagen V
tel. 11 13 25

England

Tourist Information Center
12 Regent Street
Piccadilly Circus
London
tel. 730 34 00

London Tourist Board
26 Grosvenor Gardens
London
tel. 730 34 50

Finland

Unioninkatu 26
00130 Helsinki
tel. 14 45 11

Pohjoisesplanadi 19
00130 Helsinki
tel. 16 9 37 57/17 40 88

France

Office de Tourisme and Accueil
de France
12 cours 30-juillet
Bordeaux
tel. 56 44 28 61

Office de Tourisme
4 Canebière
Marseille
tel. 91 54 91 11

Office de Tourisme de Paris-
Accueil de France
127 Champs-Élysées
Paris
tel. 47 23 61 72

Office de Tourisme and Accueil
de France
Palais des Congrès
Avenue Schutzenberger
Strasbourg
tel. 88 35 03 00

East Germany

Reiseburo der DDR (Travel
Agency of German
Democratic Republic)
1026 Alexanderplatz
East Berlin
tel. 215 41 70

West Germany

Europa-Center (Budapester
Strasse)
Berlin
tel. 2 62 60 31

Verkehsamt (Tourist Office)
Am Dom
Cologne
tel. 2 21 33 40

GNT Board Deutsche Zentrale
für Tourismus (DZT)
Beethovenstrasse 69
D-6000 Frankfurt am Main
Frankfurt
tel. 06 97 57 20

Tourist Office
Hachmannplatz 1
Hamburg
tel. 24 87 00

Greece

National Tourist Organization
(EOT)
2 Amerikis Street
Athens
tel. 322 31 11

Hungary

TOURINFORM (Hungarian
Tourist Board)
Suto Utca 2
Budapest
tel. 17 98 00

IBUSZ (State Travel Board)
Felszabadulás tér 5
Budapest
tel. 18 68 66

Ireland

Irish Tourist Board (Bord Failte)
14 Upper O'Connell St.
Dublin
tel. 73 52 09/74 77 33

Italy

Ente Provinciale per il Turismo
   (EPT)
via Manzoni 16
Florence
tel. 24 78 141

EPT
via Marconi 1
Milan
tel. 80 96 62

EPT
via Parigi 5
Rome
tel. 46 37 48

EPT
via Roma 226
Turin
tel. 53 59 01

EPT
San Marco Ascensione 71
Venice
tel. 522 63 56

Luxembourg

Office National de Tourisme
Place du Gare
Luxembourg
tel. 48 11 99

Netherlands

VVV (Vereniging voor Vreem-
   delingen Verkeer)
Rokin 9–15
Amsterdam
tel. 20 10 16

Stationsplein (Koffiehaus)
Amsterdam
tel. 26 64 44

Norway

Norwegian Tourist Board
Havnelageret
Langkaia 1 0150
Oslo
tel. 42 70 44

Oslo Tourist Information
City Hall
Oslo
tel. 42 71 70

Poland

Informacja Turystyczna (IT)
Bracka 16
Warsaw
tel. 26 02 71

Portugal

Postos do Turismo
Av. Antonio Augusto de Aguiar
   86
Lisbon
tel. 57 50 15/36 94 50

Palácio Foz
Praca dos Restaudores
Lisbon
tel. 36 36 24

Romania

Carpati
7 Magheru Blvd.
Bucharest
tel. 14 51 60

Scotland

Waverley Market
3 Princes Street
Edinburgh
tel. 557 27 27

35–39 St. Vincent Place
Glasgow
tel. 227 48 80

Soviet Union

Intourist
Marx Prospekt 15
Moscow
tel. 292 27 68

Spain

Patronat Municipal de Turisme de
 Barcelona
Passeig de Gracia 35
Barcelona
tel. 215 44 77

Gran Via de les Corts Catalanes
Barcelona
tel. 301 74 43

Plaza Mayor 3
Madrid
tel. 266 54 77

Torre de Madrid
Plaza de Espana
Princesa I
Madrid
tel. 241 23 25

Av. de la Constitucion 21 B
Seville
tel. 22 14 04

Pl. del Pais Valenciano
Valencia
tel. 352 24 97

Sweden

Swedish Tourist Board
Sverigehuset, Kungstradgarden
Stockholm
tel. 08 789 2000

Stockholm Information Service
Sverigehuset
Hamngatan 27
Stockholm 27 789 20 00

Switzerland

Blumenrain 2
Basel
tel. 22 50 50

Gare Cornavin
Geneva
tel. 32 53 40

Tour de l'Ile
Geneva
tel. 28 72 33

Offizielles Verkehrsburo
Bahnhofplatz 15
Zurich
tel. 211 40 00

Swiss National Tourist Office
 (Schweizerische Ver-
 kehrszentrale)
Bellariastrasse 38
Zurich
tel. 202 37 37

Turkey

Mesrutiyet Cad. 57
Sultan Ahmet Square
Istanbul
tel. 172 61 08

Yugoslavia

Tourist Association of
  Yugoslavia
Mose Pijade 8
Belgrade
tel. 339 753

Embassies and Consulates in Europe. The following is a listing
of embassies and/or consulates for the U.S., Britain, Canada, and Australia located in the European cities described in this guide. If an address
is not included below, this usually indicates that there is no embassy or
consulate in that city.

Austria

American Embassy
Boltzmanngasse 16
A–1091 Vienna
tel. 222 31 55 11

American Consulate
Giselakai 51
A–5020 Salzburg
tel. 662 28 601

Canadian Embassy
Dr. Karl Lueger Ring 10
A–1010 Vienna
tel. 533 36 91

Australian Embassy
Mattiellistrasse 2–4
A–1040 Vienna
tel. 52 85 80 85 89

Belgium

American Embassy
27 Bd. du Régent
B–1000 Brussels
tel. 02 513 38 30

British Embassy
Britannica House, rue Joseph II,
  28
1040 Brussels
tel. 02 217 90 00

Canadian Embassy
2, Avenue de Tervuren
1040 Brussels
tel. 02 735 60 40

Australian Embassy
Guimard Centre
Rue Guimard 6–8
1040 Brussels
tel. 02 231 05 00

Bulgaria

American Embassy
1A Stamboliski Blvd.
Sofia
tel. 288 48 01

British Embassy
Boulevard Marshal Tolbukhin
65–67 Sofia
tel. 885 361/885 362

Czechoslovakia

American Embassy
Trziste 15–12548 Praha
Prague
tel. 2 53 66 41

British Embassy
11700 Prague, Thunovska 14
Prague
tel. 533 347/533 348/533 349

Canadian Embassy
Michiewiczova 6
Prague 6
tel. 2 32 69 41

Denmark

American Embassy
Dag Hammarskjolds Alle 24
2100 Copenhagen
tel. 01 42 31 44

British Embassy
36/38/40 Kastelsvej
DK–2000
Copenhagen
tel. 01 26 46 00

Canadian Embassy
Kr. Bernikowsgade 1
1105 Copenhagen K
tel. 01 12 22 99

Australian Embassy
Kristianagade 21
Dk–2100 Copenhagen
tel. 01 26 22 44

England

American Embassy
24/31 Grosvenor Sq. W.
London W1A 1AE
tel. 01 499 90 00

Canadian Embassy
Macdonald House
1 Grosvenor Square
London, WiX OAB
tel. 441 629 94 92

Australia High Commission
Australia House
The Strand, London WC 2B 4LA
tel. 379 43 34

Finland

American Embassy
Itainen Puistotie 14B
00140 Helsinki
tel. 17 19 31

British Embassy
16–20 Uudenmaankatu
00120 Helsinki 12
tel. 64 79 22

Canadian Embassy
P. Esplanadi 25B
00100 Helsinki 10
tel. 17 11 41

France

American Embassy
2 Avenue Gabriel
75382 Paris Cedex 08
tel. 01 42 96 12 02

American Consulate
22 Cours du Maréchal-Foch
33080 Bordeaux Cedex
tel. 56 56 52 65 95

American Consulate
12 Blvd. Paul-Peytral
13286 Marseille Cedex
tel. 91 54 92 00

American Consulate
15 Av. d'Alsace
67082 Strasbourg Cedex
tel. 88 88 35 31 04

British Embassy
35 Rue du Faubourg St. Honoré
75383 Paris
tel. 1 42 66 91 42

British Consulate General
16 Rue d'Anjou
75008 Paris
tel. 1 42 66 91 42

Canadian Embassy
35, Av. Montaigne
75008 Paris
tel. 1 47 23 01 01

Consulate of Canada
Rue de Ried
F–67610
La Wantzenau
Strasbourg
tel. (011 33) 88 96 26 51

Australian Embassy
4 Rue Jean Rey
75724 Paris
tel. 40 59 33 00

East Germany

American Embassy
Neustaedtische Kirchstrasse 4–5
1080 East Berlin
tel. 220 27 41

British Embassy
108 Berlin, Unter den Linden
32/34
East Berlin
tel. 220 24 31

West Germany

American Embassy
Clayallee 170
D-1000 Berlin 33
tel. 30 83 240 87

American Consulate
Deichmanns Avenue
5300 Bonn 2
tel. 02 28 33 391

American Consulate
Siesmayerstrasse 21
6000 Frankfurt Am Main
tel. 69 28 34 01

American Consulate
Alsterufer 27/28
2000 Hamburg 36
tel. 040 44 10 61

American Consulate
Koninginstrasse 5
8000 Munich 22
tel. 089 2 30 11

British Embassy
Friedrich-Ebert-Allée 77
5300 Bonn 1
tel. 23 40 61

British Consulate General
Olympic Stadion
1000 Berlin 19
tel. 3091

British Consulate General
Bockenheimer Landstrasse
51–53
6000 Frankfurt Am Main 1
tel. 720 406/720 409

British Consulate General
Harvestehuder Weg 8a
2000 Hamburg 13
tel. 44 60 71

British Consulate General
Amalienstrasse 62
8000 Munich 40
tel. 39 40 15

Canadian Embassy
Friedrich Wilhelm Strasse 18
5300 Bonn 1
tel. (011 49 228) 23 10 61

Canadian Consulate General
Europa-Center
1000 Berlin 30
tel. (011 49 30) 261 11 61

Canadian Consulate General
Europa Carton AG
Spitalerstrasse 11
2000 Hamburg
tel. (011 49 40) 30 90 11 00

Canadian Consulate General
Maximiliansplatz 9
8000 Munich 2
(011 49 89) 55 85 31

Greece

American Embassy
91 Vasilissis Sophias Blvd.
101 60 Athens
tel. 721 29 51

British Embassy
1 Ploutarchou Street
106 75 Athens
tel. 723 62 11

Canadian Embassy
4 Ioannou Gennadiou St.
115 21 Athens
tel. (0111 30 1) 72 39 511 to 519

Australian Embassy
37 Dimitriou Soutsou St.
Ambelokipi Athens 11521
tel. 775 76 50/775 76 51

Hungary

American Embassy
V, Szabadsag Ter. 12
Budapest
tel. 12 64 50

British Embassy
Harmincad Utca 6
Budapest V
tel. 18 28 88

Canadian Embassy
Budakeszi ut. 32

1121 Budapest
tel. 76 73 12

Australian Embassy
Delibab Utca 30
1062 Budapest
tel. 53 32 33

Ireland

American Embassy
42 Elgin Road
Ballsbridge, Dublin 4
tel. 68 87 77

British Embassy
31/33 Merrion Road
Dublin 4
tel. 69 52 11

Canadian Embassy
65 St. Stephen's Green
Dublin 2
tel. 78 19 88

Australian Embassy
Fitzwilton House
Wilton Terrace
Dublin 2
tel. 76 15 17/76 24 41

Italy

American Embassy
Via Veneto 119/A
00187 Rome
tel. 64 67 41

American Consulate
Lungarno Amerigo Vespucci 38
Florence
tel. 055 29 82 76

American Consulate
Piazza della Repubblica 32
20121 Milan
tel. 02 65 28 41

American Consulate
Via Pomba 23
10123 Turin
tel. 11 51 74 37

British Embassy
Via XX Settembre 80A
00187 Rome
tel. 475 54 41/475 55 51

British Consulate
Palazzo Castelbarco
Lungarno Corsini 2
I-50123 Florence
tel. 21 25 94/28 41 33/28 74 49

British Consulate General
Via San Paolo 7
20121 Milan
tel. 869 34 42

British Government Trade Office
Corso Massimo d'Azeglio 60
10126 Turin
tel. 68 78 32/68 39 21

British Consulate
Accademia 1050
Dorsoduro, Venice
tel. 522 72 07/522 74 08

Canadian Embassy
Via G.B. de Rossi 27
00161 Rome
tel. 85 53 41

Consulate General of Canada
Via Vittor Pisani 19
20124 Milan
tel. 669 74 51

Australian Embassy
Via Alessandria 215
Rome 00198
tel. 84 12 41

Australian Consulate General
Via Turati 40

Milan 20121
tel. 659 87 27

Luxembourg

American Embassy
22 Bd. Emmanuel Servais
Luxembourg 2535
tel. 46 01 23

British Embassy
14 Bd. Roosevelt
Luxembourg Ville
tel. 298 64 66

Canadian Consulate
c/o Price Waterhouse
20 Pasteur Avenue
2310 Luxembourg
tel. 35 22 37 42

Netherlands

American Embassy
Museumplain 19
Amsterdam
79 03 21/64 56 61

British Consulate General
Koningslaan 44, 1075 AE
Amsterdam
tel. 76 43 43

Norway

American Embassy
Drammensveien 18
Oslo 2
tel. 2 44 85 50

Poland

American Embassy
Aleje Ujazdowskle 29/31
Warsaw
tel. 22 28 30 41

Canadian Embassy
Ulica Matejki 1/5
Warsaw 00-481
Poland

Portugal

American Embassy
Av. das Forcas Armadas
1600 Lisbon
tel. 726 66 00

Romania

American Embassy
Str. Tudor Arghezi 7–9
Bucharest
tel. 10 40 40

Spain

American Embassy
Serrano 75
Madrid
tel. 276 34 00/276 36 00

American Consulate
Via Layetana 33
Barcelona
tel. 319 95 50

British Embassy
Calle de Fernando el Santo 16
Madrid 4
tel. 419 02 00

British Consulate General
Edificio Torre de Barcelona
Avenida Diagonal 477 (13th floor)
08036 Barcelona
tel. 322 21 51

British Consulate General
Plaza Nueva 8 (Dpdo)
Seville
tel. 22 88 75

Canadian Embassy
Edificio Goya
Calle Nunez de Balboa 35
Madrid
tel. 431 43 00

Consulate of Canada
Via Augusta 125
Atico 3A
Barcelona 08006
tel. 209 06 34

Consulate of Canada
Avenida de la Constitucion, 30
Seville 41001
tel. 22 94 13

Australian Embassy
Paseo de la Castellano
143, Madrid 28046
tel. 279 85 04/279 85 03

Scotland

American Consulate
3 Regent Terrace
Edinburgh EH7 5BW
tel. 031 556 83 15

Australian Consulate
Hobart House
80 Hanover Street
Edinburgh EH2 2DL
tel. 226 62 71

Soviet Union

American Embassy
Ulitsa Chaykovskovo 19/21/23
Moscow
tel. 096 252 2451

American Consulate
Ulitsa Petra Lavrova 15
Leningrad
tel. 812 274 82 35

British Embassy
Naberezhnaya Morisa
Toreza 14
Moscow 72
tel. 231 855 11

Canadian Embassy
23 Starokonyushenny Pereulok
Moscow
241 91 55

Australian Embassy
13 Kropotkinsky Pereulok
Moscow
tel. 246 50 11/246 50 16

Sweden

American Embassy
Strandvagen 101
S–11527
Stockholm
tel. 08 783 53 00

British Embassy
Skarpogatan 6–8
115 27 Stockholm
tel. 08 667 01 40

Canadian Embassy
Tegelbacken 4 (7th floor)
Stockholm 16
tel. 08 23 79 20

Australian Embassy
Sergels Torg 12
Stockholm 86
tel. 08 24 46 60

Switzerland

American Embassy
Jubilaeumstrasse 93
3005 Bern
tel. 031 43 70 11

American Embassy
11, Route de Pregny
1291 Chambesy, Geneva
tel. 22 99 02 11

American Consulate
Zoliikerstrasse 141
8008 Zurich
tel. 01 55 25 66

British Embassy
Thunstrasse 50
30005 Bern 15
tel. 44 50 21/44 50 26

British Consulate General
37–39 rue de Vermont (6th)
1211 Geneva 20
tel. 34 38 00/33 23 85

British Consulate General
Dufourstrasse 56
8008 Zurich
tel. 47 15 20/47 15 26

Canadian Embassy
Kirchenfeldstrasse 88
3005 Bern
tel. 41 63 81

Australian Embassy
29 Alpenstrasse
Bern
tel. 43 01 43

Australian Consulate
56–58 Rue de Moilebeau
Petit Saconnex, 11
Geneva 19
tel. 34 62 00

Turkey

British Consulate General
Mesrutiyet Caddesi No. 34
Tepebasi, Beysglu, PK 33
Istanbul
tel. 133 75 40/144 75 45

Consulate of Canada
Buyujdere Cad 107/3
Bengun Han Gayrettepe
Istanbul
tel. 172 51 74

Yugoslavia

American Embassy
Kneza Milosa 50
Belgrad
tel. 64 56 55

British Embassy
Generala Zdanova 46
11000 Belgrad
tel. 64 50 55/64 50 34

Canadian Embassy
Kneza Milosa 75
11000 Belgrad
tel. 64 46 66

Australian Embassy
13 Cjika Ljubina
11000 Belgrad
tel. 62 46 55/63 22 61